UNHOLY ORDERS

TRAGEDY AT MOUNT CASHEL

MICHAEL HARRIS

VIKING

VIKING

Published by the Penguin Group
Penguin Books Canada Ltd, 2801 John Street, Markham, Ontario, Canada
L3R 1B4
Penguin Books Ltd, 27 Wrights Lane, London W8 5TZ, England
Viking Penguin, a division of Penguin Books USA Inc., 375 Hudson Street,
New York, New York 10014, USA
Penguin Books Australia Ltd, Ringwood, Victoria, Australia
Penguin Books (NZ) Ltd, 182-190 Wairau Road, Auckland 10,
New Zealand

Penguin Books Ltd, Registered Offices: Harmondsworth, Middlesex,
England

First published 1990

10 9 8 7 6 5 4 3 2 1

Printed and bound in Canada on acid-free paper ⊜
by John Deyell Company

Canadian Cataloguing in Publication Data

Harris, Michael, 1948-
    Unholy orders : tragedy at Mount Cashel

ISBN 0-670-83481-5

1. Mount Cashel Orphanage (St. John's, Nfld.)   2. Child molesting –
Newfoundland – St. John's.   3. Child molesting – Newfoundland –
St. John's – Investigation.   4. Catholic Church – Newfoundland – St.
John's – Clergy – Sexual Behavior.   5. Catholic Church – Clergy – Sexual
Behavior.   6. Child molesting.   I. Title.

HQ72.C3H37   1990   364.1'536   C90-094855-8

British Library Cataloguing in Publication Data Available
American Library of Congress Catalogue Card Number 90-71285

For my mother, Audrey Eleanor Harris, a great heart in the darkest hour.

Acknowledgements

THE MAIN SOURCE material for this book was the exhaustive record of the Royal Commission conducted by retired Ontario Supreme Court Justice Samuel H. S. Hughes. The author is indebted to Commissioner Hughes, who graciously granted interviews, and to his small but industrious staff who did their best to help in this ambitious endeavour. Although every member of the Commission gave valuable assistance by providing access to the videotapes of testimony, to exhibits, and to the mountain of documents compiled by staff, a few people merit special thanks.

David Day, Q.C., repeatedly made time in his demanding schedule, and in the aftermath of the grievous loss of his father, to help the project within the bounds of propriety as commission co-counsel; his unstinting assistance was greatly appreciated.

Commission secretaries Patricia Linehan and Margaret Devereaux, as well as their colleagues, Colleen Power, Virginia Connors and Sandra Burke, unfailingly unravelled informational snags with a grace not usually associated with people already taxed with heavy official duties. Their good cheer in the midst of sifting through the ashes of so much human misery was remarkable.

My main debt, of course, is due to Shane Earle, Billy Earle, Johnny Williams, Robert Connors, Dereck O'Brien, Gerard Brinston and the other twenty-five young men who took the stand at the royal commission to tell their tale of childhood lost. I have relied on their testimony before Commissioner Hughes, as well as on their accounts to the police in 1975, to recreate the nightmare they faced so many years ago, innocent, and except for each other, achingly alone.

In those parts of *Unholy Orders* dealing with subjects outside the realm of Mount Cashel, a number of people were especially generous with their time, information and services. American journalist Jason Berry freely shared his expert knowledge on the subject of priestly sex crimes in the United States, particularly in the state of Louisiana. Several members of *The Sunday Express*, where I was publisher and editor-in-chief while the book was being written, kindly assisted in a variety of useful ways. My secretary, Valerie Peckham, quarterbacked the information flow between St. John's and Toronto, and otherwise assisted in the logistics of the project. Carolyn Ryan collected the photographs for the book, while Russell Wangersky kept tabs on the hundreds of articles that were written about Mount Cashel and priestly sex crimes both in Newfoundland and in other jurisdictions. Thanks are also due to the owner of *The Sunday Express*, Harry Steele, who graciously allowed me to get on with the book at the same time as I was running his newspaper.

Morty Mint, Iris Skeoch and Cynthia Good of Penguin Books deserve mention for their enthusiasm both before and during this project as does my editor, Catherine Marjoribanks, who provided a balanced and sobre assessment of a manuscript that at times must have been difficult for her to deal with. I am also indebted to Mary Adachi for her fine copy editing and Christeen Chidley-Hill, my production editor.

Finally, there would be no book without the remarkable effort of the three researchers who assisted me on *Unholy Orders* from the December day in 1989 when we left the starting line a little unsteadily but with great expectations of meeting the most demanding deadline I have ever faced. Two of them, Philip Lee and Linda Strowbridge, are fine journalists who were already respected colleagues when the work began; by the time it had finished, they had become good friends. The third, the incomparable Lynda Harris, was as indispensable to me on this work as she has been on the wider projects of life these past twenty years.

For any errors or omissions that may come to light despite the help of so many talented and gracious people, I alone am responsible.

Author's Note

The use of asterisks beside the names of boys in Chapter 1 denotes the use of pseudonyms. The identities of Father Hickey's victims remain protected by court order.

In Chapter 2, Sidney Waters is a pseudonym for a Brother who would later be charged for incidents arising out of the 1989 Mount Cashel reinvestigation, though not involving Richard Earle.

In Chapters 4 and 9, the letters were used by the Hughes Inquiry to indicate the names of boys interviewed by the police who chose not to appear at the Commission.

In Chapter 9, the terms "Boy 1" and "Civilian 1," etc., were used by the Hughes Inquiry to protect the identities of both the victims and the alleged perpetrators named in the police and social services reports.

UNHOLY
ORDERS

Contents

Cast of Characters

Christian Brothers

John Francis Barron – Superintendent of Mount Cashel from September 1968 until June 1971.

Gordon Bellows – a former Mount Cashel resident who joined the Christian Brothers and served on the Congregation's governing council for the Canada–West Indies Province in the mid-seventies. He succeeded Gabriel McHugh as Brother Provincial of the Canada–West Indies Province in 1978.

Henry Louis Bucher – Superintendent of Mount Cashel from August 1976 until May 1983.

Douglas Kenny – Superintendent of Mount Cashel Orphanage from 1971 until January 1976.

Gabriel McHugh – the Brother Provincial of the Congregation's Canada–West Indies Province from 1972 to 1978, and, since 1978, Superior General of Christian Brothers Worldwide.

Dermod Nash – a Christian Brother and university English professor who served as Newfoundland's chief adviser to the Brother Provincial of the Congregation's Canada–West Indies Province from 1972 to 1978.

Police Officers

John Browne – Chief of the Newfoundland Constabulary from 1976 until 1980.

Robert Hillier – a detective in the assault section of the Newfoundland Constabulary's Criminal Investigation Division in the 1970s.

John Lawlor – the Chief of Police in the Newfoundland Constabulary from June 1972 until December 1976.

John Norman – the late Assistant Chief of the Newfoundland Constabulary who held the post from June 1972 until his retirement in December 1976.

Arthur Pike – a detective-sergeant with the Newfoundland Constabulary who was in charge of the Criminal Investigation Division's assault section in the mid-seventies.

Ralph Pitcher – a Newfoundland Constabulary detective assigned to the assault section of the RNC's Criminal Investigations Division in the mid-seventies.

Len Power – in 1982, staff sergeant in charge of the Royal Newfoundland Constabulary's Assault/Homocide division and the investigation into child abuse complaints at Mount Cashel orphanage. After attaining the rank of superintendent in 1987, he was placed in charge of the entire Criminal Investigation Division and the 1989 re-investigation of abuse at Mount Cashel.

Allan Thistle – a Newfoundland Constabulary detective assigned to the assault section of the Criminal Investigations Division in the mid-seventies.

Freeman Twyne – a staff sergeant with the Morals Division of the Royal Newfoundland Constabulary who was assigned to the Mount Cashel reinvestigation in 1989.

Chesley Yetman – a detective-inspector with the Newfoundland Constabulary who was in charge of the Criminal Investigations Division in the mid-seventies.

Justice Officials

T. Alex Hickman – Newfoundland's Minister of Justice from January 1972 until July 1979. In December 1979 he was appointed Chief Justice of the Trial Division of the Supreme Court of Newfoundland.

Robert Hyslop – Crown prosecutor in Newfoundland's Justice Department from 1975 to 1985, Associate Deputy Attorney General from 1985 to May 1989, Provincial Court judge since June 1989.

John Kelly – a Crown prosecutor in Newfoundland's Justice Department from 1972 to 1976. Director of Public Prosecutions from March 1976 until August 1979.

George Macauley – in Newfoundland's Department of Justice from 1968 to 1970, Assistant Deputy Minister for civil law from 1970 to January 1977, Deputy Minister and Deputy Attorney-General from February 1977 to November 1979.

Vincent McCarthy – Newfoundland's Deputy Minister of Justice from 1970 to 1977; appointed District Court judge in 1977. He died in June 1986 following a twelve-year battle with cancer.

Mary Noonan – a Crown attorney who served as legal adviser to Newfoundland's Director of Child Welfare from the early seventies until 1985, appointed presiding judge of Newfoundland's Unified Family Court in October 1985.

Lynn Verge – Newfoundland's Minister of Justice when the Mount Cashel case was reopened in 1989.

Social Services Officials

Robert Bradbury – the official liaison between the St. John's district office of the Social Services department and Mount Cashel Orphanage from 1974 until 1977.

Charlie Brett – Newfoundland's Minister of Social Services from October 1975 until October 1978 and from February 1985 until early 1988.

Sharron Callahan – the Supervisor of Child Welfare and Corrections at the St. John's district office of the Department of Social Services from 1975 until 1979, Newfoundland's Assistant Director of Juvenile Corrections from 1979 to 1985.

Sheila Devine – Newfoundland's Assistant Director of Child Welfare from July 1971 until August 1983, Assistant Deputy Minister of Social Services from April 1987 to January 1990.

Neil Hamilton – a child welfare and protection officer who served as the official liaison between Social Services headquarters and Mount Cashel Orphanage from 1966 until 1979, the Supervisor of Child Welfare at St. John's district office from October 1979 to February 1983.

Tom Hickey – Newfoundland's Social Services Minister from March 1979 until February 1985.

Vernon Hollett – Newfoundland's Deputy Minister of Social Services from December 1972 until August 1980.

Ank Murphy – Newfoundland's Minister of Social Services from April 1973 until October 1975.

George Pope – the Assistant Deputy Minister of Social Services from 1972 until 1988.

Frank Simms – the Department of Social Services' Director of Child Welfare from October 1971 until March 1989.

Alice Walters – social worker in Social Services' St. John's district office on Harvey Road in the mid-1970s.

Catholic Officials

Kevin Molloy – a former Christian Brother who joined the priesthood in 1972 and served as assistant priest at St. Patrick's parish in St. John's in the mid-seventies, later succeeded Jim Hickey as parish priest in Portugal Cove and became the official spokesman for the Archdiocese of St. John's in 1989.

Alphonsus Penney – the Roman Catholic Archbishop of St. John's from 1979 until his resignation after publication of the Winter Report on July 18, 1990.

Patrick James Skinner – Archbishop of St. John's from 1951 until 1979.

Lawyers

John Connors – Newfoundland's Director of Public Prosecutions from February 1973 until September 1975.

Michael Roche – a Crown prosecutor in western Newfoundland from 1978 until he was appointed to the Provincial Court in 1989.

Ronald Richards – a Crown prosecutor in the seventies and early eighties who served as Newfoundland's Deputy Minister of Justice from 1985 until 1989.

Colin Flynn – Newfoundland's Director of Public Prosecutions when the Mount Cashel case was reopened in 1989.

Harry Kopyto – a Toronto human rights lawyer who represented several former residents of Mount Cashel Orphanage at the outset of the Hughes Inquiry. The former residents, however, switched counsel shortly before the Law Society of Upper Canada disbarred Kopyto in the fall of 1989.

David Day, Q.C. – a St. John's drug prosecutor and family law attorney who served as commission co-counsel for the 1989–90 Hughes Inquiry.

Clay Powell, Q.C. – a former Assistant Deputy Minister of Justice in the Ontario government who served as commission co-counsel for the 1989–90 Hughes Inquiry.

Francis O'Dea, Q.C. – the St. John's lawyer who represented the Congregation of Christian Brothers at the 1989–90 Hughes Inquiry.

Gordon Seabright – a judge with the Magistrate's Court/Provincial Court in Newfoundland from 1964 until 1989. In 1978, Judge Seabright handled the Father Ronald Hubert Kelly case.

Introduction

On january 12, 1988, Father James Joseph Hickey was charged with multiple sex crimes involving adolescent boys in the various towns and villages where he had served as parish priest over his eighteen-year career. Since Hickey was Newfoundland's most celebrated priest, his case became a media sensation. But in Newfoundland, with its fiercely sectarian society and long history of denominational education, it was much more than a scandalous shooting star that streaked across the television screens and front pages of the province before sinking into oblivion. Hickey's arrest and subsequent guilty plea on twenty counts of sexual assault, indecent assault and gross indecency rocked the island to its very foundations. It was hard to tell which was worse: the crimes that sent Hickey to Dorchester Penitentiary for five years or the enormous breach of trust they represented on the part of Newfoundland's self-styled champion of youth.

As things turned out, the Hickey scandal burgeoned into a full-blown crisis for the Roman Catholic church and its 205,000 faithful in Newfoundland – over a third of the island's total population. In the year following Father Hickey's arrest, several other Catholic clergy were charged with sex-related offences involving young boys.

For generations, there was an unwritten rule in Newfoundland that crimes involving the clergy were best dealt with in the backrooms of the justice system – misplaced homage to the church's enormous prestige based on its innumerable good works. It was also testament to the immense political power of the pulpit in Newfoundland, a cultural reality dating from the island's earliest colonial beginnings. But when coverage of the Hickey scandal became a nightly ritual on the evening news, and several prominent Roman Catholic priests followed him into the dock, the shroud of secrecy in which priestly crimes were traditionally wrapped split like a sail in a hurricane. What it revealed was a Roman Catholic hierarchy that seemed unable or unwilling to deal with the crisis in its midst, a crisis that extended well beyond the borders of Newfoundland into other Canadian provinces, the United States, Australia and the United Kingdom. One high-ranking Catholic official in the United States saw homosexual pedophilia as the deadliest problem the church had faced in centuries. Regrettably, the church's response to the crisis rarely rose above simple recognition of the problem, and when it did, the result was usually self-interested chicanery rather than concern for the victims of sexual abuse by the clergy.

For months after the Hickey affair, the Archbishop of St. John's dithered while his lieutenants lamely defended his inaction: inexplicably, the church's moral leaders became moral Hamlets. Tangled in the nets of daunting legal implications, they adopted a self-serving perspective that bordered on refusal to accept any responsibility for the unfolding fiasco. Meanwhile, the victims of child abuse and their families twisted in the wind, waiting in vain for their spiritual leaders to ease the suffering they apparently could not see.

As the curious silence from the Archdiocese of St. John's became deafening, rumours abounded that Roman Catholic authorities had long been aware of the gross misconduct of some of their priests and simply failed to take action to avoid scandal. That charge, and the growing public sense that the church was evading its responsibilities, finally compelled Archbishop Alphonsus Penney to establish the Winter Commission, an inquiry charged with finding out how such widespread sexual abuse of children by priests could have gone undetected for so long.

In one documented case, a young Catholic male had complained directly to Archbishop Penney himself in 1979, claiming that he had been sexually abused by a priest. Instead of informing the office of the Director of Child Welfare or the police, the Archbishop referred the complaint to the young man's bishop and never followed up on the matter. The priest in question, Father Kevin Bennett, remained in active duty until he pleaded guilty to thirty-six sex-related charges brought against him by the police ten years after the complaint to Archbishop Penney.

It was exactly this kind of reflexive self-interest on the part of church leaders that fuelled the anger of Newfoundland's Catholics as they struggled with the systematic failure of the church to face the reality of sexual abuse by its own clergy. In the end, several victims would seek relief in court action against the church rather than in its belated spiritual ministerings.

But an even bigger test of faith awaited Newfoundland's Roman Catholics in the early months of 1989. Percolating just beneath the surface of the priestly scandal was an old story of hidden crime and secret passage through the justice system for self-confessed child molesters who belonged to a lay order of the Roman Catholic church known as the Christian Brothers. For more than a hundred years, the Brothers had been a force in Newfoundland's education system and a tribute to the island's Irish roots, housing, nurturing and educating boys that the world had somehow pushed to one side. But in the early seventies, Mount Cashel Orphanage, Catholic-run and publicly financed, became a chamber of horrors for many of its ninety-one young residents, a place where they were sexually and physically abused by a brutal coterie of Christian Brothers who disgraced the laudable work of their own colleagues and predecessors and permanently stained the lives of their young charges.

The authorities of the day were alerted to the horrors of Mount Cashel by the unblinkered police work of dectectives from the Newfoundland Constabulary who bucked the institutional prejudices of the day to get at the truth. But instead of dealing with the alleged offenders, the justice system terminated an ongoing criminal investigation that had uncovered massive child abuse at the orphanage; worse, the same authorities tried to get the police report of the Mount Cashel investigation altered to remove all references to sexual abuse. In the end, the rule of law in Newfoundland was suspended in favour of a medieval deal that banished two self-confessed child molesters for life rather than lay charges against them; at the same time, justice officials buried the alleged crimes of three other Christian Brothers named in the 1975 police investigation, including the Superintendent of the Mount Cashel Orphanage, without even allowing the police to interview them.

Fourteen years later, a soft-spoken young man named Shane Earle called the newspaper office where I was then working and asked for a meeting. Later, in the quiet gloom of a deserted St. John's hotel, the first victim of the orphanage to go public led me through the dark chronicles of Mount Cashel. Having written a book about the Donald Marshall case, the true story of a man who spent several years in prison for a murder he did not commit, I thought I had come face to face with the outer limits of human suffering. But as I listened to Shane's soft voice describing the gross invasions of his person by the very people charged with protecting him, I kept seeing the child in the man and realized that torment in this world has a multiplicity of faces.

Like Donald Marshall, Shane Earle and the other victims of Mount Cashel were survivors who had voyaged through a nightmare of the system run amok and come out on the other side thirsting for justice. Confronted by their courage in co-operating with the 1989 reinvestigation of the Mount Cashel affair, the provincial government had little choice but to establish a royal commission to find out what had gone so tragically wrong in the system in 1975. By the time the Hughes Inquiry had finished its sombre deliberations on Mount Cashel, it had laid bare a stunning, collective failure of the judicial, police, religious, media and social service establishments to protect the interests of hopelessly vulnerable and cruelly abused children. In the intervening fourteen years, at least eighty-seven people in positions of authority had learned about the dread happenings of 1975, but none took action to drag the scandal out of the shadows and into the healing light of day.

This is the story of that conspiracy of indifference, the human tragedy it engendered and its long overdue exposure under the disbelieving eyes of the nation.

Michael Harris
Three Island Pond
Topsail, Newfoundland
August 31, 1990

Chapter 1

■ *Father Jim*

> *Everybody in Portugal Cove thought he was a real nice fellow and we used to keep on going back there and it was just—like such a nice place ... Mom and them thought so much of him and it was so hard for me to tell Dad that he was doing these things to me ... I just couldn't tell them.* Male witness at Father James Hickey's preliminary trial for sexual assault, May 1988.

NEWFOUNDLAND NEVER HAD a priest quite like Father James Joseph Hickey.

Almost from the day in 1967 when he entered St. Peter's Seminary in London, Ontario, "Father Jim," as his adoring parishioners would later know him, seemed destined for a clerical career of distinction. Even as an adolescent growing up in Hoyle's Town, an old quarter of east end St. John's, the round-faced youth had been attracted to the church, helping the priests raise money for St. Joseph's parish by organizing card parties and bingo games. In his spare time, the boy who loved to be busy worked at Pike's grocery store, unconsciously emulating the heavy workloads of the priests he so admired.

When it came time to choose a career, the effervescent nineteen-year-old picked communications over the cloth, joining the CBC Radio Network then housed in the old Newfoundland Hotel, a stone's throw from the neighbourhood where he had grown up. Ten years later, Hickey's longstanding attraction to religious life prompted him to enter Roman Catholic seminaries in Ontario with the intention of becoming a priest, even though the fact that he had been born out of wedlock constituted a canonical impediment to taking holy orders. But after three years, a time during which he also pursued an arts degree at the University of Western Ontario, Hickey left the seminary. He

1

later explained that his decision to leave St. Peter's Seminary had been made on the advice of doctors who told him that he needed a rest. Hickey returned to Newfoundland and rejoined the CBC, this time in the fledgling television service.

By thirty-four, though, Hickey's secular career had left him feeling unfulfilled and restless, and, after the death of his mother, he finally embraced the profession he had been "looking at all the time" – the priesthood. After studying theology for a year at St. Peter's Seminary, Hickey was granted a dispensation from the canonical impediment created by the circumstances of his birth by the Bishop of London, G. M. Carter. Only when he felt Archbishop Skinner's hands on his head two years later in St. John's and heard the sacred words "*Tu es sacredos in aeturnum*" that made him forever a priest did he feel as though he had finally set his foot to the proper path in life. Shortly after his ordination in 1970, the animated priest with the perpetually smiling eyes was appointed assistant to the priest at the Basilica of St. John the Baptist – the mother church of the Archdiocese of St. John's.

The church proved a congenial vehicle for the talents of this educated, witty and cosmopolitan man. Between 1970 and 1976, he served as curate in a succession of St. John's parishes, including a stint as chaplain of Holy Heart of Mary High School, a Catholic girls' school in the city. He later requested a transfer to Brother Rice Regional High, then a male-only institution. Hickey founded the Basilica Youth Choir and became Archdiocesan Vocation Director, as well as Director of Communications and editor of *The Monitor*, Newfoundland's influential Roman Catholic newspaper. Then, unexpectedly, the paunchy cleric with the thinning hair and pronounced jowls gave up his high-profile position within the archdiocese to become a simple parish priest, ministering to his flock in places like Rushoon, Portugal Cove and Ferryland, outport communities that opened their hearts and their homes to this energetic and talented man of God, as they had to generations of Fathers before him.

If Father Hickey became the best known priest in Newfoundland, it was largely because of his undisputed position as the church's self-appointed champion of youth. One of his earliest works was to establish a program at the Basilica to take underprivileged children to summer camp. He served on the Newfoundland Hosteling Association, which ministered to the needs of travelling youth, and was elected first president of the Newfoundland and Labrador Association of Youth Serving Agencies–the provincial body that dealt with all youth groups in the province.

When the Prince and Princess of Wales visited Newfoundland in 1983, Hickey staged a mammoth youth rally in their honour. The self-contented smile that was Hickey's trademark was even deeper that day as he sat on the platform between the royal couple, surveying the thousands of spectators who had crowded on to King George V field to take in the royal appearance. A year later, when Pope John Paul II visited the province on his North American tour, it was Father Jim who introduced the pontiff to the leaders of other denominations in an outdoor ceremony beside Quidi Vidi Lake in St. John's. He never missed a chance to praise, promote or defend the group he felt most comfortable with–Newfoundland's young people.

"I have very few problems with youth," he was quoted as saying in a 1986 *Monitor* article dealing with juvenile delinquency. "I have a lot of problems with adults because all of the things that the youngsters are getting blamed for and are perhaps doing, very often are caused by adults. . . . Children do not put up the money to bring in the large shipments of drugs, they don't own the stores that sell the filthy magazines, neither do they publish them; that's the adults. . . ."

But there was another side to Jim Hickey that had nothing to do with the church, his calling or the desire to serve his fellow man. Carefully concealed behind the jocular and urbane exterior was a pedophile who used his position of trust to seduce and manipulate a long list of altar boys who fell under his charismatic spell. Although his unsuspecting parishioners never knew about the other Jim Hickey–a priest who had been seducing boys from behind his collar for years–the Roman Catholic church was not quite as unaware of the popular priest's dark side. It would later be documented that the Vicar General for the archdiocese of St. John's had received repeated complaints about Hickey's sexual abuse of boys as early as 1975. But the church never did anything about these complaints, partly to avoid a scandal and partly because Hickey managed to convince his superiors that the allegations against him were false. Nothing could have been further from the truth.

Jackie Sheehan* first met Father Hickey in the early 1970s when he was a student at Brother Rice High School in St. John's, where Father Hickey was a guidance counsellor. The year before Sheehan entered Brother Rice, he was sexually assaulted by an older man while on a camping trip with friends. Long after other memories of that summer faded, the ugliness of the attack in Butterpot Park stayed with him. He desperately needed to talk to someone about it and chose the cheerful priest who seemed to be everyone's friend at school – Jim Hickey. One Saturday afteroon Sheehan went to the Basilica, when he knew that Father Jim was taking confession.

It was a poignant moment for Sheehan. Since the camping trip, he had been tormented by the emotional aftershocks of the attack. His mood during confessional that day oscillated between laughter and tears as he unburdened his soul to the understanding priest. When their session was over, he was surprised to find Father Hickey waiting for him outside the box, a sure sign that the anonymity of the confessional had been broken. But Sheehan assumed that the priest had merely wanted to see if his troubled confessor had passed safely through the emotional catharsis brought on by what they had been discussing. He was deeply impressed with Father Jim's apparent sensitivity. Walking down the wide steps of the Basilica that day, with its formidable towers looking out to sea through The Narrows of St. John's Harbour, the young man felt at peace with himself for the first time in months.

A friendship developed between Hickey and his fifteen-year-old supplicant. Father Jim soon invited Sheehan to his cabin on the Bauline Line, a rural area just outside St. John's. It was in that cabin, in Father Hickey's "big double bed," that Sheehan and several of his friends learned that there was more to Father Hickey than the smiling priest who was always there with a kind word or a helping hand. Sheehan quickly became Hickey's reluctant catamite. Over the next five years, his unfortunate experiences evolved into a routine that became as predictable as it was secret.

"When I would go there with him alone, it was just, it was no longer a question of where you were going to sleep. You just knew you would sleep in the bed with him. And you would just disrobe and get in bed and he would get in bed and hold you and touch you, and you know, make you erect and then begin to just explore your body and perform oral sex on you and then kind of guide you to do the same thing to him. . . . Later he would use his hands, you know, put his fingers in my rectum. . . . He tried to enter me and I just, it was too painful and I couldn't do it and I wouldn't allow it to be done."

Apart from the pain, there was another reason Sheehan wouldn't let Hickey sodomize him; he knew from watching other boys perform with Father Jim (Hickey sometimes engaged in group sex) that the priest liked to have oral sex immediately after anal sex—a ritual Sheehan found even more repulsive than one of Hickey's other sexual oddities: licking the eyes of his adolescent lovers.

After leaving Father Hickey's orbit, Sheehan himself became a priest. But by 1987, his own confused sexuality and the phantoms of his past with Father Hickey landed him in a Toronto psychologist's office. As a result of those sessions, Sheehan eventually wrote to the Child Welfare Office in St. John's and formally complained that he had been sexually abused in his younger days by Father Hickey, information the troubled young man shared simultaneously with Archbishop Alphonsus Penney.

His purpose in writing the letter wasn't to get long-delayed justice for himself. Rather, it was to have his case on file in the event that authorities received other complaints about the priest from more contemporary victims that Sheehan was convinced had to exist. That way, the belated complainant thought, "If in the future somebody put in a complaint about Jim Hickey, that it couldn't be brushed off as being said, 'It's just a first time' or 'There must be some mistake.' "

Remarkably, Sheehan's turned out to be the only official complaint. But it was enough to expose a situation that had been festering away in the heart of Newfoundland's Roman Catholic community for nearly twenty years. After receiving Sheehan's letter, the Social Services Department turned the matter over to the Royal Newfoundland Constabulary, which launched an immediate investigation.

Two months later, on January 12, 1988, Father Hickey was charged with thirty-two counts of criminal sexual behaviour. The investigation into the priest's activities also resulted in charges against a longtime friend of Hickey's, a young man named Robert Martin. In February of the same year, Martin himself was charged with two counts of sexual assault and two counts of permitting persons under the age of eighteen to occupy his house for the purpose of engaging in sexual activities. Three of the complainants against Martin also laid charges against Father Hickey. Hickey would later testify that he introduced altar boys to Martin, occasionally bringing them for overnight visits to one of three different homes in St. John's he and Martin jointly owned.

In the incandescent explosion of publicity surrounding the case, Father Hickey told Archbishop Alphonsus Penney that the charges against him were false, just as he reassured stunned parishioners in Holy Trinity parish in Ferryland that the whole thing was a baseless slander. But by the time his preliminary hearing was finished on May 30, 1988, the charade came to a repulsive – and for Father Hickey's many supporters – heartbreaking end.

In a judicial variation on the confessional, a screen was brought into the St. John's courtroom where his case was heard so that witnesses wouldn't have to face the accused while they gave evidence. Although the province was rife with rumours about the nature of the scandal, no one in the packed courtroom was prepared for the lurid tale that unfolded over the next month as twenty men bore witness against the priest who had once so completely manipulated them for his sexual gratification. The press ban on the proceedings was almost an act of mercy for a community that was bracing for the worst and got even more than it bargained for.

Thomas Brolly,* an eighteen-year-old who served on the altar in Holy Rosary Church where Hickey had been parish priest, testified that Father Jim would fondle his genitals whenever the altar boy visited him in the presbytery. (Other witnesses described how Father Jim used to give the boys "wedgies" in the sacristy by pulling up on the waistbands of their underwear, a playful test to see who was and wasn't open to more elaborate sexual advances. Pedophiles often use some form of innocent but sexually oriented horseplay to identify "safe" victims.) Brolly also testified that Hickey would strike up casual conversation only to ask him about what stage of puberty he had reached and whether he'd ever had wet dreams or sex.

Brolly, who first met Hickey when he was nine years old, told the court that he had slept with the priest between ten and twenty times as a thirteen- and fourteen-year-old. He and Hickey would get into bed at night wearing only undershorts and after Brolly had nodded off, Hickey would perform fellatio on the sleeping boy, who testified that he would awaken just before orgasm. Although he said he was privately disgusted with what was happening, he was intimidated by the prospect of informing on the man who had blessed his sister's wedding, buried his father, christened his niece and given him a gold cross for Christmas—an outport folk-hero who was virtually worshipped for his good works.

"I was afraid to speak out for fear of pressure from my friends.... Fear of, you know, speaking out against a priest.... It was all fear of actually speaking out against everybody else's better judgment, *so-called* better judgment, and I just didn't want to be different," Brolly told the court.

Rick Hogan,* another former altar boy in Hickey's Portugal Cove parish, explained how the priest used to get boys to come over to the presbytery on school nights, ostensibly to assist them with their homework. But instead of helping them with history and mathematics, Hickey encouraged them to help themselves to the contents of his liquor cabinet. Later, when the boys were drowsy, he would take them upstairs and put them to bed—but not to rest up for the coming school day.

"I was there and I was half asleep and half awake and I looked down and he was sucking me off and I got out of the bed and I went out to the other room," Hogan testified.

Despite Hickey's incessant advances, the boys continued to visit him, partly to escape the more restrictive atmospheres of their own homes, and partly because Hickey worked so hard at winning them over. If they got drunk after a Friday night dance and didn't want to face their parents, Hickey let them stay overnight with him. Once parents found out that their sons were "at the priest's house" there were no questions asked. A chosen few of the boys had even been given their own keys to the presbytery.

The Hickey household was a well-stocked and interesting place for fishermen's sons who were unaccustomed to life's frills. There was always a supply of cigarettes, beer and vodka at Father Jim's, and the boys enjoyed playing his video games, watching the movies he would rent for them and listening to his tapes. They also enjoyed driving his car—he once owned a Cadillac that he would lend to boys who were too young to have licences. And in the drawer beside his bed was a special novelty: a silver-plated revolver the priest kept to fend off burglars.

And there was one other thing. Hickey would purposely leave money around the presbytery in small porcelain cups placed on the refrigerator and window ledges in full view of his impecunious house guests. "It wouldn't be, like, a five-dollar or a ten-dollar bill. It would be, like, a twenty or a fifty," a former altar boy testified. When the boys left and the money left with them, nothing was ever said. Jim Hickey was well versed in the sinister art of snaring his innocent prey.

On those rare occasions when the usual enticements failed to get a boy into his bed, Father Jim resorted to other methods. Terry Gushue,* a fifteen-year-old who enjoyed going to the priest's house with his friends, made a point of sleeping anywhere in the presbytery but Hickey's bedroom. He had heard from others what was expected, (the boys actually drew lots behind Hickey's back to see who would have to sleep with him) and wanted no part of it.

One night when Gushue was sleeping over, Hickey entered his room and sat down on the edge of his bed. The frightened boy sat up and drew the covers around him. Father Jim bluntly asked Gushue to sleep with him. The boy refused, just as he had resisted when the priest tried to give him wedgies in the sacristy. Hickey then reminded the stubborn object of his desire that the former parish priest had died in the house, and pointed up at the hatch in the ceiling that led to the attic.

"He said, 'If you don't come in and sleep in my room, Father Lacey is going to come down through the hatch and grab you during the night,'" the boy testified.

Another witness at Hickey's preliminary, Gary Pardy,* described how boys would clean up the gymnasium of Roncalli High School after a dance and then be taken out for burgers or doughnuts by Father Hickey. The evening always ended in the same place – the presbytery. Pardy, who would often go there after mass or school to help Father Jim with the gardening, liked the permissive atmosphere at the priest's house, but was less enamoured of the price-tag. Like the others, though, he paid his sexual dues.

"The first time I stayed there he said to me, he said, 'Do you want a French massage?' He pulled the covers down and he got on top of me and he started from my toes to my head. . . . He started to lick me. Started to go down, kept going down, right down to my feet and came back up. . . . He did oral sex on me. . . . He went down and he licked right around my privates and then he started to suck."

Pardy, who was appalled by Hickey's strange habit of grabbing the boys by the ears and quickly darting his tongue into their startled eyes, drew the line at sodomy.

"He said he had a sore bum and he went in the bathroom and took some Vaseline and he put it between the two cheeks of his bum. Then he came back out, took his shorts off and got in the bed and took mine off. He lay there for a couple of minutes and then he tried to guide my penis into his rectum. . . . It started to go inside of him and I just hauled back. It went in about an inch and I hauled back . . . I didn't want it to happen. When I refused, he kind of got pissed off and he turned over and put his shorts back on . . . ," the young man testified.

As they grew increasingly uneasy about their strange relationship with the priest, a few of the boys began to discuss the situation amongst themselves. The most detailed talk took place between Pardy and two of his friends during a camping trip to Skin Meadow, a field not far from the priest's Bauline Line cabin. The conversation was reported to Father Hickey and he moved quickly to stop what he must have realized could turn into a very dangerous rumour mill. After mass one Sunday, he made his feelings about these discussions known to Pardy in no uncertain terms.

"I was going to fix the books in the front pew and he came up and grabbed me behind the neck and he said, 'I hear you were talking about me.' I said, 'Yes.' And he said, 'Don't let it happen again and I don't want to hear nothing else.' So then I got even more frightened . . . I just froze and I turned around and walked away."

After the warning in the church, Pardy's lips were sealed. He never returned to the priest's house again.

One of the more amazing aspects of the evidence at Hickey's preliminary trial was the incredible hold he maintained over his victims long after they had grown up and married, a control that in at least one case had its roots in a carefully planted sense of guilt. One of his earliest victims, Frank Coady,* told the court about his first trip to the cabin on the Bauline Line. Shortly after going to sleep, he awakened to Father Hickey moving his penis between his thighs. After the priest had finished masturbating in this fashion, Coady performed the same act with Hickey. The next morning, while making breakfast, Hickey made an unexpected reference to the previous night's activities.

"Before I had a chance to say anything, he just said to me, 'Do you know what you did last night?' If he had punched me in the face it wouldn't have been that bad an impact. From that moment, I felt that I did this, that there was something wrong with me. I thought I was a sicko."

Far from believing he was violating his priestly responsibilities, Father Hickey felt he was observing the letter of the
First Lateran Council in 1123 when the Roman Catholic
church demanded of clergy that "service in moral leadership" required the vow of celibacy. But Hickey had a private
definition of celibacy that allowed him to pursue his fleshly
preferences with impunity: if the sex didn't involve a female,
then anything was permissible. Ten years after their sexual
liaison, Hickey would perform Coady's wedding service, and
later christen his two children. Father Jim was nothing if not
a master of keeping up appearances – and of making his
former victims do the same.

But three months after the devastating litany of evidence
against him, stark reality overtook the man who was now
being called "the cunning priest" by his former parishioners.
On September 8, 1988, the fifty-five-year-old cleric who had
twice told his archbishop that the charges against him were
scurrilous, pleaded guilty in provincial court to twenty
counts of sexual assault, indecent assault and gross
indecency. Twelve charges, which involved a second or third
incident against the same complainant, were dropped.

Wearing a dark turtle-neck sweater and navy blazer,
Father Hickey fidgeted with his eyeglass case while Crown
prosecutor Lois Hoegg summarized the charges against him
in a flat, emotionless monotone – attempting, perhaps, to
use her voice to defuse the explosive tensions building in the
packed courtroom. Several of Hickey's former flock openly
wept and the parents of the victims were locked in desperate
embraces, as if they needed to be reassured that there was at
least one reality on earth they could count on.

Father Hickey did not enter the pleas himself. Instead, he
stood silently before the bar with his lawyer, John Kelly, who
replied "Guilty" twenty times as the charges were called
out by Judge Reginald Reid. One mother sobbed loudly as
the priest's crimes – fondling, masturbation, oral and anal
intercourse – were read into the record. Another woman,
overwhelmed by events, swept out of the courtroom with
tears streaming down her cheeks. Passing close to Father
Hickey, she hissed out a single word: "Bastard!"

The next day, an emotionally charged mob of parents and

former victims waited in the lobby of the Provincial Court for Hickey to emerge from his sentencing hearing. When he appeared, the crowd broke into derisive choruses of "Bye Bye Love," and "Bye Bye Blackbird." They cheered and applauded as two policemen escorted Hickey to the cells.

Three weeks later, on September 30, 1988, Father Hickey appeared in court for sentencing and made his lone public statement of the lengthy and notorious proceedings. "I realize the pain and sorrow I have caused people . . . my remorse will stay with me for the rest of my life." Unmoved, Judge Reginald Reid sentenced Hickey to five years in prison, observing as he did so, "Your conduct appears to be without tenderness or affection. . . . The boys were exploited in their naïveté simply for the gratification of your basal sexual urges. . . . The only thing the boys have learned from you is that they shouldn't have trusted you."

Nearly a year later, the incarcerated priest would make clear to Sister Nuala Kenny during a prison visit that he felt no remorse, only a bitter conviction that he had been wronged by the system.

Father Hickey's trial sent a wave of shock and disgust through Newfoundland's Catholic community. Father Kevin Molloy, who had replaced Hickey in Holy Rosary parish in 1986, met open hostility when he tried to carry out his priestly duties. "I was told by certain people, 'Don't go to certain houses, you'll get a punch in the face.' " The angry priest said he felt like throwing Hickey's bed, and the rest of his furniture, out the window of the presbytery.

It was a dark moment for the Catholic church, but even darker clouds were boiling up on the horizon. Just two months after Father Jim was sent to Dorchester penitentiary as a protective custody inmate, another of Newfoundland's best-known priests, Father John Corrigan, pleaded guilty in Provincial Court to seven sex-related charges involving boys between the ages of ten and thirteen.

It was essentially a replay of the Hickey case. The fifty-seven-year-old parish priest would invite boys to the presbytery for cookies and beer, occasionally showing them homosexual videos and magazines. According to the complainants, they went on to have oral and anal intercourse with the priest two or three times a week over a two-year period. Judge Gordon Seabright sentenced Corrigan to five years in prison.

"Gross indecency and sexual assault," the judge said, "are probably the worst crimes against children that can be committed. They take the innocent and cause damage that ... may never be fully discovered.... When we add that these crimes were committed by a person in authority, then the defendant offends not only against the child but against the society as a whole."

Over the coming months, it was as if a decrepit wall had given way deep in the inner sanctums of the Roman Catholic church, exposing a rot no one had hitherto dreamed existed. Seven more priests were charged with sex-related offences. Overwhelmed by the epidemic of charges against his priests, Archbishop Alphonsus Penney issued a pastoral letter to be read at masses throughout the archdiocese.

"Our grief as a diocesan family helps us feel more keenly the personal distress of those who were compelled to make these complaints. We likewise share the sufferings of their families and in a truly Christian spirit assure them of our prayers and support."

Two and a half months later, in a Lenten pastoral letter published in the newspaper Father Hickey had once edited, Archbishop Penney once more addressed the sex scandal engulfing the church, urging anyone with information about sex crimes to go public. "I would much rather today have a hemorrhage within the church ... than this trickle of blood ... making the church weaker and weaker," he wrote.

The *Monitor* also reported that the Archdiocesan Pastoral Council had set up a special subcommittee "to continue dealing with the consequences of child sexual abuse scandals in our faith community." The subcommittee had already recommended "a prayer and action response" to the crisis. The church would hold assemblies in parishes "in which those who have been convicted of a betrayal of trust have been pastor." Further, parishes in the archdiocese would be asked to participate in two days of prayer "centered on conversion and on ... forgiveness."

For the time being, Newfoundland Catholics were in no mood to forgive; they were too anxious to find out how things could have gone so badly wrong in their church. Staggered by the extent of the crimes against their children, they were openly angry at the Archbishop for writing letters and setting up committees instead of visiting the affected parishes and personally consoling Catholics in their hour of need. Anger was clearly building over the church's perceived lack of response to the awful reality of the scandals, a perception that wasn't helped by the Archbishop's steadfast refusal to speak to the media.

Finally, on February 13, 1989, His Grace Archbishop Alphonsus Penney granted the only interview he would give on the escalating scandal. "No question about it," he told Rex Murphy, a local television personality, "there is something loose somewhere in the structure of the church. . . . It's a great mystery to me how such a thing could go on for so long. . . . It's astounding."

Many Catholics continued to believe that the Archbishop's response was totally inadequate. They were also angered by his statement that the scandals were greatly impeding the work of other priests, and by his request that Catholics pray for the offending Fathers. With each passing day in the ongoing crisis, his public concerns seemed more self-serving and inappropriate. It appeared that the church was more interested in damage control than it was in getting to the bottom of what lay behind the spate of sex charges against its clergy.

The tepid and tentative reaction of the church's highest officials spawned dark and disturbing rumours. Had the church known about the problem all along and engaged in a massive cover-up to save face? Was the Archbishop involved? Worst of all, could there be a pedophile sub-cult within the church, involved in systematic sex crimes against the children unwittingly entrusted to them?

Rational or Rabelaisian, irresistible forces were on the march. Following a general meeting of 180 members of St. Teresa's parish in St. John's, a press release was issued by the participants, expressing deep concern about the church's lack of response, communication and leadership in the sex scandal. The parishioners noted that there was "an over-whelming need for church structures to be responsible and accountable to the people." The release also stated that "a strong feeling of anger, frustration, helplessness and betrayal surfaced" at the meeting.

By the spring of 1989, several prominent Newfound-landers, including soon-to-be Premier Tom Rideout, NDP leader of the day, Peter Fenwick, and Portugal Cove priest Kevin Molloy were urging government to launch a public inquiry into the sexual abuse of children. On Sunday, April 23, after ten o'clock mass in the Basilica, the Roman Catholic church responded to the mounting public pressure and appointed a special blue-ribbon commission of inquiry to look into the scandal.

Headed up by former Newfoundland Lieutenant-Governor Gordon Winter, a non-Catholic, the commission's mandate was to inquire into facts that might have contributed to the sexual abuse of children by some members of the clergy. The commission was also charged with finding out how such behaviour could have gone undetected and unreported for such a long period of time. Finally, Commissioner Winter would make recommendations to the Archbishop on the spiritual healing of victims and the problems of selecting suitable candidates for the priesthood.

At the same time, Archbishop Penney established an Archdiocesan Committee on Child Sexual Abuse to deliver the necessary psychological help to the victims of sex abuse and to their families. (The offer of help would not deter the family of one of Father Hickey's victims in Portugal Cove from launching a lawsuit in the Supreme Court of Newfoundland against Archbishop Penney and Father Hickey, seeking compensation for emotional damages and financial redress for psychiatric treatment the boy had already undergone.)

However well-intentioned the church's response was, it was widely received as being too little, much too late. By the time the Archbishop made his announcements, fourteen priests, Christian Brothers and former members of Catholic orders had been charged with sex-related crimes. And to make matters worse, a Roman Catholic bishop in Nova Scotia published statements about the scandal that suggested that some of the Newfoundland boys may have willingly participated in sex acts with priests or Brothers. On May 17, 1989, Bishop Colin Campbell of Antigonish, Nova Scotia, wrote in a newspaper column that most of the "victims" appeared to be adolescents.

"If this is so, we are not dealing with classic pedophilia. I do not want to argue that homosexual activity between a priest and an adolescent is therefore moral. Rather it does not have the horrific character of pedophilia. Moreover, one can ask: if the victims were adolescents, why did they go back to the same situation once there had been one 'pass' or suggestion? Were they co-operating in the matter, or were they true victims?"

Describing the spate of sex charges in the same column as a witch-hunt, Bishop Campbell wrote that the situation represented a "real crucifixion" and that what the "Church in Newfoundland is going through is purgatory."

It was exactly the kind of self-serving commentary that was stirring up the deepest resentments in Newfoundland Catholics. On July 11, 1989, the Winter Commission held its first meeting in the fishing community of Portugal Cove, one of the parishes in which Father Jim Hickey had served before his conviction. If there was any doubt about the depth of anger Catholics were feeling, the next two and a half hours would dispel it like the summer sun burning away a mist over Conception Bay. Witness after witness cried cover-up and demanded the resignation of Archbishop Penney.

"Our shepherd and our leader, the Archbishop, didn't come," one man rasped into the microphone. "He didn't come out in support of the people. He didn't come to the parish and offer help. I know some of these people and they certainly would have welcomed him. The hierarchy fell down in their duty as leaders."

Another witness, a woman whose son had been sexually abused by Hickey for seven years, said that a sudden change had come over her boy when he was twelve. By the age of seventeen, he would sit at the kitchen table and cry without any apparent cause, unable to reveal the terrible source

of the depression that had driven him to the brink of
suicide.

"There was absolutely no way I could reach that boy," his
mother said. "I raised all my children Catholic, and today
there is not one who will go inside the church."

The next night the Commission moved its proceedings to
Pouch Cove, where Father John Corrigan had been priest of
St. Agnes' parish. The crowd was even bigger and more
boisterous than the one the night before, possibly because
the hearing opened just hours after two members of another
Roman Catholic order, the Congregation of Irish Christian
Brothers, were arraigned in Provincial Court on sex
charges.

In a raucous session that took place in the basement of the
community school, the local chapter of the most prominent
organization of Roman Catholic laymen, the Knights of
Columbus, called for Archbishop Penney's resignation.
Other witnesses urged that busloads of church members
should bring their protest to the steps of the Basilica in St.
John's. The radical tenor of the meeting was captured in the
remarks of a senior citizen who began his denunciation of
the church's response to the sex scandals with these
words:

"I perceive the clergy to be a haven for homosexuals and
perverts. If you told me twenty years ago that I would get up
and abuse the church like this, I would have told you that
you were a candidate for the mental hospital."

Over the next several hours, Gordon Winter and his fellow
commissioners spent nearly as much time on their feet as the
witnesses, defending the church's motives in establishing the
commission.

"Please don't look upon us as being under the thumb of
the Archbishop, or being unable to ask him questions,"
Commissioner Winter pleaded. But his words were swallowed up in the sea of anger, frustration and suspicion in
which he, and the Catholic church, were engulfed.

Two days after the meeting at Pouch Cove, the
Commission moved to Ferryland, where two hundred angry
Catholics argued that the only way to purge the church was
to allow priests to marry and to open the seminary doors to

women. Other radical solutions were proposed, including the abolition of confession so that fallen priests wouldn't have an easy means of homing in on their victims. Some people demanded the restriction of pay to priests so that they wouldn't be able to bribe their young charges, as Fathers Hickey and Corrigan had so shamelessly done.

The Ferryland meeting also had its share of Archbishop-bashing. Bernard Agriesti, an adviser to Alphonsus Penney who resigned from his parish council in the midst of the sex scandal, criticized Penney for failing to reprimand Father Hickey after the awful revelations of his preliminary trial.

"Jim Hickey came back to the parish and he told everyone it was lies, lies, lies. He tore this parish apart. He kept coming back and I told the Archbishop and was told nothing could be done. I ran into a cover-up and all kinds of lies. Those twenty boys and their parents were being called liars. The argument used [by the Archbishop] was that anything done would prejudice the case against Jim Hickey. That was nonsense. It's not an admission of guilt to help people," he told the cheering crowd.

Another witness who attended all three public meetings urged the commission to investigate rumours that people in Rushoon had in fact reported incidents of child abuse by Jim Hickey to the Archbishop before the priest had been transferred to his Portugal Cove parish. Randy Barnes, who was assigned by Archbishop Penney to work as an assistant to Father Hickey in the summer of 1979, would later confirm that he was uneasy about the appointment to Rushoon because he had heard that Hickey was a homosexual pedophile. He expressed his concerns to the Archbishop at the time of taking up his appointment, without going into detail.

"I didn't actually say that to him [Archbishop Penney]. I just said I didn't like the actual idea of going there because I had heard too many stories concerning Father Hickey."

Archbishop Penney never asked the reluctant seminarian to explain what the stories were about. Had he kept in touch with the young man, he would have learned that Father Hickey eventually asked Barnes to join himself and another young man in his twenties in a sexual threesome—an offer his unwilling assistant turned down.

"I said, 'No, I'm not getting involved because that's not my idea of what the priesthood stands for.'. . . I never complained about it because I never entered the room myself."

The most eloquent insight into how men of the cloth had been able to perpetrate such monstrous crimes against their parishioners' children and get away with it for so long came from a woman whose cultural eyesight was 20/20. She laid the blame for the tragedy on the traditional role of the priest in outport Newfoundland, which she said was as close to God as you could get without playing a harp. Expressing a feeling shared by many of Newfoundland's 205,000 Catholics, she told the meeting:

"If a child was born without an arm, people said it was because the mother had said something against a priest. That was nonsense, but a priest with that kind of shield could get away with anything. We are victims of our own heritage."

But if the sex crimes of an ever-lengthening list of priests had prompted a crisis of faith in the Roman Catholic community, another scandal was brewing that would make everyone in Newfoundland doubt many of the other institutions they lived by. Months before the Winter Commission began its deliberations, another victim of his own heritage emerged from the shadows to tell the story he had kept bottled up inside for fourteen years. The revelations of the twenty-three-year-old St. John's waiter were so horrific that they would alter the outcome of the then imminent provincial election, and later compel Newfoundland's new premier, Clyde Wells, to appoint one of the most controversial royal commissions Canada has ever seen.

Mount Cashel Orphanage, the institution where Shane Earle had spent most of his life as a ward of the province under the care of the Irish Christian Brothers, was about to become a household word across the country—a synonym for horrendous crimes of sex and violence against children and a tainted justice system that, instead of dealing with the perpetrators under the law, had secretly chosen to let them go.

Chapter 2

▮▮▮▮ The Brothers of Mount Cashel

You can form no idea of the enthusiasm of the entire Catholic population to have the Brothers. I am not exaggerating when I say it surpasses belief. From a letter by Brother P. D. McDonnell, written three weeks before the arrival of the first Christian Brother in Newfoundland on October 3, 1875.

SHIVERING BENEATH A Christmas moon, a child drew half of St. John's to the charity's doors with the peal of his orphan's bell.

Every December since 1923, the residents of Mount Cashel staged the year's busiest raffle in an abandoned storefront on Water Street, the city's oldest thoroughfare. Homeless boys and Christian Brothers filled a dusty room with stuffed toys, dart boards, chocolates and a freezer packed with fat Christmas birds. The Christian Brothers gingerly installed a betting wheel themselves—a large plywood board covered with a map of Newfoundland and dotted with 180 Christmas lights to mark the raffle numbers. Workmen assembled pens in the shop window so that a pair of turkeys—named after the leading politicians of the day—could strut about behind the glass to the amusement of passersby on Water Street's snowy sidewalks.

The bustle began with the pitchman's first call. Everyone—the Brothers, former orphans and local politicians—peddled strips of pink and blue tickets to the eager crowds. Lawyers, doctors and merchants passed dollar after dollar to the carnies, only to slip their tickets to downtown children who sat penniless on the outer edge of the bettors' circle. Winners declined to accept toys or turkeys. Instead, they took four-dollar cash prizes and then stayed just long enough to spend their winnings. Ladies in worn woollen coats sauntered in to press modest cheques into the palm of the nearest Brother.

By closing time on Christmas eve, the raffle's cash box would contain as much as $50,000. Walking back to the orphanage, the Brothers considered how the spirit of Christmas would stay with them for the rest of the year, while the proceedings of the annual event would see the orphanage through a few months of groceries.

But Mount Cashel's inmates were too excited to consider such practical matters. St. John's most enchanted work of Christmas magic was about to appear on their doorstep. In the small hours of December 25, unknown persons would deposit a cake in the hallway between the boys' dorm and the monastery. Shaped like a castle, a church or a whole village, the four-foot-high creation would be studded with gum-drops, cookies and peppermint canes. It was a grateful community's tribute to the Christian Brothers. After all, the Brothers had sheltered the homeless, educated the young and helped lift Newfoundland Catholics out of ignorance and want for more than a century.

The first Irish Catholics who emigrated to Newfoundland met with fierce treatment from the colony's British governors. Determined to prevent the Irishmen from settling permanently, colonial rulers fined settlers for observing religious feasts in their homes and issued edicts stating Catholics could not own property in Newfoundland. On occasion, British soldiers torched the homes of practising Catholics. Irish immigrants were forced to hold mass in vegetable cellars or fishing stages, a rite that was usually administered by a fugitive Irish Catholic priest who skulked from one impoverished and illegally erected hovel to another, under cover of darkness.

Eventually, the colony's religious intolerance eased and governors gradually repealed sanctions against the Catholics, including a tax that charged them twelve shillings for the right to be buried. Testing the limits of their freedom, a group of Irish Catholic merchants met one frosty night in February 1806 at the London Tavern, a popular pub in the seaport of St. John's. Concerned that many immigrants had failed to find prosperous lives in the New World, the men formed the Benevolent Irish Society (BIS) to provide "permanent relief to the wretched and the distressed."

From the beginning, BIS members believed education was the surest way to save children from a life of poverty in the British outpost. The Society, which would spend millions educating Newfoundlanders over the next hundred years, soon established a school at the Old Orphan Asylum on Garrison Hill in St. John's, the passport to a better life, it was hoped, for the first 206 pupils that filled its classrooms. Lay teachers, however, could never attain the high educational standards desired by their Catholic sponsors. So in 1831, the Bishop of St. John's began pleading with the Catholic hierarchy to provide its Newfoundland congregation with "even one" Christian Brother.

Across Ireland, the famous Brothers of Edmund Ignatius Rice had won the respect of the poor, the educated and the pious. Born outside Callan in Kilkenny County, Rice worked diligently for more than two decades, establishing himself as one of Ireland's most successful merchants. But his ambitions changed profoundly when, just four years after his wedding, his wife suddenly died. At the age of forty, Rice sold his Waterford business and opened a school for destitute boys. Along with nine other educated men, Brother Edmund Ignatius assumed a habit and took the vows of obedience, chastity, poverty and perseverence. This last vow, which was dropped in the early 1960s, simply meant that the Brothers would "persevere" in all tasks they were given as members of the order, particularly the "gratuitous education of male children."

The Christian Brothers were an independent lay order within the Catholic church, with their own superior in Rome to whom they reported. Nevertheless, the General Council of the Christian Brothers submitted an annual report to the Holy See about its membership and activities, and there were regular, if informal meetings between the order's senior members and the bishops. Unlike priests, the monks of the Christian Brothers could not perform such holy rites as mass or marriage, but specifically dedicated themselves to the free instruction of male children, especially those boys who were abandoned or impoverished.

By 1820, the Brothers had opened schools in the poorest quarters of Cork, Dublin, Tipperary, Thurles and Limerick. Church officials in British colonies as far away as Australia, New Zealand, Tasmania, South Africa, India and Gibraltar began petitioning the Catholic order's Superior General for the services of the teaching Brothers. Supply ran well behind demand; when the Bishop of St. John's made his first request for assistance, Brother Rice himself sadly reported that the order would not have a man to spare for several years. As it turned out, this was something of an understatement; Newfoundland Catholics would have to wait nearly fifty years for the arrival of their first Irish Christian Brother.

An advance man for the Christian Brothers reported that the Irish teachers would receive a spirited welcome to the fishing colony. In a letter to his superiors, Brother P. D. McDonnell wrote, "You can form no idea of the enthusiasm of the entire Catholic population to have the Brothers. I am not exaggerating when I say it surpasses belief."

Reverend Brother F. L. Holland—a tireless and jovial young man from Galway—arrived in St. John's aboard the S.S. *Hibernian* on October 3, 1875. Sailing out of Liverpool, the vessel had been delayed by dogged westerly gales and poor weather. But the Brother's spirits lifted when he walked down the gangway to the settlement that has been variously described as the fifth province of Ireland, or, less lovingly, a slum on a hill.

Shortly after Christmas, the S.S. *Moravian* transported three additional Brothers from Cork to St. John's. And on January 31, 1876, the Catholic lay order began educating the sons of poor immigrants in the Old Orphan Asylum.

"With a group of about five or six of my companions . . . we tramped over Theatre Hill that bright and frosty wintry morning, arriving at the school doors shortly before nine o'clock. Boys from all over the city were assembled," one of the first students of the Christian Brothers recalled. Boys from Freshwater, Riverhead, Torbay and other fishing towns travelled as much as thirty miles to meet the Irish

Brothers on the first day of classes. The Garrison Hill school, whose enrolment had slipped below seventy in previous months, was suddenly bursting with three hundred students, and anxious Catholic parents began pressing the Brothers to put their sons on waiting lists.

The first years of the Brothers in the New World were harsh. The natives of Ireland were unaccustomed to the bitter winters of St. John's, with their high winds blowing in off the North Atlantic and mountainously drifting snow. More than once during the long trek from their living quarters to the classroom, the earliest Brothers must have wished they lived in a land where the frigid Labrador current was far away. "Often, I recall, they arrived at the school covered with snow and practically frozen," one student wrote. Lectures in the overcrowded rooms of the Old Orphan Asylum were frequently interrupted by the standard request of a student whose work had been halted by the chill. "May I go thaw my slate, sir?"

The Brothers fascinated the sons of fishermen and outpost merchants with Longfellow's poems and Newton's laws. The Irishmen were masters at inspiring young boys to academic excellence. In a move that filled the Orphan Asylum with vigorous rivalries, Brother Holland divided each of the school's classes into teams of Greeks and Romans. At the end of every week, the team with the highest overall average was handed the pink, white and green flag of victory and permitted to stage a triumphant march through the corridors.

Other members of the Irish Brotherhood lured their classes through tedious hours of studying the Catechism "less by religious zeal than by the display of a large bag of confectionery placed temptingly on the teacher's desk." By such sweet-toothed appeals, Brother R. J. Prenderville even enticed boys to return to school on Saturday afternoons to study French, free-hand drawing and the marvels of electricity. Many of the Brothers' students went on to win Rhodes scholarships, and later took their place amongst Newfoundland's leading barristers, merchants, politicians and clerics.

In the years after the Christian Brothers arrived in

Newfoundland, Catholic boys stole centre stage at the
Majestic and the Casino theatres in performances of *The
Mikado, The Sorcerer, Agatha* and countless other plays and
operettas imported from abroad. Coached by the Brothers,
the sons of immigrants held choral performances in St.
John's Cathedral and several outlying parishes. Years later,
the Irishmen would goad a handful of talented students into
creating Shannahan's Band — the best vaudeville act in the
Dominion, as Newfoundland was known after World War I.
A young organist trained by the Brothers was made a Knight
of St. Gregory by Pope Pius XI for the excellence of his
playing. The people of St. John's, like the boys of the Old
Orphan Asylum, were deeply impressed by the gifted and
energetic Irishmen who brought a little Old World finish to a
colony legendary for its roughness.

In class, the early Brothers maintained discipline without
resorting to threats or violence. One former pupil recalled
that Brother A. P. O'Hurley, a Dublin man with a buoyant
disposition and a permanent smile, "controlled the boys not
by the power of his mind, nor the strength of his arm, but by
the nobility of his heart."

After class, the Brothers indulged "their boys" with
special treats and sports. The best treat was the Halloween
game of "snap apple." After dismissing class early for the
holiday, the Brothers would bring out a large tub of water
and an electric battery. One man dropped an armload of
huge, crimson apples and a few twenty-cent pieces in the
water. After the washtub was transformed into a pool of
delicacies and riches for the colonial boys, the end of a live
battery wire was slipped into the tub. One by one, the boys
plunged their bare hands into the electrified water to snatch
a prize and prove their bravery. As the novelty of the game
waned (or the high-voltage amusement grew too painful),
the Brothers disconnected the battery and distributed the
fruit to the assembled boys.

Barely seven months after the first congregation of
Christian Brothers arrived on the island, leaders of the BIS
began laying plans to construct a proper Catholic school
directly across from the Cathedral. Members of the Society
personally contributed the then enormous sum of two

thousand pounds to the project. (By comparison, the Old Orphan Asylum was valued at thirty-five pounds when it was put up for public auction.) In August 1880, BIS leaders and Christian Brothers opened St. Patrick's Hall, a school for poor men's sons that would prepare "any boy who graduated from its classes to rap at the door of any University."

Similarly, Catholics, Protestants and virtually every organization, from the Total Abstinence Society to the Bennett Brewing Company, helped raise money to build Holy Cross School, St. Bonaventure's College and several other facilities across the island. The support never lagged. Even during the Great Depression, the residents of St. John's raised more than thirty thousand pounds for the Christian Brothers in a collection that lasted little more than a week.

At times, the Christian Brothers were a little overwhelmed by the generosity of the people. After amassing considerable debts from the construction of Mount St. Francis Monastery, the Brotherhood agreed they could not become the centre of another fund-raising venture in St. John's. Instead, it was agreed that two Brothers would travel across Canada and the United States raising money by selling lottery tickets. But a layman learned of the plan and rapidly devised a means to make the lottery-ticket tour unnecessary. A charity bazaar netted six thousand pounds in six weeks, eliminated the Brothers' debt load and left the order with a tidy profit of four hundred pounds.

All through the bazaars and concerts, the Bishop of St. John's eyed the Brothers as his key to realizing a long-held dream. For years, Bishop Michael Francis Howley had wanted to convert his family's estate—twenty-six acres of prime farmland and forest overlooking the old quarter of St. John's—into an orphanage and industrial school for boys. By 1887, the Bishop's desire for a new orphanage had grown into an urgent need. An outbreak of typhoid fever had forced the Villa Nova home outside St. John's to close, leaving several dozen orphans homeless. After considerable discussion, the Christian Brothers agreed to manage the new institution. The Brothers moved into the one-hundred-year-old family cottage on the property known as Mount Cashel, named for the Howley family's place of origin in Cashel, Ireland. While the cottage was being renovated, a new orphanage was erected to house the boys.

On October 24, 1898 — the feast of the archangel St. Raphael — Bishop Howley said the first mass and blessed the house, fields and premises of Mount Cashel as the first of two boys, Richard and James Ennis, were admitted. A handful of Brothers vowed to turn the boys who occupied the beds of St. Raphael's dormitory into educated and upstanding men. After school, the Brothers taught their charges how to perform a tailor's tasks, handle a shoe-maker's tools and master various other trades. Shortly after taking charge of the orphanage, the Brothers realized that it would take a working farm to feed a family of two hundred, so they planted a vegetable garden a few yards from the chapel and raised a barnyard to house pigs, horses, chickens and a herd of thirty cows. Out of necessity, Mount Cashel boys also became skilled farmers. Each boy accepted his turn at tilling the garden and feeding the livestock — a chore that frequently sent orphans sprinting two miles across town to retrieve runaway Jerseys.

The Brothers steadily improved courses and expanded facilities at Mount Cashel until one April afternoon in 1926. Strolling down a hall in the orphanage, a Brother noticed a faint smell of smoke and anxiously tracked the scent from door to door. Bursting into a room at the rear of the chapel, the Brother discovered flames leaping from a pile of fibre used to stuff orphans' mattresses. Brothers, firemen and hundreds of townspeople came running at the sound of the alarm to evacuate the boys, free the animals and mount a bucket brigade. But the flames leapt from building to building, driven by a strong southwest wind. In less than an hour, every stick of Mount Cashel, except the Brothers' residence, was reduced to smouldering cinders.

It was a catastrophe of unthinkable proportions. More than $200,000 worth of buildings, books, clothes and supplies had been lost in the midday blaze, and the penny-poor Brothers had never carried more than $60,000 worth of insurance. In less than a week, however, the people of St. John's had miraculously raised $40,000 to erect a new home for 165 displaced orphans, and by June 1927, the new complex was ready to receive the Archbishop's blessing.

Over the years, the job of sheltering and educating Newfoundland's orphans gradually became unmanageable, as the number of residents dropped and the operating costs of running the rambling institution steadily increased. Catholics and Protestants alike still flocked to Mount Cashel's garden party and Christmas raffle, contributed to its annual collection, and donated their pocket money to the Brothers' seal-hunt sweepstakes, but their informal contributions were no longer enough to cover expenses.

However, by the 1950s, another source of income appeared. The Department of Social Services needed shelter for wards of the Director of Child Welfare, and since Mount Cashel wasn't filled to capacity, the Department began to place some of its wards there. Over the next few years the number of wards steadily increased, until there were more wards than orphans at Mount Cashel. It had become the haven of last resort for foster children no one else wanted, including former inmates of Whitbourne Boys' Home, a reform school outside St. John's. The Department of Social Services began making significant contributions to the operating costs of Mount Cashel. Although the Department would have liked a greater say in how Mount Cashel was run, the Christian Brothers continued to exercise almost total administrative control of the institution. The Brotherhood would take in children no one else wanted and, in return, demanded the authority to care for them in an environment they had created. It seemed like an equitable arrangement.

In April 1962, Brother John Murray petitioned government to increase the orphan fund. "As you know, the present [monthly] grant is $18.00 per child. This rate, I believe has been in effect for some ten years. During this time, operating costs have increased considerably. . . . From this Orphan Grant we must feed, clothe and educate a boy on little better than fifty cents a day." In a letter drafted three months later, the Vicar General of St. John's reasserted Mount Cashel's dire need for additional aid. "The Orphanage authorities have assured me that the cost of taking care of a child is approximately one dollar and fifty cents a day."

By the early seventies, Mount Cashel's finances had reached crisis proportions. Brothers apologetically told teenage boys the orphanage could provide them with no more than $2.50 a month in pocket money. Accountants warned that Mount Cashel's operating deficit would soon top $50,000 a year. In May 1971, Brother J. M. Barron informed government that Mount Cashel was about to experience drastic changes, sparked in part by its ongoing financial shortfall.

"At a recent meeting, held with the Consultants of our Congregation, it was suggested and unanimously agreed, to close this orphanage for one month during the coming summer," Brother Barron advised Newfoundland's Director of Child Welfare.

"The main purpose for closing this institution is to reduce the monthly expenditures on light, heat and maintenance of the building which we might add are very, very high. With the cost of living soaring and our allowance remaining dormant, it would be difficult for us to meet our commitments except for the fact that we are subsidized, to a great degree, by funds from our annual raffle and, further, that our religious staff is operating the orphanage without remuneration.

"In view of the above, it is suggested that you do all in your power to place as many boys as possible with relatives, and the boys remaining with us, we intend taking on a camping trip."

The move startled and embarrassed the Newfoundland government. Within months, an outside consultant hired by the Christian Brothers reported to the province that Catholic boys were receiving excellent care at Mount Cashel, even though poor financing had driven the Brothers from their St. John's home during the summer. "There is a great warmth and spontaneity in this institution," the consultant concluded. "At the summer camp, I particularly noted the good relationship that existed between the Brothers and the boys. In spite of the necessary 'regimentation,' there is a comfortable, free relaxed atmosphere. . . . The commitment of the Brothers and all their staff to the boys is very great."

Conceding that Mount Cashel required extensive repairs, government agreed to contribute nearly half a million dollars to a construction and renovation project at the Torbay Road orphanage. In a 1975 press release, the provincial government praised the Christian Brothers for saving countless boys from "the terrible disease of being unwanted." The "warm humanity of the Brothers as fathers and friends" had created a caring atmosphere in the orphanage, the release said.

"No wonder, then, that Mount Cashel boys have grown as persons strong and independent, surrounded as they have been with love and security."

For the inmates of the proud Catholic institution in the mid-1970s, the rhetoric could not have been more empty.

Chapter 3
■ The Beating

The seventy-six-year history of Mount Cashel indicates that while other approaches to child care have been initiated and implemented effectively, the alternative service offered by Mount Cashel continues to be vital and effective. The Honourable Ank Murphy, Minister of Social Services, December 20, 1974.

FOR RICK, BILLY and Shane Earle, family life came to an official end on the steps of the Mount Cashel Orphanage on April 4, 1973 – the day the boys said goodbye to their mother and father and were placed in the care of the Congregation of the Irish Christian Brothers.

At the age of thirty-three, their mother, Carol Earle, was a broken woman. Two years earlier, she and her husband, William Earle, Sr., had finally come to a parting of the ways. Over the thirteen years of their marriage, the slight woman with the long, brown hair had borne eight children – three boys and five girls, one of whom had died in infancy.

It had been a rocky road for the pretty seventeen-year-old from the very beginning of her marriage to the burly sheet-metal worker with an eye for the ladies and a fondness for rum. When the Earles separated for the first time in 1968, all of the children, except two-year-old Shane, were made temporary wards of the provincial Director of Child Welfare. Rick, age eight, and Billy, age four, were placed briefly in a United Church receiving home, a hostel for otherwise homeless people, until they could be permanently placed. After leaving the home, Rick went to Mount Cashel and spent the next few years shuttling between the orphanage and his father's home.

Just keeping her head above water was a debilitating grind for the single parent; she could barely scrape by on her modest earnings as a night cleaner at St. Joseph's school, even with a monthly allowance from Social Services. The only way she could make ends meet was by living in her former father-in-law's house on the Battery Road, a tough neighbourhood in the city's east end, carved out of a rocky cliff that rises sharply from the ocean and looks across St. John's harbour to the National Sea fish plant nestled at the base of the Southside Hills. When the icy winds of the North Atlantic blew through The Narrows, The Battery was the first place in the city to shiver; when the fog rolled in, its narrow streets echoed hauntingly with the foghorn's eerie wail.

While living at her father-in-law's house, Carol Earle allowed the Department of Social Services to use her home as a Child Welfare Clinic where the Public Health nurse gave local children vaccinations. The children remained with their mother until August 1972, when Carol Earle's father-in-law sold the house. The Social Services department would not provide a place for the large family to live, and the hapless mother, faced with responsibilities she could no longer discharge, simply ran out of emotional resources to keep going. "My mother just couldn't take it any more and she had a nervous breakdown and my father was awarded custody of us," Shane Earle recalled.

The children were loaded into a taxi and driven to another part of east-end St. John's to live with their father and his latest girlfriend, a woman they knew only as Gloria. But it wasn't long before the pressure-packed domestic situation began to test the patience of Earle, Sr.'s latest companion; with two children of her own to worry about, the addition of seven others was simply too much to handle. Gradually, the Earle children were shunted off to willing relatives or drifted into institutions – although in moments of crisis the boys, at least, sought out their mother or father.

In November 1972, at the age of eight, Billy was placed in Mount Cashel. By the following March, sickened by the physical violence he witnessed there, he had run away and returned to his father, even though he was still technically a ward of the province. Then one night after a terrible row between William Earle, Sr. and his girlfriend, the police were called to the wooden frame house on Queens Road; shortly afterwards, Billy, Shane and Rick were taken away and temporarily placed with relatives until a more permanent arrangement could be made by the Department of Social Services.

Although he didn't have the money to take care of them himself, William Earle, Sr. didn't want his sons going to a foster home. For once, he and his former wife, who now lived alone in a boarding house, saw eye to eye. They agreed that Mount Cashel was the best place for their boys, a sanctuary where they would receive the counselling and education they needed, while still having access to their parents. "I always had a lot of respect for Mount Cashel," Mr. Earle said, having himself been taught by the Christian Brothers as a boy. "They were men of the cloth."

On the dismal April day that the three boys landed at the orphanage, it was a man of the cloth who stood waiting for them in the main hallway—Brother Douglas Kenny, the Superintendent of Mount Cashel. To six-year-old Shane Earle, who was small for his age, Brother Kenny must have looked like a terrifying giant. A lean six-footer, his receding hairline exaggerated the size of his bulbous head; nor was Kenny's intimidating appearance softened by the large, slightly protuberant eyes that peered down at the little boy from under a thinning mat of grey-brown hair.

He was the son of a prominent Catholic family who owned Kenny's Marble Works, a cemetery monument business in St. John's. Kenny held a Masters degree in history from Notre Dame University and was a superb athlete. But to the inmates of Mount Cashel, it was not his intellect or hockey prowess for which he was best known, as the Earle boys would soon find out.

For ten-year-old Billy and six-year-old Shane, their nervousness that day turned to trauma when their older brother, Rick, bolted out of the building before he was signed in. Having resided at Mount Cashel during his parents' original separation, Rick knew what lay in store for Billy and Shane, a fate the thirteen-year-old boy could neither protect them from nor force himself to share.

It was, in fact, the second time that Rick Earle had run away from Mount Cashel. In 1971, he had been living in St. Aloysius dormitory, or "St. Al's" as everyone knew it. The dormitory was supervised by Brother Alan Ralph, a chunky six-footer who had an overbite that earned him the nickname "Bugs Bunny" amongst the boys. In his mid-twenties at the time, Ralph was known as an avid outdoorsman and a crude practical joker—a walking caricature who waddled through the halls of Mount Cashel like "the A&W Root Bear."

But Brother Ralph's affable exterior was contradicted by his inner temperament and secret proclivities. He once dangled a boy by the heels from a third-storey window of the orphanage, and made another walk around the dorm stark naked with his suitcase and forced him to shake hands with the other boys before leaving Mount Cashel—a cruel disciplinary joke the seven-year-old took for real until the Brother explained it was only a gag. The boys grew to fear the Brother with the deep voice who was always fidgeting with his dark-rimmed glasses, incessantly "rooting" them up and down the bridge of his nose.

But he had another trait that didn't fit the category of tasteless humour or zany eccentricity; Brother Ralph was a child molester. Rick used to watch him doing his rounds in the dormitory after prayers, making the sign of the cross on a boy's forehead and then putting his hand under the blankets and fondling his victim's penis for fifteen to twenty minutes. But Brother Ralph never stopped at Rick's bunk, and the young boy made a point of avoiding the burly Brother with the wandering hands. Still, there was only so much a boy could ignore, especially one like Rick who tried so hard to emulate his macho father who had taught him to be independent and tough.

One day Rick remembered that the boys from St. Al's went to wash up after a session in the gymnasium. Brother Ralph, who was supervising the showers, suddenly motioned one of the naked boys over to him. Rick saw the Brother embrace the boy, rubbing his bare back with his hands. Disgusted, he convinced the boy to jointly report the incident to Brother John Barron, then Mount Cashel's Superintendent. The two complainants were joined by several others and a delegation of ten boys trooped into Barron's office. One of the boys present, Johnny Williams, recalled the scene several years later—which was more than the Superintendent was able to do.

"We told Brother John Barron that Brother Ralph has been physically and sexually molesting boys in St. Al's dorm," Williams, who spent ten years in the orphanage, remembered. The offending Brother was summoned to the Superintendent's office over Mount Cashel's public address system and given a tongue lashing by Brother Barron in front of the boys. He was then dispatched to a nearby monastery, which housed Christian Brothers who taught at nearby St. Patrick's boys' school. Johnny Williams, the boy who had been dangled out the window by the cruel practical joker, watched with relief from the main entrance of the orphanage as Brother Ralph threw a large suitcase into the back seat of a car and disappeared down Mount Cashel's tree-lined driveway towards his temporary banishment. He would soon be put in charge of a Boy Scout troop at St. Pat's, and, two years later, would be back at Mount Cashel—much to the surprise of former Superintendent John Barron, who by then had left the Brothers.

After the incident with Brother Ralph, Rick Earle was more wary then ever and kept well away from the sexual and physical abuse he witnessed going on so openly around him. One person he didn't have to worry about was Brother Sidney Waters,* his favourite staff member at Mount Cashel, who befriended him and taught him how to play hockey. A brutal body-checker, Brother Waters would manhandle his charge during their practice sessions, but only in the name of tough pedagogy. As Rick later recalled, Waters was the kind of person who would "knock it into you until you had it right."

But one night Brother Waters skated offside. He came up to the dorm after prayers, sat next to Rick on the bottom bunk, and gave him a treat from the kitchen—a molasses square. They talked for a while and then the person he trusted more than anyone else in the world calmly proceeded to molest him, exactly as the youngster had seen Brother Ralph molest the other boys.

"He offered that [the treat] to me, and when I took it, that's when he put his hand down around my groin. I couldn't say nothing . . . I was just a young fellow. I just let it go."

The next morning, humiliated and afraid, Rick ran home in the driving rain. Half an hour later, coatless and drenched, he appeared at the door of his father's house on Queens Road, determined to live on the street if need be rather than return to Mount Cashel.

Now, two years later, at the sight of Father Kenny, the old memories had simply welled up and overcome him. Once more, running seemed to be the only answer.

With their older brother gone, the remaining Earle brothers were left to face their new home alone. The boys were a study in opposites – the dark-haired, green-eyed Billy, cocky and irreverent, a self-admitted "shit disturber and scrapper" who at ten was already ducking the truant officer and who made no secret of how much he hated Mount Cashel; and Shane, the blond, blue-eyed six-year-old who was painfully quiet and who liked school, though he missed his mother. Despite their different temperaments, the two boys would stick together, the back-street tough guy taking care of his shy little brother as best he could.

Compared to their previous homes, Mount Cashel must have seemed like a castle mysteriously set down in a field overlooking St. John's. In those days, the rambling, three-storey institution was painted grey with black trim, though in summer, when the trees were in full leaf, you could barely see its impressive façade from nearby Torbay Road. Just inside the main entrance, on the left, was the Superintendent's office. To the right of the entrance was the office of the Assistant Superintendent, with its imposing black door. Close by the office area were a trophy case and a Coke machine.

In addition to the executive offices, the main floor also housed the orphanage's sick room – a former classroom now equipped with four hospital beds; a broadloomed common area known as the "carpet room," where the boys watched television; and a gymnasium with a full-sized swimming pool, locker rooms and showers. There were also classrooms for grades one through three, and a reading room with a long study table and cushioned chairs.

The dining hall was down two flights of stairs from the main floor. A floor below was the basement, part of which was used as a storeroom for winter clothing. The showers for the younger children were also in the basement, which was reached by concrete stairs with no railings. The shower room included an outer area with a brown wooden bench for towels and pyjamas, and an inner room with twenty-four shower heads suspended from the walls above a concrete floor. It was here that the residents of St. Al's and St. Joseph's (St. Joe's) would shower, one dormitory at a time, under a Brother's supervision.

The study hall was located at the end of the hall in the basement, just beyond the furnace room. It contained forty desks for students and a large desk for the supervising Brother. Four project rooms were situated off the study hall.

St. Raphael's chapel was up one flight of stairs from the main floor and included a small area with pews, an altar, and a vestry for the priest and altar boys. Above the chapel were the tailor and barber shops. Twice a week a barber would visit to administer the standard Mount Cashel haircut to the younger boys—short on top and cropped above the ears in the era of the Beatles.

The second floor of Mount Cashel was reserved for senior boys. St. Patrick's (St. Pat's) and St. Pius's dorms were both large rooms with twenty to thirty beds—singles in St. Pat's and bunk beds in St. Pius's—separated from each other by rows of lockers. Adjacent to the sleeping areas, there was a common shower and bathroom for the two dorms, and individual TV lounges.

The top floor of the orphanage featured a large bathroom with twenty-four sinks and mirrors. Next to the communal washroom with its reddish brown floor tiles was St. Al's dormitory, which housed boys between the ages of five and ten. Its thirty bunk beds lined both walls, the two rows separated by a line of wooden lockers down the middle of the room. There was a large closet with slanted ceilings which housed the boys' clothes and toys. There was also a small office used by the Brother who was supervising the dorm.

At the opposite end of the top floor was St. Stanislaus (St. Stan's), a dorm for boys between the ages of ten and thirteen, which was laid out exactly like St. Al's. Sandwiched between the sleeping areas for the younger children was St. Joe's, the dorm for boys between the ages of thirteen and fifteen. There were no doors on St. Joe's; an open-air partition separated the twenty to thirty beds from the row of sinks behind it.

Completely separate from the main building, on the other side of the monastery, was St. Gabriel's (St. Gabe's), which housed the oldest boys at Mount Cashel. The monastery itself was home to the ten Christian Brothers who were at the orphanage in the early seventies. The Brothers had their own rooms, and after the boys were tucked in at night, they returned to the Monastery to sleep.

The twenty-two acres on which Mount Cashel was situated (four acres had been sold off since the original sale of the property by the Howley family to the Roman Catholic Episcopal Corporation for $3,500) had three silver-coloured barns, one of which was used as a cold-room for the orphanage's vegetables, another for storage, while a third was rented out to Green's Auto Body, a local garage. There were soccer, baseball and rugby fields on the property and excellent hills for winter sliding. The orphanage's yellow school bus and two vans were a common sight on the city streets, ferrying the boys to and from school and other outings. Brother Kenny's Ford station wagon, a simulated wood-grained Country Squire, was also a familiar sight, particularly to the ever-watchful boys he tried to catch smoking down by Rennie's River before school in the morning.

Billy and Shane were both assigned to St. Al's dorm, which helped the smaller boy make the adjustment to life at Mount Cashel. Despite Billy's constant run-ins with the Brothers (while serving on the altar one morning, he helped himself to a healthy swig of sacramental wine on an empty stomach and promptly fainted), Shane quickly adjusted to his new home. There was no shortage of children to play with, and the classrooms were small enough so that teachers could spend quality time with individual pupils. And with Brothers like T.I. Murphy around, the children never wanted for genuine affection.

"Brother T. I. Murphy used to come in every day at lunch hour and teach the Bible to us," Shane remembered. "And we always used to come up and give him a hug, and he always used to have treats for us – candies, cookies or bars, whatever he could get for us. Everybody loved him. He put his whole heart and soul into Mount Cashel."

Unfortunately for Shane and his friends, others at Mount Cashel didn't meaure up to the standards of the grand-fatherly teacher with the peaceful, moon-shaped face.

Whatever his other foibles, Brother Kenny was a good, if parsimonious, administrator. Mount Cashel's weekly routine ran like clockwork. From Monday to Friday, the day began with an optional mass at 7 A.M. Boys wishing to attend the pre-breakfast service informed their dorm supervisor the night before and were awakened accordingly. For the less spiritually observant, reveille was 7:45 A.M., which left just enough time to wash and dress under the keen eye of their dorm supervisor before heading down to the dining hall for breakfast. (Each day the supervisor checked for bedwetters, who could expect severe corporal punishment for their damp deeds.)

Breakfast was at 8 A.M., followed by school, which began at nine o'clock sharp. Up to grade three, the boys attended school in Mount Cashel itself. Older boys travelled to various Catholic schools around the city – up to grade nine, Pius X, and later, to either Brother Rice or Gonzaga – where the Christian Brothers were often their teachers.

At twelve o'clock, it was back to the orphanage for lunch and off again an hour later to complete the school day. The younger boys returned to Mount Cashel at 3 P.M., while the older students were allowed to stay out until 5 P.M. The boys then lined up for their supper, carrying their plates back to long, wooden tables where six of them took the evening meal together. Each table had its own pot of tea to help wash down the unremarkable cuisine – porridge in the morning, and some kind of minced meat at night, except on those special occasions when fancy dinners were served in honour of important guests.

Friday was chores day. After the evening meal, the dorms would take turns on clean-up duty: All sweeping, mopping, polishing and garbage collection had to be done before the boys got their weekly allowance, a stipend which increased as they grew older. While the dorm on clean-up duty did its work, the others attended study hall until 7:30 P.M. After that, everyone headed for the gymnasium or pool. Then it was time for a few favourite TV programs in the "carpet room" before going to bed. On week nights, the older boys had to be in bed by ten o'clock, the younger ones by 8:30.

Weekends were virtually free – a time when relatives or friends took the boys out of Mount Cashel for a few hours, or even overnight. But everyone had to be back in time for the obligatory Sunday mass. During the summers, no one stayed at the orphanage. Children with parents who were willing to take them went home for the vacation; boys with no place to go attended summer camps run by the Christian Brothers at Terra Nova, Ferryland and Witless Bay, all within a few hours' drive of St. John's.

There was one other ritual of note at Mount Cashel: every night, before lights out, the boys said their prayers – bottom-bunk boys kneeling on their pillows, top-bunk boys on their mattresses. Afterwards, their supervisor made his rounds of the dorm, tucking each boy in. It wouldn't be long before Billy and Shane figured out why the upper bunks were at such a premium.

Gradually the sense of well-being inspired by Mount Cashel's smoothly ordered routines, and the kindnesses of individual Brothers, gave way in Shane to a sense of stomach-churning apprehension. The physical abuse meted out by many of the Brothers terrified the little boy, who had no way of knowing that such severe corporal punishment was often the classic precursor of sexual assault, which required above all else a compliant victim. As Jordan Riak, a children's rights advocate, observed, "We cannot reasonably expect a child who is required to passively bend over for a beating on Monday to say 'No' to a pedophile on Tuesday."

It wasn't long before both Shane and Billy became the sexual targets of certain Brothers. Shane was less bothered by the sexual advances, which he didn't understand, than he was by the beatings that traumatized him. One of their tormentors was Brother Edward English, a short, blocky man in horn-rimmed, black-and-gold glasses, who taught grade eight at St. Pius X school in St. John's. Brother English had a high-pitched voice and was later described by one of the boys he molested as the spitting image of Radar on the popular television show "M*A*S*H." Several boys would later explain to police how Brother English, then twenty-seven, liked to have them crowd around him in the carpet room and massage his genitals. Billy was one of the boys whose hand Brother English would force down on his penis while the rest of the group was watching television.

"If someone else turned around, he would tell them to watch television, or grab them and hug them or rub their head. He could do anything," Billy later recalled.

Apart from his sexual appetites, Brother English was also well known for his ferocious temper. Unpopular with the boys, English could fly into rages during which he would pummel the boys with his fists or lash them with his belt or a special leather strap. Researching for a school project, one Mount Cashel resident, Johnny Williams, asked Brother English why he had become a Christian Brother.

"I had a calling from God," he remembered the Brother telling him.

Brother English wasn't the only person the boys had to be concerned about. One day when Billy was walking by the pool, Brother Kenny tried "to neck" with him, grabbing the boy by the face and asking him to bite his neck. Billy later claimed he stumbled on Brother Kenny and an older boy in a compromising situation in the shower room by the pool.

"They just had their pants undone together. He [Brother Kenny] was feeling him. They were hauling themselves."

Life at Mount Cashel was a contradictory world of caring and corruption, a place where the two boys didn't know who to trust and where they feared everyone. But early in the summer of 1974, Shane and Billy's deliverance seemed to be at hand. Their father called to say that he would come for them that Friday after work and take them out of Mount Cashel for good. The welcome news meant that they wouldn't have to go to one of the summer camps run by the Brothers, where the discipline was just as oppressive as it was at the orphanage. The boys sat on their suitcases, waiting for their father to come, while Mount Cashel residents with nowhere else to go boarded a bus bound for camp. Without so much as a phone call to explain why, William Earle, Sr. never showed up.

"I tell you," Billy later said, "you're after spending a year or two years in there and someone says to you, 'O.K., I'll be there this summer to take you out,' and you're sat down there in the fucking hallway with a suitcase waiting and you're ready to get on that bus to Terra Nova with the rest of the crew. I'll tell you, when I got on that bus and looked out that window and seen nobody coming up Torbay Road, that was it. I knew then that I was here to stay. I suppose I started to get older then, and a little wiser."

The canny philosopher was all of eleven years old.

Shane's Mount Cashel education in the ways of the world began at an even earlier age. From the moment Brother Joseph Burke entered Mount Cashel, Shane was drawn to the chain-smoking native of Vancouver who stood out amongst his colleagues for his gentle disposition and sensitive nature. He also had the physical stature to make the small boy feel as though he had found a protector in an environment that, without warning, often turned brutally violent.

"Brother Burke was a very huge man, very tall, very blocky. He looked like a dominant figure, somebody you wouldn't want to cross in a dark alley, somebody you wouldn't want as an enemy," Shane remembered. "Yet on the other hand, he was a very gentle man, very, very, gentle to the point of being there whenever you needed him."

As the months passed, the kindly Brother with the thick

mane of red hair became Shane's substitute mother and father, fulfilling exactly the same role that Brother Waters had for Rick during his stay at Mount Cashel. Brother Burke rewarded his diminutive charge with snacks and trips for good behaviour, when, for example, he made his bed so well that a dime would jump on its tauntly arranged blankets. When Shane was bad, Brother Burke sometimes gave him "a little whack" on the backside to mend his ways. But as Shane told police in 1989, Burke, like several other Brothers, had another side to him that he kept carefully hidden during the first few months of their relationship.

"I remember one particular time all of us in St. Al's dorm got the measles or chicken pox. Brother Burke used to tell us not to scratch and would smack us lightly if we did. My chicken pox got really bad from scratching, so Brother Burke got some lotion to put on me. He took me into a big closet, more or less a storage room where we kept our records and Sunday clothes and other things. He told me to take off my pyjamas. It was in the afternoon. He put a towel on the counter and had me lay down. He started at my neck and started putting the lotion on. When he got to my penis, he told me to spread my legs apart. I did. He started playing with my penis, rubbing on the lotion. Then he put his finger up in my rectum. He started moving his finger around and asked me if I liked it. I remember saying, 'Bro, it tickles.' He gave me a sucker after he done this," Shane later told police.

According to Shane's statement to police fourteen years after the fact, at least four Brothers sexually abused him, including Mount Cashel's Superintendent of the day, Douglas Kenny.

"I was sort of Brother Kenny's favourite too and he used to touch me sexually quite often. He used to get me to touch his penis with my hands and he used to have an erection. Almost always after these incidents, he would give me money. I always had money and everyone used to wonder where I got it," Shane alleged in his 1989 police statement. When another Brother, Alan Ralph, began playing with Shane's penis on a camping trip, the young boy pushed him away without really knowing what the man was doing.

None of the darker things Shane was experiencing showed up on his school records. His Mount Cashel progress report in June 1975 was glowing: "Shane is a healthy child, but small for his age—he has blond hair and a very fair complexion. Shane has no emotional problems. Attends mass regularly. Gets along well with the staff. Father visits Shane and takes him out periodically. [The progress report from January of the same year recorded that Shane's father 'rarely' visited his son.] Gets along well with the other boys in his dormitory." Under the heading, "Plans for the child's future," the objective was clearly stated: "Remain in Mount Cashel."

The report was signed by D. D. Kenny, Superintendent.

While Shane managed to stay out of trouble, his brother Billy was a different story. In early September 1975, the rambunctious twelve-year-old kicked a soccer ball through the glass protecting the fire alarms in the main hall of Mount Cashel. When he reported the accident to his supervisor in St. Al's dorm, Brother English punched him twice in the face. "He thought it was done intentionally," Billy recalled, "so he gave me two blows to the face with his fist."

Together with Bobby Connors, a boy who had a swollen eye from a recent encounter with the fists of Brother Alan Ralph, Billy decided to go to the authorities. The evening before they ran away, the two were given an even stronger reason for trying to get some help. During his nightly rounds to tuck the boys in, Brother Ralph slipped his hand down the front of Bobby's pyjamas and began fondling his penis and rubbing his buttocks. Bobby lifted his head and "could see Brother Ralph's hand under Billy's cover" too. It was the last straw.

Early the next morning the two boys "dodged" out the fire escape and went to Billy's father's house at 32 Franklin Avenue where they spent the night. The next day, after listening to his son's story, William Earle, Sr. loaded the boys into his yellow Plymouth Satellite and drove them downtown for a confrontation with authorities at Social Services.

In 1975, the Social Services district office on Harvey Road

was "a real hell hole," according to its Regional Director of the day, Jerome Quinlan. Cramped and ill-equipped, its tiny waiting room was the scene of a daily tide of human misery—the place where up to three hundred people a day, including the province's needy children, came for relief. Filled with cigarette smoke, glue sniffers and unmarried mothers trapped in debilitating poverty, the office was a "human pressure cooker" where proceedings often ended with a visit by the police to restore order. Hard-pressed social workers carrying untenable caseloads could do no more than lurch from crisis to crisis, dispensing what help and humanity they could.

With a drink or two under his belt, and even taller and more menacing in his cowboy boots, William Earle, Sr., demanded to see someone about Mount Cashel. He and the boys were quickly escorted into the office of Sharron Callahan, the new Supervisor of the St. John's District Office who had just taken up her duties on August 21, 1975. It was Callahan's job to supervise the social workers at Harvey Road, give guidance where required and report to the Director of Child Welfare at Confederation Building, the seat of the provincial legislature which housed all government departments.

Normally Callahan didn't deal directly with cases herself, except in "matters of special concern," such as Mount Cashel. Billy told her about his beating at the hands of Brother English, noting that two of the Brothers were known homosexuals who made advances to the young residents of the orphanage. They also mentioned that a Brother who had once been suspended from Mount Cashel for similar misbehaviour had returned to the institution to work with the boys.

Callahan handed the complainants over to twenty-six-year-old Robert Bradbury, the Mount Cashel liaison officer of the day. The soft-spoken social worker listened intently as the boys told their story. Once more, Billy talked about the beating Brother English had given him and went on to accuse other Brothers of sexual abuse. "We explained to him what was going on at the orphanage, that there was only a bunch of gearboxes in there." Bradbury noted down their comments on a piece of paper known as an intake referral form and assured the trio that the matter would be passed on to the "right people."

From the Harvey Road Social Services office, Earle drove the frightened boys back to Mount Cashel. "I figured we were in for a shit-knocking when we got back," Billy remembered. Instead, the boys were merely sent upstairs to their dormitory by Mount Cashel's Superintendent, while Billy's father and Brother Kenny engaged in a shouting match. Earle, Sr. confronted Brothers Kenny and English over the boys' complaints, but felt that "both would not admit the reality of what had happened," an impression that Robert Bradbury would later include in his report of the incident. Billy and Bobby waited for something to come of their trip to Social Services, but no one ever showed up to investigate their complaints, which was no mystery, considering what happened next.

Although Bradbury felt that a punch in the face was not appropriate discipline, the young social worker didn't think he had the authority to do a follow-up investigation of his own. After the Earles and Bobby Connors left the office, he consulted with Sharron Callahan and the matter was reported the same day over the telephone to Newfoundland's Director of Child Welfare, Frank Simms. (Simms would later deny this.) Bradbury was instructed to interview Brother Kenny and report back to headquarters. Although he met with Mount Cashel's Superintendent and was told by him that an investigation would be conducted, no follow-up report was ever found at headquarters and Bradbury never pursued the matter further.

"We were not responsible to supervise boys at Mount Cashel. Our immediate response was to notify headquarters and ask for direction. And the direction we got presumably was that it was being investigated from their office and not from our office," he would recall many years later.

As Sharron Callahan later testified in defence of how she and her colleagues had handled the Earle complaint in 1975, the social service workers "had done as much as we possibly could do ... we probably were intimidated to the point of not assaulting the very foundations of the religious community at that time."

Six weeks after the phone call from Harvey Road to headquarters, on October 23, 1975, Robert Bradbury filed a formal report on the visit to Social Services by the two boys and William Earle, Sr. Since he took the primary complaint to be the alleged beating of Billy Earle by Brother English, he didn't record any of the statements made to him by Bobby Connors. Even though he would later admit under oath that he would have asked the boys for the names of the Brothers who were alleged child molesters, and would probably have passed those names on to the Director's office, he said he was hesitant about formally recording the names because of his uncertainty about the truth of the allegations. For the most part, his report was an exercise in discounting the story the boys had told him, without conducting an independent investigation.

"This accusation by the Earle boy is undoubtedly partly an emotional reaction to the punishment deemed justifiable by the Brothers; and since the boy had few marks as evidence for a severe beating, perhaps little can be accomplished by bringing strong charges at this time. But just the same, charges of severe punishment by the Brothers are not new and could indicate a limited but still present level of child abuse in the institution.

"Along with this charge, the boys further allege that two of the Brothers were known (to most of the boys) homosexuals and that occasions of sexual advances toward the boys had occurred. . . .

"It must be stressed that these boys were only young, (approximately twelve) and, therefore, corroboration would have to be present before their accusations could be taken seriously. However, it would seem to be neglect on our part if some action was not taken at this time."

The Bradbury memo was forwarded to Social Services headquarters at Confederation Building, where, like every other complaint concerning Mount Cashel, it landed directly on the desk of the Director of Child Welfare, Frank Simms, marked personal and confidential. Simms would

later claim that he thoroughly discussed the Bradbury report
with both the Deputy Minister and the Assistant Deputy
Minister before instructing that Brother Kenny investigate
the matter—a contention that was denied by both senior
civil servants.

(Afterwards, the original of the Bradbury report was
placed in a confidential Mount Cashel file locked in a
cabinet in the office of Newfoundland's Director of Child
Welfare, instead of in the Child Welfare Registry where it
should have been. Nor was there a copy of the controversial
report in the Earle family file or at the Harvey Road District
Office—another breach of normal procedure. Also missing
from the official record at the district office were the intake
referral form documenting William Earle, Sr.'s visit, the
notes taken by Robert Bradbury at the time of the 1975
complaint, and the entire Mount Cashel file. Neither
Sharron Callahan nor Robert Bradbury could explain what
happened to the copies of these documents, which should
have been retained at Harvey Road.)

Over two weeks after receiving the Bradbury report, a
delay that no one in the department could later explain,
given the seriousness of the allegations, the Director of Child
Welfare recorded the action he had taken on the bottom of
the letter from Harvey Road. "Discussed with Brother
Kenny who will be investigating. FJS. 12-11-75."

The snappy bureaucratese was very strange indeed.
Simms was asking a man who had already been identified in
Bradbury's report as not believing the allegations of Earle
and Connors to investigate the matter. The Director of Child
Welfare's response also revealed how far Mount Cashel was
allowed to stray from standard procedure; a foster-care
facility was, in effect, being authorized to investigate itself.
Finally, Simms did not inform the police of the allegations
contained in Bradbury's report, even though some of them
were clearly criminal in nature.

Simms's entire handling of the affair was surprisingly
casual. Had the Earle complaint arisen in a private home, a
social worker would have conducted an immediate investigation and either the child or its alleged assailant would have
been removed at once, if any abuses were confirmed. If the

complaint had come from a regular foster home, the child would have been immediately removed until the allegations were either substantiated or disproved. Despite the seriousness of the allegations coming out of Mount Cashel, the Director of Child Welfare neither received nor pursued a written report of Brother Kenny's findings. What made that lackadaisical response even harder to understand was his later comment that he took the Bradbury report to be the first serious complaint his department had received about the treatment of wards at Mount Cashel by their custodians.

Like many of the seasoned bureaucrat's recollections, that wasn't exactly so.

Whatever else might be said about Robert Bradbury's handling of Billy Earle's complaint, he was right about one thing: this wasn't the first time that a serious allegation had been levelled at Mount Cashel or passed over without formally recording the alleged incident or independently inquiring into its validity.

On July 21, 1975 a "very angry" Mrs. Ruth Williams had shown up at the Harvey Road office of Social Services demanding an investigation into Mount Cashel. Mrs. Williams explained to social worker Alice Walters that she had three nephews in Mount Cashel, the sons of Dorothy Santuccioni, who had placed the boys in the orphanage in February 1975, a few months before her death. As it turned out, Walters herself had dealt with Mrs. Santuccioni when the terminally ill woman had first appeared at Harvey Road to find a place for her children.

"Since I was a single parent at the time, I could identify with her distress and tried to find the best homes for these children that I could possibly find," Alice Walters recalled.

Mrs. Williams had gone to the orphanage to take eight-year-old Dino Santuccioni out for his birthday. She was distressed to find a grubby little boy dressed in ill-fitting clothes and shoes waiting for her. After they had left the orphanage, Carlo, Dino's older brother, told his aunt not to bother buying new clothes or shoes for Dino, since these would only be taken away from him by the Brothers. Carlo also told her about the harsh disciplining at Mount Cashel, including a story about a Brother Kenny who struck a boy with his crutches.

Mrs. Williams was so upset by these stories and by little Dino's strange behaviour that she demanded to see Brother Kenny when she brought her nephews back to the orphange. After a strenuous argument, she was allowed to see Dino's room, which had two beds and three cotton-filled mattresses on the floor. Ripping off the bedclothes, she discovered filthy sheets that she was told resulted from ongoing renovations in progress. Infuriated, she demanded an investigation by Social Services.

Alice Walters passed along her request in a letter written to the Director of Child Welfare on July 25 and signed by both the social worker and her district administrator, Terrence Haire. Eighteen days later, on August 12, Haire received a reply from Neil Hamilton, the social worker who acted as liaison between headquarters and Mount Cashel.

"This will acknowledge receipt of a report completed by Mrs. Alice Walters on July 25, 1975, in which she indicates concern was expressed by a Mrs. Ruth Williams concerning conditions at Mount Cashel Orphanage.

"You may recall that we since discussed this matter by phone during which [talks] we requested a thorough investigation be conducted by Mr. Bradbury, since he is the worker assigned to Mount Cashel. As suggested during the course of our conversation, the investigation should be conducted as diplomatically and tactfully as possible.

"Once you [have] had an opportunity to complete an investigation we would very much appreciate receiving a report."

According to the official record, no investigation ever took place. Years later, Robert Bradbury would deny ever having received a request to investigate Ruth Williams's complaint, and Neil Hamilton would note that the words "diplomatically and tactfully" were not his but those of Frank Simms, his ultimate superior.

As for Simms, he would deny ever getting any official complaint in the Santuccioni affair, but would admit to

learning about it informally around September 1, 1975,
when Ruth Williams, his neighbour, approached him on the
matter. Simms assured her the complaint was being looked
after and assumed that her failure to call him back meant
that she understood the matter was in hand.

"The unfortunate thing is I did not follow up. . . . I don't
know how much you know about a day in the life of the
Director of Child Welfare, but during a day in the Director's
office there are many situations coming at him or her similar
to this one," he later testified.

But despite all the confusion about who did exactly what
with respect to the Santuccioni complaint, Neil Hamilton
did remember one very important fact: the ominous sense
in the Department of Social Services that all was not well at
the orphanage.

"Back in 1973 and 1974, there were rumours there were
problems at Mount Cashel . . . from within the department
. . . rumours that the children were not being well treated,"
the twenty-eight-year veteran of the Social Services
Department later testified.

One of the sources of those rumours could have been an
incident that was brought to the attention of the department
the previous year. In the fall of 1974, on a Thursday – the
night before allowance day – Brother English, dressed in his
black habit, was making his rounds in St. Al's dorm, tucking
the boys in. Stopping at one of the bunks, he slipped his hand
down its occupant's pyjamas and began groping him,
repeatedly asking the boy if he liked it. The boy loudly
objected to the Brother's advances and as English left the
dormitory, someone called out a single word that drove the
Brother to distraction: "Queer!"

Furious, Brother English snapped on the dorm's lights
and demanded to know who had called out. Unless the guilty
party confessed, he said, no one would be allowed to leave
the orphanage that weekend and their allowances would be
cancelled. Although no one came forward at the time, his
threat eventually worked. The next morning before breakfast, someone told Brother English that the culprit was
Johnny Williams.

Williams was one of Mount Cashel's characters. Most of the time he was happy-go-lucky, a cocky and confident boy who would thrust out his arm on meeting adults for the first time and pump their hands vigorously. He and his twin brother, Jerome, had been placed in the orphanage when their parents separated in 1967. Popular with the other boys, Johnny Williams had problems in school, where he would throw such severe temper tantrums that the Brothers often told him he was mentally retarded. Despite their false and cruel taunts, he remained unbowed.

When Williams came back to the dorm after breakfast, an enraged Brother English was waiting for him. The boy was kicked and punched, and his shirt was torn off in a vicious struggle. Later, when Johnny was washing up at the sink, Brother English came up behind him and struck him so hard on his bare back that the marks would last for two weeks. With Brother English dancing a furious jig in front of him, they made their way to the Superintendent's office. Johnny was determined to report the incident to Brother Kenny. Many years later, he would recount the conversation that took place in Kenny's office.

"What are you going to do about this pervert? . . . This pervert here is upstairs putting his hands down in guys' pyjamas," Williams charged.

"Get the hell out of my office," he remembered Kenny answering. To the young boy's surprise, Brother English then chimed in, addressing his remarks to Brother Kenny.

"If I go down, you go with me. You're gay too, Doug."

"Shut up, shut up," Kenny seethed, according to Williams's recollection, before he threw the pair out of his office.

But the matter didn't end there. When Johnny arrived at school that day, Christopher Hatch, a teacher at St. Pius X boys' school who had befriended Williams, noticed that he was upset. Williams told him, "Mr. Hatch, he beat the shit out of me," identifying Brother English, who also taught at Pius X, as his attacker. To back up his allegation, the fourteen-year-old opened his shirt and showed the teacher his bruises. Hatch took Johnny to his home-room teacher,

Marcella Whelan, and showed her the marks on his body. Williams broke down and cried. Later, Hatch testified that he remembered Whelan saying, "What do you expect me to do about it?"

If Williams's complaint fell on deaf ears at one of the schools where the Brothers taught, as well as at the orphanage, it was a different story with his first cousin, Brenda Lundrigan. The tough-talking seventeen-year-old with the quick temper had always been concerned about her two cousins and two brothers who lived in Mount Cashel. Unlike a lot of other people, she didn't trust the Brothers, nor did she share the widely held view that "anybody connected with the Catholic Church, whatever they did, was right." When she saw the marks on Johnny's back, arms and hip five days after the beating, she flew into a rage.

"I wanted to go after Brother English. . . . It took Dereck [O'Brien, her boyfriend who was also at Mount Cashel] and a few others to hold me back. I wanted to do the same to him as he did to that little kid."

Although Lundrigan curbed her temper, she didn't let the matter drop. She arranged to meet Dereck and Johnny the next day after school, skipping her last class at Holy Heart and walking over to Pius X to meet the two boys. She took them by cab to the Social Services office at Harvey Road, determined "to get something done about it right there and then," before the office closed. She used babysitting money to pay the cab fare.

When the trio got in to see Robert Bradbury, Brenda did most of the talking. She showed the social worker the marks, now fading, on Johnny's back and the bruises on his arms and legs. She also told him about stories she had heard from Mount Cashel boys, boys she believed would never lie to her, about physical and sexual abuse at the orphanage. Bradbury took a few notes while the angry young woman talked, but spent most of his time listening. When the interview was finished, Bradbury said that Johnny wasn't the first person to complain about Mount Cashel and that he would look into it. Brenda Lundrigan was disgusted.

"Basically, he told me it was out of his hands. He would pass it along to Confederation Building. When I called him a week or two later, he basically told me the same thing."

Years later, Bradbury would have only vague recollections of the trip to his office by Williams, Lundrigan and
O'Brien, although he did say, "I very strongly feel this report
went up" to headquarters, and may, in fact, have been the
incident he was referring to when he said in his later report
on the Billy Earle incident that such charges were not new.
Once more, he would say that if the names of Williams's
tormentors had been given to him, "they more than likely
would have been passed on" to the Director of Child
Welfare. Both Lundrigan and Williams would claim that
they had mentioned the names of Brothers English, Kenny
and French during their visit to Harvey Road.

Again, there was no official record of Johnny's complaint
to Robert Bradbury, either in the form of intake referral
notes or a formal report, although both were standard
procedure.

What none of the complainants could know was that Mount
Cashel's always unique relationship with government had
evolved into virtual independence under the stewardship of
Brother Kenny. Kenny's fierce protection of his turf was a
real departure from the attitude of his predecessor, who
acknowledged limits to the Brothers' capabilities and wasn't
afraid to reinforce them with outside professional help. In
October 1968, Brother John Barron, Brother Kenny's
predecessor at Mount Cashel, wrote to the government,
asking that a part-time social worker be assigned to the
orphanage. A few months later, his request was granted –
Leroy Norberg was assigned to Mount Cashel in February
1969.

A year later, the futility of Norberg's task was painfully
obvious. His district supervisor wrote to the Director of
Child Welfare to inform him that because of Norberg's
incredible caseload – 146 boys at Mount Cashel, and
another 63 outside the institution – he couldn't handle
the job.

"We are not providing adequate services to the boys
already at Mount Cashel and it seems that in the future we
will be providing even less service," he wrote. A request was

made for a full-time social worker for the orphanage, but it was turned down because of a lack of staff.

But in 1971, with the arrival of a new Superintendent at the institution, there was a complete change in the relationship between the orphanage and Social Services – a change that was noted in a letter from the department's regional administrator, F. A. Davis, to George Pope, then Director of Field Services.

"It has occurred to the writer on a number of occasions that Mount Cashel should have a competent person on their staff to deal with any problems that may arise with the boys. . . . I cannot say what has happened since the administration changed hands, but there appears to be a different philosophy which tends to suggest that the present administrator feels that his office can cope with the problems which are inherent in such an institution."

The "present administrator" was Brother Douglas Kenny and he was sending a clear message to government authorities – hands off Mount Cashel. In July 1972 a probation officer wrote to the Director of Child Welfare to express concern about the "break in communication" with Mount Cashel, observing that the institution was operating autonomously "without allowing for proper two-way communication" with the department.

Despite any misgivings field-level social workers had about Mount Cashel's sudden autonomy, they weren't addressed by the Director of Child Welfare, Frank Simms. In 1972, he included this note in a letter to Brother Kenny, in which he listed the proposed duties of the welfare officer assigned to Mount Cashel. It would amount to a virtual declaration of independence for the Catholic-run orphanage.

"In conclusion, it should be made clear, to the satisfaction of both the Department of Social Services and Mount Cashel, that there is no intention or desire on the part of the Director or his representative, in their relationship with Mount Cashel, to infringe upon, or threaten in any way, the structured authority, discipline, or administration of that institution."

The special status of Mount Cashel was further clarified in

a letter from Frank Simms to the St. John's district office on September 13, 1974, when he decreed that the involvement of field staff at the orphanage was to be "for administrative purposes only" — to provide comprehensive social histories, attend to monetary issues and arrange transportation home on behalf of the boys at certain periods of the year.

From that point on, Mount Cashel became a self-policing agency within the social services network of the province, demanding and getting special treatment from every level of the system — including, as it turned out, the justice system. This fact was about to become abundantly clear to a thirty-year-old handyman who would try to blow the whistle on the goings-on at Mount Cashel.

In the fall of 1975, Chesley Riche was a self-taught mechanic and jack-of-all-trades who was temporarily down on his luck. The six-foot-tall 250-pounder was a common sight at Gulliver's taxi stand on George Street, a rundown part of the inner city. It was there that he got to know Joe Kenny. Occasionally Kenny would give the man with the huge arms work at the family business, Kenny's Marble Works. One day Kenny suggested that Riche go to Mount Cashel, where the Superintendent, his brother Douglas, was always looking for volunteer workers. Riche took his friend's advice, landing a job at the orphanage as a maintenance man in the hope that it might turn into a paying position.

Riche's impressions of Mount Cashel were initially good, though as a non-Catholic, he didn't understand some of the special routines. The Brothers were "super-friendly" to him, but behind the patina of conviviality, Riche always felt he was being patronized. That, however, was the least of his problems with Mount Cashel. From his first day on the job, the lumbering maintenance worker heard disturbing stories from boys like Billy Earle and Bobby Connors. While he was repairing the furnace in the gymnasium, the boys told him that the Brothers were beating them and coming to their beds at night and "feeling them up." Two names kept coming up — Brother English and Brother Ralph. Although he had only been there a few days, Riche took the complaints to Brother Kenny who said that the boys were only "looking for attention," and not to worry. But the problem wouldn't go away.

"They had a bakery downstairs and I was down around the bakery and I got three or four more complaints. And I brought it to Joe Kenny at the Marble Works," Riche later testified. He got the same answer from his friend that he had already received from Mount Cashel's Superintendent – the boys were only looking for attention.

One morning after his visit to Joe Kenny, Riche finally gathered some information of his own on what was going on at the orphanage. He was working around the Superintendent's office when he saw Brother Kenny bouncing a twelve-year-old boy on his knee. Riche was disturbed; the boy was far too big to be bounced on anyone's knee. He returned to his work, but when he came back half an hour later, Brother Kenny had the boy by the head and was bouncing him off the wall. "The youngster was crying. I just backed off because it was none of my business," Riche later testified. "If I had've intervened, the people down at Fort Townshend [the police], would have been pleased. . . . I would have been locked up."

Although he was worried about his own past brushes with the law, and was anxious not to give the police a reason to look him up again, there were limits to Riche's sense of self-interest. A little boy named Shane Earle would quickly establish what they were.

Every Saturday, the Mount Cashel boys used to go to Gosling Memorial Library on Elizabeth Avenue to take out books. Back at the orphanage, every dorm had shelves where the books would be kept until the due date, when they were gathered up and returned. It was Shane's job to keep the books in order and to make sure they were all accounted for in time for the weekly junket to Gosling Memorial.

Just after breakfast on Saturday, December 6, Shane and a helper were collecting the books for the return trip, when he noticed that the card was missing from *Chitty Chitty Bang Bang* – one of the most popular volumes at Mount Cashel. Brother Burke asked him if everything was in order and he answered, "No, Bro, there's a card missing from one of the books." The nine-year-old was immediately sent to a small office adjacent to the storage room in St. Al's and ordered to undress. He remembered Brother Burke ordering him to pass him a belt that was hanging on a hook on the wall. Suddenly, his friend and protector, the Brother he adored because of his gentle nature, began beating him mercilessly.

"He said, 'Bend over.' So I bent over and he gave me a whack with his hand first and then folded the belt and started hitting me with the hook, the buckle part. And he kept hitting me and every time it felt like it was getting harder because I didn't realize it until after, but the hook was digging into my bottom. He said, 'Stop crying.' And naturally I stopped crying because he said, 'If you don't stop crying, I'm going to keep hitting you until you do stop.' So I was trying with all my might to hold it in," Shane remembered.

When Brother Burke finished, he ordered Shane to put his pants on and get down to the van that was waiting to take them to the library. The rest of the boys were lined up outside the vehicle waiting for Brother Burke to let them in. After loading the van, Brother Burke told Shane, who remained standing, to sit down. Ashamed to have the others know what had happened, he whispered from behind the driver's seat that he couldn't because his bottom hurt too much. Brother Burke pushed the boy down; when Shane hit the seat it was like "sitting on needles and pins." He started to cry and Brother Burke hissed at him to be quiet. Like his brother Rick before him, Shane's illusions about the one person in authority he trusted at Mount Cashel were shattered.

"At that point, I lost all faith in him whatsoever because he was no different than any of the other Brothers, not to me," Shane recalled.

That day, after returning from the library, Shane told Billy about the beating. The next day, Billy told his new friend, Chesley Riche, with whom he had already discussed the physical and sexual abuse going on at the orphanage. Riche thought "to hell with it," dropped everything and took the boys out of the orphanage that Sunday. Adding to his anger was the fact that Brother Burke, the one staff member he had come to like, had been the perpetrator.

With the Earle family living apart, Riche didn't know where to take the boys. They eventually drove to Portugal Cove, a fishing village a few miles outside the city, and caught the ferry for Bell Island, a low and imposing butte of solid iron ore a mile from the mainland, where two of Billy and Shane's sisters were living in a foster home. After returning from Bell Island across the narrow salt-water strait called "the Tickle," the threesome headed back to the Cochrane Hotel in St. John's for something to eat.

Later that afternoon, Riche took Shane and Billy to 360 Duckworth Street, to the one-bedroom apartment in City Terrace where Carol Earle then lived. When his mother opened the door, Shane started to cry, whether out of pain or relief, he didn't know. Riche told the distraught mother about Shane's beating and advised her not to return the boys to Mount Cashel. Carol Earle took her son into another room and examined him. She was shocked by the gruesome bruises on his backside. She knew the Brothers often disciplined the boys, but this was more than a mere spanking.

"Shane was bruised across his buttocks and his lower back . . . very distinct. All I can see is black . . . I was very confused at the time. I just didn't know what to do."

Despite her uncertainty, she decided on the spot not to send the boys back to Mount Cashel. Chesley Riche took care of the rest. He called Constable Gerry McGuire, a compassionate acquaintance in the RCMP, who had recently caught Riche passing a bad twenty-five-dollar cheque in Grand Bank, a fishing community on Newfoundland's south coast. The twenty-nine-year-old Mountie, who had only been in Newfoundland for five months, was just sitting down to Sunday dinner when Riche called. Half an hour later, he arrived at Carol Earle's apartment, "sort of as a favour" to Riche.

McGuire quickly realized that the situation involved possible child abuse at Mount Cashel Orphanage. Someone produced a camera and Carol Earle escorted her son into

another room and privately took Polaroid photographs of
the marks on Shane's backside. The bruises were clearly
visible in the photographs. McGuire explained that the
situation was not in his jurisdiction, since child welfare was
covered by provincial statute, and the RCMP in St. John's
upheld only federal matters. He advised them to report the
case to the Newfoundland Constabulary and gave them the
name of Robert Hillier, a detective he knew in that force's
Criminal Investigation Division (CID).

Riche, who from past dealings had "bad feelings" towards
the Constabulary, didn't want to call them. Instead, he tried
to alleviate some of the misery in the tiny apartment by
taking a picture of Carol with her two sons and explaining to
the amazed boys how the instant camera worked. McGuire,
meanwhile, entered the episode in his police notebook under
the date December 7, 1975:

"4:35 P.M. – Carol Earle, 360 Duckworth St. – Shane
Earle, age 9, hit by Brother Burke on bottom for losing a
library card and telling a lie. Billy Earle, age 11, is in Brother
Ralph's dorm and Brother English. A fellow named Bobby
Connors in Brother English's dorm, they are also fooling
around with. [McGuire would later explain this part of the
entry as a reference to sexual abuse.] Shane was beaten in
closet on 6/12/75 after breakfast."

Years later, when McGuire was reminded of Section 49 of
the Child Welfare Act, which requires that "every person
having information of the abandonment, desertion, physical
ill treatment or need for protection of a child, shall report the
information to the Director or a welfare officer," he
admitted he may have been remiss in his duty.

"Thinking back, I don't know if I'd do anything
different. . . . Maybe in hindsight, I should have taken them
to the Constabulary."

After Carol Earle took the pictures of Shane, Chesley
Riche tried to call a social worker, but since it was Sunday,
he couldn't reach anyone in authority. The wounds inflicted
by Brother Burke would have another day to heal before a
social worker or doctor saw them. Shane and Billy stayed
with their mother, and all that night Chesley Riche seethed
at what had happened to the little boy with the big, trusting eyes.

Monday afternoon Riche took his anger straight to the top. After a blunt phone call to the Director of Child Welfare, he bulled his way into Frank Simms's office at Confederation Building and told him about the physical abuse going on at Mount Cashel, including Brother Joseph Burke's beating of Shane Earle. But his most graphic charges related to the sexual abuse he had been told about by a number of boys, including Billy Earle and Bobby Connors, who had singled out Brothers English and Ralph as their worst tormentors.

Although Simms would later testify that he couldn't remember if Riche had in fact given him the names of the alleged offenders, he admitted he would have asked which Christian Brothers were sexually abusing the boys. If Riche did, in fact, give him the names, they must have had a familiar ring to them. They were the same names that Billy Earle and Bobby Connors had given to Robert Bradbury during their September 1975 visit to the Harvey Road district office, and which the social worker later testified he would have passed on verbally to the Director of Child Welfare on the day the complaints were received.

Simms must have been unnerved by another thing Chesley Riche had to say to him on the afternoon of Monday, December 8. In addition to allegations of sexual abuse and Shane Earle's beating, he also told the Director of Child Welfare that he had witnessed Brother Douglas Kenny, "the man that was running the place," physically assault a boy after bouncing him on his knee. Riche warned that if something wasn't done about all the violence and "the Brothers in bed with the boys," he would put the Roman Catholic church, and the pedestal on which Simms told him it rested, all over the front page of *The Evening Telegram*. Throughout their conversation, Riche had the impression that Simms "wanted to back off" and only took action after the threat of public exposure, a possibility that might have seemed less abstract after Riche informed the Director that he had already spoken to the police about Mount Cashel.

Surprisingly, Simms wasn't very anxious to share Riche's shocking information or commit his explosive complaints to paper. The Director of Child Welfare not only failed to inform Neil Hamilton, the liaison officer between

headquarters and Mount Cashel and the man in charge of
the province's child abuse registry, of the allegations, he also
neglected to make a written record of Chesley Riche's visit, a
clear departure from normal departmental procedure.
Instead, he referred his infuriated complainant to his
"soldiers" – social workers at the district office level who
had long been led to believe that they had absolutely no
authority to investigate anything to do with Mount
Cashel.

Years later, Neil Hamilton registered his feelings about
having been kept in the dark about the meeting with Chesley
Riche, just as he had been about the Bradbury report and
the complaints of two other Mount Cashel residents, Johnny
Williams and Dereck O'Brien.

"That's why I suggest, possibly deliberately, or for some
other reason, I was not made part of the process. I should
have, that was part of my responsibilities. . . . It was never
ever discussed or shared with me."

Under 1973 changes to the policy manual for the
Department of Social Services, there was a distinct
procedure for investigating allegations of child abuse, which
included informing the police, examining the alleged victim
at a hospital and discussing the situation with the
appropriate authority involved, in this case, Mount Cashel's
Superintendent, Brother Douglas Kenny. Luckily for Riche,
the social worker he drew was Alice Walters, who had
already dealt with a complaint about the orphanage in the
Santuccioni case.

The former Dutch war-bride came to Newfoundland just
before its entry into Confederation in 1949. The mother of
seven had been widowed while four of her children still lived
at home. She went to Memorial University and earned an
English degree and was later hired by the department of
Social Services in 1974. A foster home specialist, with a
caseload of 90 to 120 children, Alice Walters took more than
a professional interest in her clients.

"I handled them more like a mother than a social worker,"
she would later say.

The social worker listened attentively to Riche's story
and, in contrast to Robert Bradbury, prepared a detailed

report of his visit, or what the department called a "running record," a printed form attached to the cover of a family's file where all important information was noted. When Chesley Riche arrived, he took Walters and Bradbury to Carol Earle's Duckworth Street apartment. Shane reluctantly showed Bradbury his bruises, which now covered the lower part of his left buttock. After some discussion, Walters requested that Shane and his mother accompany her to the Janeway Children's Hospital in St. John's for a medical examination – the regular procedure in cases of suspected child abuse.

While waiting for a doctor to examine Shane, Carol Earle, who had always felt guilty about putting her sons in Mount Cashel, explained to Walters why she didn't have custody of her children. The distressed mother then gave her more details on Shane's beating, an account that would make its way into the social worker's report: "Shane had been beaten by Brother Burke with a belt on Saturday morning because he had lost his library card and consequently lied about a book which he should have returned. . . ."

Walters explained the situation to the nurse on duty, who, in keeping with hospital procedures, called an outside doctor to conduct the examination. When Dr. Paul Patey arrived, Walters told him why they were there. Dr. Patey, an assistant professor of Family Practice at Memorial University, then examined his young patient in the presence of Carol Earle between 7 and 8 P.M. on the evening of December 8, 1975 – two and a half days after the beating by Brother Burke. The ever-vigilant Alice Walters recorded the event in a memo.

"He [Dr. Patey] said it appeared the boy had been hit with a blunt, flexible object, (most likely a leather belt) about six times and that the bruises were more than a day old but less than a week."

In his medical report, which included a piece of cellophane on which he made a tracing of Shane's bruised buttocks, Dr. Patey stated, "He [Shane] had a 1 centimetre bruise on . . . the left calf. This appeared to be a week or more old. On his buttocks, there were several superficial bruises. The skin was intact. There was minimal swelling. These bruises were approximately an inch in circumference, but had a linear extension from them. They were red with very slight green colouration, suggesting more than one but less than five day old bruises. . . . There were more on the left side than on the right side. . . . These bruises could have resulted from pressure from a flexible strip of material between one and two inches in diameter; the bruises occurring when the skin was contacted by the tip and adjacent three or four inches [of the strap]. Six blows, [Shane would later claim 52] could have accounted for all the bruises on his buttocks. Other possible mechanisms of injury cannot be ruled out."

Dr. Patey performed one other invaluable service that night at the Janeway. Upon arrival at the hospital, he called the Criminal Investigation Division of the Newfoundland Constabulary. Ralph Pitcher and Jerome Corcoran, two CID detectives working the 6 P.M. to 2 A.M. shift, answered the call.

The detectives spoke with Chesley Riche, who not only told them what had happened to Shane, but related information about sexual assaults at Mount Cashel carried out against the boys by the Brothers. Riche recalled one of the policemen saying to him, "You don't really believe this is going on?" Leading them down to the basement of the Janeway, Riche handed over one of the Polaroid photographs of Shane's bruised backside.

"If I never believed it, I wouldn't do it," he told them.

The detectives left the hospital without taking a statement from Riche, nor did they seek a warrant for Brother Burke's arrest, even though they had reasonable and probable grounds to believe an offence had taken place.

Instead, when they finished their shift early that morning, Pitcher and Corcoran recorded the night's routine activity on blue citizen complaint forms – "blue-prints" in the jargon of the force – back at Fort Townshend: a break-and-entry in Shea Heights at 8:10 P.M.; a bad cheque at a local store at 10 P.M.; and finally, at 10:30 P.M., an aerial twisted off a parked vehicle. They left the blue-prints with the duty officer at the Water Street police station who would later type them into the Occurrence Book, the official daily record of each shift's activities.

A complaint had finally made it through the administrative thicket of Mount Cashel and the Department of Social Services. But the Occurrence Book contained no reference to Shane Earle or Mount Cashel and a "blue-print" of the alleged act of child abuse was never found. The orphanage's tawdry secret would now be snagged in the much finer nets of the justice system, a system which a senior police officer would later testify had special protocols for dealing with the powerful or prominent.

In the Newfoundland of the 1970s, the Roman Catholic church was the essence of both.

Chapter 4

■ *The Investigation*

> *Brother Kenny is all right. He only asks me to bite his neck. . . . Brother English used to feel up the boys and then give them the gift from the corn flakes box.* A nine-year-old Mount Cashel boy to police investigators, December 14, 1975.

ON DECEMBER 9, 1975, three days after Shane Earle's beating, Detective Robert Hillier climbed the winding staircase to the CID offices on the second floor of Fort Townshend, the former police barracks in the heart of St. John's, and reported for work.

The thirty-two-year-old fisherman's son with the grey-blue eyes was a seasoned veteran of the Newfoundland Constabulary. Seven of his eleven years of service had been spent in the Assault Section, one of seven units of the force's Criminal Investigation Division. The trim six-footer from the tiny community of Point aux Gaul had left home on his seventeenth birthday to find work – a rite of manhood on the economically depressed south coast of Newfoundland where, if the fishery is bad, life is bleaker than the boulder-strewn barrens of the Burin peninsula that stretch to the horizon like desolate prairies of the moon.

On the advice of his high-school teacher, Hillier joined the police force in 1964. The twenty-one-year-old had recently married Daphne Foote, his childhood sweetheart from Lamaline, a fishing community next to Point aux Gaul. Intense and emotional, the rookie policeman took his work seriously, seeing himself as something of a loner, a man with "no friends and no enemies"; even so, he enjoyed the company of his fellow officers. On Friday nights, he and Daphne would go to the Apollo Club on Torbay Road for dances and darts – weekly respites from the pressures of a job that only other policemen and their spouses could understand.

In those days, the 216-member Newfoundland Constabulary worked primarily within the city of St. John's, leaving the Royal Canadian Mounted Police (RCMP) to patrol the rest of the province. The key word on the force was loyalty – to your Chief, the Constabulary, the Minister of Justice and your Church – and the young policeman honoured the code religiously.

For his first year and a half as a policeman, Hillier was assigned to foot patrol with a senior constable. His star rose when he and another young constable, Len Power, were transferred to the thirty-one-member CID on special assignment to investigate a series of mysterious arsons involving Roman Catholic schools in St. John's. The pair solved the case in just over a year, earning Hillier a reputation as a shrewd arson investigator. Following a brief transfer back to foot patrol, he became a permanent member of the CID in 1968. It was a tough assignment. In 1975, the plainclothes investigators of the CID's assault section handled 700 cases, only 250 of which they were able to complete because of a crippling shortage of manpower and a crushing workload.

Hillier was known by his fellow officers as a tough customer who kept himself in good shape (he especially enjoyed floor hockey) and a solid investigator. He played a central role in a high-level blackmail case involving Ches Pippy, one of Newfoundland's wealthiest men, and worked on two homicide cases and two attempted murders after joining the CID. As former Staff Sgt. Arthur Pike, his immediate superior in the assault section, recalled, "Hillier was a good fellow I could depend on. . . . He took his work seriously." By the time Bob Hillier got around to saying something, he could usually back it up.

That December morning, Hillier wondered what awaited him as he passed through the Dutch door into the general CID office and was informed that Det.-Insp. Chesley Yetman wanted to see him. Hillier would normally have taken his orders from Staff Sergeant Pike, the man in charge of the CID's assault section, but Pike was heavily involved in a complex fraud investigation and was working out of a different office. Hillier listened quietly as he was briefed on the Shane Earle file and formally assigned to the Mount

Cashel investigation. His partner on the case was to be Det. Allan Thistle, a greenhorn who had joined the CID from the uniformed service just a week before.

Although he never mentioned his misgivings to his superiors, the young detective knew he had a potential tiger by the tail. If the assault allegations against a Christian Brother turned out to be true, he would soon be on a collision course with some of the most powerful forces in the province. And as fellow police officer Robert Pearcey would later testify at the Hughes Inquiry, the Newfoundland Constabulary of the day only laid informations themselves, "depending on what the charge was and depending on who was going to be charged. . . . If there was any person in a high position in the community, there's no way. That report had to go to the Chief's office. . . . You couldn't just walk down to court and say, 'Well, I'm going to charge somebody. . . . People were treated differently. . . . It was quite obvious."

Hillier, too, had seen other cases where special consider-ations had smothered police investigations, and knew that the Roman Catholic church was about as special a case as you could get in Newfoundland. As he left Detective Inspector Yetman's office that day, Hillier was convinced he would have to work fast if he were to complete the case, believing as he did that it was just a matter of time before the investigation would be called off. And even if he could complete his inquiries, and felt charges should be laid, there was still no guarantee that anything would ever be done. "Reports would fade away," one policeman would later testify, "and would never be seen no more and you could never ever find out where they went."

Hillier's first stop was at the 360 Duckworth Street apartment of Carol Earle, where he interviewed little Shane to satisfy himself that the complaint against Brother Joseph Burke was valid. The child was upset and difficult to deal with, particularly when it came to showing the stranger the bruises that had sent him to the Janeway the previous Sunday. After seeing the bluish green marks that were still there three days after the alleged beating, Hillier knew that the incident required further investigation. He didn't take a statement from Shane because he was under the age of ten, but made reference to the interview in his December 18 police report.

"The boy appeared to be very bright for his age and when asked if he wished to go back to the Orphanage he replied, 'no,' he would rather be home because he was afraid of the Brothers."

Detective Hillier's next stop was the Harvey Road district office of the Department of Social Services, where he and Detective Thistle officially informed the department that they were conducting a police investigation into the Shane Earle incident. They also interviewed the social worker who had dealt with Shane's complaint. Alice Walters advised the detectives to contact Chesley Riche, who was angry about the beating and, in her opinion, a "man with a vengeance" about getting to the bottom of the Mount Cashel situation.

After talking to the detectives, Mrs. Walters had the feeling that Detective Hillier felt the same way, an impression she recorded that day, December 9, in her running record of the Earle case:

"Office visit from CID officers Thistle and Hillier. More questions about yesterday's happenings. Mr. Hillier said complaints about Mt. Cashel had been coming in steadily for the last two years, and he would not be surprised to see the lid blown off this time." (Years later at a royal commission, Alice Walters would reinforce the picture she had painted in 1975 of a frustrated detective determined to crack the case. "He went with his hand like that [striking her fist into her palm], and he said, 'My God, I know it's been going on for a long time and I haven't been able to nail them down, but this time I'll get them.' ")

No one knew better than the police that all was not well at Mount Cashel. The Morals Section of the Newfoundland Constabulary was responsible for missing persons and would often be called in to find boys who had run away from the orphanage. The favourite hideaway for runaway Mount Cashel boys was in the woods behind the Zellers Mall on Torbay Road, where they would build bough houses and cook their food over open fires. The police would either apprehend them there or in the mall itself, where they went for spare change and warmth.

One member of the Morals Section, Robert Pearcey, later recalled what it was like returning runaways to Mount Cashel.

"I remember one particular day we brought one young boy back. . . . Most of the young boys that were at Mount Cashel from my observation were too frightened to say anything to anybody about anything. They seemed like they were . . . they had a lot inside but they wouldn't give. So we brought this particular boy back and we went in the main entrance and brought this particular boy over to the Brother. With this, the Brother asked him where he was and what not. And we just stood there and listened. He ordered him upstairs. Before he ordered him upstairs, he struck him across the face and told him it better not happen again and the boy went upstairs. We left. . . . It was the language the Brother used on the boy that I didn't like. When we got into the car . . . I mentioned it to my partner. I thought it was terrible that a man of that calibre, and what he was representing, could say such things to a young boy."

In the wake of Shane's beating, a call went out from the Harvey Road office of Social Services to William Earle, Sr., who was by then living with his new wife, Rosemary, and eldest son, Rick, in Pasadena near Corner Brook. Earle seemed to have found his niche in life in the paper-mill city on Newfoundland's west coast, providing security at two Corner Brook hospitals. When the call from Social Services came in one night after supper, his first thought was that Shane or Billy had gotten into some kind of trouble.

"My wife answered the phone and my son Richard was there and I asked my wife who it was and she said it was long distance from St. John's. The lady revealed that there were some more problems at Mount Cashel Orphanage and that my son Shane had been beaten.

"She asked me if it was possible I could come to town and I told her yes, I could come to town. She didn't have too much to say and she said she would explain it to me when I got to town," Mr. Earle recalled. But the voice on the other end of the line did mention a Brother Burke and the fact that the Brother had given Shane "a few blows with his hand." The social worker also mentioned that the police were involved.

After he hung up, William Earle, Sr. immediately tried to call Brother Burke, first at Mount Cashel, and then at St. Bonaventure's College where he finally caught up with him. The Brother was coy, neither admitting nor denying that he had beaten Shane.

"I asked him over the phone, 'Brother Burke, did you beat Shane?' And he refused to answer. He gave me no explanation. . . . He and I got into an argument and there were some choice words used, by me, not by him. . . . I was very upset." Earle told Burke that he was six foot two and over two hundred pounds and if the Brother wanted to hit someone, he should try hitting him. Burke hung up. The angry father called right back, but the line was busy.

The next day, William Earle, Sr. and his son got on an Eastern Provincial Airlines flight to St. John's, where they rented a car at the airport and drove to Rick's grandmother's house in the Battery. There they began calling St. Bon's, looking for the man who had beaten Shane. After a few drinks, they finally drove over to Mount Cashel, itching to even the score.

On their arrival at the orphanage, they found three Brothers in their robes standing by the entrance. Rick took a few swings at one of them and in the ensuing scuffle tore off his collar. Earle, Sr. and his son then stormed the front steps, intent on confronting Brother Burke. Rick was restrained by two of the Brothers, but there was no stopping his burly father who stormed into the orphanage. He was met just inside the door by Brother Douglas Kenny, Mount Cashel's Superintendent, who was on crutches and had his leg in a cast from a serious hockey injury. The Superintendent calmly asked his distraught visitor what he wanted. Earle, Sr. replied that Shane had been beaten and that he wanted to see Brother Burke. Brother Kenny said that wouldn't be "wise," adding that Brother Burke was not there. When Earle, Sr.

asked why Shane had been beaten, Brother Kenny informed him that the matter was now being handled by the police.

As Shane's father was leaving the orphanage, a boy lingering by the door whispered that Brother Burke was up in one of the dormitories. But when another child pointed to what looked like an unmarked police car parked at Mount Cashel's front gates, the Earles decided it was time to go. At least if there had been any wrongdoing, William Earle, Sr. had the consolation of knowing that the police would take care of it.

"When I spoke to the gentlemen, Mr. Kenny, at the orphanage regarding these few incidents, he told me it was being looked after by the proper people and that sort of satisfied my mind."

More consoled than angry now, William Earle, Sr. and his son left town without visiting Shane, or finding out that he and Billy were no longer at the orphanage but staying with their mother on Duckworth Street.

Heeding the advice of Alice Walters, Detective Hillier tried to reach Chesley Riche. Riche, who was leery of the Constabulary from past dealings, refused to come to the police station and failed to keep two meetings with Hillier outside of police headquarters.

"To date, I have not discussed the matter with him in person," Hillier noted. "He stated by telephone that he knew what was going on at the Orphanage and said it's up to the police to do something about it. He said he was a volunteer worker at the Orphanage."

Not for long. When Riche returned to Mount Cashel, he heard that several Brothers were being moved out. But his curiosity about where they were going was as unwelcome as he was; when he asked what was going on, one of the Brothers abruptly told him to leave.

"He said I was a negative influence and would appreciate it if I never came back any more. . . . He made it very plain that I made him uncomfortable and wasn't welcome there," Riche remembered.

The headstrong heavyweight was just as unpopular at

Kenny's Marble Works. For the time being, there would be no more work from his former friend, Joe Kenny. Riche returned to doing odd jobs, one of them in the house of a school teacher, Kathryn Burry, Carol Earle's sister. The teacher remembered Riche being "very disturbed and very vocal" about the scandal at Mount Cashel. Burry, a staunch Catholic, was so upset by Riche's accusations that she reported them to Father Kevin Molloy, the chaplain at the school where she taught.

That same afternoon, Father Molloy drove over to the orphanage to find out what was going on. He was met at the door by Brother Kenny. "You are too late," he remembered the Christian Brother telling him. "The police are already investigating."

With Hillier and Thistle barely into day one of their investigation, the Mount Cashel case was already making waves in the senior levels of the Newfoundland Constabulary and the Justice Department. The Chief of the day was sixty-four-year-old John Lawlor, a career policeman who had climbed to the top of the ladder one rung at a time, starting on the spring day in 1932 when he joined the force. His promotions were regular and unspectacular, taking him from constable, supervisor of street patrol, acting prosecutor at the Magistrate's Court, Deputy Assistant Chief to Assistant Chief of Police in September 1970. By the time he donned the gold-braided Chief's cap in 1972, the tall, silver-haired man with the thick St. John's accent, whose prototype could still be heard on Grafton Street in Dublin, had forty years service on the force.

In the mid-seventies, the Newfoundland Constabulary was unofficially organized along religious lines. If eight graduates were hired from the police academy, four would be Catholic, four Protestant. If the Chief of Police were Catholic, the Assistant Chief would be Protestant, and vice versa. This denominational balancing act wasn't restricted to the police force but applied to the whole society. The fierce separation of the island's two principle religious groups didn't lessen with the passage of time; instead, it was institutionalized. The principal support of the sectarian status quo was a system of education that was totally church-controlled.

It would be hard to find a man better attuned to the denominational realities of St. John's — or more potentially compromised by them in the circumstances — than Chief John Lawlor. A staunch Roman Catholic, he attended daily mass at the Basilica, a short walk from Fort Townshend down Bonaventure Avenue to Military Road, where the huge cathedral looked out over the harbour. His brother was Father Eric Lawlor, later a Monsignor in the Archdiocese of St. John's. His spinster sister, Elizabeth, devoted her life to her cleric brother, keeping house for him and travelling with him on his church duties. Chief Lawlor's daughter, Maureen, was a nun, a Sister of Mercy stationed in St. Lawrence on the island's rugged south coast. His son Edward was a Christian Brother, while another son, John, had been a Christian Brother before leaving the order to get married. Lawlor himself was a member of the Patricians, a club whose members were former students of St. Patrick's Hall, a St. John's school run by the Christian Brothers.

Chief Lawlor learned about the Mount Cashel investigation on or about December 9 from his Assistant Chief, John Norman, the senior administrative officer responsible for the CID. Norman informed the Chief that they had a "serious problem" at the orphanage, including suspected sexual acts involving some Christian Brothers and some of the boys. Lawlor, known by his men as an approachable and gentlemanly person, was shocked — and worried. It was not a happy turn of events for a man who was set to retire in a few months' time, and who was also deeply involved in planning celebrations to mark the one-hundredth anniversary of the Christian Brothers' apostolate in Newfoundland.

"I was concerned because of the involvement of the Brothers whom I had known down over the years, who taught myself as a young boy. I had great respect for . . . all the Brothers," he would later testify.

Chief Lawlor ordered his Assistant Chief to continue the investigation and to keep the Deputy Minister of Justice informed. Even though Lawlor would later say that it was part of Norman's duties to maintain liaison with the Justice Department, Lawlor himself then called the Deputy Minister – his good friend, former Constabulary member and staunch fellow Catholic, Vincent McCarthy.

"When it came to light," he said, "I immediately made him [McCarthy] aware of what was going on. I . . . related to him that we had some information concerning a nasty situation involving Christian Brothers at Mount Cashel."

Lawlor instructed John Norman, who would resign from the Constabulary when the search committee looking for a new Chief of Police bypassed him, to keep McCarthy, and the Chief of Police, informed of the investigation's progress on a daily basis.

Years later, Lawlor remembered practically nothing about the Mount Cashel affair and did not explain why he felt it necessary to call the Deputy Minister of Justice about a police investigation that was less than a day old.

By the evening of Wednesday, December 10, Detective Hillier had cleared up his other files and was working full time on the Mount Cashel investigation. He returned to 360 Duckworth Street and took a statement from Carol Earle, who was more determined than ever to find out what was going on at the orphanage. The still distraught mother gave Detective Hillier two photographs of Shane's buttocks that she had taken the previous Sunday, clearly showing the marks of the beating. She also confirmed for the detective that there was more to the case than Shane's ugly beating, telling Hillier that "sexual passes had been made toward Billy," a claim that Chesley Riche had made when he brought the two Earle boys home to their mother on December 7. Although she didn't know Riche well enough to trust him, his words brought back a disturbing memory of what another of her sons had told her after leaving Mount Cashel.

"My older son Ricky, who is now sixteen years of age, was also in the Mount Cashel Orphanage over seven years ago and since he has got out he has told me that the Brothers in the orphanage was a bunch of queers," she said in her

statement to police. "I would like to have the matter investigated to find out if my children have been abused by the
Brothers at the orphanage. . . ."

That night on his way home, Hillier planned the next day's
interviews. He reasoned that if he could officially gather
enough evidence, it would be harder for his superiors to
suppress the investigation. He decided to ask one of his most
experienced colleagues, Det. Ralph Pitcher, to assist him in
the case. The two had worked together before, and Hillier
had a lot of respect for the stocky, five-year veteran of the
CID's Assault Section. But by the next morning, the
investigation had hit its first bureaucratic snag. By the time it
was untangled, nearly an entire working day would be
lost.

On Thursday, December 11, Detective Hillier was
summoned to a meeting with John Lawlor and John
Norman. Ironically, the sensitive meeting took place in the
hallway of Fort Townshend, since it was improper
procedure for a detective to go directly into the Chief's
office. It was unusual for Hillier to be dealing directly with
the Chief and the Assistant Chief on an investigation rather
than with Detective-Inspector Yetman, who was the officer
in command of the CID. Noting the fact that his superior
had been taken out of the loop, Hillier listened in silence as
he was told to halt the investigation until further notice. The
two senior police officers said that the Justice Department
had not yet determined whether the matter would be
proceeding − bald confirmation that justice operated very
differently in Newfoundland than it did in other jurisdictions, where the police themselves routinely determine what
is to be investigated.

Detective Hillier wasn't the only person who noted the
peculiar reporting procedures on the Mount Cashel investigation. Det. Insp. Chesley Yetman, the fifty-nine-
year-old career policeman who was in charge of the CID,
objected to being shunted to one side as the sensitive
case developed.

"I was being bypassed with regards to the investigation as
they were speaking to Detective Hillier. When I say 'they' I
mean the Chief and the Assistant Chief. I told him I was

disturbed by it and Assistant Chief Norman said: 'You weren't being bypassed. It was a matter of getting the information quickly and first-hand,' which I thought was a little unusual," he would later recall. No one ever explained to Yetman who wanted the news on Mount Cashel in such a hurry. Although he would later sign the December 18 police report into the Mount Cashel affair, his only real job in the investigation was approving Detective Hillier's overtime.

Many years later, John Lawlor acknowledged that Hillier had indeed been temporarily pulled off the case. He testified that Assistant Chief Norman had been instructed by the Justice Department to "hold" the operation until he received further word. According to Lawlor, Norman had asked the Chief to place a call to Justice to find out what the problem was — a call the Assistant Chief could easily have placed on his own. Lawlor, who testified that he had spoken only once with Deputy Minister Vincent McCarthy about the Mount Cashel case, then placed a second call, allegedly to find out why the investigation was being delayed.

"I called the Deputy Minister and I told him that we were a little concerned about this being held up and was there any reason why. 'I don't know offhand,' he said, 'and I'll find out who's prosecuting and get back to you.' " Lawlor didn't explain why a prosecutor would have already been assigned to a case where the investigation itself had just begun, and where there was not even a police report. "Sometime later I did get a call (maybe a day or two later) saying, yes, they did ask to hold it over. . . . Arrangement had been made with the Christian Brothers to have the Brother Superior who was stationed in Toronto, no, a place called Mono Mills, and that he had been advised about this and in turn that he was coming to St. John's to see what it was all about."

Hillier wasn't given these details at the time, but he didn't need them to figure out which way the wind was blowing. The young detective's premonition of interference in the investigation had simply come to pass faster than he'd expected.

It had been Hillier's intention to interview everyone at Mount Cashel, complainants and suspects alike. Given that there were ninety-one boys and ten Brothers at the orphanage, there was no time to waste. But the pale winter afternoon was already fading in the sombre windows of Fort Townshend before he finally got the official go-ahead to continue the investigation. Someone in the upper echelons of the system was clearly troubled by the investigation, but for the time being had not yet decided how to handle it.

Detectives Hillier and Pitcher drove straight to Mount Cashel to arrange interviews with the boys. They were greeted by a clutch of curious youngsters gathered in the institution's hallway, anxious to find out what was going on. Detective Hillier had made official calls on Mount Cashel before, including a 1972 visit to investigate a theft. The money in question had been powdered and the suspect boys had been trooped in to have their hands held under an ultra-violet light that would expose the culprit. It had been a depressing assignment, watching the boys file in to be scanned, but nothing like the one that would soon be unfolding before the horrified detective's eyes.

"I went there and had a look to see the atmosphere and so on, as I recall it, and decided after I arrived there that it wouldn't be a good idea to interview the boys at Mount Cashel Orphanage."

The boys to be interviewed were selected at random, though Detective Hillier did obtain some names from his interview with Shane Earle. He arranged for Brother Kenny to bring the boys to Fort Townshend for questioning the following morning. He did not have any reason to be concerned about Mount Cashel's Superintendent personally bringing the boys to CID headquarters. That would soon change.

On Friday, December 12, the CID investigators got a shocking introduction to the situation they were facing. Eight boys were brought to the CID Assault Section office in the northeast corner of the second story of Fort Townshend. Hillier and Pitcher sat on opposite sides of a desk, taking down statements, while the boy being interviewed sat in a chair off to their left. The others waited their turn in a room at the top of the stairs. At times, the two detectives would split up, with Pitcher taking one of the boys down the hall to record his statement. In the joint interviews, although Hillier led the questioning, Pitcher put queries of his own. Each interview lasted about half an hour, depending on how long it took them to make their subjects relax – a task that wasn't always easy, given the mental state of the boys.

"Most of the boys when they came to my office, it took us some time to settle them down. I think pretty well all of them was crying. . . . They were completely exhausted children," Hillier remembered. The detective assured the boys that the police were there to help and that if anything was amiss, they could count on something being done about it. In almost every case, the tall detective with the steady gaze won their trust.

Hillier selected as his first interviewee a boy who came from the Burin Peninsula, not far from where the detective himself had grown up. "A" was a thirteen-year-old from St. Lawrence, a fishing community on the south coast of Newfoundland which was also the site of a major fluorspar mine. Sitting above the small community was a graveyard studded with the bone-white crosses of miners who had died of silicosis, or "miner's lung," as the deadly disease was locally known.

A, one of a family of fourteen, had been placed in Mount Cashel with three of his five brothers after his mother was diagnosed in 1975 as having a kidney disorder and had to move to St. John's for bi-weekly sessions on a dialysis machine. Her husband's prolonged drinking binges resulted in several visits to the family home by social workers, who discovered that the remaining children were ill-clothed, undernourished and infested with body lice. On the advice of their social worker, they were taken out of their home and transported to the hospital at nearby Grand Bank, where they were de-loused and treated. Afterwards, they were placed in foster homes. Their father was escorted to the same hospital by his parish priest, who later made arrangements for the man to stay at the Harbour Light mission in St. John's, where he could be close to his wife.

Part of A's statement to the detectives outlined his experiences at the orphanage:

"During the night when I am doing study, Brother English

comes in and feels around me, he puts his hand on my leg and rubs it all the way up to my privates. When I go to bed at night time and Brother English is working, he usually come to my bed and sits down talking to me. He puts his hand inside my pyjamas and feels my bird. He feels me all over my body. Brother English also does this with other boys. . . . My brother also haves [sic] problems with Brother English doing the same thing to him."

Half an hour later, the detectives interviewed B, A's younger brother. The boy told the detectives a story remarkably similar to the one they had already heard:

"The only problem I have is with Brother English. He is always feeling me up with his hands. On many occasions he has been lying on my bed and he has called me and told me to feel his leg. I told him no, but had to do it as he would call me back if I left. He would take my hand and move it on his bird outside his pants. Many times when I've been in the carpet room, he has come up behind me when I been watching TV. He catches my hand and puts it behind my back. He then moves it on his bird and starts moving his body. He is always putting his hand inside my pants and puts it on my bird. On one occasion in Holyrood [a seaside village off the Trans-Canada Highway northwest of St. John's], we were swimming and he did it."

If the two detectives thought they were dealing with a lone deviant, their next interview with nine-year-old Ian Pumphrey shattered that theory. Placed in the orphanage that summer along with two of his four brothers, the youngster told them that two Brothers had been abusing him.

"At the home it's pretty good, but Brother English and Brother Ralph does things to me that I don't like. About four or five times Brother Ralph put his hand inside my pants and felt me. . . . Brother English is the worst one as he is always putting his hand inside my pants and inside my shirt; once he put my hand on his stomach. When I am running around he grabs me and makes out he is fooling around and he then put his hand inside my pants."

The little boy's testimony was backed up half an hour later when twelve-year-old Bobby Connors repeated similar complaints about Brother English and Brother Ralph. Connors had already made the same complaints of physical and sexual abuse by the Brothers a few months before to social worker Robert Bradbury, but to no avail. "We have a name on Brother English because he feels the boys up," Bobby told the detectives. "We calls him 'Jigger.' " (Jigging in Newfoundland is a method of fishing in which a hand-held line is jerked up and down in the water.)

The detectives then interviewed Bobby's brother, eleven-year-old Gregory Connors, who told them about physical as well as sexual abuse and added yet another name to the list of alleged offenders amongst the Brothers – the same person Shane Earle claimed had beaten him the previous Sunday.

"I don't like Brother Burke because he beats me for every little thing, he beats me across my bare backside with a stick. About three days ago Brother Burke took me into a closet and made me pull down my pants. He hit me five or six times across my backside with a stick. He beat me because I threw a after-shave tin into the garbage can – it made a noise and Brother Burke was watching TV. Both Brother Ralph and Brother English on seven or eight times have caught hold of me and have felt my legs and felt my bird; sometimes this has happened when I have been in bed. Brother Ralph would sit down on the bed and feel my bird inside my pyjama pants. Most times Brother English would feel my bird when I was in the dining hall, he would do it sometimes when I was in bed."

The detectives were devastated by what they were hearing. The next two interviews sounded a new and disturbing note in what had already been a sickening day's work.

"P", a nine-year-old who had been at Mount Cashel for a year and a half, identified Brother English as his regular tormentor.

"He feels me up all the time and puts his hands inside my pants. He tells me to play doctor with him and when I do, he puts my hand inside his pants and makes me play with his bird. He tells me to fool with the hairs and to move my fingers on his thing. I does this for him because I'm afraid he will hit me if I don't do it."

Then the little boy added a new and surprising detail.

"Today, dinner hour, Brother Kenny called me in a room at the orphanage and questioned me. He asked me if I had any trouble with any of the Brothers and I told him 'Yes' and told him that it was Brother English. He told me not to discuss it with anyone."

It appeared as though the police weren't the only ones conducting an investigation. The detectives noted the information and from that point on watched for interference in their work by Mount Cashel's Superintendent. Their vigilance was reinforced by the last interview of the day, in which Douglas Kenny's name came up again.

"J" was as sorry an inmate of Mount Cashel as the detectives would come across during their week-long investigation. He had been placed in the orphanage in 1971 at the age of six. He had already lived in eight homes by then — three of them in his first three months of life. His last move before entering the orphanage had been to his aunt's home on Torbay Road in St. John's. According to a social worker's notes, "He was a very good boy until recently but his aunt is now very troubled keeping him away from Zellers and getting him in at night. He has, also, an inclination to 'possess' other people's property."

The boy's father had spent time in prison and was legally prohibited from entering his own father's house. J's mother had been an illegitimate child who was herself raised in a succession of foster homes, including the Belvedere Orphanage, a church-run institution for homeless and destitute girls in St. John's. After working briefly as a domestic, J's mother was committed to the Waterford Hospital, an institution for mental and nervous disorders. Three years after her son was placed in Mount Cashel, the rootless mother showed up at Social Services to inquire about her own foggy family background; she did not ask about her children.

The ten-year-old's story reinforced the detectives' conviction that very serious crimes were being committed against Mount Cashel's children by some of the very men who were supposed to be their moral and spiritual guardians.

"Since last year, a lot of times Brother [English] has got me to feel his bird. Sometimes when 'P' and I are together, Brother English would get the two of us to feel his legs and his bird outside his pants. Some nights when I am in bed Brother English . . . begins feeling my bird. He does this inside my pyjama pants. When 'P' and I are watching TV Brother English won't let us watch it. He always wants us to feel his bird for him. I am quite happy in the orphanage except for Brother English. Today Brother Kenny called me into his office and asked me if I had any problems with any of the Brothers. I told him about what Brother English was doing. Brother Kenny told me not to tell anyone about it."

After the little boy signed his statement, the last one of the day, Hillier and Pitcher informed Chief Lawlor of what they had learned. Years later, the Chief wouldn't remember anything about the Mount Cashel investigation, including the contents of the statements his detectives had taken. Hillier remembered a different John Lawlor — a man who had been smack in the middle of the affair — and stuck to his story that both Lawlor and Assistant Chief Norman were well aware of the details of the investigation.

"He had to receive it. I couldn't keep stuff like that from them," he said.

The two detectives worked straight through the weekend, taking twelve more statements at CID headquarters in Fort Townshend — five on Saturday and seven on Sunday. The first boy they talked to on Saturday, December 13 was Billy Earle, Shane's older brother. Like the others, the eleven-year-old described how both Brother English and Brother Ralph had sexually molested him during his last two years at Mount Cashel. He related how another Mount Cashel boy, Gerard Brinston, had witnessed Brother Ralph "feeling up" Billy and urged him to report the incident to Brother Burke. The older boy warned Billy against telling Superintendent Kenny about Brother Ralph because, as he put it, "he is also a bit like it." Just before the beating that would lead to Shane and Billy leaving Mount Cashel, Billy got some first-hand confirmation of Gerard Brinston's suspicions about Brother Kenny.

"About two weeks ago, I was at the swimming pool at Mount Cashel with Brother Kenny. There was no one else around and Brother Kenny started kissing me on the lips. He told me to bite his neck and I did it once. He said it was good. He told me to do it again. Another time I went to his office to get some money from my bank and he again kissed me on the lips. I didn't like it, but I did it because I thought he might say something to me if I didn't do it," Billy said in his statement.

The next boy, "O", added to the picture that was emerging of Brother English as a pedophile who, in addition to sexually molesting his victims, regularly brutalized them. The twelve-year-old described how both Brother English and Brother Kenny had "big rubber straps" and strapped "very hard," leaving blisters on the boys' hands and arms. O said that Brother English tried to stop the boys from telling anyone about the beatings.

Hillier and Pitcher were now seriously concerned about Mount Cashel's Superintendent and decided to re-interview Greg Connors to see if he could corroborate what Billy Earle had told them. Connors gave a second statement to the investigators on Saturday afternoon. Like Billy Earle, Connors told the detectives that Brother Kenny had asked him to bite his neck on three or four occasions and that he had witnessed other Mount Cashel boys – Derm Ryan and Craig English – doing the same thing. Greg's brother, Bobby, also gave the detectives a second statement in which Brother Kenny and Brother Burke figured prominently.

"About four months ago Brother Kenny was fixing the swimming pool and he asked me to come near and clean the floors in the dressing room. Brother Kenny sat down on the stool to take a rest. He called me to come over and have a rest. I sat down two or three feet away from him and he moved closer to me. He told me to bite his tongue which I did about three times. He also put his tongue in my mouth. He told me to bite the tip of his tongue. He also kissed me several times on the mouth the same day. The day before this, again in the same place, he told me to bite his neck, which I did. I didn't want to do anything like this but I was afraid he would get mad if I refused.

"Last Saturday Brother Burke hit me six times with a leather belt on the backside with my pants up. He then took me into a closet and made me take my clothes down, including my shorts. With a round stick about a foot long he hit me on my bum. The same night when I was getting ready to go swimming, the other boys told me I had blisters on my bum which was caused by the stick. There is a stick got written on it, 'Ouch' [Mr. Ouch, as Shane Earle would later describe it] and he have also hit me with this one once before. . . . I have heard the Brothers are not allowed to have these things."

The last boy the detectives interviewed on Saturday was Gerard Brinston, one of the few real orphans at Mount Cashel. Born in St. Lawrence, Gerard lived at home with his parents and four brothers and sisters until he was three. In November 1963 his mother was killed in a car accident, and two years later his father, who worked in the fluorspar mine, died of miner's lung. The graveyard in St. Lawrence had one more white cross, and the Brinston children had run out of protection. They were put into foster homes, where little Gerard was a real favourite.

"Gerard is a delightful little boy," his social worker reported. "He has dark brown hair, freckles, blue eyes and long-lashed. He is a little 'chubby' and makes one think of a lovable 'teddy bear'. . . . Gerard is of normal intelligence. He is not the least bit shy but is the outgoing, affectionate type."

The picture had changed dramatically by the time Gerard turned twelve. Still in foster care in St. Lawrence, the affectionate cherub had grown sullen, difficult and fretful, a transformation that his social service progress report for 1972 soberly reflected.

"A nervous boy when it comes to sleeping alone or being in the dark. He has a great fear of death or being injured. . . . Gerard failed Grade IV. His marks were very low. This may be due partly to the change of schools in March and then a further change in teachers. . . . Gerard has a tendency to play with girls because of fear of injury."

The social worker recommended that the adolescent see a child psychiatrist at the Janeway "to investigate Gerard's unwarranted fears." In April 1973, Gerard and his sister were removed from their home in St. Lawrence at the request of their foster parents. After a brief stay in another foster home, in which he was viewed as sullen and disobedient, the moody fourteen-year-old was transferred to Mount Cashel, where he would remain for the next three years.

When his turn in the interrogation room came, the sixteen-year-old made no effort to disguise his dislike of the orphanage, complaining to the detectives of beatings by Brother Kenny and sexual abuse from other Brothers. He told Hillier and Pitcher about having seen Brother Ralph in bed with Billy Earle, and of his suspicions about Brother Kenny. According to the story he haltingly related that afternoon, the young man's own initiation into the orphanage three years earlier had not been any kinder.

"The first week I was at the orphanage I was out in the porch when Brother English came. He put his hands inside my pants and began to feel me up. He wanted me to put my hand inside his pants, which I did. At this time, another boy came and he stopped. A little while after, Brother English, he got me to go out to the Goulds [a rural area west of St. John's] with him to bring out some tapes. On the way out Brother English began feeling me up. He asked me to give him a blow. He forced my head down on his penis and I took it in my mouth. I don't believe he came, as a car came and he got up. . . . Malcolm Baird, one of the boys, told me Brother English did the same thing to him a little while ago, just before Malcolm left the orphanage.

"The incident with Brother English and I took place in by a overpass by a drive-in. I was fourteen years old when this took place. That was the first week at the orphanage."

Of the eleven boys Detectives Hillier and Pitcher had randomly selected to interview since Friday morning, ten had made complaints of either physical or sexual abuse against the Brothers. The two policemen knew that they had a full-blown scandal on their hands that could tear the city apart. And there were still eighty boys to interview — and, of course, the Christian Brothers.

That night on the way home, Hillier thought about his own three children and shuddered.

After breakfast on Sunday morning, Brother Douglas Kenny assembled the seven boys the police wanted to interview that day and loaded them into Mount Cashel's Ford station wagon, saying only that they were "going somewhere." The roads were empty and the trip through the sleepy city streets passed quickly – up Elizabeth Avenue, with its orderly rows of frame bungalows, left at the lights by Churchill Square, past Brother Rice High School and into the parking lot by the fire station beside Fort Townshend. One of the passengers, Dereck O'Brien, recalled what Brother Kenny told them on the way to the police station.

"He had said to me that we were going to talk to some police officers and they were going to ask us some questions and he said that he didn't want his name mentioned or Brother English's name mentioned. . . . I just looked at him in the eye and he never said anything."

A policeman met the boys at the entrance to Fort Townshend and the boys walked in single file up the stairs to the second floor, where they would be individually interviewed by Detectives Hillier and Pitcher.

The burly O'Brien, who just the year before had gone with Brenda Lundrigan to Social Services to complain about the beating Johnny Williams had received from Brother English, was the first to be interviewed.

The seventeen-year-old was no stranger to cruelty before coming to Mount Cashel. Placed into care at the age of four, O'Brien and two of his brothers lived in a succession of foster homes. In one of them, just west of St. John's, they experienced nightmarish abuse. They were regularly beaten, submerged in icy bath water, and dispatched to a chilly basement when they misbehaved.

"They would put food on a tin plate and call us by dog names . . . I can remember the name Fido and names of that sort," he recalled. He had one other recollection that he would later share with the Hughes Inquiry: when the boys had to use the bathroom, their foster mother would sometimes hand them a wad of toilet paper and send them outside to use the Mount Pearl dump, which was a short distance down the road from their house.

"She told us that we were kids that nobody cared about and somebody was paying her . . . to care for a couple of kids that nobody wanted."

The husky boy grew fiercely protective of his hapless family, a characteristic he would bring with him to Mount Cashel when he and his brothers were placed there in 1974. O'Brien told the detectives that he himself hadn't had any trouble at the orphanage, possibly because he was too big for the Brothers to abuse. But he knew the same wasn't true for many of the other boys, including his two younger brothers.

"About the first two weeks we were there, Roy came to me and told me Brother English got him in the dorm and wanted him to give Brother English a blow. I told Roy if Brother English tried it again to let me know. As far as I know, it didn't happen again. My other brother, Ronnie, age thirteen years, came to me because he was hit by Brother English. I looked at Ronnie's back and I saw marks across his back like they were made by a broom handle. I went to Brother English and told him not to hit Ronnie again. I went to Brother Kenny about it but he didn't do anything about it as far as I know. . . ."

Although Dereck avoided the fate of many of the other boys at the orphanage, he was often a witness to the abuse going on all around him.

"One time last year I saw Brother English and Joey Boland in the carpet room. Brother English was feeling Boland up. They then went upstairs to the dorm. Myself and some other boys went to the dorm and looked in. I saw Brother English going right to town on Boland, he was kissing him. He had Boland's pants down around his knees. Brother English was doing homosexual acts on little Boland. Boland heard us and told Brother English someone was coming, so we beat it downstairs and waited as if nothing was going on. . . . It's a common occurrence to see Brother English with his hands inside the smaller boys' pants. . . ."

Dereck finished by telling the detectives about his trip to the Harvey Road Social Services office after Johnny Williams had his back "beaten to pieces" by Brother

English. Hillier stored away the information and wondered why nothing had been done about what appeared to be a much earlier complaint of physical abuse at Mount Cashel than Shane Earle's. The detective made a mental note to follow up the incident with Williams, Lundrigan and the responsible Social Services authorities.

After their interview with O'Brien, Hillier and Pitcher got a personal look at a case of physical abuse, when they interviewed fourteen-year-old Andre Walsh. The social worker's notes on his case provided a stark picture of the boy's background on the Burin Peninsula before his arrival at Mount Cashel in 1968 at the age of seven.

"A visit to the Walsh home at Lawn has produced further evidence of deterioration. The two-storey wooden structure is in a state of complete ruin and can boast of a leaky roof, very poor windows, and no doors. As well as this extremely apparent lack of repair, the house is untidy and furnished very poorly.

"At present there are eleven children between the ages of two to fifteen years in the home. . . . She [the mother] seems to have lost all control of the family."

Although he hadn't been sexually assaulted, Walsh related a story of gross physical abuse during his years at Mount Cashel.

"I got beaten a number of times but most times I deserved it. But once I got beaten about a year ago by Brother English who strapped me on the hands with a leather strap. He hit me about sixty times and I begged him for mercy but he wouldn't stop. This was just because I called a friend out [by] his name. My hands were really bruised and just above my hands on my wrist they were really beaten up as a result of the strap. Both of my hands are continuously peeling and cracks open up since these strappings. My hands are now a mess, and I haves to put Vaseline on them to keep them from drying up."

The young boy held out his hands while he talked, as if to convince the policeman he was telling the truth. Fourteen years later, Detective Hillier would still remember the pathetic sight.

"His hands were badly swollen and split, cracked. I

haven't forgotten the look of his hands since that time. . . . His hands were split lengthwise with the fingers. . . . The splits were lengthwise with his hands. . . . He had been strapped, badly strapped."

Their next interview provided more horrific tales of sexual abuse and a bitter historical irony. Seventeen-year-old Leo Gerard Rice was a direct descendant of the family of the founder of the Irish Christian Brothers, Edmund Ignatius Rice. Orphaned in April 1961 when his mother died (his father had died a month earlier), the three-year-old boy lived with his maternal grandmother until her death in August 1966. The eight-year-old and his four brothers were then placed in Mount Cashel; he would remain there for the next eleven years. His initial problems with Brother English were similar to the ones experienced by the other boys, but the day came when English upped the ante.

"About three months ago, Brother English got me in his room. He was in bed and he got me to get in bed with him. Both of us had our clothes off. Brother English tried to kiss me but I kept pulling away from him. He got on top of me. I was face up. He had his penis between my legs, he was going in and out. He then took it out and put it on my stomach and he 'came' on my stomach. He tried to pull me off but I didn't want to so I left.

"About three weeks ago Brother English took me for a ride one night. He went out by the new Arterial Road. He pulled down his pants, he kept putting my head down to his penis for to take it in my mouth. At this time he was trying to pull me off but I didn't want to. He didn't come when I had it in my mouth, so I gave him a few pulls; he then got horny and slid on top of me and he 'came' on my stomach. I didn't like what Brother English was doing, but I didn't feel like telling anyone about it.

"About four years ago, another Brother, Brother Short, who is at St. Pat's now, got me to pull him off three or four times when he was at Mount Cashel giving the other Brothers a break on Saturdays."

Yet another Brother had been added to the list of the two detectives, and with the seriousness of Rice's allegations,

Hillier was beginning to wonder if he could wait to interview all of the boys before taking further action.

One of the last statements that Sunday came from "R," a nine-year-old who gave what were probably the most pathetic quotes contained in the statements recorded by Hillier and Pitcher. R had been placed in Mount Cashel a year after his father's death, following an interval of disintegration for the young boy during which he became a disobedient bully who threw rocks at the children around him, threatened his babysitter with a knife and began setting fires behind his house. When his mother told him she was thinking of putting him in Mount Cashel, he enthusiastically agreed, insisting on leaving home as quickly as possible. With the exception of a two-year stretch when he returned to live with his mother, he stayed at Mount Cashel until he was sixteen.

After describing how the boys had "a big laugh" watching Brother Ralph feel up Greg Connors in the little boy's bunk, R told the investigators, "Brother Kenny is all right. He only asks me to bite his neck. . . . Brother English used to feel up the boys and then give them the gift from the corn flakes box."

R also told the detectives that the boys at the orphanage "is saying they [Brothers English and Ralph] is left and I hope they are." The police were already aware that some staff at Mount Cashel had suddenly left the institution just as the police investigation began.

One boy who didn't make complaints against the Brothers during the investigation even though he spoke to police was Gregory Preshyon, a fourteen-year-old, who, along with his brother, Gideon, had been in Mount Cashel since 1971. Shortly after he entered Mount Cashel, Preshyon was sexually assaulted by both Brother English and Brother Kenny, but he was too frightened of the Brothers to tell the story he would later relate at the Hughes Inquiry.

"He [English] would more or less feel me up. He would put his hands down in my pants. . . . I didn't know, to be honest, what a homosexual or a gay was until I went there."

One of Preshyon's sexual encounters took place with Brother Douglas Kenny. One day when the boy was in the reading room, Brother Kenny came in, shut the door, and began kissing Preshyon and asking him to bite his tongue. The incident was repeated as many as fifteen times, occasionally in Kenny's office and sometimes by Mount Cashel's swimming pool.

Greg was terrified of the strong, cruel Brother. Kenny used to take Preshyon on drives, parking by the ocean to kiss and pet him, telling the boy, "I want to be like your mother." Preshyon went along, particularly after the day Kenny lost his temper with him, grabbed him by the throat, banged his head off the wall and kneed him in the stomach as he crumpled to the floor. When the detectives asked him about Brother Kenny, though, Preshyon repeatedly denied that anything had ever happened.

"I was really scared because the man [Kenny] was just after driving me to the police station and I felt if I said something he would beat me," he would later testify at the Hughes Inquiry.

After the boys finished giving their statements to the detectives, they trooped down to the Ford station wagon where Brother Kenny was waiting behind the wheel to take them back to Mount Cashel.

Later that afternoon, Detective Hillier travelled to 46 Donovan Street in Mount Pearl, a suburban community just west of St. John's, to interview Carol Baird, whose children had previously been at Mount Cashel and who had been referred to in statements by other boys at the orphanage. Fourteen-year-old Malcolm Baird, who had been mentioned by Gerard Brinston in his session with the detectives, confirmed that he, too, had been sexually assaulted by Brother English, as Detective Hillier's notes of their interview record.

"He was in the orphanage about two months. Brother used to go to his bedside occasionally and feel him up. He used to put his hands inside Malcolm's clothes and fool around with his private parts."

If Malcolm's brother Frankie had spoken to Hillier, he could have reinforced the sense of revulsion that was threatening to overwhelm the troubled detective. But Frankie refused to talk because of a recent encounter with police over what was happening at Mount Cashel, an encounter that had ended disastrously for the boy who had dared to tell them the truth, only to be returned to the very tormentor he had identified.

Sick of the physical and sexual abuse at the orphanage, Frankie and a few other boys had planned to run away. But when the time came, he was the only one who crept through Mount Cashel's empty corridors "bright and early" one morning in November 1975 – just a week after social worker Robert Bradbury submitted his report to Newfoundland's Director of Child Welfare on allegations of physical and sexual abuse at Mount Cashel. The grass crunched beneath Frankie's feet, as the small and scrawny ten-year-old hurried towards the town, shivering in the frosty, pellucid air.

He passed like a shadow through the empty avenues where the silent houses sent plumes of smoke into the dawn sky, an image of order and warmth that made him shiver even more violently inside his thin summer jacket. When he reached Water Street, not far from St. John's Harbour, the diminutive escapee's few hours of freedom came to an abrupt end. Spotted by a police patrol, Frankie was ordered to stop. Instead, he "took off running" in a desperate attempt to avoid being sent back to the orphanage.

"They chased after me and caught up with me. . . . They tackled me to the ground. . . . I fought like you would never have seen a ten-year-old boy fight, and they handcuffed my wrists, they handcuffed my legs and they took me and literally threw me in the back of the car," he would later testify.

Once inside the police cruiser, Frankie broke down, kicking and crying as he related what was happening to the children at Mount Cashel. Over and over again, the sixty-five-pound boy told the policemen that he didn't want to go back to the orphanage. Once Frankie had settled down, his captors unshackled him and he was taken to the Child Welfare office on Harvey Road, where he was interviewed by a tall, dark-haired social worker whom Frankie thought "looked like somebody who would care." It was a physical description that closely matched Robert Bradbury, one of only a handful of males working at the district office. His

wrists swollen and marked from the handcuffs, the desperate
boy poured his heart out to the kindly stranger.

"I went in there and he asked me what was wrong, and I
explained to him, I told him that I didn't want to go back to
Mount Cashel. When he asked why . . . I told him what was
happening, what was happening to myself, my brother and
the rest of the children in Mount Cashel. And I explained to
him in great detail, in detail I'll never explain again, what
was happening. . . . And I tried to explain that in a
ten-year-old child's form to the police and the social
worker. . . . The most unbelievable thing . . . I explained to
him about one particular person mostly at Mount Cashel . . .
and I brought up his name continuously in my conversation.
This man was the one that scared me the most. And they
took me, put me in a taxicab with this social worker
presumably, and they brought me back to Mount Cashel
Orphanage and they brought me in the front door and they
literally picked me up and handed me to the same man I told
them about."

Years later, Frankie Baird recalled the impact of being
turned over to his tormentor. It was "like taking me and
throwing me into a fire."

Given what had already happened, by the time Robert
Hillier showed up at Frankie's house, the detective was just
another face of the enemy. Unaware of Frankie's previous
ordeal, Hillier recorded the trip to the Bairds in his
December 1975 police report.

"Written statements were not taken from the three last
named, Malcolm Baird, Edward Strickland, and Frank
Baird. These three brothers are now at home with their
mother, Mrs. Carol Baird, 46 Donovan Street, Mount Pearl.
The boys were taken from the orphanage by their mother
because she was told by her son Malcolm of Brother English,
who was feeling him up when he was in bed at night."

Carol Baird would later say she first learned of sexual
abuse at Mount Cashel from Detective Hillier.

The two detectives completed three more interviews on
Monday, December 15, unaware that these would be their
last with Mount Cashel boys.

"D" was a difficult boy who wouldn't do his homework and wouldn't accept punishment. Social Services initially referred the "problem child" to the psychiatric unit of the Janeway hospital, where it was found that the boy was normal. It was then theorized that his problem was a "lack of proper management at home."

"I feel that this boy will benefit greatly in a stable, calm, ordered atmosphere away from the complaints of family and neighbours. He also needs a place where he will receive firm, consistent discipline, without all the excitement and perhaps hysteria, of his home environment. I firmly feel," his social worker wrote in February 1975, "that this boy would present a challenge as I do not feel that this is a 'bad' boy, but a victim of his home circumstances. . . . Placement at Mount Cashel may just be what this boy needs right now."

Ten-year-old D would have disagreed.

"Since I have been in the orphanage, Brother English has been doing dirty things. One time when I was out in Placentia for a long weekend, Brother English got me on the floor and held my arms. He took my hands and began rubbing them against his privates; he would then be going in and out on my hands. Several times in the orphanage, Brother English has rubbed my privates with his hands and has taken my hands and rubbed against his privates. Brother English grabs me and squeezes me close to him and he goes in and out with his body. I have seen Brother English doing this to lots of boys at the orphanage but I can't remember who they were. I told my father about this. He told me to stay away from Brother English."

The last two boys interviewed by the detectives – fourteen-year-old John Pumphrey and fifteen-year-old Johnny Williams – also identified Brother English as a violent pedophile who had tormented them during their stays in Mount Cashel. Williams told the detectives about the savage beating from Brother English, which he had duly reported to both Brother Kenny and Social Services, without any result. He also told them about a sexual encounter with the Brother.

"One time Brother English took me for a drive outside the city. He put his hand on my leg and tried to feel me up but I pulled away from him," Williams said. "He offered me a Coke to lie on top of him but I didn't do it."

Pumphrey described how Brother English had tried to molest both him and his brother Ian, adding that one of the boys had told their father about what English was doing.

John's father, Ron Pumphrey, was the host of a popular talk show on radio station VOCM in St. John's. Hillier was concerned that the investigation would be jeopardized if the scandal became public before he had completed his work, so he tried to reach Pumphrey to seek his co-operation in keeping the matter temporarily out of the media.

"The message I wanted to get across to him," Hillier remembered, "was to explain the situation to him . . . and probably try to keep the thing quiet for a little while at least. . . . I thought that he would go public with it."

The radio personality never returned the detective's urgent telephone messages, but Hillier needn't have worried about Pumphrey breaking the story. After receiving word that the Mount Cashel scandal would be exposed on VOCM's "Open Line," Hillier went out in a patrol unit, waiting for the program to begin. Although a few callers tried to raise the matter, they were cut off, in keeping with the station's policy of not permitting criminal allegations to be made on the air. (Ironically, the reinvestigation of the Mount Cashel affair would be sparked fourteen years later by a call to the same show, which by then had a different host.)

Ron Pumphrey would later say that the police had downplayed the whole affair and that he had no idea of what was really happening at the orphanage. Hillier would firmly deny Pumphrey's story, maintaining that he had never spoken to the talk-show host. As in so many other instances of contradictory testimony, it would be up to a retired judge with a weakness for Havana cigars and esoteric points of law to determine where fact left off and self-interest began.

By Tuesday, December 16, Detective Hillier decided it was time to start interviewing suspects and making arrests. He also wanted to obtain a search warrant and seize as evidence the various sticks and straps the boys had referred to in their statements. On both initiatives he was stymied by the Chief of Police, John Lawlor.

"I didn't do it, because I was ordered not to do it," Hillier would later say, claiming that the command came jointly from the Chief and Assistant Chief of Police. "I was told not to take steps until they got back to me." No reason for the delay was offered. The two-tiered system of justice in which there was one rule for the socially prominent and another for ordinary citizens had kicked in with a vengeance.

Incredibly, the rest of the day was taken up with arguments about whether to interview Brothers English and Ralph, the two men who were whisked out of St. John's as soon as they had confirmed the allegations made against them by several Mount Cashel boys. After it was agreed that they should be interviewed, the debate shifted to where the sessions should take place. Word had spread through Fort Townshend that the two Brothers were about to leave the province. Hillier, who had been given the same story by Lawlor and Norman, insisted that they must be interviewed before they left the jurisdiction. Tuesday ended without a final decision by the Chief.

At his weekly Wednesday morning meeting, during which Chief Lawlor met with Detective-Inspector Yetman and the officers in charge of the CID's seven sections, the hottest investigation the Constabulary had conducted in a long time was not even mentioned. As Chief Lawlor would later explain, "That was kept as sort of a private thing between Assistant Chief Norman and myself."

That day, when Hillier was finally given the green light to interview English and Ralph, he was ready. According to normal police practice, they would have been picked up and brought to Fort Townshend. Again, John Lawlor intervened.

"I'm not sure what time of day, but I was informed by the Chief that the interviews would not be done at police headquarters and that a place would be sought for us to go outside police headquarters to do the interviews."

The "place" turned out to be McAuley Hall, part of the Roman Catholic parish located near Holy Heart of Mary School on Bonaventure Avenue. Hillier was furious. He knew that a good investigator always conducted interviews on his own ground, not on the turf of the suspect. The message was coming through loud and clear: the Brothers were not to be embarrassed by being dragged into the police station for questioning. Hillier remembered being given one more disconcerting order: since the Brothers were on their way out of the province, he should get through the interviews as quickly as possible.

Ralph and English were already waiting in a downstairs office at McAuley Hall, with their luggage, when detectives Hillier and Pitcher arrived. Both detectives distinctly remembered the luggage, a blunt reminder that they had to conduct their interviews expeditiously.

"When we interviewed the Brothers, their bags were packed. They were leaving to go somewhere. Their bags were packed, that's the thing that stands out to me," Detective Pitcher would later recall.

Detective Hillier remembered the same rushed scene.

"They were both ready to leave," he testified at the Hughes Inquiry, "and we were hurrying it up, trying to get the interviewing done and trying to get to the scene and interview them and get it over with so they could leave the city. . . . I know that before I left the office, the Chief told me . . . I think I knew one of them was supposed to be going to the United States."

The two Brothers were congenial, co-operative and very nervous. After being given the standard police caution, Brother Ralph gave a written and signed statement, but Brother English would only agree to answer questions orally. Hillier took notes during his interview with Brother English. He recorded his impressions of both interviews in his police report, astonished that the Brothers would so matter-of-factly admit to the allegations that had been levelled against them.

"During my interview with Brother English, I made particular reference to statements given me by the following boys: namely, Andre Walsh, Johnny Williams, Leo Gerard Rice and Malcolm Baird. Brother English was questioned considerably on these statements and he admitted that what these boys have stated in their statements is true. He also admitted having been involved with the following boys and states that he was involved with them as they have stated in their statements: William Earle, Robert Connors, Peter Brown, J, P, Ian Pumphrey, B, Gregory Connors and O.

"Brother Ralph admitted to feeling up four boys and names them in his statement. Reference was made by me to the statements given by the boys and he admitted the boys were telling the truth."

The final portion of Detective Hillier's police report amounted to a half-hearted confession by Brother Ralph.

December 17th, 1975;
Statement of Brother Alan Ralph;
Cautioned.

I am 31 years of age, D.O.B. Oct. 22nd, 1944 and presently residing at Holy Cross, Patrick St. I have been a Brother for the past 12 years and has been staying at Mount Cashel Orphanage since September 1974. About October 1975 I became involved with a boy Robert Connors one night while he was in bed. All I did with him was rub his backside. This has been done by me with Robert on several occasions since October. I have also been involved with boys, namely, Robert Connors, Ian Pumphr[e]y, Gregory Connors and William Earle. I did not become involved with the boys as far as homosexuality is concerned. All I did was rub their backsides, except for Billy Earle — I did touch his penis. I did not hurt either of the boys sexually. I know that I was seen by two boys, namely Jerry Brenston and R when involved with the other boys.

Physically, I have not injured any of the boys at the orphanage at any time. On occasions when I felt it necessary to punish a boy, I did use the strap on the hands or the backside. I usually have faith in what I'm doing and at no time has told them to cover it up by refraining to tell anyone about it.

I have never used a stick on the children in a physical way. I have had a stick for chastising the boys, but never beat them with it.

The statement was witnessed by Detectives Hillier and Pitcher and signed by Brother Alan Ralph at 10:35 in the morning. Hillier's sense that he was running against the clock was reinforced by a telephone call he received at McAuley Hall, ordering him to return to headquarters.

When the detectives got back to the CID offices, fresh from confirming with the suspects themselves many of the allegations against them, they got the word that Detective Hillier had been expecting all along. Expected or not, the news still left Hillier thunderstruck. Chief of Police John Lawlor pushed through the door of the CID office, accompanied by Assistant Chief John Norman, and informed them that their investigation was over. Lawlor promptly turned on his heel and left the office, with Hillier in hot pursuit.

"I can't do that Chief, there's more work to be done."

"There'll be no more work," he remembered Lawlor telling him.

"Chief, we can't do this, we can't let these people go, we just can't stop the investigation," Hillier persisted. The desperate detective knew many more interviews had to be conducted. Nor was he satisfied with the way he had handled the two Brothers, who were now leaving the province with the apparent blessing of the Chief of Police. But Lawlor was implacable. The investigation was over and he wanted Hillier's report immediately.

Detective Hillier demanded to know why.

"They told me there's no further investigation, that was it, that the church or the parish was going to look after matters pertaining to the Brothers from here on in and it was all in their hands." Hillier was mortified.

"I just thought it was horrible," he recalled. "I didn't think they would shut it down after what we got. I figured that there would be some interference, but I didn't suspect it would be shut down completely. When I had what I did have, I couldn't see for the life of me how they could just squash it under the carpet then."

In Hillier's opinion, the system had simply "let the boys go down the chute."

But the worst was yet to come. Detective Hillier quickly

put on paper what had been accomplished to date in the Mount Cashel investigation. On or about the morning of Thursday, December 18, he submitted his report entitled, "Homosexual acts and Child abuse at Mount Cashel Orphanage, Torbay Road, St. John's, NFLD."

The report was a combination of facts and a none-too-subtle protest aimed directly at senior police officials. Affixed to the hastily written three-page document were copies of all the statements Hillier and his two partners had taken since they began questioning children on December 9 – as much dynamite as could be packed into sixty-two pages. Brothers English, Ralph and Kenny figured prominently on the first page of the report. Hillier was careful to point out details of his rushed interviews with the two Brothers. He also emphasized that several other Brothers had been mentioned in the boys' statements, Brothers who had not yet been questioned by police.

"Brother Kenny was mentioned by some boys who [were] displeased with the way in which they were being kissed by him. They also stated that they have made complaints to Brother Kenny about the way they have been treated by other Brothers and he would not look into the matter and instead would apparently try to cover up by telling the boys to say nothing about it.

"Brother Burke was mentioned by three boys, namely Shane Earle, Robert Connors, and Gregory Connors, who states they have been beaten by him with a stick which on occasions has caused blistering to their backsides.

"Brother Short, who is now at St. Pat's, use to relieve the Brothers about two years ago by filling in for them on Saturdays. Leo Gerard Rice, age 17 years, states that about two years ago Brother Short got him to masturbate him three or four times when at Mount Cashel Orphanage."

Detective Hillier then drove home his point in a direct appeal to the Chief.

"Sir: Neither Brothers Kenny, Burke, or Short has been interviewed by me concerning these incidents and at this time the investigation is discontinued, pending further instructions."

If the Mount Cashel investigation was going to be buried,

then at least the frustrated detective was going to make his superiors say it again, and say it for the record.

Less than an hour after he handed in his report, they went one better: Assistant Chief John Norman, acting on instructions from Chief John Lawlor, returned Hillier's report and ordered him to change it.

"I was told to rewrite the report and leave out the sex matters, just put in the physical abuse," Hillier recalled, noting that Lawlor's order represented the lowest point in his career as a police officer. He had always believed in the loyalty code of the Constabulary, but he now realized that the only kind of person who could be loyal in the circumstances was someone without principles.

With Norman standing in front of him, waiting for an answer, Hillier reeled with the magnitude of what was happening. Following Shane Earle's complaint, he had interviewed a total of twenty-six boys who were either at Mount Cashel or who had recently lived there. Of twenty-three who had given statements, twenty stated that they had been sexually or physically abused by some of the Christian Brothers, two told police they had witnessed such abuses, and only one denied any direct knowledge of wrongdoing by the Brothers.

Instead of permitting the detective to interview the remaining sixty-eight boys at the orphanage, and the Brothers who had been named but not yet questioned by police, the Chief had arbitrarily halted the investigation. Despite the fact that Hillier and Pitcher had already documented prima facie evidence of dozens of criminal offences, attested to in part by none other than two of the alleged perpetrators, Brother English and Brother Ralph were allowed to leave the province. Worst of all, the detective was now being asked by none other than his Chief of Police to destroy evidence of the criminal offences his investigation had brought to light.

The dumbfounded detective flatly refused, telling Norman that he didn't think he should be changing a police report. Norman, who later that day would commiserate with Hillier over Lawlor's outrageous demand, said that he had no choice but to order him to make the changes. Again Hillier refused. Norman then took the report and walked back to the Chief's office. When he reappeared, he once again ordered the investigator to change his report by expunging all reference to sexual abuse at the orphanage. The stand-off had escalated to the breaking point. Hillier felt that if he disobeyed a third time, he would be sacked on the spot.

"We have orders we must carry out. And when you're ordered to do something, you do it or you could be fired. I had already gone beyond where I should have gone. I could have been fired right there."

Stunned and upset, Hillier thought about quitting the force. He left Norman and returned to the general CID office where he raised the subject of the Chief's order with his boss, Staff Sgt. Arthur Pike. Pike was an idealistic and outspoken supporter of his men, and despite his reputation for binge drinking and occasionally impolitic cockiness, he enjoyed their respect as a man who "told it like it was." The blocky forty-two-year-old detective with the razor-thin moustache didn't mince words when the younger man asked him what to do. "I said, 'Don't change a goddam word.' "

Between the two of them, Hillier and Pike worked out a clever compromise. They left all the sex-related evidence in the report, and made only a cosmetic change in the text so that if Hillier were ever charged under the Police Act for disobeying a direct order, he could say he had, in fact, changed his original report. Hillier then signed the report and made four copies – one for the Chief of Police, one for the investigators, one for Records and one for the Department of Justice, which was delivered by the police mail carrier on one of his two daily trips to Confederation Building.

As he drove home that night, Hillier was crushed. He knew that due process had been violated and that no decision should have been made on what to do with the Brothers until his investigation had been properly completed and his report tendered. He was also convinced that the order to change the report had been flatly illegal.

Someone had wanted the facts of an official investigation changed, and that someone appeared to be in the very Justice Department he had always served and trusted.

Although he was frustrated and depressed, the detective also had the feeling that night that he hadn't heard the last of the Mount Cashel Orphanage affair. Even so, he could not have dreamed that it would take fourteen years for the truth to emerge about the secret machinations that had been going on without his knowledge for the past few days at senior levels of the Attorney General's Office, in the Social Services Department, with the Irish Christian Brothers and the police.

Whatever was astir in the institutional shadows, it had nothing to do with justice.

Chapter 5
■ The Deal

*As a young lawyer, I was appalled that this
interruption in the normal process of the justice
system should have taken place. And I often
wondered in passing by Mount Cashel Orphanage in driving home, what secrets this place held
within its four walls.* Albert John Noel,
Crown attorney in 1975, testifying in 1989 at
the Hughes Inquiry.

ON MONDAY, DECEMBER 8, 1975, the day that Chesley Riche
roared into Social Services headquarters at Confederation
Building complaining of "the Brothers in bed with the boys"
and threatening to blow the scandal wide open, Newfoundland's Director of Child Welfare immediately placed a call to
Brother Dermod Nash of the Irish Christian Brothers.

It was a call that clearly should have gone to Mount
Cashel's Superintendent, Brother Douglas Kenny. After all,
when nearly identical complaints by two Mount Cashel
boys, Billy Earle and Bobby Connors, had reached Simms's
desk six weeks earlier, he had disposed of them by asking
Brother Kenny to investigate. But this time Simms had his
reasons for turning elsewhere for assistance. Judging from
the graphic report he received from Chesley Riche of
continuing sexual abuse at Mount Cashel, the Director of
Child Welfare now knew that Brother Kenny hadn't gotten
to the bottom of the complaints that formed the basis of the
report filed by Robert Bradbury following the visit of Billy
Earle and Bobby Connors. And there may have been
another reason Simms was reluctant to call Kenny. Chesley
Riche would later testify that at the same time as he made his
allegations of sexual abuse at Mount Cashel to the Director
of Child Welfare, he also told Simms that Brother Kenny
himself was involved in the physical abuse of at least one boy
in his care.

In the circumstances, the man Simms chose to contact

about the brewing scandal in which the police were now involved was fifty-five-year-old Brother Dermod Nash, a Memorial University English professor who also occupied the powerful post of "consulter" within the Christian Brothers. The consulter was the chief adviser in Newfoundland to the lay order's Brother Provincial, Gerard Gabriel McHugh, the executive head of the Christian Brothers in Canada and the West Indies. At the time of Simms's call, Nash was on a one-year leave of absence from his university post to oversee the planning for the centennial celebrations of the Christian Brothers in the province. Although Simms would later describe his call to Brother Nash as an "appropriate" courtesy, it could just as easily have been a warning — particularly since Nash would later tell police that Newfoundland's Director of Child Welfare gave him the names of the Brothers involved in the wide-ranging sexual abuse allegations made by Chesley Riche.

Sometime later, probably the next day, Simms called the police. He wanted to find out if they were indeed working on the Earle case, as Chesley Riche had intimated during their hour-long meeting. The Constabulary confirmed that an investigation was about to get under way. Even though Newfoundland's Director of Child Welfare knew the CID was investigating possible sexual abuse at Mount Cashel, he never shared the Bradbury report with them, or passed on the names of the alleged abusers that he had already made available to the Christian Brothers. Making his decision even less defensible was the fact that Simms himself linked the two complaints — the allegations contained in the Bradbury report of October 23 and the subsequent Shane Earle charge of physical abuse made on December 8.

"Having come weeks after this report [the Bradbury report] I tended to tie the two of them together because they dealt with the same family, they dealt with the Earle family," he would later testify.

After his call to the police, Simms engaged in a flurry of further phone calls and meetings whose exact sequence has been lost in the mists of time. What is known is that over the next few days he summoned Sheila Devine, the Assistant Director of Child Welfare and his closest adviser, to his office on the third floor of Confederation Building and told her what was going on. During the same meeting, he informed her of the Bradbury report into earlier complaints of abuse at Mount Cashel, a report he had never previously shared with her. Simms told Devine that the police were conducting an investigation and that the department would await its outcome before taking any action. It was a departure from normal procedure that wasn't lost on Devine.

"The usual practice was for the Child Welfare Division to continue its own investigation. Where the police have a mandate to determine whether a crime has been committed, the mandate under the Child Welfare Division is to protect children," she later testified.

In the unsettling wake of Chesley Riche's visit, Simms also tried to contact his immediate superior, George Pope, the Assistant Deputy Minister of Social Services, and, later, the Deputy Minister himself, Vernon Hollett.

"I felt this particular incident was sufficiently serious to share it with the Executive and also to, of course, advise them what action was taken." By chance, both officials were unreachable. In such circumstances, it was procedure to go directly to the Minister, but Simms, a career bureaucrat who knew the rules, would later be unable to recall if he tried to contact Charlie Brett. Brett had replaced Ank Murphy as Minister of Social Services after the September 1975 provincial election.

"I cannot state that I went to the Minister's office. I don't know if I went to the Minister's office or not," he would later testify.

Unable to reach Brett's immediate deputies, Simms would later remember calling his legal counsel in the Justice Department, Mary Noonan, through whom he claimed to have repeatedly – and unsuccessfully – tried to get a copy of Det. Robert Hillier's report of the Shane Earle incident. He also claimed that he acquainted his legal adviser with the details of the abuse case as reported to him by Chesley Riche. Noonan would later remember only a single call asking her to get the police report, and denied ever being briefed on the details of the Shane Earle incident or feeling any unrelenting pressure from Social Services to access the document.

"I certainly don't ever recall having heard a description of any injuries that may have been suffered by that particular child. And I feel very certain that if I had received such a description, I would not have forgotten. . . . If Mr. Simms detailed to me injuries a child suffered, I am quite certain I would recall that. I don't forget these things," she would later testify.

Noonan, then thirty-two, was born and educated in Buchans, a small mining town of 2,000 in western Newfoundland, where she attended St. Theresa's Academy. She graduated from St. Francis Xavier University in 1964 with a Bachelor of Science degree, but after working for a year in the field of chemistry, she gave up science and entered law school. In her third year at Dalhousie University in Nova Scotia, she wrote a paper on the battered-child syndrome.

"One of the problems was the failure to report, the conspiracy of silence which existed around this particular problem," she would later testify at the Hughes Inquiry.

In 1967, while still in law school, Noonan began articling in the Newfoundland Justice Department. The lawyer she articled under was Vincent McCarthy. George Macaulay, her superior after she joined the department in December 1968, described her as efficient, capable and independent. She was extremely interested in family law, especially in matters involving children. By 1968, most American states had passed mandatory reporting laws with respect to child abuse, and after returning to Newfoundland from law school Noonan pressed to have similar legislation enacted in her home province. She was ultimately responsible for the inclusion of Section 49 in the Child Welfare Act of 1972, which required every person having "information of the abandonment, desertion, physical ill treatment or need for protection of a child" to report that information to child welfare officials.

Following the passage of the act, Noonan launched an energetic campaign to educate Newfoundlanders about child abuse and the need to report incidents to the proper

authorities. As she would later testify, "We were really
promoting, you know, the fact that people must turn their
mind to the problem of child abuse. It exists and we can't
hide it."

Passionate interest had its rewards. Although George
Macaulay made a practice of shuffling his lawyers around in
order to give them broad experience in all aspects of the
department's work, he left Mary Noonan in her post as the
attorney handling all Social Services matters. Ironically, she
would become one of the central figures in the most serious
travesty of child care in the history of Newfoundland,
playing a far different role than one might expect from
someone who realized so clearly the need for full reporting of
child abuse cases and who deplored "the conspiracy of
silence" that all too often surrounded them.

After receiving the request from Social Services for
the police report of the Shane Earle incident, Noonan
immediately went to the Justice Department's registry where
all incoming reports were received and logged by the office
manager, Eileen Maloney. "The official [Frank Simms] who
called me seemed quite concerned and I had a sense of
urgency," she later testified.

Detective Hillier's Mount Cashel report wasn't in the
registry. Noonan then went to Vincent McCarthy's office to
request the report, a logical choice since he was the acting
Director of Public Prosecutions. She was totally unprepared
for his response.

"I went into his office to request the police report. And I
recall he stood when I came into his office. And I made my
request that I had had a call from the official, and I probably
named the official at the time [Frank Simms], from the
Department of Social Services who was requesting a copy of
the police investigation report into an incident at Mount
Cashel. And I recall that he said to me, 'I've dealt with the
matter. You don't need to see it.' "

From McCarthy's body language, Noonan had the idea
that the document in question was in the Deputy Minister's
desk. The solicitor for the Director of Child Welfare was
taken aback. She was also embarrassed at being denied
information about unnamed public wards whom the

appropriate authorities in Social Services believed may have been in need of help. She would now have to tell Social Services that she couldn't get them the police report. It was the first time she had ever been refused access to a Justice Department report or document. Despite her unease, Noonan neither discussed nor argued about the matter with the man she had articled under, believing that if Vincent McCarthy, a man she trusted implicitly, didn't want to disclose the report he probably had a very good reason. She was, of course, right.

Despite her deference to McCarthy, Noonan wasn't pleased at being taken out of the loop on the Mount Cashel police report, as she made clear to Justice colleague, John Kelly.

"I recall that she was, perhaps upset is too strong a word, but she was concerned that she had not been consulted. She was the solicitor for the Department of Social Services. . . . Mrs. Noonan had an interest and an expertise in child abuse matters and in the reporting and consultation in those matters. And I think she expressed that she should have been involved in this matter in some way." Kelly, who would become Director of Public Prosecutions on March 6, 1976, was also "miffed" at not being consulted on the case by Vincent McCarthy, a man who had little working experience in criminal matters.

Although they had some reservations about the Mount Cashel file, neither lawyer made any concerted effort to garner more information about the mysterious case or to insist on being briefed on the contents of the police report that was so fastidiously kept out of all but a very few hands. Had Mary Noonan wanted to find out more about the case, she was well positioned to do so: Police Chief John Lawlor was her husband's uncle, and she had worked closely with Assistant Chief John Norman on a juvenile diversion program designed to keep young offenders from further run-ins with the law. But like John Kelly, Noonan was satisfied that Vincent McCarthy was within his rights as Deputy Minister to dispose of the matter as he saw fit. The problem had been remedied and the file was closed.

"That sounds perhaps inadequate," Kelly later testified. "But it was a matter for the Deputy Minister and he chose to deal with it and that's where the matter rested after our conversation. I was aware that the decision had been made by Mr. McCarthy not to proceed with prosecutions and I never went behind that decision or looked behind it."

In a temperament different from Mary Noonan's, simple curiosity would have supplied the impetus to delve into McCarthy's ruling. After all, at that time, a Social Services official would simply have requested access to the police report and it would have been automatically granted. This was the first occasion where normal practice had not been followed and Vincent McCarthy's explanation for the procedural departure was, at best, cryptic.

Simms later told Assistant Director Sheila Devine that Social Services had simply run into a roadblock on the Mount Cashel case, a roadblock that neither Newfoundland's Director of Child Welfare nor his legal counsel in the Justice Department were able to surmount. It was the beginning of a pattern of secrecy that would be exhibited at every turn when requests for information about the report were raised by Social Services, a secrecy that aroused remarkably little official inquisitiveness.

"What he indicated was that he was unable to access the police report himself and that even our legal adviser was unable to obtain or view the report," Devine testified. Devine also recalled being told by Simms that since he had not been able to get the police report through normal channels, he would be discussing it with "the executive" — the Deputy and the Assistant Deputy Minister.

Justice's refusal to allow Social Services access to the report wasn't the only irregularity surrounding the investigation into the orphanage. Once she learned of the police investigation, Sheila Devine was disturbed by the fact that police had not informed social workers that Mount Cashel boys were going to be interviewed by detectives from the CID. "Our practice and our preference was to be present whenever children under the age of sixteen were being interviewed by police," she subsequently testified.

On December 9, 1975, the day Det. Robert Hillier was assigned to the Mount Cashel investigation, and three full days before he interviewed any boys who would make sexual allegations against specific individuals at the orphanage, Brother Nash called Christian Brother headquarters in Mono Mills, Ontario, and reported that Brothers English and Ralph had been accused of sexually abusing a number of children in their care. From this point on, the Brotherhood's entire reaction to the crisis would focus directly on episodes of sexual abuse at Mount Cashel that had already come to the attention of the responsible Christian Brother authorities and officials of the Department of Social Services, including Frank Simms. Shane Earle's beating was merely the wind that blew the top off the institutional Pandora's box of Mount Cashel. Once the demons were out, sexual abuse was the plague on their house, or at least the only plague they were worried about.

The man on the other end of the line with Brother Nash, Gerard Gabriel McHugh, had been born in St. John's and educated by a teaching order known as the Presentation Sisters. The erudite and soft-spoken forty-four-year-old joined the Christian Brothers in 1950, beginning his religious career in the Brotherhood's New York centre before taking on a brief teaching assignment in Washington. He returned to Newfoundland in 1953–54 to pursue his career as an educator, teaching at Holy Cross School in St. John's. He later became principal of St. Michael's School in Grand Falls, the paper-mill town in the central region of the province that was the first Newfoundland community to be built out of sight of the sea.

After a brief return to New York for further studies, he began his ascent through the administrative hierarchies of the Christian Brothers that would eventually take him all the way to Rome as the Superior General of the Congregation of Christian Brothers Worldwide. In 1975, though, McHugh was Brother Provincial, a post where he was responsible for the overall administration of the Canada–West Indies Province of the Christian Brothers, one of thirteen administrative regions established by the order. The Canada–West Indies Province was comprised of twenty-one educational institutions, including sixteen schools, nine of them in Newfoundland. McHugh monitored the religious and spiritual life of the Province's 168 members (the Christian Brothers were 3,000-strong worldwide) and assigned them to various institutions associated with the lay order. The experienced administrator understood the seriousness of what Nash was telling him, and issued clear orders to his subordinate on how to proceed.

"I instructed Brother Nash to remove the two Brothers who were named, immediately from Mount Cashel, but not from the province. And to interview both Brothers to ascertain whether these allegations had any foundation," he would later testify.

But the situation was far too serious for long-distance damage control, and Brother McHugh decided to fly to St. John's immediately. Before leaving Christian Brothers headquarters in Mono Mills, McHugh informed the other three members of the four-man Christian Brother Council about the Mount Cashel situation.

Shortly after his plane landed at Torbay Airport on or about December 10, 1975, Brother McHugh went directly to Brother Rice Monastery in St. John's. Awaiting him there were Brother Nash and Brother Gordon Redfield Bellows, the former Superintendent of the Roman Catholic school board who had recently been promoted to the post of Provincial Director of Education for the Christian Brothers. McHugh had earlier called Bellows, who by a coincidence was visiting Newfoundland in the course of his new official duties, and asked him to interview Brother English about the allegations that were being made against him.

Brother Bellows, himself an orphan who had been raised at Mount Cashel, called Brother English and asked him to come to Brother Rice Monastery to discuss "an urgent matter." English, who was teaching at St. Pius X School, excused himself from classes and hurried to the monastery, burdened, perhaps, by a premonition of what awaited him.

"He showed up in the morning and I went into the room and without any formalities whatsoever, because the news itself was terribly distressing, I simply put the question to him. I said, 'Is this particular allegation of sexual abuse at Mount Cashel, is it true or is it false?' And he said that it was true. . . . I indicated to him that he could expect to be transferred from Mount Cashel immediately," Brother Bellows later testified.

Bellows, who was "flabbergasted" by the confession, informed Brother English that the facts would be reported immediately to the order's Brother Provincial, Gabriel McHugh. They would not, however, be reported to the Director of Child Welfare as required by Section 49 of the Child Welfare Act.

Later that same day, on or about December 10, Brother Bellows sat in on the interview conducted by Brother Nash with the other person named in the scandal, Brother Alan Ralph. Like English before him, Brother Ralph readily confessed to sexually abusing boys at Mount Cashel.

"Brother Nash put the same question very simply and very straightforwardly to the man. 'Is this allegation true, [this] allegation of sexual abuse?' And the second Brother said 'Yes,' " Bellows recalled. Once more, the confession would not be reported to authorities at Social Services or to the police.

After their admission, the accused Brothers were immediately sent out of St. John's, one to Grand Falls, the other to Corner Brook on the west coast of the island. The two grim-faced monks who had interviewed them briefed Brother McHugh on the situation shortly after he arrived at Brother Rice Monastery. McHugh later called Rome and reported the known details of the Mount Cashel affair to the order's Superior General, Brother J. L. Kelty, who was due to come to St. John's in less than two months to take part in a gala dinner celebrating the one-hundredth anniversary of the Christian Brothers in Newfoundland.

The day after his lightning trip to Newfoundland, the head of the Christian Brothers in Canada paid a visit to the Chief of Police in St. John's. McHugh would later claim that he had requested the meeting to tell Chief John Lawlor that the Christian Brothers took the situation seriously and that the order would co-operate in the police investigation.

It was a strange comment coming from a man whose first

directive, on learning of the Mount Cashel affair, had been to send suspected child abusers out of the city where their offences had been committed before the Constabulary could begin their investigation into the Shane Earle complaint, that might well lead them to Brothers English and Ralph. Nor did McHugh give the CID the names of the Brothers his own investigation had already confirmed had molested boys at Mount Cashel. The two staunch Catholics, who knew each other socially, spoke for about ten minutes. Although John Lawlor would later claim that he could remember practically nothing about the meeting, he did admit to a vague recollection that he may have called the Justice Department to arrange a meeting for Brother McHugh with Deputy Justice Minister Vincent McCarthy.

According to Brother McHugh, he did very little in the week between his meeting with the Chief of Police on the day after his arrival in St. John's and his session with the Deputy Minister of Justice on the morning of December 18. At some point during that interval, McHugh paid two visits to Mount Cashel, meeting with Superintendent Kenny and several other Brothers to discuss the allegations and to determine if anybody had prior knowledge of the scandal.

"My recollection is they were in a state of shock," McHugh later testified, "and nobody could come forward with any information or any knowledge about the allegations."

Again, such protestations of total ignorance on the part of the Brotherhood about allegations of sexual abuse were hard to understand. Just a few months before, Brother Douglas Kenny had been asked by Frank Simms to investigate allegations of physical and sexual abuse by certain Brothers arising out of the Bradbury report. Just a few weeks before the Shane Earle incident, Chesley Riche had also brought allegations of physical and sexual abuse to Kenny after hearing disturbing stories from Billy Earle and Bobby Connors. And if Mount Cashel kept internal records of disciplinary actions taken against individual Brothers, Kenny would have known that Brother Alan Ralph had once been sent away from Mount Cashel for alleged sexual abuse of boys in his care.

Although Brother McHugh was apparently diligent about delving into the crisis with the Brothers themselves, he didn't interview a single boy at Mount Cashel to identify alleged victims, discover the precise nature and scope of the allegations or find out how the children were coping with the situation. Based on his one-sided investigation, he concluded that, although the allegations of sexual abuse were well founded, they were only isolated incidents.

According to Brother McHugh's version of events, he couldn't recall either informing P. J. Skinner, then Archbishop of St. John's, about events at Mount Cashel, or asking anyone else to brief His Grace — despite the fact that Christian Brothers could only teach in a school or serve in a monastery at the invitation of the archdiocese. If a teacher left in disgrace, particularly in the middle of term, the Archbishop would surely have to know about it. McHugh would later acknowledge that he did not inform the Archbishop. He also could not recall discussing details of the Mount Cashel situation with the Archbishop at their next annual meeting, although he did admit that the scandal got passing mention.

McHugh would also acknowledge that he didn't approach Social Services at any time during this week in St. John's, either to garner information or to provide any. Instead, the Brother Provincial of the Canada–West Indies Province of the Christian Brothers had apparently flown to St. John's and spent the better part of a week virtually incommunicado. Meanwhile, a scandal swirled around him that had the potential of destroying his order in Newfoundland — particularly if the police investigation prompted by the beating of Shane Earle were to turn up the sexual abuse that had already been reported to both Frank Simms and Brother Douglas Kenny.

"During that week I was just waiting for the other shoe to drop and I didn't know which shoe it would be or how it would come," he testified many years later.

Towards the end of McHugh's week of alleged inactivity, the chain of events slips into the shadows of a fascinating mystery. On Wednesday, December 17, Brother Nash made the arrangements for Brothers English and Ralph to have their brief interviews with CID Detectives Hillier and Pitcher at McAuley Hall. During those sessions, the two Brothers admitted to illicit sexual contact with some of the boys, just as they had to Brothers Nash and Bellows a week earlier. Detective Hillier then received a call from Fort Townshend ordering both him and Detective Pitcher back to CID headquarters. What happened to Brothers English and Ralph after the detectives left, though crucially important, is far from clear.

According to Brother McHugh, they spent a couple of days in two different monasteries in St. John's — English at St. Francis and Ralph at Holy Cross — before following him to Christian Brother headquarters in Mono Mills. But there is evidence to support another version of events — namely that English and Ralph proceeded to the airport directly after their police interviews and left the province immediately.

The evidence for that view is circumstantial but stubborn. According to the testimony of Det. Ralph Pitcher, both Brothers had luggage with them when they arrived at McAuley Hall for their interviews with police. So if they weren't on their way out of the province, why would they have their luggage?

A possible answer might be that since they were arriving in St. John's from Grand Falls and Corner Brook, the Brothers might have come directly from the airport to McAuley Hall to meet the detectives. In that case, they may well have had their luggage with them. But that doesn't square with another fact. Detective Hillier recalled being told by Chief Lawlor to hurry up with his interviews because the Brothers were leaving the province. Detective Pitcher, too, remembered that there was a "time-frame" element to their interviews, a sense of having to hurry, because the Brothers were leaving the city.

Interestingly, Hillier's investigation was called off on the same day that the Brothers were interviewed. At that point, not only was there a mountain of incriminating evidence against them, the two Brothers had freely confirmed most of the allegations that Mount Cashel boys had made to police. So if an agreement hadn't already been worked out to send the pair out of the province, why were English and Ralph not arrested the same day they gave their statements, Wednesday, December 17? And why did Hillier and Pitcher get a call from headquarters during their interview ordering them to return to the office?

There were other questions that suggested that the two detectives were dealing with a *fait accompli* of which they were as yet unaware. Why would the same order that had hustled English and Ralph out of the city before a police investigation in which the Brotherhood knew the pair figured prominently bring them back to St. John's at the height of the investigation, when the threat of their arrest was much greater than it had been on December 8? It was an inscrutable decision if the intention was to keep them there; but if the deal that would send them out of the province to receive treatment had already been struck, bringing them back for a token police interview made a lot more sense.

The recollections of a former Justice employee further support the theory that the Brothers may have left Newfoundland the same day they were interviewed by police. John McGrath, a Crown prosecutor in the fall of 1975, testified at the Hughes Inquiry that he was told at the time that some Christian Brothers were being questioned by the police that day on allegations of sexual abuse at Mount Cashel Orphanage. The next morning, McGrath recalled, he was advised by someone in the Justice Department that the Brothers in question had already left the province. The young lawyer remembered being shocked because Mount Cashel was a very significant institution in St. John's, and he himself had been taught by the Christian Brothers at St. Bonaventure's College and Brother Rice High School.

The issue of exactly when the two Brothers left St. John's has a crucial bearing on the next episode in the sequence of events — the meeting on Thursday, December 18 between Brother Gabriel McHugh and Brother Dermod Nash of the Christian Brothers, and Newfoundland's Deputy Minister of Justice, Vincent McCarthy. According to McHugh's often hazy testimony many years later, it was at that meeting that the Deputy Minister instructed him to send the Brothers out of Newfoundland.

But if they had already left the day before, and the police

investigation had already been terminated, it raised the puzzling question of what was really done that day in the privacy of Vincent McCarthy's fifth-floor office.

Vincent Patrick McCarthy, a staunch Catholic, had pulled himself up by his own bootstraps. Born in Placentia Bay, a remote area on Newfoundland's south coast, he was educated at the Roman Catholic school on Red Island, a tiny fishing community that disappeared after Joey Smallwood's controversial "burn your boats" resettlement program of the 1960s in which rural Newfoundlanders were encouraged to leave remote outports and move to more developed centres elsewhere on the island. After a brief stint in the Newfoundland Constabulary, McCarthy enlisted in the Royal Artillery, later the Royal Newfoundland Artillery, which was ultimately reorganized as the 166th (Newfoundland) Field Regiment and saw action in North Africa and Italy during the Second World War.

After his discharge in 1945, McCarthy resumed his interrupted education, attending St. Bonaventure's College in St. John's, where his teachers were the Christian Brothers. Although his religion was not something he wore on his sleeve, McCarthy's ardent Catholicism was deeply ingrained. As one of his colleagues in the Justice Department would later remark, "Vince was the kind of man who would jump to his feet if a priest walked into his office." McCarthy went on to get a Bachelor of Arts degree from Dalhousie University in Halifax, and in 1952 added a law degree to his academic credentials. Two years after he graduated from law school, he married Teresa Healey. During the long and happy marriage the couple would have ten children, as McCarthy worked his way up through the Justice Department from Crown prosecutor in 1953 to Deputy Minister of Justice seventeen years later at the age of fifty-one.

For six months in 1975–76, McCarthy also served as acting Director of Public Prosecutions as well as Deputy Minister of Justice. John Connors, blind, brilliant and abrasive, had resigned the post in September 1975 after repeated run-ins with the Director of the department's civil division, George Macaulay. Shortly before Connors resigned, Macaulay actually seized control of part of the criminal division and began vetting files. Connors' replacement as Director of Public Prosecutions, John Kelly, wasn't appointed until March 1976, although there was an interim period of a few months when he functioned as the *de facto* D.P.P.

Two types of criminal files were funnelled through the Deputy Minister's office on their way to the prosecutors. In cases where they believed that the evidence warranted criminal charges, the police themselves laid an information. In those cases, the prosecutors were simply instructed to master the files, prepare their cases and make the necessary court appearances. But in the mid-seventies, the Newfoundland Constabulary only laid charges in the most blatant or routine of cases and never when a prominent person was involved. The more common practice was for the Constabulary to simply compile a police report and refer the matter to the Department of Justice for a decision on charges – a clear abdication of police independence within the justice system. This servile and suspect system would persist until April 1989 when Associate Deputy Attorney General Robert Hyslop wrote to Police Chief Ed Coady ordering him to put an end to it.

". . . This is a practice which can be unhealthy both for the police and the department as it tends to interweave each of our respective roles and functions," Hyslop wrote.

McCarthy was known in the department as the kind of Deputy Minister who went by the book, rarely taking part in the process of deciding on charges, and restricting his role to distributing files to prosecutors and relaying their advice back to the police. Given his lack of expertise in the criminal law, that was probably just as well. Former Director of Public Prosecution, John Connors, later remembered McCarthy as a man who was "a fine fellow to know" but who could "goof" in criminal matters because he tended to misapply legal principles.

McCarthy's unease with making unilateral decisions dictated caution in all aspects of his duties, including civil matters, where he was more at home as a lawyer. Keith Mercer, a prosecutor in the department's civil law branch, had daily meetings with McCarthy when McCarthy was Deputy Minister, and later attested to his ingrained habit of consulting with prosecutors or the Minister before proceeding on complex legal matters. A consensus seeker who wasn't given to going off on his own frolics, McCarthy was also extremely cautious about not exceeding his authority.

"On the occasions when I was dealing with him," Mercer testified, "he was most careful to ensure he had authority to proceed on any matter before he proceeded. . . . I would find it difficult to imagine that he would make a significant decision in a sensitive matter without discussing that part with other people in the department, and I would have expected that he would have consulted the Minister."

By December 1975, McCarthy's well-known penchant for consultation may have been frustrated by events in the Justice Department. After the departure of John Connors as Director of Public Prosecutions in September, McCarthy was left in charge of "a very infantile" contingent in the criminal division − four or five inexperienced prosecutors who were "rudderless," operating without direction for several months. McCarthy couldn't offer the sage legal advice on criminal matters that Connors had regularly dispensed, let alone seek any from his junior staffers. Had the expertise been available to him, the overworked official still would have had trouble finding the time to forge a consensus on how the Mount Cashel situation should be handled. The constitutional conferences between the provinces and Ottawa were just beginning, and McCarthy's first priority was to attend them on behalf of the Justice Department and the government.

Harassed and overworked, not all of Vincent McCarthy's preoccupations were professional. In 1974, cancer had developed around his eyes and nose, necessitating first an operation, and later a long succession of painful cobalt treatments and chemotherapy. But if spiritual rather than temporal matters were on his mind because of his physical condition, he didn't show it. Despite his serious illness, he missed very few days at the office and wouldn't share the enormous workload that was weighing him down. Instead, he would close his door at lunchtime and rest for an hour before resuming work; at night, he would carry off suitcases of files to finish at home what he had been unable to complete at the office.

"Night after night when I would see him leaving, the man would be carrying piles of files and briefcases home. I don't know how he ever coped with it all," one of McCarthy's former prosecutors, Barry Hill, recalled.

Perhaps, in the end, he didn't.

The mid-morning meeting on December 18, 1975 that included Vincent McCarthy, Brother McHugh and Brother Nash took place in McCarthy's office on the fifth floor of Confederation Building, where the Minister and Deputy Minister of Justice shared a suite. A joint doorway opened into a reception area where their secretaries were stationed. Through a doorway to the left of this common area was the Minister's private office, while to the right, through another doorway, was the office of the Deputy Minister.

The meeting took place on a slow day in the Justice Department, just a week before Christmas. Although T. Alex Hickman's office door was open, the light was off. This was the normal sign that the Justice Minister was not in his office and would not likely be coming in. On days when he was attending meetings, he came into the office to collect papers and left the light on, signifying his intention to return later — an idiosyncracy well known to his secretary, Pearl Lombard.

Despite Gabriel McHugh's claim that he and Brother Nash met alone with Vincent McCarthy, another version of events would surface many years later. Pearl Lombard would testify that four men, not two, walked into the reception area that morning, removed their coats and hung them on a coat tree between a filing cabinet and Vincent McCarthy's door. As they chatted with McCarthy's secretary, Lombard noted that two of the men were dressed in clerical robes and two in police uniforms. "I recall thinking to myself, 'I wonder why they're here?' because it wasn't something I had seen before with the two [groups] together and I just passed it off. I thought it was something to do with religion."

Lombard, who had seen John Lawlor in the office on several occasions, would testify that the two policemen were John Lawlor and John Norman, and the two men in clerical robes were Brother McHugh and Brother Nash, although she could only tentatively identify them when she picked them out of a Christian Brother centennial history book many years later. For their part, McHugh and Lawlor vehemently denied they had attended the McCarthy meeting together.

As strange at it may have seemed for the Deputy Minister of Justice to be meeting with representatives of people who were facing possible charges with the express purpose of talking about the case, it was not the first time that Vincent McCarthy had held such meetings and not the first time that Roman Catholic officials had been present. In the fall of 1975, the RCMP began investigating complaints of sexual improprieties in Conception Bay South, a rural community west of St. John's. Late in 1975, possibly in December, two "complainants" and two Roman Catholic priests from the town visited McCarthy's office. The Deputy Minister called one of his prosecutors, Barry Hill, into the meeting. McCarthy explained to the delegation that the police had completed an investigation into the alleged sexual offences and recommended that the department press charges against several young men – a clear breach of the confidentiality of police reports. In front of the delegation, McCarthy then passed the police file to Hill and announced that the young lawyer would deal diligently with the matter. Indeed he did. On January 6, 1976, twelve males between the ages of seventeen and twenty-five were charged with a total of twenty-seven sexual offences.

The Mount Cashel meeting on December 18 had been set up following a personal call from an unidentified woman in the Justice Department to Brother McHugh. Although McHugh would later leave the impression that the Justice Department had initiated the meeting, the call in turn had likely been prompted by Police Chief John Lawlor's request for a meeting between the head of the Christian Brothers and the Deputy Minister of Justice.

Brother McHugh had never met McCarthy before, but

knew that his family was highly respected in Placentia Bay, where McHugh also had family roots. After exchanging pleasantries, McCarthy, according to Brother McHugh, quickly focused on the subject of their meeting.

With a file folder in front of him, which McHugh took to be the Mount Cashel police report, McCarthy said that detectives had uncovered evidence that two Brothers had sexually abused children at the orphanage. (Hillier's report in fact named three other Brothers, Kenny, Short and Burke, in addition to English and Ralph as either having sexually or physically abused boys. Why McCarthy would happen to pick the same two individuals the Christian Brothers already knew about, while neglecting the others, is a mystery). Although McCarthy didn't share any photographs or documents with the Brothers, he did tell them that both suspects had admitted to sexually abusing some of the boys – confirming for Brother McHugh exactly what Brothers Nash and Bellows had already told him.

"He indicated . . . that no charges would be laid at that time and the report would be placed in the file," McHugh later told the Hughes Inquiry. "Then . . . he told me to transfer the two Brothers from communities in Newfoundland to elsewhere within the Canadian Province. . . . It was more than a suggestion. It was a direction."

McHugh never retained legal counsel or questioned McCarthy's alleged directive, accepting it instead as normal practice. As he would later testify, "This for me was a totally and absolutely unfamiliar situation, my very first experience in this sort of thing."

Brother McHugh then told McCarthy that the Canada – West Indies Province of the Christian Brothers had a policy of providing counselling to any Brother in difficulty, and that Brothers English and Ralph would be sent to treatment centres outside Newfoundland – a course of action the Brotherhood had already settled on before the meeting with the Deputy Minister. McHugh would later deny that his compliance with McCarthy's alleged directive amounted to a deal between the Christian Brothers and the Justice Department in which the two Brothers wouldn't be charged provided they, in effect, got out of town.

"I had the clear impression," he testified, "that the case was unfinished . . . I was only aware that charges could have been laid in the future," McHugh testified. If that were true, it was passing strange that Brother McHugh never contacted the Newfoundland Justice Department after December 1975 to check on the legal status of the Mount Cashel file. Even stranger would be the recollection of two other people integrally involved with the Mount Cashel affair that Brother McHugh categorically told them in early 1976 that no charges would be laid in the incident. The deal was in place.

If the meeting happened the way Brother McHugh described it, Vincent McCarthy had another side to him that his colleagues in the Justice Department had never seen. In dictating such a bizarre arrangement to private citizens – in effect, banishment for life in lieu of criminal charges – the senior bureaucrat would be taking an awful chance. It would mean playing fast and loose with the law, revealing the contents of a police report to interested parties and risking monstrous civil and criminal consequences if McCarthy were ever found to be personally responsible for enabling child abusers to evade the justice system.

Finding a motive for McCarthy to enter unilaterally into such a scandalous arrangement with the Christian Brothers requires some imagination. If his behaviour were to be attributed to misguided religious zeal, it would also have to be explained why he would later commit his theoretically clandestine actions to paper in a letter to a new Chief of Police, with a copy for Justice Department files. For a man who would be appointed to the bench in 1977, such a course would, on the face of it, appear to some observers to be nothing short of an act of folly.

There was also the possibility that the cautious Mr. McCarthy was acting on the authority, and in the interests, of others. It is worth noting that just a few months earlier, in February 1975, the government of Premier Frank Moores had given the Christian Brothers $450,000 for renovations to Mount Cashel and agreed to pay the interest on a loan by the Brotherhood for another $450,000. Government had also approved $300,000 for the Brothers to build a new hockey arena. Finally, the government was heavily involved in the elaborate centennial celebrations of the Christian Brothers in Newfoundland, which were by then already under way.

In the circumstances, if a sex scandal involving the orphanage, which former Social Services Minister Ank Murphy referred to as a "footstep to heaven," would be ruinous for the Christian Brothers, it would also be highly embarrassing for the government of the day. One cabinet member from that era, James Morgan, expressly remembered whispers in late 1975 or early 1976 of a damaging scandal surrounding the orphanage that was about to break.

"There were rumblings around the political circles of something going on in the wrong way at Mount Cashel . . . I mean, we were all politicians. We follow what's going on politically. And there was a rumbling that something was going to break. I recall that quite clearly. Something was going to break that might be really embarrassing."

The fact that it didn't was to the benefit of more than one public figure of the day.

Although the confidential discussions between Brother McHugh and Vincent McCarthy remained private, they did become the topic of speculation in the Justice Department. Albert Noel, a Crown attorney working in the legislative drafting section of the department would later testify that he was advised about the Mount Cashel affair by office manager Eileen Maloney – a longtime Justice worker who knew everything about the day-to-day happenings in the department and enjoyed a close working relationship with the Deputy Minister.

Miss Maloney, who was upset about Mount Cashel, told Noel at the department's 1975 Christmas party that the police had conducted an investigation into allegations of sexual and physical abuse at the orphanage, but that after they had filed their report, no charges were laid and the Brothers in question were sent out of the province. Although all letters and reports coming into the department were recorded as a matter of policy in the daily mail diary,

Hillier's report was never entered. While it was not a matter of general knowledge in the department, Noel recalled that the Mount Cashel deal later became a topic of discussion among Crown prosecutors, with the apparent exclusion of Mary Noonan, who might have been expected to have the keenest interest in the subject.

"As a young lawyer," Noel testified, "I was appalled that this interruption in the normal process of the justice system should have taken place. And I often wondered in passing by Mount Cashel Orphanage in driving home, what secrets this place held within its four walls."

Noel and the rest of St. John's came tantalizingly close to finding out about some of the secrets the day after the private meeting between Brother McHugh and Vincent McCarthy. Bill Kelly, the crusty, chain-smoking city editor of Newfoundland's leading daily newspaper, *The Evening Telegram*, received a tip that police were investigating allegations of improper conduct by Christian Brothers at Mount Cashel Orphanage. An aggressive journalist and a devout Catholic, Kelly immediately understood the implications of the story and tried to chase it down.

He called the police and asked about an investigation into Mount Cashel, but the CID refused to comment, either on or off the record. Acting on their advice, Kelly then called the Justice Department and interviewed Crown prosecutor, and soon-to-be Director of Public Prosecutions, John Kelly. The interview produced only slightly more information. As the journalist would later testify, "They confirmed in a roundabout way that there were some problems at Mount Cashel without going into any detail. And the main point that came out of it was that there were no grounds for criminal charges. The impression we had was there was inappropriate behaviour but no criminal activity."

The journalist had no way of knowing that the assurances that there had been no criminal activity at Mount Cashel had come from a person who hadn't even seen the police report into the matter.

Still not satisfied, Bill Kelly assigned his friend and fellow reporter, Bob Wakeham, to the Mount Cashel story, instructing him to call the orphanage and try to arrange a meeting with the Superintendent. An hour later, Kelly and the rough-and-tumble Wakeham were on their way up Torbay Road, hot on the trail of what could turn into a major story. But when they arrived at Mount Cashel's front steps, it was not Brother Kenny who greeted them but Brother Ignatius Moore.

The congenial Brother took the two journalists on a tour of Mount Cashel. As they walked through the dorms and study halls, Kelly and Wakeham peppered their guide with questions. Brother Moore answered in generalities, acknowledging that there had been some problems at the orphanage, but emphasizing that they had been dealt with. When pressed for more details, he refused to comment, insisting that the reporters speak to more senior officials in the Brotherhood. The meeting ended cordially, but Kelly and Wakeham left the orphanage more convinced than ever that they had a story.

"I do recall very distinctly leaving Mount Cashel thinking that we were definitely onto something," Bob Wakeham later told the Hughes Inquiry.

After returning to *The Evening Telegram*, Kelly tried to reach Brother Provincial Gabriel McHugh in Mono Mills, only to discover that the most senior Christian Brother in the country was visiting Newfoundland. His curiosity piqued by what might or might not be a coincidence, Kelly finally tracked down Brother McHugh in Grand Falls, where he had gone the day after his meeting with Vincent McCarthy.

The Christian Brother confirmed that there had indeed been a problem at Mount Cashel, but assured the journalist that the Brotherhood had settled it themselves. The party line had been clearly established. McHugh was "very anxious" that no story be printed, since it would do more harm than good. After Kelly made it clear that, in the public interest, he fully intended to pursue the matter, Brother McHugh gave him a few more details, so that any story that did appear would at least be based on the facts — or as many of them as the shrewd administrator was willing to share with the persistent journalist.

He told Kelly that two Brothers had been involved in the

Mount Cashel affair, which involved excessive corporal punishment and some minor problems in the Brothers' relationships with the boys that Kelly was led to believe involved "fondling." McHugh's characterization of the incident was telling; in fact, English and Ralph were being secretly banished for gross sexual abuse of children in their care. Excessive corporal punishment had nothing to do with their being sent away, and the Brother who was accused of physical abuse by Shane Earle had not been disciplined at all. It was top-spin that bordered on deceit.

McHugh gave Kelly the names and ages of the two Brothers in question, explaining that he didn't want innocent members of the order to be implicated by a vague story. McHugh also stressed that the problems had been detected quickly, and that no damage had been done — strange words from a man who would later privately inform Brother Douglas Kenny that his only mistake was in not moving quickly enough once the problem at Mount Cashel had been brought to his attention, and who would himself admit that he had no idea of the terrible consequences of sexual assault on its child victims. Just before the conversation ended, Brother McHugh once again urged the reporter not to run a story that could do so much harm to a worthy institution.

After the conversation with Brother McHugh, Kelly was convinced he had a legitimate news story. He and Wakeham pooled their notes and Wakeham began pounding out a first draft on one of *The Evening Telegram*'s ancient typewriters, while Kelly, puffing on an ever-present cigarette, walked up to the fourth-floor office of the publisher to tell him about the story they intended to run.

Tall and aristocratic, with a salt-and-pepper beard and wise wrinkles around the corners of his eyes, Stephen R. Herder looked every inch a newspaperman. His grandfather, William J. Herder, had founded *The Evening Telegram* in 1879, and it had remained in the family until 1970 when Stephen Herder and other family members sold out to the Thomson newspaper chain. The publisher listened attentively to his editor and quickly decided not to run the story.

"In many ways," Kelly later testified, "he took much the

same position Brother McHugh had. His position was that the story could do more harm than good, that we could undo the good that the Brothers had done for eighty or ninety or one hundred years through a story like this. . . . In the end, he felt very strongly that we could do an awful lot of damage to the institution and he felt that the circumstances were such that it wasn't warranted. . . . We were dealing simply with two Brothers involved in what we thought were a couple of isolated incidents and that swayed Mr. Herder in the other direction. . . . At that point, the story was dead."

Although Kelly strongly disagreed with the decision and said so, he dutifully trudged back down to the third-floor newsroom and informed Bob Wakeham that the Mount Cashel story had been killed.

Upset as they were at Herder's decision, neither Kelly nor Wakeham pursued the story any further. On the morning of Saturday, December 20, Kelly called Brother McHugh in Grand Falls to inform him that there wouldn't be a story on Mount Cashel after all. For a long time afterwards, when Kelly and Wakeham walked down Duckworth Street from *The Evening Telegram* and descended the cement stairs to The Ship Inn for a beer, they would discuss Herder's controversial decision. They were convinced that the publisher had made the wrong call, although Kelly, at least, could see that there were reasonable grounds for having made it at the time. When he later learned the extent of sexual abuse at Mount Cashel known to the Christian Brothers at the time of his interview, Kelly would feel deceived by Gabriel McHugh.

In a few short weeks, the paper that had killed the Mount Cashel story in the public interest would use the occasion of the Christian Brothers' centenary to publish a glowing editorial tribute to the order. Temporarily, at least, news had taken a shameless backseat to a misguided exercise in public relations in the pages of *The Evening Telegram*.

After returning to Christian Brother headquarters in Mono Mills, Brother McHugh interviewed Brothers English and Ralph to personally confirm that they were indeed admitting to the sexual abuse allegations, to express his concern over the Mount Cashel affair and to enforce his wish that the two submit to treatment. He would later be unable to recall whether he asked the Brothers if any other adults were mistreating children at Mount Cashel, testifying only that "no information was forthcoming."

In January 1976, Brother Ralph was sent to the Emmanuel Convalescent Home in Aurora, Ontario, or "Southdown," as it was more commonly known. The 110-acre farm, deep in the rolling hills of King Township's horse country, opened in 1965 as a treatment centre for priests with alcohol problems. The Canadian Conference of Catholic Bishops supported Southdown, which expanded its care beyond treatment of alcoholism in 1974 to include the psychological and emotional problems of priests. Many of these problems multiplied sharply after the sudden emergence of dizzying new personal freedoms for clergy after the Second Vatican Council in 1965, from raising the hemlines of nuns' habits to the abolition of self-flagellation at the Chapter of Faults.

Brother Ralph was assessed by two doctors – Dr. Mark Eveson, a clinical psychologist who was also Southdown's Director, and Dr. William Hughes, a consulting psychiatrist. Both doctors agreed that Brother Ralph needed treatment, and recommended that he enter the clinic's residency program for a period of three to five months, a program that did not include specialized treatment for pedophiles. In fact, the nature and impact of child abuse were not well understood at the Southdown of the mid-seventies.

"It happened. It was considered sort of a strange anomaly that was probably geared to other factors like alcohol or loneliness or whatever," Father John Loftus, the clinic's current director, said in an interview.

Accordingly, Brother Ralph was treated with, among other clinical approaches, "bio-energetic therapy," according to Father Loftus "a kind of psychiatry . . . instead of just expressing yourself verbally or on the emotional level, you go for the physical in order to get to the source of the feelings. So it's a very physically based therapy." With its walking trails and a pond for skating, Southdown was well equipped for this radical advance in psychiatry.

Brother English, meanwhile, was receiving treatment at the House of Affirmation in Whitinsville, Massachusetts, a similar, Catholic-run centre for troubled clergy forty-five miles west of Boston that opened its doors in 1973. The institution's Director, Rev. Dr. Thomas A. Kane, ran extensive tests on English and advised Brother McHugh that he would "definitely benefit" from at least a six-month retreat at the centre. Although Kane insisted on the title Reverend Doctor, he was not a medical doctor. Like Southdown, the House of Affirmation had no specialized treatment for pedophiles. In fact, neither the House of Affirmation nor Southdown was geared to deal with the problem of pedophilia in 1976, despite their carefully cultivated reputations as legitimate treatment centres. For proper treatment, patients would have to go to facilities like the Sexual Disorders Clinic at Johns Hopkins Hospital in Baltimore, Maryland.

Since individual Christian Brothers, unlike priests, take a vow of poverty in addition to their other vows, they draw no salary from their order. Any money Brothers earn from outside sources such as teaching goes into the general fund of the order. The order in turn then pays all of the expenses of individual Brothers, including medical costs. Accordingly, the Brotherhood paid for the treatment of English and Ralph and covered their living expenses. In early January, the Canada – West Indies Council of the Christian Brothers was informed that the two Brothers were receiving psychiatric care. When asked many years later if the council ever discussed the possibility of identifying the child victims of Brothers English and Ralph with a view to providing them with treatment, Brother Gordon Bellows testified, "I certainly don't recall any such discussion, to my shame."

With English and Ralph safely institutionalized, Brother McHugh called Brother Nash from Ontario and instructed his consulter to set up a meeting with the Department of Social Services. McHugh was anxious to determine the standing of the Christian Brothers with the provincial government in the wake of events at Mount Cashel, which he felt was somehow "under attack." In January 1976, Deputy Social Services Minister Vernon Hollett; his assistant,

George Pope; the Director of Child Welfare, Frank Simms; his assistant, Sheila Devine; Brother Nash and Brother McHugh met in the office of the Deputy Minister of Social Services. The meeting had been called on very short notice and lasted approximately forty-five minutes.

According to Brother McHugh, the meeting did not focus on the December investigation into Mount Cashel, but rather on the need for the Christian Brothers to work more closely with the Social Services department to ensure that the "incident" was never repeated. He denied that the status of the police investigation was ever raised at the meeting, and couldn't recall if representatives of Social Services offered any special assistance to the boys involved in the incident.

It was not the meeting that Newfoundland's Director of Child Welfare, or his Assistant Director, remembered attending. Frank Simms clearly remembered the Christian Brothers informing the meeting that no charges would be laid as a result of the police investigation at Mount Cashel.

"He [McHugh] did give information about the fact that the police report had been completed and a decision had been made not to lay charges. . . . I think Brother McHugh and Brother Nash came to the meeting to state that the investigation had been completed."

Sheila Devine, too, distinctly recalled that Brother McHugh briefly assured the Social Services officials that a complete and thorough police investigation into the affair had produced no grounds to press charges, a gross deception if true, because McHugh knew full well that two Brothers had already confessed to sexually abusing children in their care. If accurate, there was bitter irony attached to the recollections of both Social Services officials. When Newfoundland's Director of Child Welfare finally got some information about the disposition of the police report into Mount Cashel, it came not from the Justice Department but from a representative of the very group that was under investigation.

"What was merely passed along at that meeting was what seemed to be factual information – that the investigation had been concluded and no charges were to be laid. . . . He [McHugh] definitely said there would be no prosecutions," Devine testified.

At one point in the meeting, which was largely given over to the future direction of Mount Cashel, Devine asked for the names of the boys who had been interviewed by police. To her surprise and dismay, Brother McHugh replied that, given what had already been said, there was no need for the department to be concerned, or to know specifically how many or which boys had been interviewed.

"I then rephrased my question to indicate that I was not suggesting that abuse had been proven or had happened, but that rather, knowing that boys had gone through an interviewing process with police, and that can be very traumatic, and this had happened without a social worker being present, that I felt that if we knew the names of the boys that our staff or even psychologists or somebody that we could recommend could become involved with the boys to help them just with the trauma of having gone through a police investigation."

According to Devine's recollection of events, her own Deputy Minister then parroted the answer Brother McHugh had previously offered: given what had already been said, there was no need for the department to know the names of the boys. Devine was not surprised by Vernon Hollett's answer, knowing from her own experience that Mount Cashel had a special status within Newfoundland's Social Services network. She also knew that Brother Kenny did not welcome or encourage any hands-on involvement by social workers with the boys at Mount Cashel. Nevertheless, she was bitterly disappointed. Devine was appalled at what she saw as the total insensitivity of the Christian Brothers and her own superiors to the trauma the boys had gone through, and found it incredible that the Director of Child Welfare could not even get the names of the public wards who had been interviewed by police, let alone the green light to assist them. Fifteen years later, when a policeman finally showed her a copy of Detective Hillier's report, she understood why.

In keeping with the recent decision to reorganize the

orphanage by bringing in more outside expertise, Brother McHugh asked Brother Nash to serve as chairman of the new Mount Cashel Advisory Board. The Board would consist of three Christian Brothers and Newfoundland's Director of Child Welfare, Frank Simms, and was designed to help the Superintendent of Mount Cashel formulate and administer policy in the areas of discipline, admission and efficient operation. House mothers were introduced to give the orphanage the atmosphere of a "warm, secure, caring Christian family."

The cosmetic administrative changes were in keeping with plans for a redesigned Mount Cashel, which would see the large and impersonal dormitory system replaced by a series of more personal and private apartments. When social worker Stead Crawford first visited Mount Cashel, he noted that the dormitories were exactly like the ones in photographs of the orphanage from the early 1900s that hung in the institution's halls − twenty-five to thirty iron beds in a huge and dingy room, "an awful place for anybody to have to live."

In October 1975, the Provincial Council of the Christian Brothers had already decided to appoint a new Superintendent to take charge of the remodelled orphanage, which would be completed the following year. For some reason, about the same time that social worker Robert Bradbury filed his report alleging sexual and physical abuse at Mount Cashel, the man who was charged with investigating those accusations, Brother Douglas Kenny, no longer figured in the Brotherhood's future plans for the institution. His departure from Mount Cashel by the end of January 1976 was premature, coming halfway through his second three-year term.

With the two confessed Christian Brother child molesters safely out of the way without a scandal and the order's relationship with the Social Services department reaffirmed, there was only one thing left for Brother McHugh to do. On January 23, a week before the gala dinner for the Christian Brothers in St. John's, McHugh wrote to Vincent McCarthy to inform him of "the community's action concerning

Brother Ralph and Brother English":

"Brother Ralph was interviewed by Drs. Hughes and Eveson of Emmanuel Convalescent Home, Aurora, Ontario. It is the opinion of both doctors that Brother is in need of psychiatric care. He has entered the Convalescent Home and will probably need from three to five months treatment.

"Br. English received a three-day intensive evaluation from doctors of the House of Affirmation. . . . It is the opinion of Father Kane that Brother will require at least six months therapy. I am enclosing a copy of one of the letters received in reference to Br. English.

"I thank you sincerely for giving Br. Nash and myself the opportunity to discuss the Mount Cashel situation with you. Whenever it is appropriate, I will appreciate hearing from you."

They were hardly the words of a man who claimed to have been summoned to the office of the Deputy Minister of Justice and told what to do.

Vincent McCarthy never replied.

Between September 1975 and August 1976, hundreds of Christian Brothers, their former pupils, Roman Catholic dignitaries and assorted officials participated in a string of events to commemorate the one-hundredth anniversary of the Brothers' apostolate in St. John's. The theme of the centennial year of the Irish Christian Brothers in Canada was "Journey into a New Century – To Do and To Teach."

Some interesting names appeared on the list of guests and centennial organizers. Brother Dermod Nash was chairman of the centennial celebration. Nash's close personal friend from boyhood, the Honourable Ank Murphy, was chairman of the "Bring the Brothers Back" committee, a group whose task was to raise money to pay the travel expenses of thirty-one Christian Brothers who had taught in Newfoundland but who now resided in New York, Rhode Island, California, Massachusetts, Illinois, Washington, Ontario and British Columbia. As a former student of St. Patrick's Hall, Police Chief John Lawlor, another friend of Ank Murphy's, was also on the committee.

The celebrations began with a special mass of thanks-giving for the Brothers and their ex-pupils at St. Patrick's Hall at four o'clock on Saturday, September 20, 1975 — a few weeks after Billy Earle and Bobby Connors complained to Social Services that certain Brothers were physically and sexually abusing children at Mount Cashel. Archbishop P. J. Skinner presided over the official celebrations. And while Brother Gabriel McHugh would later insist that the Christian Brothers maintained only nominal ties with the Roman Catholic church, Archbishop Skinner left a very different impression that afternoon with his homily:

"The strong role of the Brothers in Catholic education in Newfoundland is an abiding one. I am particularly grateful at the present time for the tremendous co-operation and enlightened counsel I receive, and we all receive, from the wisdom and the experience of the Brothers who are definitely foremost in the ranks of Catholic educators and whose voice carries authority and prestige in our community."

A former pupil of the Christian Brothers, Archbishop Skinner abandoned his general discussion of the Brother-hood to "pay personal gratitude to the Brothers whom I have known so well throughout a lifetime and with whom I have had such close association in St. John's, in Halifax, and back in St. John's."

The centennial celebrations included an education conference, an entertainment program, an international convention of Christian Brothers and a visit from Mother Teresa. Visitors from England, Ireland, the United States, India, South Africa, Australia, New Zealand and the islands of Dominica and Antigua flooded into St. John's to take part. Media coverage was intense, including two television documentaries, a special edition in one of the city's two daily newspapers and blanket coverage by the Roman Catholic newspaper, *The Monitor*.

The Evening Telegram expressed its feelings about the Christian Brothers on the editorial page. After noting that the Christian Brothers had been a shining example to all who had been entrusted with the education of children in Newfoundland, the editorial writer concluded, "It is the sincere hope of the community, we feel sure, that the Order will long remain in our midst to continue an outstanding record of service and dedication, not just to the cause of education, but to the growth and integrity of the community, the province and the nation."

The most prestigious event of the centennial was a black-tie dinner in St. John's, held at Memorial University's dining hall on January 31, 1976. Five hundred and eighty-three guests braved a severe winter storm to attend the tribute to the Christian Brothers. As the guests nibbled at their cod au gratin and sipped their champagne, a blue-ribbon line-up of speakers regaled them with the exploits of the famous Catholic teaching order.

Provincial Finance Minister William Doody, a prominent Catholic, and Premier Frank Moores' right-hand man, praised the Brothers for their compassion during their first, harsh years in Newfoundland.

"The definition of poverty as we know it today would pale by comparison with the poverty as experienced in those days. The scope and extent of abuse of children and the utter lack of social welfare outside of the churches cannot even be imagined today," Doody said.

Newfoundland's Chief Justice, R. S. Furlong, proposed the toast to the Brothers. The Chief Justice had been one of the Congregation's former pupils, and he described the Brothers as "the great men of my boyhood and my youth. . . . I am totally the product of these men, and I thank God that His chosen instrument in my development were [sic] the Irish Christian Brothers."

After Archbishop Skinner had offered his response to the toast, another reply was given by the Superior General of the Congregation of Irish Christian Brothers, Brother J. L. Kelty, who had flown in from Rome for the glittering occasion. It was almost as if Brother Kelty was thinking about the turmoil of the past month and a half instead of the order's glorious past.

"It is inevitable, I suppose, over one hundred years, that there would be periods of despondency, periods during which things might run against one, when it might look as though work was in danger, when there might be obstacles and opposition. There might be disappointment in friends, and there might at times seem to be no light at the end of the tunnel. It is on occasions like this that the Christian Brothers here have appreciated the support, the assistance, material and spiritual, that they have been given by the whole population of this land, whether they be Catholic or non-Catholic."

Obscured in the sea of faces, provincial Justice Minister T. Alex Hickman, Lieutenant-Governor Gordon Winter, federal Cabinet Minister Don Jamieson, provincial Cabinet Minister John Crosbie, his protégé Brian Peckford, Father Kevin Molloy and Police Chief John Lawlor took in the Brother's inspirational, if somewhat ominous, address. With a blizzard howling outside, Father Molloy's mind had been on a storm of a different kind. He had been feeling "a bit of apprehension due to the fact that this big celebration was due to go ahead, was scheduled, and yet there were rumblings that this thing could indeed have a tragic overtone."

The parish priest needn't have worried; the day was still distant when the horrors of Mount Cashel would be made public. But he was right about one thing. It would have been a very different evening if several members of the order had been charged with sexually and physically abusing their charges just a few weeks before the gala dinner in honour of the Christian Brothers.

With the enchantment of answered prayers, the dinner came off without a hitch.

Chapter 6
■ *The Second Report*

I knew keep down that nothing ever was going to be done about it. As a police officer, I knew there was going to be no further steps. Det. Robert Hillier, in his March 3, 1976 report into sexual and physical child abuse at Mount Cashel.

IN NEWFOUNDLAND, JANUARY is the cruelest month. The Labrador current rolls down the northeast coast, chilling the land and carrying huge icebergs into the shipping lanes farther south, driven by gales that can take your breath away. In January, there is no forgetting the island is ringed by the icy waters that claimed the *Titanic* and the *Ocean Ranger*. Fierce storms blow up with deadly suddenness over the shallow waters of the Grand Banks, spawning waves the size of three-storey buildings. In the unforgiving waters of January, a man overboard is a man thirty seconds from eternity. Even in the snug comfort of St. John's Harbour, the power of the North Atlantic winter is visible in the frozen rigging of ships at berth along the quay. Picturesque on a moored vessel, the weight of frozen sea spray on the superstructure of a ship at sea can cause it to "turn turtle" and go to the bottom like a stone.

In the early days of the New Year, Det. Robert Hillier was feeling as raw as the weather. Shortly after he had filed his December 18 report on Mount Cashel, he and Detective Pitcher were assigned to investigate a case of attempted rape that took them to Gander and kept them occupied for the next few weeks. But it wasn't long before Hillier found himself brooding over the Mount Cashel investigation again, chafed by his conviction that it had been covered up. Haunted by the pathetic evidence he and Pitcher had gathered from the boys at the orphanage, the normally taciturn Hillier found that it was easier to talk about the case than to keep his frustrations inside. He wasn't the only police officer at Fort Townshend who was unhappy at the way the investigation had been handled by higher authorities.

"It was common knowledge in the division . . . I would say all of us knew about it in the division. We spoke about it frequently. I had conversations with Art Pike over different things and we spoke about what was going on at Mount Cashel," CID veteran Robert Pearcey would later testify.

Unaware of the dealings between the Justice Department and the Christian Brothers, Det.-Insp. Chesley Yetman, for one, was anxious to find out what had happened to Hillier's report.

"When I asked the Assistant Chief about it, he said he was working on instructions from the Department of Justice. . . . I was continuously asking about the report that Detective Hillier sent in."

It was routine for Yetman to get feedback from Justice Department lawyers and he was disturbed by the deafening silence that surrounded the Mount Cashel investigation. As for Bob Hillier, his bitterness at having been called off the case before his investigation was finished drove him to follow up on something that had been bothering him since before Christmas: what had been done about the 1974 complaint against Brother English by Johnny Williams, when Johnny's cousin, Brenda Lundrigan, had taken him to the Child Welfare office on Harvey Road?

The experienced detective was well aware that he was disobeying a direct order in pursuing the matter on his own. But he had to find out why no action had apparently been taken about a serious complaint of abuse at Mount Cashel that had come to light more than a year before Shane Earle's beating. Although his immediate superior, Detective-Inspector Yetman, didn't give his official blessing to Hillier's follow-up, he privately approved of the unauthorized action and winked at it.

When Detective Hillier went to Social Services a second time, he "came on strong," upset by his suspicion that nothing had been done about the earlier complaint against Brother English. None of that emotion made it into the laconic record of his visit to Harvey Road.

"A check at Child Welfare showed this complaint had been made by Miss Lundrigan and apparently the information passed on to the Department of Child Welfare at Confederation Building."

Hillier was determined to locate Brenda Lundrigan to find out exactly what she had reported to authorities. On January 10, 1976, he finally contacted her, three weeks after the police investigation had been officially terminated. Lundrigan, who had been working in Toronto, arrived back in St. John's at 6:30 P.M. on December 23 to spend Christmas with her family. She decided to stay a few weeks longer when, in early January, her mother, Veronica (Lundrigan) Tobin moved house from Quidi Vidi Road to St. Clare Avenue in St. John's.

When Lundrigan got home on the night of January 10, her mother told her that Detective Hillier from the CID wanted her to call him. Veronica didn't know what the police wanted. Brenda got in touch with Hillier the next day and agreed to an interview about events she had officially complained about more than a year before. Surprised by the belated police interest in Mount Cashel, she couldn't help wondering why it had taken them so long to respond.

Detectives Hillier and Thistle listened as the young woman recounted her trip to the Child Welfare office on Harvey Road with Johnny Williams after his beating at the hands of Brother English. It certainly appeared that Lundrigan and Williams had expressed their complaint to the proper authorities, just as Johnny Williams had stated in his December 1975 police interview. But Lundrigan then took the interview a step beyond where the police may have thought her knowledge of the situation ended.

"Another time while at Mount Cashel I was going to speak to Jerome Williams. I wasn't visiting at this time but was swimming at Mount Cashel when I decided to drop along and see him. When I went in I saw Jerome in the hallway with Brother Kenny. Jerome was crying at the time. I asked Jerome what was the matter but he wouldn't say anything. I asked Brother Kenny what was wrong and he said nothing was wrong. Brother Kenny then said it was none of my business what was wrong. I told him it was my business and told him I wanted to know but he wouldn't tell me. . . . From talking with the boys at Mount Cashel I am convinced the boys are treated bad by the Brothers."

Completely unaware of Detective Hillier's December investigation into Mount Cashel, Brenda Lundrigan was determined to let police know about the sexual abuse various boys at the orphanage had complained about to her.

"I am, as well as others, aware of other things that's going on and if the police did an investigation they would find out about it."

Detective Hillier decided to take a second statement from her concerning these "other things."

"Further to my previous statement, I am aware of homosexual acts taking place at Mount Cashel Orphanage. I have not witnessed these things, but was told by boys at Mount Cashel. Johnny Williams, who is my first cousin and who lives at Mount Cashel, told me that he saw a fellow, Jimmy, whose last name I forget, with Brother English. The words he used was that one night while the rest of the boys were asleep he saw Jimmy 'jerking off' Brother English near his bedside. There is also other boys involved with homosexual acts. The boys is in a position whereby there is very little they can do about what's happening but a lot of people knows about it now and something should be done to help them."

Lundrigan's last words were like a dagger in Detective Hillier's heart, as he remembered his promise to the boys he had interviewed − that if anything was wrong, the police would help them. He took down this second statement on a separate sheet of paper and had Lundrigan sign it at 12:20 P.M. On her way back home from Fort Townshend, the young woman with the irrepressible urge to defend the downtrodden had the same feeling she'd had a year earlier after leaving the Child Welfare office with Johnny Williams and Dereck O'Brien − the frustrating sense that nothing would be done.

When the time came to unravel the dismal tale yet again, Brenda wouldn't be the only member of her family to take the stand.

Veronica (Lundrigan) Tobin was a woman who had taken life on the chin and come up swinging. The small, stocky firebrand from Cuslett, Placentia East, a rural community about three and a half hours by car from St. John's, could be counted on to stand up and fight for people who had fallen by the wayside in life's pitiless race. The mother of ten — five sons and five daughters — was the president of the Newfoundland and Labrador Anti-Poverty Association, whose office was located on New Gower Street in downtown St. John's, next door to Gosse's Tavern. A social worker would later suggest that she was so busy standing up for others she ended up neglecting her own children.

By 1974, the thirty-six-year old woman had been ground down by personal reversals and the very poverty she so passionately fought against on behalf of others. She was separated from her husband and was seeing a psychiatrist, having lost one of her sons in a car accident a few years earlier. The five children who were still at home were becoming more than she could handle. Her sons Joey and Larry, "two little devils," were running wild; Joey would be out all hours of the night, and little Larry would lower himself out of his second-storey bedroom window on bedsheets and run around Bannerman Park stark naked. Acting on the psychiatrist's advice, the impoverished woman eventually contacted Child Welfare, which at first gave her some domestic assistance at home and later placed five of her children into care. Three daughters, including Brenda, went into foster homes, and Joey and Larry were placed in Mount Cashel.

Despite the severe depression brought on by the "anti-social behaviour" of her children, Veronica still reacted vigorously when she came across instances of human suffering or abuse. In the autumn of 1974, her two nephews, the twins Johnny and Jerome Williams, paid her a visit at her Barnes Road home off Bonaventure Avenue. When she tried to hug Johnny, the small boy recoiled. Opening his shirt, she saw "long welts" on his body. Outraged, Veronica marched into the Child Welfare office on Harvey Road where she remembers being told that if the boys at Mount Cashel didn't deserve the punishment, they wouldn't get it.

Not satisfied with that answer and disturbed by the stories Johnny and Jerome were telling her, she went down to the baseball field behind Mount Cashel and convinced four boys to talk to her about what was going on at the orphanage. The boys agreed, with the proviso that she wouldn't tell the Brothers what they said. She and an associate at the Anti-Poverty Association, Peter Harrington, who ran a small newspaper called *The Town Crier*, took a tape recorder and tapes from the association office and went to Mount Cashel to record the boys' stories.

The taping session was held in the carpet room on the main floor of the orphanage, with Harrington doing the interviewing and Veronica standing watch at the door, ready to sound the alert if any Brothers happened along. An hour later they were back at the Anti-Poverty Association listening to the boys' allegations of physical and sexual abuse at Mount Cashel. Harrington apparently decided against using the tapes, a call that didn't sit well with his more combative accomplice.

"If it had been left to me I would have brought them both to the TV and radio stations," she would later testify at the Hughes Inquiry.

Instead, she told the story to Detective Hillier after he had submitted his first report on Mount Cashel. Although Hillier would later officially record the information about the tapes, he didn't pursue the matter – possibly because he had already gathered the same information from five times as many boys during his investigation at Mount Cashel, including three of the same residents Tobin and Harrington had interviewed.

Many years later, in evidence studded with inconsistencies of time and place, Veronica (Lundrigan) Tobin would testify at the Hughes Inquiry that Social Services Minister Ank Murphy advised her to leave the province after she threatened to go to the media about abuse at Mount Cashel.

"He said, 'You put your children in [care] with a letter from your psychiatrist.' So he said, 'We will use that against you. . . . If you pursue this any further you'll end up in court and probably in jail yourself and you won't get the children back any more.' "

Tobin testified that Murphy's threats convinced her to leave the Mount Cashel affair alone and suppress the tapes she and Harrington had made. Eventually she would decide to move to Nova Scotia.

Ank Murphy would deny her allegations, claiming that he had never met Veronica (Lundrigan) Tobin and that the encounter described in her testimony had never taken place. The tapes were never recovered.

In February 1976, Detective Hillier had another chance to make a point with his superiors about the quashing of the Mount Cashel investigation; his action in turn gave someone in authority an opportunity to make something equally clear to him.

Every year police officers submitted a tally and brief description of their investigations, which were then incorporated into the CID Annual Report. In Hillier's report, which he submitted on February 24, 1976, he stated that he had been assigned 269 investigations, 107 of which he completed. One of his investigations appeared under the heading "Child Abuse and Homosexual Acts" and recorded the fact that he had looked into twenty-five complaints — a clear reference to Mount Cashel. When Staff Sgt. Arthur Pike submitted his general report for the Assault Section, he included Detective Hillier's contribution exactly as it had come to him.

But by the time the Newfoundland Constabulary's Annual Report was submitted to the Department of Justice before being made public, the reference to Mount Cashel had been deleted. On the list of offences reported each month, there was no mention of child abuse or homosexual acts. Nor was there any sign of Hillier's submission in the report's monthly listing of occurrences. Under the heading "Common Assault on Males," the report listed twelve occurrences for the month of December; under "Indecent Assault on Males," only one.

The same forces that wanted all references to sexual abuse at Mount Cashel removed from Detective Hillier's December 18 police report were still keeping a very close eye on the situation.

Two and a half months after he was ordered off the Mount Cashel investigation, Bob Hillier found himself back in the middle of the most demoralizing case of his career.

When he reported for work at Fort Townshend on the morning of March 3, 1976, he was greeted by Chief of Police John Lawlor with an urgent message: Newfoundland's Justice Minister, T. Alex Hickman, had requested a second report on the Mount Cashel case and Lawlor wanted it sent up the line that day. If the detective felt a momentary sense of relief that the justice system had finally decided to deal with the serious matters he had unearthed at Mount Cashel, it was immediately tempered by Chief Lawlor's final instructions.

"I was told by the Chief to write a report pertaining to physical abuse at Mount Cashel Orphanage but to keep sex-related matters out. . . . He told me because the Minister was requesting it."

For months the CID office had been buzzing about the Mount Cashel investigation, and the surprise request by the Justice Minister sent the rumour mill into overdrive. When Hillier told Det.-Insp. Chesley Yetman what had happened, the senior police officer thought the request "made no sense." He was dead right. If the Minister wanted to see the Mount Cashel report, all he had to do was request the one that had already been sent to Vincent McCarthy. Yetman went to Assistant Chief Norman for an explanation and was informed that the force was merely following orders from Justice. Years later, T. Alex Hickman, the man who allegedly asked for it, would flatly deny having requested the report.

The episode of the request for a second report raised some fascinating possibilities. Interestingly, March 3, the day the new report was requested, was the same day that John Kelly was officially appointed to the post of Director of Public Prosecutions. According to his colleagues, the outgoing D.P.P., Vincent McCarthy, was not only cautious in his judgments, he was also careful to act within his authority. In the case of the Mount Cashel police investigation, McCarthy's decision not to lay charges flowed directly from his authority as D.P.P. to determine such matters.

Vincent McCarthy knew that the Department of Social Services had already tried to obtain the report through their contact in the Justice Department, Mary Noonan – a request he had personally turned down as D.P.P. But with John Kelly's appointment, he too would have every right as D.P.P. to access the Mount Cashel police report. If McCarthy were suppressing the report because he wanted to hide the widespread sexual and physical abuse reported at Mount Cashel, Kelly's appointment could present a major problem. What grounds would there be for refusing the D.P.P. access to the police report if Mary Noonan asked Kelly to find out on behalf of Social Services which boys had been interviewed for Detective Hillier's December police report? And if Kelly obtained the report for Noonan, she would have to inform Frank Simms of the monstrous allegations of sexual abuse against his wards that the Justice Department had decided to sweep under the rug rather than investigate, prosecute or share with Social Services. The scandal would in every sense be declared. Unless, of course, a second report could be obtained, one that documented only physical abuse at Mount Cashel. This was exactly what Detective Hillier was asked to produce on March 3 for someone purporting to be the Minister.

Detective Hillier was at a loss to explain the latest turn of events and his emotions were divided. Although he was upset at being asked to launder his report yet again, he also hoped that Hickman's alleged request meant that the Justice Department might finally be planning to do something about the Mount Cashel case. The key task as far as he was concerned was to comply with Chief Lawlor's request to remove, or at least understate, references to sexual abuse at the orphanage, but to make crystal clear between the lines that more than physical abuse was involved. With the assistance of Staff Sgt. Arthur Pike, he prepared a second report that he hoped would both get past the Chief and wake up the country club. If someone in the Justice Department was looking for a dry-cleaned report, they must have been disappointed with the "scarlet-worded" document that shortly landed on their desks.

Anxious to foil the cover-up they believed was in progress,

Hillier and Pike pored through the Canadian Criminal Code and stumbled across a rarely used section dealing with the corruption of children: "Everyone who in a home of a child participates in adultery or sexual immorality or indulges in habitual drunkenness or any act of vice and thereby endangers the morals of the child or renders the home an unfit place for the child to be, is guilty of an indictable offence and is liable to imprisonment for two years."

The two detectives used the archaic statute to come up with a new title for Hillier's second report: "Further to my report dated December 18, 1975 concerning 'Corrupting of Children' at Mount Cashel Orphanage, Torbay Road, St. John's, Newfoundland. (Refer Br. Sec. 168(1) C.C.C.)"

As Hillier later told the Hughes Inquiry, "The words 'corrupting children' should have opened the eyes of someone reading the report. . . . [The Minister] couldn't help determining that something is astray here, something is amiss, something has gone wrong and perhaps come back for a further report where sexual activities would have to be involved."

In his opening paragraph, Hillier wanted to emphasize the point that the Minister of Justice had requested the second report. Arthur Pike urged his colleague to spell out Hickman's name in the report, but Hillier settled for using his official title when referring to the highly unusual request.

"I respectfully report that as requested by the Minister of Justice I am forwarding this report on child abuse regarding assaults on a number of children by Christian Brothers at Mount Cashel Orphanage."

Detective Hillier then compiled a "run down" on the Brothers and some of the boys they had allegedly abused. He dealt first with the victims of Brother English, beginning the pathetic litany with a description of Andre Walsh's cracked hands.

"He said he cried for mercy for him to stop and he refused to do so. . . . The boy's hands at the time of my interview were obviously abnormal as they were peeling and cracked. Since the strapping, he has to use Vaseline on his hands to keep them from drying up. This boy cried as he held his hands out for me to view."

Hillier then reported that Peter Brown had also been beaten by Brother English.

"This boy shows his feelings very much and it is my opinion he is in bodily fear of Brother English. He has been called names such as bastard and bitch and tells Peter he is going to kick the shit out of him. The boy reported the matter to his father, who visits him regularly and his father asked Brother English about it but Brother English denies having said or done such things and this has made the boy more nervous."

The detective reported that he had interviewed eighteen boys who gave statements telling of "frightening experiences" they had with Brother English.

"These statements were attached to my original report and the complete contents are not covered in this report," he wrote, hoping that any concerned reader would be driven to find out what was contained in the December 18 document. To further encourage the reader to follow up, the frustrated detective wrote that Brother English had "admitted verbally that the boys did tell the truth."

When Hillier turned to Brother Ralph, he stopped worrying about Chief Lawlor's request for a laundered report and outlined several sex-related complaints. He clearly stated that four boys made complaints concerning sexual abuse by Brother Ralph, adding, "He [Brother Ralph] admits in a statement attached to my original report of having been involved with the boys sexually."

Hillier then dealt with Brothers Kenny, Short and Burke.

"In their statements, five of the boys tell how they are displeased about Brother Kenny, who has been kissing them on the lips and having them bite his neck and the tip of his tongue. [G]erry Brinston tells how he has been hit in the face and stomach by Brother Kenny and also slapped around by the hair on his head."

Hillier added additional details of alleged assaults on Bobby and Greg Connors by Brother Burke.

"Robert Connors states he was beaten by Brother Burke who struck him several times with a leather belt. He was then put into a closet used to punish boys, told to take off his clothes and his bare back side was beaten with a round stick about a foot long. . . .

"Gregory Connors also complains of having been beaten by Brother Burke with a round stick and claims this took place in a closet and the boy had off his clothes."

Having raised the issue of Brothers Kenny, Short and Burke, the investigator then made his point to the Justice Minister.

"Brothers Kenny, Burke and Short were not interviewed by me concerning these incidents due to a slowdown in the investigation as requested by both the Chief of Police, J. F. Lawlor, and Assistant Chief, J. R. Norman."

Hillier made note of Shane Earle's beating and the fact that Billy Earle "complained of sexual passes by the Brothers." He then outlined his trip to Social Services, including the fact that Johnny Williams's complaint had been passed on to the Department of Child Welfare at Confederation Building. Finally, the detective included a paragraph on Veronica (Lundrigan) Tobin's private investigation, which he hoped would prompt Justice Department officials to take action, laden as it was with the spectre of a sensational exposé.

"Since my original report, informed sources tell me that people of the Human Rights [Hillier misapplied the name of the provincial body to the Anti-Poverty Group in the hope of forcing the politicians to act] have taken reports from some boys at Mount Cashel Orphanage and have taped conversations they have had with the boys. These tapes were done with the purpose of revealing the matter to the public. . . ."

Hillier closed the report with another pointed reminder that he had not been allowed to complete the Mount Cashel investigation.

"To date I have not gone to the Mount Cashel Orphanage for the purpose of carrying out an investigation. The boys were conveyed to my office for interviews. The straps and sticks mentioned in my report were not confiscated and this will await further instructions from headquarters."

Attached to the report were the two statements Brenda Lundrigan had given Detective Hillier in 1976, as well as

Dr. Paul Patey's report on Shane Earle written after his December 8, 1975 examination at the Janeway Hospital, and three photographs of the little boy standing with his pants down to his knees, back to the camera, self-consciously displaying the bruises on his buttocks. Hillier handed the report to Arthur Pike who took the short walk down the corridor to the office next to Chief Lawlor's where he passed it to Carol Power, one of the Chief's stenographers.

Later that day, after Detective Hillier signed the typed version of his report, bearing the same reference number as his first report — 7855 — another CID officer was detailed to hand-deliver a brown envelope containing a copy of the report to the Justice Minister's office at Confederation Building. The detective held his breath.

Nothing happened. Like a stone dropped off the stern of a boat, the report vanished into the depths of the justice system, where it would remain until both it and Hillier's original document were returned to police in 1977. Both Hillier and Pike knew that justice hadn't been done, but they had carried the Mount Cashel affair as far as they dared without sacrificing their jobs. Detective Hillier's hopes, so fiercely kindled by the Minister's unexpected request, were as quickly extinguished in the long days of silence after the second report was filed.

"I knew deep down that nothing ever was going to be done about it. As a police officer, I knew there was going to be no further steps."

Later that spring, the detectives of the CID would sullenly consider taking independent action in what they believed was one of the most scandalous cases the Newfoundland Constabulary had ever investigated — an initiative that Chief of Police John Lawlor would snuff out with the vigour of a man extinguishing a flame licking a keg of dynamite.

While several members of the CID were left scratching their heads over the latest turn of events in the Mount Cashel affair, the chain of events that would see Shane and Billy Earle returned to Mount Cashel was working its way through Newfoundland's courts.

On May 16, 1974, Shane Earle's temporary wardship had

expired (temporary wardship orders were good for only twelve months), prompting Newfoundland's Director of Child Welfare, Frank Simms, to set the wheels in motion to have the boy's status reviewed by the court. Billy had already been made a permanent ward of the Director of Child Welfare in 1973. The Department of Social Services advised William Earle, Sr., who was still on the province's west coast, that the boys' wardship would have to be determined. Earle, Sr. informed social workers that he wasn't able to look after Shane and Billy. On November 14, 1975, Frank Simms wrote to his District Administrator in Corner Brook and instructed Henry Anthony to arrange to have the wardship case presented to court.

It was a surprising request. Not only did Shane, Billy and their mother live in St. John's, there was also a lengthy social services court history of the family there. So why, as commission counsel would later ask, would the Director of Child Welfare want somebody four hundred miles away on the other side of the island to handle a case involving the wardship of two little boys living in St. John's? The social worker dealing with the file at the field level, Geraldine Stapleton, had no ready answer.

"Based on my experience, when I saw this letter it raised a question in my mind. . . . I don't ever remember . . . having been involved in transferring cases similar to this for review elsewhere."

(Interestingly, Frank Simms requested that the wardship hearing be moved to Corner Brook two days after he officially disposed of Robert Bradbury's report containing Billy Earle's allegations of physical and sexual abuse at Mount Cashel against the Christian Brothers — a coincidence that raised the possibility that the two events were related.)

After Shane's December 6 beating at Mount Cashel, Carol Earle, who had taken her sons back, received careful attention from the Department of Social Services. Although social workers had never regularly called on her before, she now received frequent visits from Geraldine Stapleton. It was from these visits that she finally got some information about the police investigation into her son's beating.

Although it was "normal procedure" for the Newfoundland Constabulary to notify the person who made a complaint about the results of an investigation, no one ever informed Carol Earle about what had happened with the Mount Cashel case – possibly because the police themselves were so totally in the dark about the fate of Hillier's report.

"I was under the impression that it [the police investigation] had ended but the only thing I knew was that three of the Brothers had been sent away. . . . " she would later testify.

While Carol Earle and her new companion, Gus Summers, were trying to make a home for her two boys, William Earle, Sr.'s new beginning in western Newfoundland was coming to a familiar end. On the morning of January 13, 1976, Earle pulled up stakes once more, piling his wife, their new baby, and his son Rick into the family car and heading east along the empty stretches of the TransCanada Highway back to St. John's.

On the same day William Earle, Sr. and family were leaving Corner Brook, Geraldine Stapleton was informing her counterpart on the province's west coast, Henry Anthony, that Shane and Billy Earle had left Mount Cashel under "unusual" circumstances and would be placed with their mother until a wardship hearing could take place. The hearing was originally set for February 4, 1976, but in fact wouldn't be heard until over a month later. Stapleton asked for an update of William Earle, Sr.'s circumstances and directed that he should be notified of the hearing, without realizing that Shane's father had already left the west coast and was on his way back to the capital.

Earle never quite made it to St. John's, stopping instead in Admiral's Beach, his wife's hometown in St. Mary's Bay. On the day of his boys' wardship hearing, he telephoned the Department of Child Welfare to inform them of his change of address. The hearing was postponed and William Earle, Sr. went to see the Child Welfare workers two days later when he arrived in the city. On February 6 he signed a notice stating that he had been notified of a court hearing on February 13 to review Shane's and Billy's wardship. At the bottom of the notice, social worker Geraldine Stapleton wrote: "It will be my recommendation at the hearing that William and Shane remain in the care of their mother, Carol Earle." William Earle was dead against such an arrangement. Although he couldn't take care of the boys himself, he was prepared to contest any wardship agreement that would place Shane and Billy with their mother, whom the estranged husband vowed to "put in the mental" rather than see take charge of the children.

Meanwhile, behind the scenes, the Department of Social Services was preparing its brief for the Earle boys' wardship hearing, now set to take place on March 18, 1976. It was a serious court proceeding. In a wardship hearing, a judge must decide whether to make a child a permanent ward of the province, a decision that cuts all legal ties to its natural parents forever and clears the way for formal adoption proceedings. In order to help the judge make this grave determination, he must be provided with all material evidence relating to the individual in question, particularly when both natural parents are still alive, as they were in the case of Shane and Billy Earle.

The Department of Social Services would routinely go to their contact in the Justice Department to request counsel for upcoming wardship hearings. Accordingly, on March 4, 1976, the Deputy Minister of Social Services, in a letter signed on his behalf by Frank Simms, officially asked the Deputy Minister of Justice, Vincent McCarthy, to assign a lawyer for the Earle wardship hearing. The request was passed along to Mary Noonan.

In reviewing the file, Noonan noted that Geraldine Stapleton had written in her report that "Mr. Earle was residing in Pasadena, outside Corner Brook, when the allegations arising from mistreatment of Shane at Mt. Cashel necessitated his removal from that institution." With the memory of the mysterious events at Mount Cashel fresh in her mind, Noonan wondered if Shane and his brother Billy had been two of the children involved in the police investigation.

Curious, Noonan asked her colleague and newly appointed Director of Public Prosecutions, John Kelly, to see if he could obtain a copy of the police report into the Mount Cashel affair, the report she had been unable to get from his predecessor in the job, Vincent McCarthy. With Noonan sitting in his office, Kelly called Fort Townshend and asked Staff Sgt. Arthur Pike for information from Detective Hillier's report. Pike was surprised by Kelly's request and told the new D.P.P. that the Justice Department already had the report.

"... I thought this was unusual and I said, 'Sure the report,' I said, 'should be in your office concerning this matter,' and he said that he hadn't seen the report and he couldn't get it. But he was requesting the names ... or he asked me to check ... he gave me two names of children and asked me to check and see if these two children were two of the children involved in the investigation, because I think it was Mrs. Noonan, he told me ... had a custody case in family court and she was wondering if the custody case involving these children were the same children involved in the investigation."

Although Kelly asked Pike to find out what he could, the policeman never followed up, possibly because working-level officers in the CID were still smarting over the way the Justice Department had smothered the Mount Cashel investigation. As he would later testify, "I think he [Kelly] may have asked me if I would find out, but I didn't. I did nothing further on that."

For the second time, the solicitor for the Director of Child Welfare had been unable to obtain any details from the mysterious police report dealing with Mount Cashel. But just as she had not seen any "red flag" when she read Geraldine Stapleton's account of Shane Earle's mistreatment at Mount Cashel, she was not particularly alarmed at failing to get the police report a second time, as she would later testify.

Overburdened with other work, Mary Noonan assigned the Justice Department's oldest and most inexperienced lawyer to the Earle wardship hearing, which she viewed as an "exercise" for him. Fifty-year-old Herbert J. Buckingham, who from his earliest education was a self-described "product of the Christian Brothers. . . . In every sense . . . a

Christian Brother boy," had in fact never appeared in court before. Although he would later say he had no direct knowledge of alleged mistreatment of Shane Earle at Mount Cashel, he did admit that he had a "feeling" that something was amiss at the orphanage. "I picked it up," he testified.

Buckingham's vague awareness of trouble at the orphanage received no airing at the brief wardship hearing on which he cut his legal teeth. Despite the fact that the lawyer had the Social Services file on Shane Earle in his possession, including Geraldine Stapleton's report mentioning Shane's mistreatment at Mount Cashel, there was no reference in Buckingham's notes from the hearing to indicate that the issue of physical abuse was ever raised in open court. Nor did social worker Geraldine Stapleton raise Mount Cashel when she gave her brief testimony, which included the fact that plans were now being made for placement of Shane and Billy outside their mother's home.

As the hearing approached, and with it the spectre of an ugly confrontation with her husband, Carol Earle had thought better of keeping the boys. Billy was hard to discipline, and there were hard feelings between her common-law spouse and her high-spirited son, who kept in close touch with his natural father. At the last moment, she had asked her social worker to place the boys elsewhere. On March 18, 1976, Shane Michael Earle was made a permanent ward of the Director of Child Welfare and Billy Earle's permanent wardship was reconfirmed by Judge M. R. Reid of the Newfoundland Provincial Court.

The learned judge made his routine order without being informed of either the Bradbury report, which was in the possession of the Director of Child Welfare and contained complaints from Billy Earle of physical and sexual abuse at Mount Cashel, or the Social Services documents and police report relating to Shane Earle's beating, documents that showed how widespread those abuses were at the Christian Brother institution.

On March 31, 1976, Newfoundland's Child Protection Officer, Neil Hamilton, wrote a memo to Sheila Devine, the Assistant Director of Child Welfare, informing her that both boys were to be returned to Mount Cashel. A few weeks later, the Department of Social Services reinstated the monthly payments to the orphanage for the Earle brothers — $89 for Shane and $99 for Billy.

When Mary Noonan read Geraldine Stapleton's March 30, 1976 note on the Earle file stating that the two boys were about to return to Mount Cashel, she was mildly surprised. But instead of reflecting on the fact that a child who had been removed from Mount Cashel for alleged mistreatment was being returned to the same institution, or that the proper authorities in Social Services had been flatly refused access to a secret police report into the mysterious affair, she took comfort from the fact that Shane's mother seemed to approve of the arrangement.

"It suggests to me, though, if I may say," she later testified, "that Mrs. Earle must have been satisfied that the problem at Mount Cashel had been resolved or she wouldn't have asked to send her boys back."

One would have thought that the opinion of a person who self-admittedly couldn't look after her own children was not the most reliable guide to Mount Cashel's suitability for Shane and Billy, reflecting as it did exasperation with her own situation rather than a balanced analysis of what was best for her boys. More to the point, Noonan's comment neglected a few simple facts: the boys' natural mother was basing her satisfaction with the decision to place the boys in Mount Cashel on assurances she'd received from social workers that the problems there had been dealt with and the offending Brothers had been sent away. Besides, Carol Earle hadn't been legally responsible for Shane and Billy since 1973, and nothing that happened on March 18 changed that. The decision to send the boys back to Mount Cashel, and the responsibility for that decision, belonged to one person and one person alone – Newfoundland's Director of Child Welfare.

For quite some time to come, Simms's legal adviser, Mary Noonan, would continue to get ominous indications that pointed back to the mysterious police report of 1975. Sad to say, none of them made her question her faith in Vincent McCarthy's judgment, or spurred her to inquire into the matter further.

On April 7, 1976, almost four months to the day after Shane and Billy left Mount Cashel with Chesley Riche, the boys were returned to the orphanage. For twelve-year-old Billy, his stay would be little more than a year, but nine-year-old Shane would be calling Mount Cashel home for the grey and lonely stretch of another decade.

In a less trusting and bureaucratic soul than Mary Noonan's, the sad case of Frankie Baird, who had run away from Mount Cashel in November 1975, would have set off alarm bells that might even have been heard in the Department of Social Services.

A little over a month after the Shane and Billy Earle wardship hearing that sent the boys back to the institution where they had been physically and sexually abused, Noonan began dealing with the Baird case on behalf of the Director of Child Welfare. On April 23, 1976, she wrote a letter to the Deputy Minister of Social Services asking for ten-year-old Frankie Baird's file to prepare for an upcoming contested wardship hearing.

The request to make Frankie a ward of the Director was partially the result of the recommendation of Dr. U. Sreenivasan, the Director of Child Psychiatry at the Janeway Hospital. On March 4, 1976, Dr. Sreenivasan wrote to social worker Sharron Callahan recommending that Frankie be "removed from his mother's custody." Dr. Sreenivasan depicted Mrs. Baird as a completely unreliable and untruthful woman who had rejected Frankie and was blighting his future. "I hope that your Department will have Francis removed from his mother's custody and placed in a foster home far away from her. This is his only hope."

Carol Baird's own life was no less desperate than her troubled son's. At eighteen she had married Malcolm Baird, two years after their first child was born. The stormy relationship that began in 1957 lasted seven years. During that time, Malcolm served six months in jail and was temporarily committed to a mental institution for abusing his wife. On one occasion, he hit her so hard that she was unconscious for three days. In the wake of the beating, Carol Baird suffered recurring seizures and underwent psychiatric care for "poor nerves." Whenever she talked about leaving him, Baird would threaten to cut off the heads of their children and roll them into her mother's house like human bowling balls.

In 1969, Carol Baird met Francis Strickland, who would become her common-law husband. Once more, the relationship was painful and tumultuous. It came to an end six years later in April 1975, when her husband threw her out of a window during a terrible fight. Mrs. Baird (Strickland) was hospitalized and her nine children were put into care. On October 7, 1975 she signed a non-ward agreement with the Social Services Department which placed her three sons in Mount Cashel without making the province their official guardian. Just under two months later, she removed the boys from the institution and brought them home. Two months after that, ten-year-old Frankie made his first appearance at the Janeway Hospital. The little boy had tried to kill himself by taking a quantity of drugs, including Valium. Two weeks later he was admitted again. Janeway social worker Catherine Foster explained why in a letter to Sharron Callahan.

"Francis was seen in the Emergency Department of this hospital on February 15, 1976. Mother advised the attending doctor that her son had allegedly attempted to kill her with a knife and was threatening to do the same with himself."

The incident was repeated a week later, and Frankie was eventually examined by Dr. Sreenivasan, who advised Social Services to offer the child protection. Frankie was apprehended under the provisions of the Child Welfare Act, but his temporary wardship was delayed pending a request for legal representation from the Social Services department. It was during this delay that his mother told social worker Patricia Roberts that Frankie had been abused by certain Christian Brothers during his brief stay at Mount Cashel the previous autumn.

". . . She is claiming now that his problems really started last year when he was first placed in care. . . . She was hospitalized . . . because of injuries suffered in a fight between her and her common-law spouse, Frank Strickland.

She further claims that Frankie's problems got worse when she put him into Mount Cashel and is making the claim that he was abused by the Brothers."

Roberts "walked" her report into the Department of Social Services and hand-delivered it to the Assistant Director of Child Welfare, Sheila Devine. The social worker was never asked to follow up on the report of child abuse at Mount Cashel. After Mary Noonan took on the case for the Department of Social Services, she dealt directly with social worker Patricia Roberts.

"I think it would be safe to say there was consultation between myself and Mrs. Noonan about the case," Roberts would later testify.

On June 24, 1976, two weeks before Frankie Baird's temporary wardship hearing, Dr. Omesh Kashyap wrote a report, at the request of the court, dealing with the troubled family. Fourteen years later, a copy of the document would be found in the files of the Justice Department. Once more, Kashyap's report contained direct reference to allegations from Mrs. Baird (Strickland) of physical and sexual abuse of Frankie during his stay at Mount Cashel, references that failed to stir anyone in the system to investigate.

"She indicated he was beaten a lot at the orphanage, sexually assaulted. Father Molloy investigated. Got call from Det. Hillier. Ron Pumphrey also told her that the Brothers were suspended. He was badly beaten, threatened and sexually assaulted. . . . They [Baird's three sons] finally returned home in early December."

On July 8, 1976, Mary Noonan went into court on behalf of the Social Services department and made application for a temporary wardship of Frankie Baird. The presiding magistrate dismissed the application. Nowhere in Noonan's extensive notes on the proceeding was there a reference to allegations of physical and sexual abuse at Mount Cashel. In fact, Noonan would later testify that the subject wasn't raised. When asked years later if she made any connection between the fact that Frankie had attempted suicide twice in the two months following his departure from Mount Cashel and the fact that his mother told officials her son had been

Noonan merely noted how odd it was that Mrs. Baird
(Strickland), not Frankie, made the allegations.

As oddities go, it was also strange that someone as well
informed as the legal adviser to the Director of Child
Welfare wouldn't relate the tragedy of Frankie Baird to the
mysterious contents of the police report on Mount Cashel
that she had twice been forbidden to see – especially since
Detective Hillier was mentioned by name in Dr. Kashyap's
report as having visited Frankie's house during his
investigation.

But then Mary Noonan was a lawyer, not a social worker,
and that wasn't her job.

Early in March 1976, the Brother Provincial of the Canada–
West Indies Province of the Christian Brothers received yet
another disturbing telephone call from his lieutenant in
Newfoundland. Brother Dermod Nash informed Gabriel
McHugh that allegations of abuse had been made against
three other Brothers at Mount Cashel, in addition to
Brothers English and Ralph – information that almost
certainly came from Detective Hillier's March 3 report.
Someone in either the police force or the Justice Department
was keeping the Brotherhood very closely informed about
developments in the Mount Cashel affair. Precisely who
would be cleared up a few weeks later, when Brother Nash
wrote a remarkable memo to Brother McHugh. The memo,
written on the same day as Shane and Billy Earle's wardship
hearing, outlined a far more comprehensive deal between the
Justice Department and the Christian Brothers than
anything contained in the arrangement allegedly dictated by
Vincent McCarthy on December 18, 1975. Once again,
McCarthy was front and centre.

SUBJECT: Reminders re Mt. Cashel
At the most recent meeting with the Deputy Minister
of Justice, Mr. McCarthy, the following points were
raised. I have already communicated such to you by
phone and am including again as reminders re situation at
Mt. Cashel:
1...Brs. Ted English and Gerry [Alan] Ralph are not to

return to the Province of Newfoundland.

2. . .Brs. Kenny and Short are not to be assigned to Mt. Cashel.

3. . .Br. Burke's continuance at Mt. Cashel is questionable re record of punishment.

4. . .There seems to be a need (strongly expressed) that the Congregation make public in some form the fact that the Mt. Cashel scene is very definitely under change and review. This will serve to assure all (friends and otherwise) that the "situation" at Mt. Cashel is definitely at an end and that definite action has been taken.

The reference to "the most recent meeting with the Deputy Minister of Justice, Mr. McCarthy" indicates that there was at least one more session after the December 18 meeting between the Christian Brothers and the Justice Department over the Mount Cashel affair. But if the man who attended that meeting, Brother Dermod Nash, recalled the event accurately, it was a puzzling event indeed. Nash would later say in a sworn deposition that the second meeting had been called by Vincent McCarthy to deal with allegations of physical abuse made against Brother Joseph Burke. Nash explained that McCarthy was concerned about Burke's alleged physical brutality because the Deputy Justice Minister's own son attended the high school where Burke taught. But if that was why Vincent McCarthy had called the second meeting, why hadn't he been concerned about Burke when he first learned of his alleged physical abuse? After all, Vincent McCarthy knew by December 18 that allegations had been levelled against five Brothers, including Brother Burke, not just the two who had been banished from the province. Yet McCarthy hadn't dealt with Brothers Burke, Kenny and Short at that time. He knew about them in December but did nothing. A second report of the Mount Cashel affair is requested in March and suddenly the justice system, in the person of Vincent McCarthy, is dealing with the same Brothers for the same allegations that had been made against them more than two months earlier. The question is why?

Depending on the timing of the meeting with Vincent McCarthy referred to in Brother Nash's memo, it might have had to do with Det. Robert Hillier's second report, which contained information that hadn't been mentioned in his previous report. In the March 3 report, Hillier made reference to the fact that a lady involved with "Human Rights" had made tapes with boys at Mount Cashel and intended to make them public, pending "the decision of the Justice Department on this matter." Faced with the possibility of a major public scandal, and the fact that he had already decided not to lay charges, Vincent McCarthy would have been in a difficult spot.

As long as the extent of the scandal lay hidden in the Deputy Minister's own files, he had this comfort: even if the abuses of Brother English and Brother Ralph became public through another source, McCarthy could make a reasonable defence of his decision. In the interests of preserving public faith in an important institution, he had exercised prosecutorial discretion by not charging the two Christian Brothers, but he had also taken very definite action in the interests of both the boys of Mount Cashel and society at large. The Christian Brothers were to provide psychiatric care for their fallen members, and English and Ralph were never to return to Newfoundland. It was still a very dicey proposition, but in terms of damage control, the exposure of government from both a Justice and Social Services perspective would be reduced by the conditions McCarthy could argue he had imposed on the Brothers.

But if allegations against other Brothers named in Hillier's December 18 report were to become public from another source, such as the tapes of Mount Cashel boys mentioned in the detective's second report, McCarthy would be dangerously vulnerable. In such circumstances, the Deputy Minister would have to explain why he hadn't taken action against the other three Brothers mentioned in Hillier's first report. That, in turn, would have led to the extremely compromising fact that the detectives of the CID had been called off on the orders of the Justice Department before these very serious allegations had been properly investigated, an action that would fuel allegations of a cover-up. Beyond that, McCarthy would also have to explain why he had refused to share information requested by Newfoundland's Director of Child Welfare respecting the welfare of children under his care, children who had been grotesquely mistreated.

Given that English and Ralph were already in treatment outside the province and the deal with the Christian Brothers was done, one of McCarthy's only options would be to set up another meeting to deal with the remaining Brothers who were mentioned in Hillier's first report but whom he had not dealt with in his December 18 meeting with Brother Nash and Brother McHugh. Then if the story broke, McCarthy could at least say that, although he had exercised prosecutorial discretion in not laying charges as a result of Hillier's investigation at Mount Cashel, he had taken other strong measures to protect the residents of Mount Cashel and the public. Otherwise, his arrangement with the Christian Brothers would make it appear that he had sent two Brothers away to avoid a scandal and assisted others to escape justice because of their standing in the community.

As for item number four in Nash's March 18 memo to McHugh, could the "strongly expressed" need for the Congregation to make public the fact that Mount Cashel was undergoing real change be aimed at the lady with the tapes who was, as Detective Hillier put it in his report, "awaiting the decision of the Justice Department in this matter"?

Whatever the explanation for the strange events of March 1976, Brother Gabriel McHugh wasn't slow in carrying out his end of the bargain as dictated by Vincent McCarthy – either on his own initiative or on the instructions of others. On April 10, McHugh wrote a very telling letter to Mount Cashel's Superintendent, Brother Douglas Kenny, who was by that time in Rome on a tertianship, or sabbatical. McHugh's letter gently informed him of the outcome of the Mount Cashel investigation and the fact that he wouldn't be going back to the orphanage. Kenny had adopted a religious name – DePaul – and McHugh shortened it in his affectionate salutation:

Dear Dip,
Greetings from Canada where "spring has sprung."

The weather has warmed up and all signs of life have returned. No doubt the Italian countryside is magnificent at
this time.

I sincerely hope that the tertianship is a good experience
for you. God knows, you needed a rest! It is probably only
now that you realize how tired you were after years
without a proper vacation.

The final report on the "Mount Cashel affair" is
completed. You will be happy to know that no accusations
have been levelled against you whatsoever. As you will
recall our discussing so many times, your only implication
was not moving on the situation soon enough. That was an
error of judgement which any of us could have and may
have made. I pray that you will have peace of mind now
over the whole matter. Many thanks for your support
and cooperation during that difficult time and indeed
throughout your term of office in Mount Cashel. You
have much to be proud of and thankful for.

It was a strange way of telling Brother Kenny that
Newfoundland's Deputy Minister of Justice had ordered
that he not be reassigned to Mount Cashel. It was also a
strange way of depicting the information contained in
Detective Hillier's second report, which in fact contained
allegations from five boys that Kenny had both sexually and
physically abused them.

McHugh then informed "Dip" that his new assignment
for the next year would be at Vancouver College, where the
Brother Provincial hoped Kenny would be "able to assist
with the boarders. . . . I feel sure, also, that for awhile you
will not want too many reminders of the painful experience
of December. Vancouver will take care of that too."

April 10 must have been Gabriel McHugh's day for tying
up loose ends in the Mount Cashel affair. On the same day
that he informed Brother Kenny of his new posting, he wrote
to the principal of St. Thomas More Collegiate, a Christian
Brother institution in Burnaby, British Columbia, and
revealed his plans for Brother Edward English.

"He [English] will prove to be a more flexible and dynamic

personality. He has been quite successful at Pius X. He became involved in a Mt. Cashel situation during the year primarily because of his overemphasis on corporal punishment. This has been rectified and will not be a difficulty."

Brother Gabriel McHugh knew very well that Brother Edward English hadn't been ordered out of Newfoundland "primarily because of his overemphasis on corporal punishment," just as the pedophile's lengthy psychiatric care hadn't been arranged because he'd gotten carried away with a strap or stick.

But there was something even more surprising about Brother McHugh's letter to Brother C. H. Slattery than its blatant lie: Despite the fact that the minimum six-month treatment that Reverend Doctor Kane of the House of Affirmation had said Brother English would require was less than half over, Gabriel McHugh was already putting the deeply troubled monk back into the system.

With the psychiatric treatment still ongoing, how could he possibly know that Brother English would be cured?

By spring 1976, the investigators of the CID had fresh cause to discuss the place that still left a bad taste in their mouths — the Mount Cashel Orphanage. CID investigators were looking into the allegation that certain Christian Brothers were taking residents out of the orphanage and driving them to the Harbour Arterial Road, a new highway under construction that ran west from the city to the TransCanada Highway, where they were beaten. Over coffee, Art Pike mentioned to the customary group gathered in the general CID office that an investigation into the situation was about to get under way. Another officer, Det. Robert Pearcey from the Morals Section, quickly brought up the previous investigation into Mount Cashel.

"It will be the same as what went on before," he said. "You'll get nowhere with it because we have too many Roman Catholics."

Another CID investigator chimed in that they should go down and lay informations at the Magistrate's Court, get warrants, and go over to Mount Cashel and arrest the

Brothers involved. Afterwards, the Justice Department could do whatever it wanted. As Pearcey was enthusiastically seconding the idea, a tall figure walked out of the Inspector's office, which was close to the door of the CID office. His scowl made clear that the walls indeed had ears. Chief John Lawlor was not amused.

"... He overheard this general conversation. ... His eye contact focused on me, for what reason I don't know," Pearcey later recalled. "I didn't care less anyway. But he let me know, and the rest of us in the office, that if we continued stuff like this, that he was the Chief of Police and we'd be charged under the Police Act. So the conversation was more or less hushed."

As it turned out, Chief Lawlor wasn't the only person who didn't appreciate Pearcey's disdain for the Brothers and the Justice Department's handling of the Mount Cashel scandal. A few weeks later, Pearcey met Father Kevin Molloy in Fitzpatrick's Body Shop on Blackmarsh Road. Pearcey knew the Catholic priest from his work on a drug education program offered by the police. A brief conversation was struck up and the subject turned to Mount Cashel.

"I told him that I didn't feel what was going on was right or proper. And as I recall, Kevin Molloy said to me, 'Bob,' he said, 'They can't all be blamed for one or two. The good name of Mount Cashel has done good.'

"And I said, 'Kevin, I don't agree with you. I think they should be arrested.'. ... His body language told me that he didn't agree with me."

The final official act in the Mount Cashel affair belonged to Vincent McCarthy. On January 26, 1977, more than a year after the Mount Cashel investigation, he wrote a brief note to then Chief of Police John Browne. It was the first and only official word from the Justice Department on what had been done as a result of Detective Hillier's reports.

"I return herewith your reports dated September 18, 1975 [sic] and March 3, 1976, respecting child abuse at Mount Cashel. If McCarthy had indeed used the Justice Minister's name falsely in requesting the second report, it was odd that he sent documented proof of that serious offence to another official source.

"I also enclose copies of letters received from Brother McHugh and Reverend Dr. Thomas A. Kane which are self-explanatory. In view of the action taken by the Christian Brothers, further police action is unwarranted in this matter."

Sixteen days later, on Feburary 11, 1977, Vincent Patrick McCarthy was appointed a judge of the District Court. On vacating the Justice Department, the only trace of the Mount Cashel affair he left behind were copies of the two letters from McHugh and Kane, and his own note to Chief Browne referring to "child abuse" at the orphanage. In a flagrant departure from normal practice, no copies of either of Hillier's reports were retained for the Justice Department file.

Although it could be argued that sending the reports to Browne and retaining a letter to that effect in the files of the Justice Department was not the act of a person anxious to conceal what he had done, either on his own or at the behest of others, there was really no choice. To destroy the file or take it with him would have been clear proof of stealth and a guilty mind on McCarthy's part, should the scandal ever resurface. But by sending it to the police, with the clear instruction that no further police action was warranted, the case was closed, and Hillier's reports effectively became dead letters within the system.

Given the slavish relationship between senior police officers and the Justice Department, it was very unlikely that Chief Browne would challenge the Deputy Minister's decision, particularly since the police already had copies of the Hillier reports and weren't getting anything from McCarthy they hadn't seen before. In effect, McCarthy had both dealt with the Mount Cashel reports and taken them out of the system in the same stroke. He could never be accused of covering up Hillier's police reports, but at the same time, no one who might take exception to how he had handled the matter, like the solicitor for the Director of Child Welfare, would now be stumbling across the documents in the files at the Justice Department.

By the time Judge McCarthy took up his place on the bench, Brother English and Brother Ralph had been back in their teaching careers for months, Brother Douglas Kenny had been reassigned to the Vancouver College, Brother Joseph Burke had been transferred out of Mount Cashel to St. Bonaventure's College in St. John's, and Brother Kevin Short would soon be leaving his teaching position at St. Patrick's Hall to become principal of St. Thomas More Collegiate in British Columbia.

At last, the deal was done.

Father James Hickey organized a mammoth youth rally for the Prince and Princess of Wales during their royal visit to Newfoundland in 1983.

Carol Earle with sons, six-year-old Shane Earle (left) and ten-year-old Billy Earle (right).

Mount Cashel Orphanage, founded in 1898 by the Congregation of Irish Christian Brothers.

R.N.C. detective Robert Hillier feared his investigation into child abuse at Mount Cashel would be quashed by authorities.

It was Brother Joseph Burke's alleged beating of Shane Earle in 1975 that touched off the Newfoundland Constabulary's investigation of physical and sexual abuse of Mount Cashel boys.

In 1989, shortly after the R.N.C. reopened the 1975 Mount Cashel case, former Superintendent Douglas Kenny was charged with eleven counts of physically and sexually abusing boys at the orphanage.

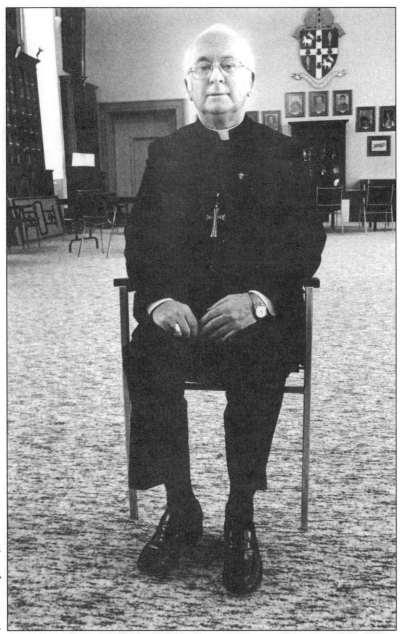

(Ned Pratt photo)

Archbishop Alphonsus Penney, after failing for several months to provide counselling to victims, called upon Catholics to participate in two days of prayer designed to encourage forgiveness for accused priests. His handling of the scandal would later lead to his resignation.

Days before Gordon Seabright passed sentence on Father Ronald Kelly, the Provincial Court judge discussed sentencing options with the Bishop of Corner Brook, Richard McGrath.

In December 1975, Gabriel McHugh made a lightning trip to St. John's to arrange the removal of two Christian Brothers who had confessed to abusing boys. At that time he made a deal with then Deputy Justice Minister Vincent McCarthy that sent two self-confessed abusers out of the province for life in lieu of criminal charges.

Mary Noonan was legal adviser to the Director of Child Welfare from the mid-seventies until 1985. Noonan was refused access to the 1975 police report documenting physical and sexual abuse of boys at Mount Cashel, but did not challenge her deputy minister's decision.

St. John's lawyer David Day is one of two lawyers who acted as co-counsel to the Hughes Inquiry.

Samuel Hughes heard evidence from 258 witnesses at the Hughes Inquiry. At the end of the inquiry, the seventy-six-year-old commissioner, a retired Ontario Supreme Court Justice, said that the "evil" exposed in 1975 had been in the system for a long time.

Chapter 7
■■■■■ *Keeping the Lid On*

Over a week has passed since the news outbreak. At the moment, all appears calm. However, last night, Premier Peckford called a provincial election for June 18. I'm worried that in the hurly-burly of politics, the Liberal Party may play it "dirty" and the Mount Cashel episode . . . [may be] used to embarrass the Government and still further embarrass our Congregation. I'm afraid we're in for a very difficult month of June. Please keep us in your prayers as we try to weather the shocking revelation. Brother Provincial Gordon Bellows writing to the Superior General of the Congregation of Irish Christian Brothers in Rome concerning the unexpected public re-emergence of the Mount Cashel scandal in 1979.

RISING MODESTLY ABOVE the neat rows of bungalows that surround it, the Elizabeth Towers apartment building in central St. John's was home to more than a few of Newfoundland's most prominent figures in the 1970s. High-rolling land-developers, old outport money in need of a winter home in the capital city and out-of-town political potentates all kept luxury apartment suites there, relishing the privacy and prestige of the city's best high-rise address. Frank Moores, then Premier of Newfoundland, had the use of an apartment in Elizabeth Towers, as did his Minister of Industrial Development, Dr. Tom Farrell, the hard-drinking Irishman Moores cajoled into leaving Corner Brook for St. John's, and medicine for politics. Ironically, it would be a fire at the exclusive apartment complex that would bring the Mount Cashel scandal to the surface, if only briefly, three years after the Justice Department deal with the Christian Brothers that buried it.

At 6 A.M. on the morning of April 26, 1978, Dr. Farrell

awakened to flames licking up around his mattress and engulfing the drapes in his bedroom. Although he had been drinking heavily the night before and was still feeling the effects, he quickly jumped out of bed and staggered through the thick, acrid smoke that filled the apartment, fighting his way to the hall outside. There, between coughs and clad only in his underwear, the bear-like Farrell sounded the alarm. Shortly after the fire department had doused the blaze and those puffy-eyed residents who were permitted to had returned to their apartments, the Criminal Investigation Division of the Newfoundland Constabulary arrived. Det.-Insp. Donald Randell ordered the Assault Section of the CID, headed up by Arthur Pike, now Detective Sergeant, to take part in the investigation. Pike, in turn, assigned Det. Robert Hillier to the case.

The Assault Section assisted in fire investigations only when there was a strong suspicion of arson. In the case of the Farrell fire, the Minister was then embroiled in a political scandal swirling around his involvement with flamboyant mining promoter John C. Doyle. Doyle had been one of the industrial kingpins in former premier Joey Smallwood's development dreams for Newfoundland. It had been Doyle's promotional flair that founded one of the largest iron ore mines in the world at Wabush in Labrador. The Stephenville Linerboard Mill, another of Doyle's castles in the economic sky of the province, ended less auspiciously in a huge and scandalous bankruptcy.

The cigar-puffing Chicagoan was eventually charged with more than four hundred counts of wash trading (a pretended sale to make the market appear active, thereby inflating a stock's price) in the stock of Canadian Javelin, a mining company headquartered in Montreal. Rather than answering the charges, Doyle fled to Panama where he took up residence in a luxurious, two-floor penthouse suite in downtown Panama City. But the millionaire fugitive with a fondness for beautiful French-Candian women and a maestro's touch at the organ kept up his contact with Newfoundland, principally in an effort to have the wash trading charges against him dropped by the provincial Justice Department – a decision that would clear the way for his return to Canada. He was already banned from entering his native United States because of a former conviction for selling unregistered stock through the mails.

Documents tabled by the Liberal Opposition in the House of Assembly just before the Elizabeth Towers fire showed that Farrell's recent stay in Panama had been paid for by John C. Doyle. As word of the Farrell fire spread through St. John's, fuelled by stories that former premier Joey Smallwood, who remained very close to Doyle, had been desperately trying to get in touch with Frank Moores on the eve of the fire, more than one political hand assumed that the beleaguered Minister had set the fire himself to destroy other documents that would link him to the fugitive promoter.

Public interest in the case was intense. The Progressive Conservative government of Frank Moores was lurching from scandal to scandal, and there was a sense that the Farrell fire might be the straw that would break the political back of the rascal from Harbour Grace who had knocked off Joey Smallwood after two decades of his Liberal hegemony. As a former associate of Moores put it, "There are bastards and charming bastards. Frank is a charming bastard."

Detective Hillier's first task on the morning of the 26th was to disperse a crowd of municipal and provincial politicians who wanted to tour the scene of the controversial fire. Hillier told a nearby fireman that he would charge the politicians with obstruction of justice if they came near the scene. Having already seen the fishtailing pattern of accelerant (the substance believed to have started the fire) on the floor leading from Farrell's bedroom to the apartment's front door, the policeman had little doubt that he was investigating a blatant case of arson. The last thing he needed was gossipy curiosity seekers poking around in potential evidence.

Three months after the fire, on June 7, 1978, Detective Hillier sent his report to Newfoundland's Director of Public Prosecutions, John Kelly. After reading the report, Kelly forwarded it to senior Crown prosecutor Robert Hyslop, requesting his written opinion on the file. Kelly believed the investigators had reached a premature conclusion in deciding that Farrell himself had set the blaze; he also thought their police work had been poorly done. Hyslop came to the same conclusion. On June 14, Kelly wrote to Chief of Police John Browne and asked that twenty-four points in Hillier's report be clarified before the Department of Justice decided what action, if any, to take.

It had not been easy for Det. Robert Hillier to deal with the memories of his investigation into the orphanage, and Kelly's request left him "feeling like it was Mount Cashel all over again." On July 12, Hillier forwarded a second report to the Justice Department, a document that answered many, though not all, of the questions Kelly had raised. As he had in his first report, Hillier once again concluded that the Elizabeth Towers fire had been deliberately set by Farrell. Although Kelly and Hyslop were satisfied that a crime had been committed, based on the evidence Hillier presented to them, they were still not "completely satisfied" with his conclusions and decided to consult the Deputy Attorney-General, George Macaulay. It was Macaulay's opinion that Detective-Inspector Randell himself should be put in charge of gathering the additional information justice officials agreed was still missing from Hillier's second report.

The handling of the Farrell fire report provoked a shoving match between Detective Hillier and the Director of Public Prosecutions, John Kelly, when the pair ran into each other in a hotel bar after the policeman had handed in his reports.

"This gentleman was very critical about the Elizabeth Towers fire investigation and also there was comments made about Mount Cashel. . . . Well, he wasn't happy with it and said I should be quiet about it," Hillier recalled. Kelly confirmed the confrontation, explaining that he was "a bit perturbed" by comments Hillier was making about Vincent McCarthy, who was by then a judge.

Chief John Browne was given ten days to have Randell, his senior CID officer, produce a third report on the Farrell fire. On July 31, Detective-Inspector Randell was ordered to discuss the case with the Deputy Attorney-General, who told him that he wanted the report back within a week. Randell also talked to Crown prosecutor Robert Hyslop about the case before commencing his reinvestigation. None of the justice officials had kind words for the police work done on the politically sensitive case, and George Macaulay was openly angry about the slipshod approach investigators had, in his opinion, so far exhibited.

The detective quickly realized that it would be impossible to finish the investigation according to the schedule laid down by the Justice Department. He was expected to interview Dr. Farrell again, but the Cabinet minister was by then vacationing at his summer home in the Codroy Valley on the west coast of the province. Another needed interviewee, Dr. Farrell's son, was already back in Ottawa. Finally, Robert Hillier, whom Randell wanted to see before the final report went up to Justice, was also on vacation.

It would be twenty-two days before Randell's reinvestigation of the Farrell fire would be completed. As Randell's work dragged on, public opinion hardened that a cover-up was in progress — a suspicion that was carefully nurtured by the political Opposition, which sniffed a provincial election in the air and believed the Farrell fire was a controversy that could carry the Grits to power.

On or about August 1, Det.-Sgt. Arthur Pike was called back from his vacation in St. Anthony to speak to Randell about the controversial case. Pike made the fateful decision to fly back to St. John's on the provincial government aircraft. While waiting to board his flight, Pike got into a conversation with the Premier's private secretary, Barbara Nugent, in which he mentioned the Farrell investigation. Nugent immediately informed senior Cabinet ministers of her discussion with the detective, who in turn reported Pike's unprofessional indiscretion to the Minister of Justice. When Pike got back to St. John's, he was promptly pulled off the case by Detective-Inspector Randell.

"I did speak to Mrs. Nugent and Dr. Farrell's name did come up briefly at the airport before we left. I attempted to explain this to Inspector Randell. . . . He didn't ask me what happened. I tried to explain to him but he didn't appear to want to listen," Pike would later testify at an inquiry into the matter.

Disgruntled and suspicious, Pike surreptitiously made

copies of Hillier's first two reports into the Farrell fire and took them home, determined to use them if the necessity ever arose.

On August 16, 1978, Detective-Inspector Randell submitted the third CID report on the Farrell fire to the Justice Department. Once more, officials weren't satisfied with the quality of the police work. Yet another report into the controversial case, the fourth, was ordered by the Deputy Attorney-General. It was too much for Arthur Pike, who had been through the Mount Cashel cover-up and wasn't prepared to tolerate what he believed was another one in the making. On September 16, he invited the editor of *The Daily News*, a newspaper of Liberal persuasion in St. John's, to come over to his house for a chat.

The detective showed editor James Thoms copies of Hillier's two reports, convinced that the Justice Department was refusing to act because Farrell was a prominent member of Cabinet. Thoms took his notes of the meeting with Pike to his publisher, William Callahan, a former Smallwood Cabinet minister. Callahan telephoned Deputy Attorney-General Macaulay and informed him that the newspaper had the two police reports and asked when charges would be laid against Farrell. Macaulay said he didn't know if Justice would be taking further action in the matter. On September 21, *The Daily News* published a story about the investigation, but didn't mention Dr. Farrell's name.

Having leaked the contents of Hillier's reports to the press, Pike next got in touch with the leader of the Liberal Opposition, William Rowe, the handsome young lawyer who was widely expected to defeat Frank Moores at the next provincial election. Rowe, also a former Smallwood Cabinet minister, picked up Pike at his house and drove around the streets of St. John's, discussing the Farrell situation. The politician had the impression that the policeman had been drinking, although there was no smell of liquor on Pike's breath. Neither man realized that both of their careers would very shortly be ruined by their involvement in the Farrell case.

"He was talking to me about a cover-up, about the fact that the investigation into the Elizabeth Towers fire ...

because he knew there was a cover-up and foot-dragging going on. He indicated that there were a couple of incidents . . . in early August . . . whereby he may have divulged some information and that this may also have led to his dismissal from the case as an investigator," Rowe later testified.

Rowe asked Pike if he could see the reports he suspected the detective had already leaked to *The Daily News,* an accusation Pike vehemently denied. Pike refused to produce them. Rowe dropped off his coy informant but later that same Saturday night received a telephone call from Pike, who said he had something to show him. Rowe picked up Pike for a second time and they parked in the city's west end to discuss the matter further. Pike finally agreed to give the police reports to Rowe.

On September 26, 1978, the eager politician made several copies of the two reports and then telephoned the most senior news reporters and editors in St. John's, offering copies of the explosive documents. All of them wanted the leaked police report, although few, as it turned out, would use them. Rowe placed the reports in brown envelopes and had them delivered to various newsrooms around the city by his executive assistant of the day, and now federal Liberal MP, Brian Tobin.

The next day, *The Evening Telegram* ran a front-page story quoting from the police reports which unequivocally fingered Farrell as the person who had set the fire in his own apartment. A little over two weeks later, after the fourth police report into the Farrell fire had been submitted to the Justice Department by the CID, the Conservative Cabinet minister was charged with arson. Two months later, with the future Newfoundland Premier, Clyde Wells, representing him, all charges against Farrell were dropped at his preliminary hearing. Under questioning from Wells at the preliminary hearing, Pike said he leaked the report because of "other investigations which had been shelved," a comment he was later asked to explain by Chief of Police John Browne.

"He asked me what I meant when I said I was aware reports were shelved and nothing was done. . . . I told him about Mount Cashel, what had happened. I told him about the investigation that was done by Detective Hillier and how it had been stopped, and how it was covered up. . . . His reply to that was, 'I wasn't Chief of Police at the time of the Mount Cashel investigation. Anyway, these fellows were sick and they've been sent away for treatment.' I said, 'We have not received any communication' – 'we' meaning my section – 'informing us as to the disposition of these reports.'. . . He said, 'From now on I will make sure we get a reply on any reports we send to the Justice Department.' "

Incensed by the smear tactics against a minister of the Crown, and alive to the political opportunity the Farrell scandal presented to destroy William Rowe for his ill-considered role in the affair, the Moores government quickly appointed an inquiry to look into the circumstances surrounding the unauthorized release of police reports concerning the Elizabeth Towers fire. The inquiry was headed up by Judge Lloyd Soper, a Provincial Court judge. A total of twenty-one witnesses gave testimony in a makeshift courtroom in a building at Torbay Airport in St. John's. One of the star witnesses was Detective-Sergeant Pike, who would be demoted to Patrol-Sergeant for life for leaking Hillier's police reports on the Elizabeth Towers fire.

Pike told the Soper Inquiry that he felt there was a possibility of a cover-up going on at the time because of "the fact that the investigation was being dragged out so long." He also testified about "other investigative reports where action was recommended, had gone to the proper channels to the Justice Department where no action was taken." Judge Soper reluctantly decided that the hearings should go "in camera" to hear Pike's evidence about the "other cases" that concerned him.

Although he cited three cases, his key example of the system gone wrong was the 1975 Mount Cashel investigation. Pike explained that the investigation had started out as an assault complaint by a child resident of Mount Cashel, but turned into a nightmare of widespread sexual and physical assault allegations against the Christian Brothers, which were officially covered up.

"Hillier complained to me that the Chief of Police at the time had asked him to change the report to make two reports out of the one, to separate the assaults from the sexual activities. And he didn't feel that he should do this because it was all contained in the one. . . . I, in turn, spoke to the Assistant Chief at the time and he told me that this request had come from the Deputy Minister. . . . As far as I know, the reports were not changed. . . .

"Well, you know, when this thing began to drag out in the Farrell case, I said, 'Well, what's going to happen to this, you know, [is] the same as some of these other . . . the Mount Cashel [case],' and if I remember correctly, Hillier said, 'You know, this could end up the same as Mount Cashel.' "

Pike outlined his dealings with John Kelly, including an alleged threat by Kelly that he would stay proceedings against Farrell if the police charged the politician on their own. Pike also testified that Kelly had called the CID, looking for information on the 1975 police report into Mount Cashel that he had apparently never seen. Specifically, Kelly asked Pike about two children who were facing wardship hearings, and who may also have been involved in the 1975 police investigation into the orphanage.

Kelly was later called to the Soper Inquiry to defend his department's treatment of various cases mentioned by Pike, including Mount Cashel. Ironically, Kelly never tried to obtain the police reports Vincent McCarthy had sent to Chief Browne in 1977, even though the purpose of his testimony was to defend the manner in which the Justice Department had dealt with controversial cases like Mount Cashel.

Kelly explained that all he could remember about the Mount Cashel case was that the solicitor for Social Services, Mary Noonan, had once asked him if he knew about the 1975 incident at the orphanage. Kelly told her he had no knowledge of the case. A year or so later, he said that he learned that the Deputy Attorney-General at that time, Vincent McCarthy, had agreed with the Chief of Police that no charges should be laid in the case, and that they had an undertaking from the Christian Brothers that the offending Brothers would be sent away, never again to be in charge of young boys.

"I have never seen the report," Kelly testified, "other than knowing or hearing from one of the detectives that no action was taken on that report but again, that is a prosecutorial discretion . . . charges would not be laid if psychiatric steps were taken or if sometimes the accused gets out of the jurisdiction. You know, he is out of our hair. This is a decision that prosecutors make quite often."

Judge Soper and commission counsel Fred Woolridge were both apparently satisfied with Kelly's woefully inadequate answer. The proceedings moved along, paying little heed to testimony that would, fourteen years later, prompt Newfoundland's Premier of the day to call a royal commission.

A little over a month after it was taken, Arthur Pike's in camera testimony was made public by Judge Soper. On May 17, *The Daily News* reported Pike's testimony essentially as he had given it − the first public reference to the 1975 Mount Cashel investigation that had ever been made.

"The policeman who was demoted after admitting he leaked the fire reports gave instances of investigations being carried out and then shelved − as he came to suspect the Elizabeth Towers investigation might be . . . the case of three Christian Brothers alleged to have sexually assaulted two children at Mount Cashel in 1975."

CBC Radio gave the same coverage as *The Daily News*, broadcasting the bare fact of an alleged 1975 cover-up of a sex scandal at Mount Cashel. *The Evening Telegram*'s Ron Budgell took a different approach, perfectly in keeping with the paper's 1975 decision to suppress the story that two of its own reporters had unearthed. All references to Mount Cashel and the Brothers were expunged from the copy, an editorial decision whose impact the Christian Brothers themselves quickly realized was to their advantage. The *Telegram* story was conveniently vague.

"The second case Pike brought up was one involving an investigation into alleged assault and sexual assault

incidents on the part of three men against young boys. No
charges were laid as a result of the investigation, although,
Pike reported, the investigator thought there was sufficient
evidence. . . .

"Kelly said it is not unusual for a prosecutor to decide not
to press charges, 'if psychiatric steps were taken or if
sometimes the accused gets out of our jurisdiction.'

"In this case, the three men were transferred to the
United States and would not be in a position to repeat
the offences."

Although this belated public reference to the Mount
Cashel affair didn't blow up into a public controversy, it
didn't escape the vigilance of the Christian Brothers, who
were still extremely nervous about the three-year-old
skeleton in their closet. A week after the public disclosures at
the Soper Inquiry, Brother Gordon Bellows, one of two
Brothers who had met Gabriel McHugh when he flew from
Mono Mills to St. John's in 1975 to deal with the Mount
Cashel crisis, wrote the Superior General of the order in
Rome a detailed letter informing him of the latest turn of
events.

Dear Gabe,

I have the sad task of informing you that the Mt. Cashel
incident of the fall of 1975 (involving three monks) became public last week in St. John's and was reported in the
media. It happened this way:

A Sergeant Pike of the St. John's police force – who did
the original investigation of the Mount Cashel case – was
involved in the Dr. Tom Farrell episode concerning a fire
in Elizabeth Towers. Before the Justice Department's
report on the Farrell case was officially released, Pike
slipped a copy of it to Bill Rowe, Leader of the Opposition, on the pretext that the Justice Department intended
to bury the Farrell Report. After Rowe had given the
details of the Report to the media, there was a hue and cry
in the police department about the release of confidential
documents and Pike was identified as the "leak." He was
demoted consequently and suffered a loss in salary. In

retaliation, he indicated he had acted to prevent "cover ups" similar to the ones that he alleged had taken place in the past. Because of this allegation, he was called before an "in camera" court session presided over by Judge Soper. Later, Soper released Pike's testimony which identified three cases of "cover-up": including that of Mount Cashel. In reference to Mount Cashel, Pike revealed that "three American CB's had been involved in improper behaviour, that their Superior had acted immediately and that one was sent to a psychiatric institution and the others back to the U.S." CBC-Radio repeated this item verbatim, *The Telegram* edited it circumspectly to render it harmless, but *The Daily News* quite clearly reported it unchanged.

You can imagine the shock and embarrassment of the monks in Newfoundland at this unexpected revelation – since so many of them had absolutely no inkling whatsoever of the episode. Over a week has passed since the news outbreak. At the moment, all appears calm. However, last night, Premier Peckford called a provincial election for June 18. I'm worried that in the hurly-burly of politics, the Liberal party may play it "dirty" and the Mount Cashel episode, (together with other confidential Justice Department Reports) [may be] used to embarrass the Government and still further embarrass our Congregation.

I'm afraid we're in for a very difficult month of June.

Please keep us in your prayers as we try to weather the shocking revelation. I'll keep you posted of further happenings.

In Christ,
[Gordon]

Another interested party in the events coming out of the Soper Inquiry was Crown prosecutor Robert Hyslop. Disturbed by Pike's allegations, the future judge decided to look into the matter to see "what the commotion was about" over Mount Cashel. Hyslop approached Mary Noonan, the solicitor for the Social Services department, and was taken to see a file on the fifth floor of Confederation Building. At the time, Noonan handled all files dealing with cases of child abuse.

"I recall she showed me a brown file folder. . . . She opened a filing drawer in the main office and [took out] a brown file folder containing three pieces of correspondence. [The] folder was labelled: 'Mount Cashel: Child Abuse,' " Hyslop would later testify.

It contained Vincent McCarthy's letter to Chief Browne informing him that no further police action was required, the letter Brother Gabriel McHugh had written to McCarthy in January 1976, and a letter from the House of Affirmation attesting to the fact that Brother English was receiving psychiatric help in the United States. Hyslop handed the file back to Noonan, satisfied that the matter had been properly concluded by the head of the department, and that Noonan's knowledge of the case was restricted to the documents in the file. But the Crown prosecutor did note a few oddities – the police report on the Mount Cashel affair, which should have been in the justice file, was missing. And Vincent McCarthy's letter to John R. Browne was marked "personal and confidential," an "unusual" departure from the normal way of addressing mail to the Chief of Police, since all correspondence between them was considered to be private.

For her part, Mary Noonan would later deny Robert Hyslop's very clear recollection of having been shown the Mount Cashel file. Neither, apparently, did Noonan read newspapers, listen to the radio or talk to colleagues about the then public details of Arthur Pike's in camera testimony. Had she become aware of the fact that Robert Hillier's investigation into Mount Cashel dealt with wide-ranging allegations of sexual and physical abuse against children, she would, no doubt, have quickly connected it to the events of 1975, when she had twice been denied access to the same mysterious police report. But just as she had been one of the only people in the Justice Department who hadn't heard rumours of what was happening at Mount Cashel in 1975, Mary Noonan was once more completely unaware of developments in a story in which she had a declared professional interest.

On August 16, 1979, Judge Soper submitted his report to Newfoundland's Lieutenant-Governor, Gordon Winter. The judge tore a broad strip off Patrol-Sgt. Arthur Pike.

"There was no justification for his releasing police reports to William Rowe or to any other person. . . . It appears to me at the time Pike was not in that emotional state which would enable him to take a completely objective view of the investigation. Indeed, his approach brings into question his usefulness as an investigating officer . . . Pike conducted himself in a manner unbecoming to a member of a police force. He was reduced in rank from a detective sergeant to a patrol sergeant, with a consequent reduction in rate of salary. He considered that he was 'severely punished,' to use his own description of the consequences of his actions, but in my view he was treated leniently. His conduct would have justified dismissal."

In rejecting Pike's claim that he leaked the Farrell fire report because he feared another cover-up, Judge Soper rejected the so-called "other instances" of judicial interference alluded to by Pike.

"In each instance, he [Kelly] was able to give an acceptable reason for not prosecuting. The only possible criticism that may be made was the failure of the Department to ensure that the police knew why the prosecutions had not been proceeded with."

If Pike's promising future in the Newfoundland Constabulary was now blighted, so too was Bill Rowe's brilliant political career. In the wake of his involvement in the Farrell scandal, he was deposed by his own caucus on the eve of the provincial election and replaced as party leader by federal war-horse Don Jamieson. But the Liberals remained under a cloud and the Tories were quick to take advantage of their dilemma. Less than a month after the inquiry began, Frank Moores officially stepped down as Conservative leader to be replaced by a fiery newcomer from Green Bay, suddenly shifting the political balance in favour of the previously wobbly PCs. At the end of the day, Jamieson lost both his voice and the election to the PC's young lion,

Brian Peckford. Tantalizingly close to power before the Farrell fire, after June 18, 1979, the Liberals faced another decade in the political wilderness.

"If there was no justification for Pike's actions there was still less for those of William Rowe," Judge Soper sourly observed, issuing both his verdict on the politician's behaviour and his political epitaph.

Sitting on the sidelines, Det. Robert Hillier had mixed feelings towards his former boss and colleague, Arthur Pike. Pike's theft and subsequent leaking of Hillier's reports had ruined the close friendship between the two police officers. But Hillier still felt a sense of loyalty to the man who shared his anger at the interference in the Mount Cashel investigation. Hillier went to bat for his disgraced colleague with Newfoundland's new Justice Minister, Gerald Ottenheimer.

"He [Pike] had been charged with leaking police documents . . . which I believe led back to the Mount Cashel investigation. And I was trying to convince these people, 'Please don't let him fall by the wayside.' I know he did wrong, he breached the Police Act. . . . I was trying to convince them to give him a pension. And I flew from St. John's in the government aircraft with both these gentlemen and . . . tried to convince these people that Mr. Pike was wrong, but he was partly right."

The scandal had run its course. Although Tom Farrell would be cleared of setting the blaze at his Elizabeth Towers apartment, and awarded what at that time was the largest defamation settlement in Canadian history, the "crime" that justice officials were convinced had been committed was never solved, raising the question of whether it had ever really been a case of arson at all.

But one thing was certain: the echo of Mount Cashel raised by the Farrell affair was quickly stifled in the judicial humiliation of the two men who choked on the whistle they tried to blow.

Chapter 8
Fatherly Treatment

He stated that he didn't believe that he should be treated in this way . . . just the arrest and search of him. He did not believe he should be treated this way because of his position. . . . His immediate response was something to the effect that 'Don't matters such as this have to be cleared through the Department of Justice?' . . . RCMP Sgt. Kenneth LeBreton, describing the reaction of Father Ronald Hubert Kelly after being arrested on ten charges of indecent assault.

IN THE SPRING of 1979, Newfoundland's publicity-shy Roman Catholic hierarchy had more things to worry about than the potentially damaging revelations of the Soper Inquiry.

At nine o'clock sharp on the morning of April 30, 1979, Corporal Gerald Tabor, supervisor of the Piccadilly detachment of the RCMP on the west coast of the island, received a complaint that a Father Ronald Kelly had indecently assaulted a fifteen-year-old boy in his parish. After a preliminary investigation, Corporal Tabor turned up unsettling rumours about Father Kelly and several other youths in the small community of De Grau where the priest lived – whispers of forbidden activities that had even reached the ears of Sisters in a local lay order of the Roman Catholic church. Strongly suspecting that he wasn't dealing with an isolated incident, and feeling, perhaps, that such a sensitive investigation was too much for the three junior constables assigned to the tiny Piccadilly detachment, Tabor requested assistance from the General Investigation Section (GIS) of the RCMP in Corner Brook.

A few days later, on Thursday May 3, Sgt. Kenneth LeBreton and Constable Murray Urquhart began the breathtaking drive down the winding road that leads from

Corner Brook to the Port au Port Peninsula, with its awesome cliffs and rolling hills falling away gently to the sea. The local communities, home to the peninsula's 7,000 scattered residents, are strung like beads along the lone highway. Constable Urquhart noted in his diary that when you travelled to Port au Port, you always had to leave exactly the same way you came in. Cape St. George, their destination that morning, was where the road came to an end in a spectacular vista of sea and sky. The heart of the community was Our Lady of the Cape Church, where thirty-six-year-old Father Ronald Hubert Kelly had been parish priest since 1973.

The RCMP officers weren't long in finding out that Father Kelly was no ordinary mortal as far as his adoring parishioners were concerned. To the francophone residents of Cape St. George the tall, strikingly good-looking Roman Catholic priest with the shock of blond hair and sparkling blue eyes was a local hero. In addition to his religious duties, he was chairman of the Port au Port school board. He also founded the first Community Council, brought the Girl Guide and Brownie movements to the community, founded the Corps of Army Cadets at Cape St. George, and established a French immersion program – an invaluable service considering the fragile state of Newfoundland's isolated francophone community. In 1978 the provincial government had recognized his talent and industry by appointing Father Kelly to the post of Vice-Chairman of the Bay St. George Community College.

Raised in St. John's, Kelly used the political influence of his father, Hubert Kelly, to lobby for various community improvements in Cape St. George, including the town's first ambulance, in which the sick were often driven to hospital in the middle of the night by Kelly himself. Of independent means, Kelly was generous with his parishioners, the sort of person who could be depended on to lend money in a pinch and not to complain if the borrower were slow in repaying it. Although there were whispers about another side of Kelly, an unspoken foible that dwarfed his serious drinking problem, every door in Cape St. George remained open to him. For the RCMP, it was like investigating Robin Hood.

Luckily for the investigators, the champion of the down-trodden was holidaying in Florida when they arrived in De Grau. "Because of his stature in the community and the immense respect and deep, maybe even at times blind, trust that the people had in him . . . we were probably fortunate that he was out of the community at that time," Sergeant LeBreton later testified.

After talking to the first complainant, who had been fourteen when the priest sexually assaulted him, the RCMP investigators also realized that in all probability one of Father Kelly's favourite community pursuits was young boys. Sitting alone with these boys in their squad car, LeBreton and Urquhart listened in disbelief as a parade of Father Kelly's male victims described their sexual encounters with the often drunken priest.

The policemen preferred to talk to complainants in their car or back at the detachment office in Piccadilly because the boys' parents were plainly "entranced" by Kelly. Had they been able to listen in on what their children told the RCMP investigators, their opinions would have changed faster than the capricious winds that blew across Cape St. George from the shimmering expanse of the Gulf of St. Lawrence, where most of them made their living.

One sixteen-year-old described how Father Kelly had called his house at 4 A.M. in the fall of 1978 summoning him to the rectory. When he arrived, Kelly, who had already been drinking, gave his young guest two glasses of rum before taking him upstairs, ostensibly to watch television. Dragging the boy to the bed, the priest tried to put his hand into his reluctant companion's pants. Unsuccessful, Kelly then groped at the boy's privates through his jeans, exclaiming rather quixotically, "I do not love that, but I love your heart."

Another boy told police about an incident that had taken place during De Grau's annual Garden Party in August 1978. The boy was sent home by his parents for fighting. A little while later, Father Kelly showed up and got into bed with him. Almost immediately, the priest tried to force his hand into the boy's pants. Kelly's own pants were undone and he thrust his exposed penis near the face of his prone companion. The boy pretended to be asleep, and half an hour later Father Kelly got up and left. When the boy later told a friend what had happened, he was advised not to repeat the story to anyone, "because a Priest is a high man" and no one would believe him.

A fifteen-year-old who had been with Father Kelly on at least three separate occasions told police that he and the priest had performed mutual fellatio in the rectory, after which the boy was given five dollars. On one of these occasions, Father Kelly showed no signs of having been drinking.

Perhaps the strangest case involved a young boy who had been sexually assaulted by Father Kelly on a number of occasions with the inadvertent blessing of his mother. After showing up drunk at the boy's home one night, Father Kelly was put to bed by the lady of the house. The priest then asked that her thirteen-year-old son be sent to sleep with him. His hostess obliged, and no sooner had the boy got into bed with the priest than Kelly began fondling his genitals. Kelly told the boy how much he loved him and how much money he had in the bank and that it was the anniversary of his entering the priesthood – all the while continuing his unwelcome stroking.

On another occasion, the same boy was awakened at three or four o'clock in the morning by muffled conversation between his family and Father Kelly. The priest presently appeared in the bedroom, and although the boy's mother tried to convince him to sleep in another room, he climbed into the lower bunkbed with the thirteen-year-old and immediately began fondling the boy after his hostess left. Father Kelly also asked his companion's brother, who was sleeping in the upper bunkbed, to join them; he then lay between the two boys fondling their privates and talking to them. On his way out of the house, he gave one of the boys ten dollars.

A few months later, the same two boys watched in growing apprehension as Father Kelly and their parents played cards late into the night. The priest drank steadily from a bottle of Bacardi rum. When their mother sent them to bed at 4:30 A.M., the boys pushed their bed up against the door so the priest couldn't get into their room. But their sleep was soon disturbed by someone banging on the bedroom door. The frightened boys then heard their mother's voice telling them to let the priest in.

After Kelly had gotten under the covers with them, one of the boys got up and, putting on his jeans, told the priest he had to use the washroom. When he returned, he left his jeans on and purposely lay on top of the covers because Father Kelly was under the blankets, wide awake and waiting for him. Despite his precautions, the young boy soon felt the priest groping at his privates and telling him, "I don't care what's below, it's what's in your heart that counts."

After a short nap, Father Kelly left the house. The boys didn't tell their parents about the incidents because they were afraid no one would believe them. Judging from the response the RCMP got from adults during their investigation, the boys weren't far wrong.

"All the people we interviewed in connection with the victims, all parents expressed dismay and disbelief at the allegations," Sergeant LeBreton later testified.

After interviewing the complainants, their parents, an informant and twenty others who had indirect knowledge of the situation, LeBreton and Urquhart met with top RCMP officials in Corner Brook, including Superintendent William Halloran, to discuss the case. The decision was made to proceed with ten counts of indecent assault. Their commanding officer told the two RCMP officers to treat the priest as they would any other individual — a stark contrast with the instructions given by senior officers of the Newfoundland Constabulary to their men during the 1975 investigation of Mount Cashel Orphanage. As Judge Michael Roche, the Crown prosecutor in the Kelly case, would later testify, his instructions were that police officers not contact him prior to the laying of charges, a right that was jealously guarded in any case by the RCMP.

Constable Urquhart swore an information against Father Kelly alleging ten criminal offences contrary to Section 156: "Every male person who assaults another person with intent to commit buggery or who indecently assaults another male person is guilty of an indictable offence and is liable to imprisonment for ten years."

Believing that the priest was still out of the jurisdiction and fearful that he might not return to Newfoundland if he found out about the police investigation, Urquhart also obtained a warrant for his arrest from Judge Gordon Seabright, which would be needed to apprehend Kelly outside Newfoundland. But while the police were still at the Magistrate's office laying the charges, LeBreton and Urquhart got a call informing them that Father Kelly had returned unexpectedly from his trip and had driven to the RCMP detachment in Piccadilly, "demanding to know what the police were doing asking questions in his parish. . . ."

The two RCMP officers got in their car and drove to Piccadilly. Corporal Tabor telephoned Father Kelly at his home in De Grau and Sergeant LeBreton then asked the priest to come in to the detachment. Shortly after his arrival at 5:10 P.M., the plainclothes RCMP investigators identified themselves to the priest, showed their badges and placed Kelly under arrest. In explaining the charges against him under Section 156 – seven offences alleged to have occurred in De Grau, and three others in Cape St. George, Sergeant LeBreton cautioned the priest. He further explained that the offences against five different boys ranging in age from thirteen to seventeen took place between August 20, 1977, and April 16, 1979. LeBreton was struck by Kelly's reaction.

"His immediate response was something to the effect that 'Don't matters such as this have to be cleared through the Department of Justice?' Or, 'Has this gone through the Department of Justice?' . . . I just told him that was incorrect. . . ."

Kelly, who gave the RCMP the impression that he had many influential friends, including Pierre Trudeau, was then searched by the police officers. In fact, Trudeau and Kelly had become acquaintances after the Prime Minister visited the Port au Port Peninsula in the early seventies to open a French school.

"He stated that he didn't believe that he should be treated

in this way . . . just the arrest and search of him. He did not believe he should be treated this way because of his position," LeBreton later recalled.

Ten minutes after the arrest, the three men began the hour-and-a-half drive from Piccadilly back to Corner Brook, with Urquhart behind the wheel. Corporal Tabor immediately called Superintendent Halloran in Corner Brook and asked what he should do if the media called about Father Kelly. He was told to confirm the fact that an arrest had been made but to decline all further comment until after a court appearance by the accused. The media never called.

Judging from the priest's rambling soliloquy as they drove down the deserted highway, Sergeant LeBreton had the feeling that he was in for a lengthy interview with Father Kelly when they reached "B" Division. After they arrived, the priest was taken to a green-carpeted interview room with two fluorescent lights set in the ceiling. Although the single door to the room had a window, the blind was pulled, sequestering the three men from the outside world for the next five hours. At 6:50 P.M., the priest was again cautioned, and with Urquhart taking notes, LeBreton conducted a remarkable interview in which Kelly, an Export A cigarette dangling from his left hand, talked about his private life in intimate, and telling, detail.

After some preliminary remarks, LeBreton broached the subject of Kelly's alleged indecent assaults on boys.

"How many incidents?" the priest asked.

"I think you have a better idea of that than us. But you have been charged with ten charges."

"Oh. My God. I didn't think it was that."

After initially declining to talk about the charges, Kelly ventured a tentative opinion on what he might have done.

"I can remember being with people, things could have happened. Nothing that went that far to constitute a crime."

Asked if he wanted to make a statement, Kelly snuffed out his cigarette, took off his glasses and rubbed his eyes. With his elbows on the table, he looked at LeBreton, who was sitting across from him, and answered softly.

"I was at people's places and laid down for a rest before going home. . . . Was there anyone that cleared me?"

"Not that I can recall."

Looking nervous for the first time, Father Kelly put his boyish face in his hands and lowered his head to the table. Sergeant LeBreton asked him about putting his hands down boys' pants.

"I been down this road before with regard to other people in the school. I've cleaned up with regard to disease, crabs. . . ." Kelly broke off to rub his eyes and then asked if he could speak to the policeman without the oath. LeBreton gently declined.

"Do you feel you have a liquor problem, Father?"

"No I don't think. I may have before. No, I drank at staff parties." Pausing, he added hopefully, "I look after the ambulance, operate it."

Soothing but insistent, LeBreton gingerly led Kelly back to the sexual assaults. The priest listened in silence, picking at his fingers, his eyes averted.

"We went in with an open mind. Very disturbing what we came away with," LeBreton told him.

Kelly was unresponsive, replying in oblique one-word answers. Once again he was holding his head in his hands. LeBreton described the kind of incident that had happened at various homes in De Grau and Cape St. George.

"No sir, that's not true, not a number of nights. I can count the number of times on one hand."

The interrogator's patience had finally been rewarded. For the first time, Father Kelly was acknowledging at least some of the allegations against him.

"Oh my God, the fact you've been going around my parish asking these questions."

"The boys came from good homes."

"How old are they?"

"They're not being untruthful. All without exception came from good homes."

At ten minutes after seven, Kelly opened a fresh pack of Export As and balled the cellophane wrapping between his thumb and forefinger. He lit a cigarette and momentarily withdrew into himself. Sensing that the priest might be ready to break, LeBreton reminded Kelly that it would be pretty well impossible to forget such sensitive matters.

". . . Your memory couldn't fail you."

"No, really, I took people for what they're worth. I didn't crawl into bed with every boy in the Cape. If there are a couple of incidents mentioned there, I don't know."

Heading towards the net, the fish had suddenly veered away. LeBreton gave him line, before jerking back on the inquisitorial rod.

"We know the people think highly of you. . . . Do you recall putting your hand down a young boy's pants and feeling his privates?"

"Well, not that I thought there was something medically wrong — medically, physically. It was drinking maybe," Kelly answered disjointedly.

LeBreton's subject was still having trouble facing the consequences of his actions, but he was circling closer. Kelly denied he had done anything criminally wrong, and said that putting his hands down other people's pants wasn't his cup of tea. LeBreton tried a different tack.

"This isn't going to help the church and parish."

"If my resignation tonight would help the problem I would."

Kelly's will to resist was weakening, and he embarked on a rambling description of his life, claiming that he had never had any intention of going to bed and "doing these things." He talked of the loneliness and hardship of a priest's life.

"I wouldn't think I did anything to want to hurt them. . . ."

At 7:20 P.M., LeBreton detailed the numerous occasions when Kelly had sexually abused young boys. The handsome priest leaned forward, visibly upset by the policeman's words and then sat back in his chair, coy or resigned, LeBreton had no way of knowing.

"Maybe in my sleep or subconscious," he theorized a little wildly. "Even then I can't buy the way it's being put . . . I have a blind trust with people and put myself in embarrassing situations."

LeBreton patiently explained how Kelly had turned down available empty beds in order to sleep with ones occupied by young boys when he visited their homes.

"... If I got in bed and did this I wouldn't force them to stay."

"This is what happened," LeBreton said, laying down one of the statements.

"What does he mean by advances?" the priest asked.

"Hand on a leg could mean a friendly gesture; but handling the privates . . ." LeBreton didn't finish, and Kelly lit up another cigarette.

"Unless I'm mixed up in my mind, it was someone else. I know the laws, and liquor isn't an excuse."

Kelly asked for coffee and told the policemen that he sometimes had so much to drink that members of the RCMP had had to escort him home. LeBreton reminded him that there are degrees of indecent assault.

"If you touch a girl's breasts it is an indecent assault."

Kelly puffed on his cigarette and said that several young girls had crushes on him.

"Do you feel you set up a mental block and don't want to believe you're doing it?"

"When you know psychology, the thing you don't do is analyse yourself," Kelly replied, explaining to LeBreton that he held a degree in the subject.

LeBreton was beginning to wonder if Kelly would ever face the unpleasant facts before him.

"In your time in De Grau, do you remember things that you regretted?"

"I don't believe things went that far, the fondling of hands in shorts. I may have put my arm around them. I can say I know how far to go."

"Is there things you have done?"

"Talked about alcohol. I spoke about homosexuality."

Father Kelly asked to go to the washroom. When he came back with his escort, Corporal Urquhart, the RCMP officers raised the issue of a nun who was Kelly's girlfriend. The emotional barriers shuddered, then broke, and Kelly began to weep. Urquhart brought him a glass of water and he was allowed a phone call to the convent in De Grau where his girlfriend lived.

At 11:00 P.M. Father Kelly began his statement in his own hand. Twenty minutes later he signed the document in which he admitted to the crimes with which he'd been charged, and, to a degree, tried to rationalize them.

> Regarding the complaints I have heard, I can say in some cases I realize that I have been at fault, however there was no deliberate attempt to hurt any person or to break any laws of church or state. I do not think I forced any person at any time . . . I have been involved with the people named. . . . In nearly all cases there was no extreme involv[e]ment. I have worked very hard in Cape St. George during the past 6 years. I guess I was not fully conscious of the fact that I had broken the law. I have no previous involvement with the courts insofar as prosecutions are concerned. I think I was overly emotionally involved with my parishioners and work and this may have led to my becoming too involved with them.
>
> Ronald H. Kelly

The two RCMP officers signed Kelly's statement and he left the RCMP detachment at 12:15 A.M. in the company of another priest, Father William Boone. Urquhart noted in his account of the interview that Father Kelly admitted, under caution that anything he said could be used against him, that the names the police had presented to him accounted for most of the boys he'd been involved with, though there may have been a few more. Kelly also stated that there was a "young guy" the police hadn't mentioned with whom he "went further" than with the other boys. Before leaving the detachment, Kelly said that he intended to get things over with as soon as possible, plead guilty and do some soul searching about his life.

The next day, in front of the brawny and bombastic figure of Magistrate Gordon Seabright, another echo of Mount Cashel would float through the strange proceedings involving the Catholic priest.

Just after 9 P.M. on the same evening the RCMP were interviewing Father Kelly, Michael Roche, the lone Crown prosecutor on the west coast of Newfoundland, received a call from RCMP Superintendent William Halloran. Halloran advised Roche that there was a Roman Catholic priest in custody in Corner Brook named Father Ronald Kelly, who had been arrested earlier that day on sex-related charges. The RCMP officer explained that Father Kelly was going to be released later that night into the custody of Bishop Richard McGrath of the Diocese of St. George's and would be spending the night at the Palace on Hammond Drive in Corner Brook. Halloran wanted to know if Roche would be available the following morning to prosecute the case. Roche, whose brother was a priest and who had been educated by the Christian Brothers, confirmed that he could schedule the matter and arranged to meet the arresting officers the following morning for a briefing.

On Friday, May 11, 1979 the two RCMP officers showed up at Roche's seventh-floor office suite in the Sir Richard Squires Building, which housed the Magistrate's Court, the District Court, the Supreme Court, and the west coast office of the Premier of Newfoundland. LeBreton and Urquhart briefed Roche on the charges and informed him that, as far as they knew, Father Kelly planned to enter a guilty plea.

"I was appalled. Particularly I was struck ... by the possible element of collusion between the parents of the boys and Father Kelly," he later testified.

Uncertain about what the Crown's position on sentencing should be, Roche called the senior Crown attorney for the Eastern region, Robert Hyslop, to get some authorities.

"I felt strongly at the time that obviously a period of incarceration was in order, but I had absolutely no idea of what the possible range of sentence might have been," he recalled.

Hyslop, who promised to send the appropriate authorities out on the first available flight from St. John's the next morning, conveyed some rough guidelines to Roche over the telephone: most lenient, six months; average, two years. Roche then chatted briefly with counsel for the defence,

Michael Monaghan and Gerard Martin, who had been retained by Bishop McGrath after a brief meeting at the Palace earlier that morning. Kelly's lawyers confirmed the RCMP's information that their client would be entering a guilty plea and that the defence was prepared to get into a sentencing hearing sometime that afternoon.

After a series of delays, the case was set to proceed at four o'clock in Courtroom 2, in front of Magistrate Gordon Seabright. Seabright, a swashbuckling and legendary figure in outport Newfoundland, was a product of Newfoundland's unusual method of dealing with the fact that, until very recently, few people practised law outside the city of St. John's. To deal with judicial matters in the rural districts of the province, a system of magistrates was devised that placed para-legals like Seabright on the bench, even though they didn't have law degrees. (On December 14, 1979, Magistrates were renamed Provincial Court Judges, in spite of the fact that the old Magistrate's Courts had been replaced by Provincial Courts on July 15, 1974.)

Seabright, who had also been a welfare officer and a teacher went to the bench in 1964, eventually taking advantage of a program that sent him to law school between 1975 and 1978 at the province's expense. At the time of the Father Kelly trial, the big man who entered a room like a bull moose breaking through the alders had recently spent a month articling with the Corner Brook firm of Wells, Monaghan, Seaborn, Marshall and Roberts. Michael Monaghan had been his principal. During his next two annual holiday periods, in 1980 and 1981, Seabright would continue his articling with Monaghan and, if the other parties didn't object, continue to preside over cases in which Monaghan was involved.

At 4:20 P.M., Roche and the two RCMP investigators were still waiting in Courtroom 2 for the other parties to arrive. When Magistrate Seabright appeared, he told Roche that there was a telephone call for him outside. The Crown prosecutor took the call in the vacant office of Judge Arthur Cramm and was astonished to find the Director of Public Prosecutions (D.P.P.), John Kelly, on the other end of the line.

"His first question to me, I can't possibly forget this, was

'What is going on out in Corner Brook?' I explained to Mr. Kelly that there was a Roman Catholic clergyman charged with ten counts of Section 156. I explained to him the circumstances of the case. And I then asked Mr. Kelly why he had phoned me, because I was obviously a little concerned at that time that there might have been some political interference."

The astonished prosecutor was then informed that the defence lawyers had been trying to reach the Attorney-General of Newfoundland, T. Alex Hickman, to get the charges against Father Kelly withdrawn. Astonished that Monaghan and Martin had undertaken such action without giving the Crown prosecutor the slightest inkling of what they planned to do, Roche explained that the charges were too serious to simply drop. Kelly agreed and gave his official consent to proceed with the matter.

(On Monday, May 14, Monaghan would in fact speak with Newfoundland's Attorney-General about the disposition of the Kelly case. In what Alex Hickman would later describe as both a "very professional" but nonetheless unusual call, Monaghan asked Hickman to review the decision by John Kelly and prosecutor Roche to proceed against Father Kelly rather than grant an unconditional discharge in exchange for a promise by the church to put the priest in psychiatric care in another province. Monaghan made it clear he was acting on the instructions of his client, Bishop McGrath. Hickman declined.

Before hanging up, though, Monaghan made reference to Mount Cashel or the Brothers, an allusion that meant nothing to the Justice Minister. When he subsequently asked John Kelly about the case, Hickman was assured that it had been properly handled by the Deputy Minister of the day, Vincent McCarthy. Moreover, Hickman knew that Mount Cashel was one of the cases that was being examined at the Soper Inquiry, so if there had been any wrongdoing by the Justice Department, Judge Lloyd Soper would be dealing with it – or so Alex Hickman thought.

(Years later, Monaghan would claim that his partner, Gerard Martin, had made the call to Newfoundland's Justice Minister while he listened in.)

After Roche finished speaking with John Kelly, he took

the elevator to the sixth floor of the Sir Richard Squires Building and found the two defence lawyers in the robing room, which, coincidentally, was equipped with a telephone. Without mentioning his conversation with John Kelly, Roche told them that he had been waiting for them downstairs on a matter that was already half an hour late in starting. They followed the prosecutor down to Courtroom 2 where the case proceeded in front of Magistrate Seabright, Father Kelly, the two defence lawyers, the two investigators, Roche, the court reporter and the sole member of the public to witness the trial, Father William Boone.

To protect the identities of the youthful victims, the case was heard in camera. Father Kelly elected trial by magistrate without a jury and entered a guilty plea to each of the ten charges against him. Sergeant LeBreton and prosecutor Roche presented the facts of the case, including Father Kelly's signed statement. After LeBreton finished his summary, Magistrate Seabright questioned him about the condition of Father Kelly's victims.

"When he was finished I turned to him and I questioned him very thoroughly on what the effect was, if any, on these children. . . . Was there any such thing as bedwetting? Was there any such thing as inverted behaviour? Was there any such thing as people having to go to psychiatrists or anything along that line? And he assured me that nothing of that nature had happened," former Magistrate Seabright would later testify.

Forty-five minutes after the matter began, it was over. Roche informed the court that he had been in touch with St. John's and arrangements were being made to have sentencing precedents flown out to him the next morning. Since he was not in a position to make final submissions on sentence, he requested an adjournment until the following week — a motion that was vehemently opposed by one of Kelly's lawyers.

"The reason was that they, or Mr. Monaghan I should say more specifically, was prepared to make his final sentencing submissions at that time, and as well, he advised the court that Father Kelly had plane reservations to leave Stephenville airport on the afternoon of Saturday, May 12, at approximately 1:30 in the afternoon."

Roche was shocked. Monaghan's stated reason for proceeding immediately on sentencing took for granted that Father Kelly would be going somewhere other than jail. The defence counsel explained that arrangements had already been made for Kelly to fly to Ontario and receive psychiatric help at Southdown – a replay of the drill that had forced Det. Robert Hillier to rush his interviews with Brothers English and Ralph during the 1975 Mount Cashel investigation.

Magistrate Seabright then inquired when Roche would next be available for court and was told the afternoon of Wednesday, May 16. Not satisfied with that date, the Judge asked Roche where he would be on Monday, May 14. Roche replied that he was prosecuting a case in District Court before Judge Lloyd Soper. When Seabright further asked the prosecutor what he was doing on Tuesday, May 15, Roche explained that he had a case set down for 10:00 A.M. in Woody Point, 115 kilometres north of Corner Brook. Seabright inquired how long it would take the prosecutor to drive from Corner Brook to Woody Point. When Roche answered an hour and a quarter, Magistrate Seabright ruled that the sentencing hearing would be held on May 15 at 8:00 A.M., a highly unusual time to convene a judicial proceeding, but one at which the absence of the press would virtually be guaranteed.

"I was floored by that," Roche later testified. "I mean, I thought it was an eminently reasonable request to ask that it be set over until the following Wednesday afternoon, a mere day and a half difference. I cannot for the life of me conceive why it had to be set for that particular date at that time. . . ."

Roche's sense of uneasiness with the case didn't diminish as the day wore on. Over the lunch period, his secretary, Helen O'Brien, had received a call from a man who wanted to speak to Roche but who wouldn't leave his name. Nevertheless, she was able to tell her boss who the caller was because of his very familiar voice – her parish priest, Father William Boone, whose sermons she faithfully took in every Sunday. The Crown prosecutor couldn't help wondering if the call had been made to subtly influence his conduct in the Kelly case. As Roche left the courthouse after the priest's trial, he was approached by Father Boone near the elevators. After exchanging pleasantries, Roche looked straight at Boone and asked him a single question.

"Father, why did you try to telephone me today?"

The priest flushed and began to stammer.

"But, but, but, I did not leave my name." Roche smiled at the befuddled priest until his red face vanished behind the closing elevator doors. (Ironically, the priest who sat through the Kelly trial, Father William Boone, would himself be charged ten years later with gross indecency involving a young male.)

But more was on the way to convince Roche that the Kelly case was not being handled the way it should be. After dropping off his files at the office, the lawyer went to the Glynmill Inn for a drink. Shortly after he arrived, Magistrate Gordon Seabright, Michael Monaghan, and Gerard Martin entered the bar together to have a drink. Without finishing his beer, Roche left the hotel immediately.

"I obviously was upset by the way things were unfolding. . . . I felt that the appearance of justice was being compromised."

On Tuesday, May 15, at the unusual hour of 8:00 A.M. the sentencing hearing of Father Ronald Kelly began in front of Magistrate Seabright. Present were exactly the same people who had been at the priest's trial four days earlier. For at least one of the participants, Cpl. Murray Urquhart, the whole proceeding took place in an atmosphere suggesting that it was a foregone conclusion that Father Kelly would not be going to jail.

"I got the distinct impression that the plans had been made. And that he, if he walked out of that courtroom, that he would be catching the next flight out. My impression of it was that . . . the disposition had been made up before court was . . . to commence. . . . There was not going to be a jail term and he was to be leaving the area and going to Toronto and going to Southdown." That impression was reinforced by the exchanges that were taking place between Father Boone, defence counsel and Magistrate Seabright.

Father Boone testified to the prodigious amount of work Father Kelly had done in his parish and entered his curriculum vitae into evidence. Father Boone also produced a telex from Southdown confirming that arrangements had been made for Father Kelly to become an in-patient of the treatment centre. The priest told the court that Kelly would be on his way to Southdown later that same afternoon – a statement that vexed Michael Roche, based as it was on the cavalier assumption that Father Kelly would not in fact be incarcerated.

Just the day before, Roche had prosecuted the case of Regina v. Piercey in which a fifty-three-year-old man had pleaded guilty to a charge of indecently assaulting a seven-year-old girl. Although it was a first offence, and the crime had been committed under the influence of alcohol, the married man with eight children was sentenced to three months in jail, plus two years' probation. The judge's sentencing notes explained the rationale: "Although the accused has shown remorse and has already punished himself emotionally, a term of imprisonment was necessary as deterr[e]nt to the accused." Roche fully intended to use the Piercey case as a precedent in his own sentencing submission on Father Kelly.

After Father Boone had finished, Michael Monaghan made his sentencing submission for the defence, in which he accused Michael Roche of an abuse of prosecutorial power for allowing the charges to proceed. According to Roche, the defence attorney also referred to a precedent which had been set in a 1975 case, where three Irish Christian Brothers had left the province to receive psychiatric treatment in lieu of having sexual assault charges laid against them.

"There was a clear reference to 1975, St. John's, three Irish Christian Brothers, and no charges being laid and their being shipped out of the province . . . I am absolutely 100 per cent certain," Roche would later tell a public inquiry into the Mount Cashel affair. (Although there is no definitive evidence to explain Roche's recollection of the mention of three Brothers having been sent out of the province, Brother Douglas Kenny had, in fact, left Newfoundland for his tertianship in Rome in early 1976. Like English and Ralph, Brother Kenny was also accused of sexual abuse in Detective Hillier's 1975 police report into the Mount Cashel affair.)

What was so fascinating about Monaghan's alleged reference to Mount Cashel during the Kelly case was that it came a full day before Judge Lloyd Soper released Sgt. Arthur Pike's in camera testimony from the Soper Inquiry — the first time the orphanage scandal was ever put on the public record. The question was, where had Father Kelly's lawyers learned about the details of a case so secret that even the Justice Minister of the day said he was unaware of it? If it was from the man who had hired them, Richard McGrath, the Bishop was taking a dangerously intrusive step into the justice system by getting Father Kelly's lawyers to press the 1975 deal as any kind of legal precedent.

Unknown to Michael Roche, Bishop McGrath had already taken an even bigger step on Saturday, May 12, three days before Father Kelly's sentencing hearing. On Friday night, the Bishop had called Magistrate Gordon Seabright at home, leaving a message with the absent judge's wife that he would call back. At 11:30 the next morning he called again and told the judge he wanted to speak to him. Seabright invited McGrath to his house, where amongst other things, the Bishop asked the judge about the range of sentencing available to him in the Kelly case. Seabright explained that his options ranged from unconditional discharge to ten years' imprisonment. Seabright's eminent guest was invited to stay for lunch and the men shared a bowl of pea soup at the kitchen table; Bishop McGrath left a few hours later.

Angered by Monaghan's remarks in court, Roche made his own submission on sentence, reading from notes written on a pad entitled "Dumb Things I Gotta Do," a present from his secretary. Noting that there was absolutely no pre-sentence report filed before the court other than Father Kelly's curriculum vitae, Roche described the Crown's position as both "ethical and adversarial." He rejected arguments by counsel for the defence that the Roman Catholic church was in any way on trial in the Kelly case.

"I further went on to state that Father Kelly first and foremost was a man, and was standing there as a man accused of having committed criminal offences."

Roche also expressed in open court his concern that Father Kelly was getting preferential treatment — late appearances one day, early ones the next. His remarks prompted Magistrate Seabright to declare: "If there is any thought that this matter was done in a secret way I would dispel them completely."

On the main point at issue, Roche told the court that sentencing precedents indicated that even for first offenders a period of incarceration was warranted. For example, in 1974 a corrections officer at a boys' home had received a year in jail on appeal for similar offences. In asking for a jail sentence for Father Kelly, the Crown prosecutor cited individual and general deterrence, protection of the public and the seriousness of the offences. He stressed the fact that the boys involved had been frightened to report Father Kelly's sexual assaults because of his vaunted position in their community.

"Most importantly, I urged Magistrate Seabright that it is a basic value that confidence of the public in the administration of criminal justice be maintained. To treat a sexual offender, albeit a first offender, with excessive leniency would increase the risk that such confidence may be eroded and the criminal justice system be brought into disrepute."

In the case of Father Kelly, Roche's review of the precedents indicated that a jail sentence of three months to two years was in order.

Without an adjournment, Magistrate Seabright dealt immediately with Father Kelly straight from the bench, ordering a suspended sentence on all ten counts against him and a period of probation of two years. In addition, Kelly had to enter Southdown "until results were satisfactory." All reports from the institution were to be sent to that well-known medical expert, Magistrate Gordon Seabright. Before adjourning the court, Seabright gave a short statement from the bench indicating that he didn't agree with incarceration and emphasizing the need for rehabilitation. Ten years later, this same man, hearing the case of Father James Corrigan, would describe gross indecency and sexual assault as "the worst crimes against children that can be committed." In the intervening decade, Seabright's judicial vision had clearly evolved.

Roche hurriedly left the courtroom to make the hour drive to his next case at Woody Point, feeling strongly that the case had to be appealed. When he later learned about the luncheon meeting between Magistrate Seabright and Bishop McGrath that preceded Father Kelly's sentencing hearing, he was convinced that he could win it.

He was wrong.

The next unusual step in the Father Kelly case was taken immediately after the trial. Magistrate Gordon Seabright sent a letter to Southdown informing authorities there that he would be personally monitoring the probation progress of the priest, normally the role of a probation officer. In asking for copies of progress reports on Father Kelly, Magistrate Seabright made his opinion of what was wrong with the priest very plain.

"The problem is a combination of liquor, loneliness and celibacy. One can see that there is a problem which needs to be treated. I felt that no useful purpose would be served by a period of incarceration if the process of rehabilitation is to be given a chance to work."

Despite the fact that Magistrate Seabright specified that he wanted to personally monitor Father Kelly's progress, the first report from the Catholic-run treatment centre would be sent to Bishop McGrath at the Palace.

On May 31, 1979, Michael Roche filed a Notice of Application to appeal the sentence in the Father Kelly case. Early the next morning, Corporal Urquhart of the RCMP served the notice of appeal on Judge Seabright before he went into court. The policeman later recalled part of their conversation.

"At the time of the serving . . . he had mentioned to me that there had been a petition from the community of Cape St. George and that area, De Grau, with regard to wanting Father Kelly returned by the church to that parish. And my response at that time was the fact that, yes, I could understand that because he was highly thought of. He did a lot of community work. He was well known. But that it was also obvious that the community at large did not know of the crimes he had committed. And I don't believe that Judge Seabright responded to that."

In the two weeks after Father Kelly's trial, complaints began to trickle in about the way that Magistrate Seabright had handled the case, from his pea-soup confab with Bishop McGrath to the 8 A.M. sentencing hearing. In a June 27 letter to Magistrate Seabright, the Chief Magistrate of the Provincial Court, Cyril Goodyear, asked for a full accounting of the Father Kelly trial, including the meeting with Bishop McGrath. In his return letter, Magistrate Seabright confirmed the facts that had come to the attention of the Chief Magistrate, ending the letter with "I write this to you without excuse or explanation so that you can get the total picture."

Goodyear was furious.

"I had some very serious concerns about the fact that while the matter was before him, somebody representing the church and the superior of the defendant had come to visit him with a view to discussing the matter."

Goodyear considered taking the matter before the Judicial Council, an intention he expressed in writing to Magistrate Seabright on August 6, 1979. But when he checked at the Department of Justice, he discovered that government had let some of the appointments to the body lapse, leaving the Judicial Council without a quorum. No further action was taken against Magistrate Seabright, who felt he had done nothing wrong in meeting with Bishop McGrath and discussing the sentencing aspect of the Kelly case.

Ten years later, retired Judge Seabright would remain unrepentant when he recounted how he had responded to the Chief Magistrate.

"I said fine. *You* may not have done it. But I can tell you now I did no wrong, and if the opportunity came, I'd probably do it again."

After receiving Roche's case report, the Director of Public Prosecutions, John Kelly, asked senior Crown prosecutor Robert Hyslop to review the file to see if he thought the sentence should be appealed, a move he quickly recommended. As he would later explain at the Hughes Inquiry, "I made that decision on the basis of the police report involving the allegations and obviously what I had been told had been brought before the court. . . . It was what I considered to be a very lenient sentence, extraordinarily so for the circumstances of which I was aware."

But by mid-summer the pending appeal of the Father Kelly case was delayed by John Kelly's resignation as Director of Public Prosecutions and two medical reports from Southdown that arrived at the Justice Department. The clear intention of the reports, as Justice officials quickly surmised, was to quash the Crown's appeal by showing what good progress the fallen priest had been making. Once a permanent replacement for John Kelly was found, it was hoped that he would see things differently than his predecessor, a hope that the report from Father Canice Connors, the Executive Director of Southdown, was designed to encourage.

> . . . The medical assessment indicates that it is no small wonder, given the combinations of alcohol and Valium consumed over a period of years, that he survived to receive treatment. . . . The entire staff is convinced that he has achieved adequate insight into himself and has begun to develop a lifestyle that augurs well for a problem free future. . . . In the past two weeks, at the suggestion of the staff, he has requested a temporary pastoral assignment from Bishop Lacey, the Personnel Director for the Archdiocese of Toronto. Beginning on 1st of October he will take up residence with Bishop Lacey and will continue as an out-patient under the care of George Freemesser, M.D., a priest-psychiatrist on the staff at Southdown. . . . The professional staff at Southdown is comfortable that Ronald Kelly's progress has verified the prudence and wisdom of your decision to place him here on probation. We are confident here that with Fr. Kelly's co-operation we have uncovered the fundamental causes of his problems and that he is well on his way to complete recovery.

Cheerleading to one side, the bottom line was clear – four and a half months after being admitted to a treatment centre, a priest who pleaded guilty to ten counts of sexual assault was being reassigned to active duty.

Frustrated by the delays on the Kelly appeal while the new D.P.P., Cyril Goodyear, studied the case and the Southdown reports, Michael Roche finally wrote to the Justice Department to bring the matter to a head. In a subsequent Friday afternoon telephone call with Goodyear, Roche learned of Magistrate Seabright's "infamous pea-soup" letter of July 4. Roche felt strongly that it should be brought to the attention of the Appeal Court should the case proceed. Goodyear said he would consider releasing a copy of the letter to Roche and told him to be in his Corner Brook office at 8 A.M. Monday morning. At that time the prosecutor would be given "the green light or the red light."

Roche spent a "nerve-wracking" weekend, wondering what the decision would be. That Sunday night, after discussing the ethical dilemma he found himself in with two lawyer friends, he came to a momentous decision.

"I resolved that Sunday night that, if I were to be given a red light . . . I had no honourable recourse but to immediately resign the following day, Monday, from the Department of Justice and call a press conference."

When the call came in from St. John's first thing Monday morning, Cyril Goodyear uttered but two words: "green light." In giving his written blessing to the appeal a few days later, the new D.P.P. made clear what he thought of the post-sentencing reports from Southdown.

"I have reviewed the documents which you forwarded in this matter. It is obvious that your decision to appeal sentence in these cases was completely objective, based on the law, and not influenced by any other consideration. Please proceed with it.

"The reports from Southdown, which are being circulated widely, appear to have an obvious intent. It should be noted that Southdown is not an independently operated clinic."

The appeal of sentence in the Father Kelly case was set down for November 21, but postponed at the request of the Crown until November 30. In the interim, Roche had sent a copy of his notice motion to Kelly's lawyers, including a personal affidavit outlining Magistrate Seabright's luncheon with Bishop McGrath before the sentencing hearing. The agitated lawyers showed up at Roche's office in Corner Brook before the hearing of the appeal, upset that he was jeopardizing Seabright's career.

"Their position was quite simply, 'How in the Christ, Roche, can you do this, because a man's job is at risk? Judge Seabright, if it ever comes out, is going to lose his job.' And my attitude, my response to them was . . . 'He should have exercised better judgment. When receiving that call on May 12, he should have politely declined such a request to meet. . . .' "

Monaghan and Martin needn't have worried about Gordon Seabright's judicial future. When Michael Roche arrived in court at 10:30 on the morning of November 30, 1979, to argue the appeal on sentence of the Father Kelly case, the learned Justices ordered all the lawyers into chambers. All three judges – Mr. Justice Robert Furlong, Mr. Justice James Gushue and Mr. Justice Herbert Morgan – "vehemently" impressed upon Roche that they refused to hear his application as set out in the notice of motion dated on November 21, which included the affidavit outlining Magistrate Seabright's out-of-court discussions with an interested party to the proceedings in the lower court, namely Bishop McGrath. Roche argued in chambers that the appearance, at least, of justice being done in the case had been jeopardized by the pre-sentencing luncheon.

"They specifically referred to that May 12 meeting and said that meeting was of no significance or relevancy whatsoever with respect to the fitness of the sentence being appealed from."

The appeal itself lasted a little over an hour. The three judges listened in stony silence as Roche made the argument that the trend in courts in Newfoundland and other provinces was to provide jail terms when faced with serious crimes of a sexual nature. His arguments were received in "an aura of hostility," as he would later describe it.

"They were clearly, clearly unreceptive to the Crown's position. I can recall one specific comment made as I sat down after going through the experience. The Chief Justice leaned over to Mr. Justice James Gushue, and in a loud whisper audible to everybody in the courtroom, he said, 'Do we even need to hear from Monaghan?' "

After defence counsel gave a brief presentation, two post-sentence reports which closely followed the information laid out in the Southdown reports were received.

"There was no mention of pedophilia, absolutely none in the post-sentence reports. They just basically said this man had problems, exacerbated by drink and drugs. What kind of mental illness to this day I'm at a loss to describe," Roche later recounted.

After retiring for fifteen minutes, Newfoundland's Supreme Court of Appeal upheld Magistrate Seabright's suspended sentence for Father Kelly. In his judgment, Mr. Justice James Gushue said Father Kelly's offences were "serious" and "this factor cannot be minimized," but proceeded to do just that. He noted that Father Kelly was "no criminal in the commonly understood meaning of the word, but in fact suffers from a type of mental illness aggravated by drink and drugs which could very well respond to proper treatment.

"To confine him to prison at this stage is not going to cure this illness, or even begin to do so. In fact, it would most likely have a decidedly adverse affect on him. . . . The respondent's aberrations are undoubtedly an illness, so the public is also better served by his being placed in a curative institution, subject to strict supervision as was ordered by the magistrate."

After his brief stint at Southdown, Father Kelly was afterwards re-assigned to the Archdiocese of Toronto, where he was eventually appointed Vice Chancellor of Temporal Affairs, one of the most senior positions around Gerald Emmett Cardinal Carter. No one outside the administrative hierarchy in his new parish was informed of Father Kelly's criminal record in Newfoundland. As for his former parishioners in Cape St. George, seven hundred of them, many of whom still didn't know what had happened to the popular cleric, signed a petition asking that Father Kelly be returned to the area as parish priest. Despite more than a few close encounters with the justice system, the Catholic Church and the Christian Brothers had gotten out of the seventies in Newfoundland with barely a scratch.

The next decade would not prove as lucky.

Chapter 9

■■■■■■ *Dark Harvest*

Brother Burton would enter the room wearing a housecoat [and] sit on the edge of W's bed. W said he would pretend to be asleep and cover his head with his pillow. Brother Burton would take off W's pyjamas, top and pants, and then he 'would begin kissing his body.' . . . The duration of these incidents would extend anywhere from twenty minutes to over an hour and Brother Burton would perform 'Oral' sex almost every night. . . . On two or three occasions, W could not remember exactly, Brother Burton, according to him, entered his rectum area with his penis and performed anal sex. . . . Notes from a social worker's interview with W.N., a fifteen-year-old who was sexually abused by a Christian Brother at Mount Cashel Orphanage in 1982.

IN THE AFTERMATH of the Soper Inquiry, the Christian Brothers held their breath but nothing happened. Just a few months after Brian Peckford vanquished the hapless Liberals in an election that passed without mention of Mount Cashel, Mobil Oil announced a major oil find on the Grand Banks. Newfoundland's inexhaustible faith in the brass ring was revived, and few people were interested in anything but the "Newfie tea" their politicians boasted would transform the province into the Alberta of the Atlantic. Suddenly Stetsons and cowboy boots were hot items in the stores along Water Street, as everyone geared up to get in on the coming boom Hibernia was expected to bring.

The fixation on Hibernia intensified as Brian Peckford engaged Ottawa in an increasingly bitter struggle over ownership of the offshore El Dorado. By 1982 the struggle had become a war. At home, Peckford was lionized for refusing to agree to a resource giveaway that would make outsiders the principal benefactors of the province's natural wealth – as they had been from the time of the English fish merchants, who built mansions in Exeter and Poole with fortunes made on Newfoundland cod while local fishermen lived in abject poverty. With Peckford's rhetorical guns trained on Ottawa and Newfoundlanders massed behind him like an angry fist ready to strike his opponents down, a minor incident at the Mount Cashel Orphanage slipped past like a dory adrift in the fog.

Around noon on January 26, 1982, two thirteen-year-old boys ran away from Mount Cashel to avoid being punished for a fire authorities believed they had started at the orphanage the previous day. The runaways walked and hitchhiked until dark and then bedded down in the woods, rising early the next morning to continue their journey to St. Bride's on Placentia Bay, 185 kilometres southwest of St. John's. Cold and wet, they finally arrived at the door of Sarah (Sadie) Murphy, whom they knew from happier days when they still lived in the small fishing community.

Murphy called the Social Services Department and Shirley Stephenson from the Placentia District Office came to the house to interview the boys. During the interview, the boys complained that they had been mistreated by adults at Mount Cashel. Stephenson recorded the interview and, in spite of the boys' complaints, arranged to have the pair returned to Mount Cashel on February 6. On February 11, Sarah Murphy wrote a letter about the runaways to the Minister of Social Services, Thomas Hickey, in which she referred to the allegations made by the boys in their interview with the social worker.

> [Boy A] complained Bro Bucher was always on his back alike if he did some thing and was bunished for it. It dident end Bro Bucker kept buging him for weeks. . . .
>
> the boys Also told the lady in my presents that they dident like the fireing of pelet guns in the building
>
> They also didn't like the idea of a movie that was showing in there to boys from 8 years old to the 16 years – Beleve it or not this move was showing nothing less than

the stripers and thats a fact because [Boy A] told the social worker He almost droped when his mother and another ladie walked in to visit them right in the middle of the show

... Hope the whole matter would be looked in too by the time the boys would go back and very little as far as I know was done about it I do know [Boy A] got to set on his bed for 30 days Some people don't get that punishment for robbery and I think those poor children are hurt enough by being sent from their parents and home not to be treated like this by Christian Brothers where is charity our government pay 60 per cent of the cost of running that place. . . .

And who do you think would be responsible for those boys if they died in the woods that night. . . . Mr. Hickey I am asking you to have some one look into this matter as soon as possiable. . . . I listened to you on Open Line this morning and you lifted my Heart when you spoke of the people on welfare you got a heart of gold. . . .

> Yours Truely
> Sarah Murphy

Six weeks later, the Social Work Program Co-ordinator at Confederation Building, Sandra Morris, wrote to the Placentia District Office and asked for comments on the enclosed copy of Murphy's letter to the Minister. A week later, Shirley Stephenson, who had interviewed the boys at Murphy's house, relayed her impressions of their complaint.

"From observing the boys' facial expressions and body movements it appeared that they were telling the truth. However, when considering the home's good reputation and the valuable service which has been and is presently being provided, these complaints are indeed questionable."

Based on Stephenson's novel logic, headquarters then wrote a letter to Sarah Murphy, smoothing the matter over without any independent investigation.

"It would appear everything has been settled in a satisfactory manner for all concerned. . . . Thank you for bringing the matter to our attention."

Things hadn't changed much in the Department of Social Services since 1975. But the next time a complaint about Mount Cashel came Sandra Morris's way, a quick bureaucratic burial would be out of the question.

On Thursday, October 7, Henry Louis Bucher, who replaced Brother Kenny as Superintendent of Mount Cashel in 1976, telephoned social worker Sandra Morris with a disturbing report. He told her that he had received complaints that a sixteen-year-old who had been a resident of Mount Cashel since 1975 was sexually harrassing two younger boys at the orphanage. Bucher had no way of knowing that he was setting in motion a chain of events that would end in the first criminal conviction in Newfoundland of an Irish Christian Brother.

Morris, who by this time had left her administrative post at headquarters for a social work position at the district office where she functioned as the liaison with Mount Cashel, recorded Bucher's call and then interviewed the alleged offender, a dishwasher at the local Holiday Inn who lived in St. Gabe's dormitory at the orphanage. A year and a half earlier, the boy had dropped out of school — grade five special education class at Pius X. Boy 3 readily admitted his sexual involvement with two other boys at Mount Cashel, explaining that the encounters took place late at night, usually around 3:30 A.M., when he would enter St. Stan's dormitory through the fire-escape door, which would be left open by one of his partners.

Sandra Morris wrote to Newfoundland's Director of Child Welfare, reporting on the call from Brother Bucher and her subsequent interview with Boy 3. It was decided that social worker Karen Alexander should interview both of Boy 3's sexual partners. The brothers confirmed that the older boy had been sexually abusing them and one said that Boy 3 had scared the "wits" out of him. They also mentioned that another Mount Cashel resident, Boy 5, had been sexually involved with Boy 3. Alexander informed Simms of her interview with Boy 3's victims and the police were made aware of the report the same day. That much, at least, had changed since the days of Robert Bradbury.

During a subsequent interview with Det.-Sgt. Len Power at CID headquarters, Boy 3 revealed the nature of the encounters that had been going on for eighteen months with the two boys, aged fourteen and twelve. No social worker was present when the youth was interviewed.

"What would you do?" Power asked.

"I was sucking him, his penis, pulling him, each other."

"Would he suck you?"

"No."

"If he didn't go along with you, what would you do?"

"I would sorta force him." Boy 3 explained that he would visit St. Stan's approximately three times a week, where he would occasionally have sex with his regular partner's brother.

"Why would they let you do it to them?"

"Something to do, I don't know. They're sort of that type too, gay."

"Do you understand . . . the meaning of homosexuality?"

"Yes."

"Are you homosexual?"

"I am not sure. I don't really think so."

"Were you involved with anyone else at Mount Cashel?"

Boy 3 recounted his experiences with another partner, Boy 7, who demanded sex from him on at least 20 occasions.

"He used to stick his penis in my 'rectum.' He said hole, and [would] get me to suck his penis."

". . . About how often did he insert his penis into your rectum?"

"About ten times at most."

By Thursday, October 14, Neil Hamilton, the Supervisor of the St. John's East District Office on Harvey Road was in a panic. With each interview, a more grotesque picture of Mount Cashel took shape out of the rough-edged accounts of its inmates, a place where older boys were sexually using younger ones and where there was an inordinately high level of homosexual activity amongst orphanage residents. Remembering the whispers he had heard about the orphanage in 1975, Hamilton started to assign social workers to interview Mount Cashel boys without going through the office of the Director of Child Welfare.

"After hearing problems back in '74, '75 by way of the rumour mill, this time as a Social Work supervisor I wanted to make sure that the matter was addressed, that the Director was made fully aware, and that the police should be alerted," he later said.

Sandra Morris was dispatched to interview Boy 5, while Karen Alexander was sent to look into new and explosive allegations from a Mount Cashel resident who was officially known as Boy 6, or "W.N."

W.N. was a fifteen-year-old who had been a permanent ward of the Director of Child Welfare since December 2, 1980. The boy had been placed in Mount Cashel three months later, on March 18, 1981. On October 8, 1982, W.N. failed to return to Mount Cashel after a weekend visit with his family on Bell Island. By 2:30 Sunday afternoon, Gerald Power was getting worried. It was part of Power's part-time job at the orphanage to keep track of when boys left the institution for visits and when they returned. Power, a retired thirty-year veteran of the Social Services department, called W.N.'s social worker and asked her to make a home visit to find out what had happened to W.N. At 3 P.M. social worker Sharon Jesso called Power and told him that W.N. didn't want to return to Mount Cashel.

When he heard the reason – W.N.'s shocking allegation that he had had anal sex with a Christian Brother at Mount Cashel three times in the last month – Power suggested that they not discuss the matter over the telephone. After telling Jesso to call her supervisor, Fred Powell – something the social worker had already done only to get the order to call Mount Cashel directly – Power agonized over what to do next. Since he was paid by Mount Cashel and reported to its Superintendent, he desperately wanted to inform Brother Henry Bucher of the crisis. But Brother Bucher was out of town. Given the gravity of the situation, Power decided to bypass normal reporting lines and place a direct call to the Department of Social Services. He picked up the telephone and called Neil Hamilton.

Power went to work early the next morning to personally inform officials at Mount Cashel of W.N.'s allegations. Perhaps part of the reason the retiree wanted to follow through as quickly as possible on the matter was a rumour he had heard several years earlier. In 1975–76, when he was Assistant Director of Social Assistance, Power had been told during a coffee break about two Brothers who were removed from Mount Cashel because of "misbehaviour." Without knowing the details of that case, he was anxious to pass on what he knew of this latest allegation against a Christian Brother in the event that decisive action would have to be taken again. What he had to report didn't make Brother Henry Bucher's day.

"He was devastated," Power recalled. "He was upset and he was very much concerned. . . . He didn't engage in any conversation whatsoever. . . . I told him I had already contacted Social Services."

Meanwhile, Neil Hamilton called the Director of Child Welfare and it was decided that because Karen Alexander had just interviewed Boy 3's sexual partners, she should look into the Bell Island complaint, "in case it was connected" to investigations that were already under way.

The Director of Child Welfare then paid an informal visit to Mount Cashel to tell Brother Bucher in general terms about the allegation against Brother Burton, and the fact that it was being investigated. Simms, it seems, was as big on courtesy in 1982 on matters touching the Christian Brothers as he'd been in 1975, when he alerted the order to the pending police investigation into alleged sexual abuse at Mount Cashel by Brothers English and Ralph.

In a "rambling interview" the disconsolate boy told Alexander that he had been involved in both oral and anal intercourse with forty-three-year-old Brother Burton, who was known to most Newfoundlanders as the famous teacher of the St. Pat's dancers, a troupe that had gained acclaim for public performances of their Irish folk dancing. The twenty-five-year veteran of the Christian Brothers had been assigned to Mount Cashel in 1976 as part of the new regime replacing the draconian administration of Brother Douglas Kenny.

The relationship between the boy and the Brother began innocently enough. Brother Burton gave W.N. a pair of roller skates for his birthday. After presenting the boy with the gift, Burton patted him on the bottom, an action he occasionally repeated when he met W.N. on the stairs at Mount Cashel. Later, the Christian Brother started going to W.N.'s bedroom, which the boy shared with three other Mount Cashel residents. Alexander recorded the pattern of Brother Burton's escalating physical demands in a report she prepared the day after her interview with W.N.

"Brother Burton would enter the room wearing a housecoat [and] sit on the edge of W's bed. W said he would pretend to be asleep and cover his head with his pillow. Brother Burton would take off W's pyjamas, top and pants, and then he 'would begin kissing his body.' I asked for clarification of 'his body' and was told that it would be his face, stomach, privates, 'all over my body.' W, when questioned if he responded in the same manner, said 'No' he would continue to pretend to be asleep until Brother Burton would leave. The duration of these incidents would extend anywhere from twenty minutes to over an hour and Brother Burton would perform 'Oral' sex almost every night. . . .

"On two or three occasions, W could not remember exactly, Brother Burton, according to him, entered his rectum area with his penis and performed anal sex. W stated only one occasion giving detail of the experience. The incident supposedly took place one night on a weekend when he had the room to himself as his room-mates had gone home for visits. Brother Burton supposedly entered W's room and proceeded with oral sex – kissing W's body – and this act led to anal sex when W states that Brother Burton entered his rectum at least half-way. The sexual act lasted approximately twenty minutes according to W, but W continued to be vague when describing the actual experience. He 'thought' Brother Burton 'enjoyed the experience.' I questioned him as to whether ejaculation occurred but W said 'No.' He still lay pretending to be asleep and made no responses of a similar nature to Brother Burton. He said he never made any sexual advances toward anyone at any time."

W.N. also reported that a thirty-year-old volunteer worker at Mount Cashel, officially known as Civilian 1, was "a queer too."

W.N. told Alexander that he also took exception to the strappings he received on his hands and buttocks by Brother Bucher. The social worker noted one of these occasions in her report.

"He [W.N.] shoplifted at Canadian Tire and received four–five straps on palms and two–three on his bottom. He proceeded to say that lots of the boys received this punishment, 'it's something you accept.' "

Alexander concluded her three-page report with a personal assessment of W.N. with a view to establishing his credibility.

"He avoided questions and rambled and was somewhat inconsistent. This could be that he was uneasy discussing the issue and preferred to blot it from his memory or that the incidents were indeed fabricated."

The report, marked confidential, was sent to Newfoundland's Director of Child Welfare, Frank Simms, and was signed by Karen Alexander and Neil Hamilton. In the wake of the allegations against Brother Burton, Hamilton requested a high-level meeting of Social Services personnel including the Director of Child Welfare, Frank Simms; the Assistant Director, Sheila Devine; and the department's legal adviser, Mary Noonan. Noonan advised the Director to refer the matter to the Royal Newfoundland Constabulary (the Newfoundland Constabulary got its new name in 1979, though it wouldn't be officially proclaimed until December 4, 1981) and not to contact Brother Bucher before the police began their investigation. Although she would later describe her role during the entire affair as that of someone holding "a watching brief," it was Noonan who actually placed the call to police. Frank Simms didn't bother informing his legal adviser that he had already informed Brother Bucher about the Brother Burton investigaton.

At four o'clock on the afternoon of October 15, Neil Hamilton invited Brother Bucher to a meeting in his office with Karen Alexander in which the precise contents of the social worker's report were revealed to Mount Cashel's

Superintendent. Shocked by the detailed allegations he was seeing for the first time, he hurried back to the orphanage to look for the offending Brother.

"I immediately returned to Mount Cashel and presented the facts to Brother [Burton]. And there was an immediate acknowledgement and admission of the misconduct, and then he met with the community at his request. He wanted to meet with the Brothers that he was living with to admit his failure and then from there he left the building," Bucher later explained.

Meanwhile, Sandra Morris's interview with Boy 5, whom she described as "mentally backward," had turned up the names of several more boys who were either sexually abusing younger boys or homosexually active amongst themselves. Morris documented the numerous examples in which Boy 5 had been involved in oral sex with other Mount Cashel residents, ending with her impressions of the young boy.

"[Boy 5] presents a pathetic picture. Before our interview concluded, he said to me 'What will I do if it happens again?'. . . [He] is more to be pitied than anything else. The boys involved with him range in age from 16–18 years and [Boy 5] could be easily manipulated by them. . . . From what [Boy 5] says, there would seem to be a lot of sexual activity amongst the boys at Mount Cashel which should be substantiated or otherwise."

On October 18, 1982, Det-Sgt. Len Power, who now held Arthur Pike's former post as supervisor of the Assault Section of the CID, was assigned to the Brother Burton case. The tall, angular police officer with the salt-and-pepper hair had spent eighteen years in the Constabulary, seven of them as a detective. His entire police career had been spent in St. John's. He and Det. Cyril Simms quickly confirmed Karen Alexander's information after an interview of their own with W.N. They shuddered as the boy described how he would cover his head with his pillow, plug his ears and pretend to be asleep while the sexual assaults by Brother Burton took place.

"He would try to put his penis in my rectum and a couple

of times he did get it in half-ways. Sometimes he would take my penis in his mouth . . . ," W.N. told them.

W.N. said that the sexual relationship with Burton had been going on for about a year and that it only stopped when the boy threatened to tell a social worker. W.N. also told the detective that three other Mount Cashel residents had told him that Civilian 1 had had sexual contact with them.

The day after the detective took down W.N.'s side of the story, he interviewed Brother Burton. As had been the case with Hillier's interviews with Brothers English and Ralph, their meeting did not take place at CID headquarters in St. John's, but on the church's turf – in the parlour at Holy Cross Monastery on Patrick Street. The interview began at 2:30 P.M. with the standard police caution. To Power's surprise, Burton, who was "physically and emotionally in terrible shape," quickly stated, "I want to tell you the truth."

The detective showed the Christian Brother W.N.'s police statement. Although he admitted to the various sex acts complained of by W.N., the forty-three-year-old Burton claimed that his fifteen-year-old partner had initiated their affair. He described the beginnings of the relationship, which he said dated from a summer trip he and W. N. had taken in August 1981 – the same trip during which Civilian 1 had allegedly molested other Mount Cashel boys.

"I was in the back seat of a van resting from driving. . . . W.N. was sitting next to me. There were sleeping bags there, and W.N. had one over him. He threw it over my lap and lay across me. He put his hands under the sleeping bag and started to touch me near my penis. I got aroused, but never made a serious effort to stop him. He felt my penis a couple of times, and that was all that happened. I knew I was really to blame because I should have stopped him and he was only a little boy. Sometime, maybe in September, I dropped the boys off maybe at the Stadium, I'm not sure, but W.N. came for the ride. After we drove them and dropped them off, we went on down Forest Road and W.N. started to touch me and I got aroused. I opened my zipper and he or I, I'm not sure, took out my penis. He put it in his mouth. I started then touching him. We kept driving through, on through the village around through Pleasantville and back to Mount Cashel. After that I would sometimes find him in my room at bedtime. I never really made a serious effort to send him out. At times like that, I would take off his clothes, but ... sometimes he took off my clothes, but most of the time I took off my own. I would play with his penis and sometimes put it in my mouth. He would always tell me to 'pull him.' I would do it. Sometimes, but not often, he would 'pull me.' On three or four occasions, I tried to put my penis up his rectum, but couldn't really do it. [W.N.] never objected to anything. . . ."

The detective then asked the Christian Brother how often he had had sexual relations with the boy since August 1981.

"God, it must have been more than fifty times."

"Did you have any other sexual relations with any of the other boys at the institution?"

"No."

"Do any of the boys know about this?"

"No," the Brother answered without hesitation. "I don't think they would even believe it."

The statement, written in Burton's own handwriting, was signed by the Christian Brother and the policeman at 3:25 P.M. Despite his confession, Burton was never arrested.

"I don't think I would have seen the need to arrest this person at that time in order to compel his appearance in court. . . . I was satisfied that he was in a position where offences of the nature he was suspected of committing could not be continued," Power later explained.

From all appearances, the Christian Brothers took the same steps in the Burton case as they had in the Mount Cashel affair in 1975. Gordon Bellows, who became Brother Provincial of the order in August 1978, was informed of developments and immediately flew to Newfoundland from his headquarters in Mono Mills. The Brothers informed police that Burton was staying at the order's monastery in Freshwater, Placentia Bay, and that he had been relieved of all official duties pending the outcome of the investigation.

The Christian Brothers made it clear that they were fully aware of his involvement with W.N. and promised that at the conclusion of any criminal prosecution, Brother Burton would be re-assigned to another post outside Newfoundland.

Power's report on the Brother Burton affair was sent to the Justice Department on October 25, 1982. The next day, Newfoundland's Deputy Minister of Justice, Cyril Goodyear, wrote on the top right-hand corner of the report words that echoed back to 1979 and the questionable way the Father Kelly case had been handled by Magistrate Gordon Seabright: "This person is to be treated like everybody else."

When asked several years later what had prompted the notation, Goodyear had a crisp reply.

"I remembered the [Father Ronald] Kelly case in 1979 and also at that time I had almost thirty-five years' combined experience as a policeman and as a magistrate. . . . I had learned to be wary of matters involving the clergy or oganizations of that type. . . . My experience had taught me that they were prone to exert whatever influence they might possibly exert in situations where they were having difficulties."

Ronald Richards, the senior Crown prosecutor in the Justice Department, got Goodyear's message. On November 2, he wrote to Det.-Sgt. Len Power with a clear set of instructions for charging Brother Burton.

"Further to our telephone call of today's date, please be advised that the above captioned individual should be charged with a breach of Section 157 [Acts of gross indecency] of the Criminal Code of Canada.

"The accused should be summonsed to appear in the St. John's Provincial court on November 17, at 3:30 P.M. It is anticipated at this time that the accused will be electing Magistrate without Jury and pleading guilty. We will therefore speak to sentence and the whole matter will be terminated on that day hopefully."

A week after his interview with Brother Burton, Detective-Sergeant Power turned his attention to the allegations against Civilian 1. Three different Mount Cashel boys confirmed in statements that they had had sexual encounters with the volunteer worker, both in Newfoundland and during a camping trip to Maine during the 1982 summer vacation. One of them, Boy 13, described his encounter at a campsite in either Nova Scotia or New Brunswick on the way to the United States.

"I was sleeping on one of the bunks in the trailer. . . . We were in bed about one hour. I was asleep and woke when I felt someone touching my privates.

"When I awoke I found that Civilian [1] was touching my penis. He was awake, must have been, but I didn't say anything or let him know I was awake. I was too afraid. He kept touching me even though I kept moving from side to side. He did make me hard and fluid came. He kept feeling around my ass after that but after a while he stopped. . . ."

When Power brought Civilian 1 to CID headquarters and confronted him with the three statements from the Mount Cashel boys, the man tersely replied, "I have read the statements given by the three individuals and deny the allegations. I feel that they have misinterpreted any contact with them during the past summer holidays while on our trip. That's all I think I should say for now."

Crown prosecutor Hyslop would later dispose of the allegations against Civilian 1 in a letter to the Chief of Police.

"I do not believe we have sufficient evidence to proceed against the above noted person. I have no doubt whatever that offences were committed by him; however anything provable occurred outside of our territorial jurisdiction and no action can be taken."

After the smoke of the 1982 investigations cleared, Civilian 1 fulfilled his ambition to join the Christian Brothers, but left the order a short while later to return to his former profession as a pharmacist.

Power himself would later acknowledge the woeful inadequacy of his 1982 investigation at Mount Cashel. Burton's claim that W.N. had been his sole sexual contact at Mount Cashel was never independently investigated.

Feeling at the time that it would be somehow "intrusive" to interview people who did not come forward of their own volition, Power shied away from fully investigating allegations that older juveniles at the orphanage were sexually abusing younger residents. As for the allegations against Civilian 1, they were not even pursued with police authorities in other jurisdictions.

Once again, the children of Mount Cashel had proven to be institutionally invisible.

A week after Richards forwarded his written instructions on the Burton case to Det.-Sgt. Len Power, social worker Stead Crawford wrote an alarming memo to Newfoundland's Director of Child Welfare, Frank Simms, who was now being inundated with reports about Mount Cashel. The memo made reference to widespread homosexual activity amongst boys at Mount Cashel. To make matters worse, some of the victims of 1975 had apparently become the victimizers of 1982. A vicious cycle of sexual perversion had moved up to the next generation of abusers, and Newfoundland's justice and social service systems were about to reap the dark harvest.

Boy 14, a twelve-year-old resident of Mount Cashel, told Crawford that he had become involved in frequent oral and anal sex with his room-mate, Boy 5, who would sometimes bite his penis. Boy 3 once caught Boy 14 and Boy 5 in a sex act and reported them to Brother Bucher who he said "slapped them both" but took no further steps to prevent their sexual trysts. Crawford detected no sense of remorse or wrongdoing in Boy 14.

"He doesn't feel that it was all that wrong but is embarrassed about talking about it. He obtained pleasure out of it as the sexual behaviour either oral sex or anal sex lasted until each party had received a climax. [Boy 14] was even able to describe the flavour of the sperm fluid.... Though [Boy 14] is considered slow, he was able to give vivid detailes [sic] of homosexual activity including mutual masturbation, thigh intercourse, oral intercourse, and anal intercourse. His descriptions were too accurate to be fabrications or stories told him by other individuals."

Crawford was puzzled by one thing: how had the rampant homosexuality amongst boys at Mount Cashel gone undetected by authorities for so long?

"I have no reason to doubt what he [Boy 14] told me. He was engaged in sexual activity every other night. Surely if this behaviour was so prevalent, sometime down the road some adult in an official role would have seen something going on? . . . The homosexual activity was way above what would be considered normal to expect and . . . I feel there seems to have been a complete neglect of acceptable sexual education in this institution and possibl[y] supervision."

Two days later, senior Crown prosecutor Robert Hyslop wrote to Mary Noonan, the solicitor for the Social Services Department, to confirm that she had been fully informed about the facts surrounding the police investigation into homosexual abuse at Mount Cashel. Regrettably, Hyslop would neglect to inform Ronald Richards, the prosecutor in the Brother Burton case, of the 1975 incident at Mount Cashel, presumably because he failed to connect the two events in his own mind.

"For my records," Hyslop wrote, "it was my understanding that Detective Power was given a clear direction as to how his further investigations should proceed, since he sought our advice in that regard. We advised that older children victimizing younger children and persons in authority should be clearly investigated and charges laid if warranted.

"On a more serious matter, having read the memorandum of Mr. Stead Crawford to the Director of Child Welfare, it was decided among us that there were only two viable options which could be put to the Director of Child Welfare. You undertook to follow this up with the Department of Social Services, and I would appreciate it if you would informally advise me of any decision made by the Director in this regard."

Exactly what the two options were is unclear. Years later, Hyslop, Noonan and Frank Simms would claim that they could not decipher what the memo meant, although social worker Neil Hamilton recalled that the closing of Mount Cashel had been under discussion at the time. As for the investigative situation they were faced with, the CID was not interested in aggressively pursuing criminal investigations involving young people at Mount Cashel.

"There came a point in that investigation . . . that I recall the feeling that 'this is getting out of hand, there's so much of this happening down there.' And I recall feeling that it was a matter for Social Services as opposed to the police. . . ," Det.-Sgt. Len Power later recalled.

Robert Hyslop in the Justice Department apparently agreed. As he would later explain, the Justice Department was not particularly anxious to "criminalize or prosecute" children who were sexually active with one another. Instead, the Crown opted to bring the aberrant behaviour going on at Mount Cashel to the attention of the Director of Child Welfare for modification, direction and guidance. Still, if there were strong indications that older children were victimizing younger ones, a strange qualification for justice officials to make given the evidence police and social workers had already gathered, then the older children would have to be brought to court in the interests of protecting their victims. But the desire to protect young victims never rose above the level of Justice Department rhetoric.

One older boy Det.-Sgt. Power tried half-heartedly to interview in relation to an allegation of abuse from a young Mount Cashel resident was Shane Earle, who had himself been molested at the institution as a small boy. Word had come back to Shane through Brother Bucher that one of Shane's older sexual partners had seriously implicated himself in possible criminal acts during an interview with police.

"Brother Bucher came to me and told me that E.J. hung himself [figuratively] and I don't want you to do the same," Earle remembered.

Bucher took Earle to see the Christian Brothers' lawyer, William English, to advise him what to do if the police called for an interview.

"And I knew what I was there for. I felt I could be charged. He asked me at one point am I a homosexual. And I just looked at him and said, 'I don't know, I really don't.' So he said, 'I'll tell you what to do.' He said, 'Go home, don't go down to the police station and give a statement. Go home.'"

When the police called the orphanage looking for Earle, he told them that he had been "strongly advised not to make a statement."

"That was the end of that. . . . But during the time that we were having sexual encounters with each other and with the younger kids . . . the Brothers knew and nothing was done. . . ." Earle later recalled.

Brother Bucher strongly denied that he had any first-hand knowledge of sexual activities amongst the boys at the orphanage. And he claimed that the only reason he took Shane Earle to a lawyer was that he believed the boys had the right to legal counsel, given that the police had informed him that some of them could be charged.

"I can tell you and I swear before Almighty God that my motivation was solely to provide this young person with the services he had a right to so he could make an intelligent decision as to what he wanted to do and what he didn't want to do," he said in an interview with *The Evening Telegram*.

In the end, although thirteen separate reports were written about Mount Cashel in the autumn of 1982, nine by Social Services and four by the police, no one except Brother Burton was charged.

There was talk of providing four more social workers at the institution, but they never materialized. Even though the Social Services Department had irrefutable documentation of a major sex scandal at the orphanage, and copies of the reports had been forwarded to Frank Simms, there was no follow-up contact with the residents of Mount Cashel, no counselling and no medical help. Once again, Newfoundland's Director of Child Welfare did not review the police reports into the activities of his wards, just as he hadn't in 1975 – partly because the Justice Department didn't forward them to Social Services as it should have. Despite the graphic information Mary Noonan received on the 1982 investigation, she still didn't connect the horrors going on at Mount Cashel with the 1975 police reports she had been forbidden to see. Social Services Minister Thomas Hickey, who knew about the Brother Burton incident, claimed he was never advised of complaints against Civilian 1 or any of the reports on sexual activity amongst the boys. Seven years later, when it came to explaining why the system had failed to respond to yet another tragedy at Mount Cashel, social worker Neil Hamilton was at a loss.

"It baffles me. . . . It just didn't happen."

The trial of Brother David Burton began on November 17, 1982, before Provincial Court Judge E. J. Langdon. Almost immediately, the manoeuvring of defence counsel William English made it clear that his principal task in representing Brother Burton was to keep all reference to the facts of the case and to Mount Cashel off the public record.

When Judge Langdon asked Brother Burton to elect trial by judge or jury, English quickly intervened with a request to have the court order an in camera session so that he could privately make his case for hearing the substance of the proceedings in an in camera hearing – a highly unusual application. What English was requesting was the right to bar the public from even hearing his arguments for conducting the Burton trial in secret. With the startled judge looking on, counsel for the defence handed him written affidavits that made clear that Burton would be entering a guilty plea. The Crown immediately objected, wondering if it too would have to make its arguments in writing. The judge asked again for an election and plea from the accused. Burton chose to proceed in front of a judge, without jury, and entered a guilty plea.

English then asked for three things: an in camera hearing, a publication ban on all evidence relating to the charge against Brother Burton and a permanent seal on the proceedings that would forever prevent them from being publicly scrutinized. The defence lawyer went on to urge the court to accept written submissions on the need for judicial secrecy in the case from Brother Gordon Bellows, by then Brother Provincial of the Canada–West Indies Province of the Christian Brothers.

Crown prosecutor Ronald Richards objected. He argued

that the public had the right to be fully informed of the reasons a hearing is to be held in camera. Judge Langdon ruled that English could make arguments for a Section 442 in camera order (a request to exclude the public and hear a legal matter in a judge's chambers), but that those arguments would have to be made in open court. Reluctant as he was to lead evidence in a public forum, English nevertheless called Brother Bellows to make the case for holding Burton's hearing in secret. Bellows pleaded his case from every angle, but his last and strongest argument revealed a greater concern for Christian Brother public relations than for justice, or compassion for Burton's youthful victim.

"Well, I think really that the key reason that I would object to publicity would be the terrible, detrimental effect it would have upon eighty-five innocent children at Mount Cashel," Bellows testified. "These youngsters, many of them, are emotionally disturbed, disadvantaged in so many ways. They are totally incapable of handling the pressures or any additional pressures that would be brought upon them. I think that the slurs and the innuendo that would be hurled at them by their classmates and even by insensitive adults would crush a great number of them."

Bellows went on to describe Burton's connection to Mount Cashel.

"Brother Burton specifically has charge of some twenty youngsters. He is their guardian, he is their parent, and they love him. They love him deeply. Not only these twenty, but the other sixty-five in my judgment would be just damaged in so many ways were this thing to go public."

But damage to the boys wasn't the only, or even the primary, thing on Brother Bellows's mind as he helped English support his case for an in camera hearing.

"I think it would also have a very unfortunate effect upon Mount Cashel itself. It is an institution that has been in existence since 1898. It has a prestigious record. . . . Its reputation is a very, very high one indeed. I think it would have a damaging effect on the relations between the staff, the Christian Brothers and the lay staff – men and women that are there – by reflection, by association it would impinge upon them and certainly that extension is something that can't be taken lightly, and for that reason, therefore, the effect on the orphanage itself, the effect that it would have on the Congregation of Christian Brothers, a body of men who have given their lives to education here in Newfoundland. . . ."

Even as he gave his testimony, Brother Bellows was well aware that Mount Cashel's "very, very high" reputation wasn't quite as untarnished as he wanted the court to believe, knowing as he did of the previous sex scandal at the orphanage and the subsequent deal that kept it secret. In 1975, Bellows had been the Christian Brother who confronted Brother Edward English with the allegations of sexual abuse against him, and later passed on English's confession to Brother Provincial Gabriel McHugh. Under cross-examination from Richards, Bellows made it crystal clear that his main concern in asking that the hearing be heard in camera was to protect the reputation of the Christian Brothers at all costs. His testimony provided a reprise of what may well have been the elements of the argument that were made to Vincent McCarthy seven years earlier, when the Congregation and the Justice Department closed ranks over the Mount Cashel affair and cut a deal. But this time around, the Crown, in the person of Ronald Richards, wasn't accepting those arguments uncritically.

"Would you not, in your capacity, feel that Mount Cashel's reputation would exceed the one incident that would be published?" Richards asked.

"I think that the kind of damage that would be done by an incident of this type would be irreparable, and I think that the good work that has been done over eighty-four years is such that I would strongly urge the court to keep it in mind that the entire community of Newfoundland has benefited. There are hundreds of people who have gone through this institution and who look upon it with respect and with admiration and affection; and hence to slur the name of that institution in the public media at this time, in my judgment would have a devastating effect. . . ," Bellows answered.

"And then, Brother, you know the charge that is before the court. I understand you know the facts of the charge." Richards was trying to focus Bellows' mind on the grotesque breach of trust represented by Burton's serious crimes, instead of their public-relations impact on the Brothers if they were revealed.

"Yes, sir."

"Would you say that's the kind of conduct that would add to the benefit and the adjustment of the children?"

"I certainly would not. And for that reason, therefore, we indicated that the individual has been taken – he was immediately removed from the scene. I've indicated that he would receive competent and professional psychiatric help and assistance at the desire of the court. There certainly wasn't any – none whatsoever – no temporizing with this at all. There was immediate action on the part of the authorities at Mount Cashel for the well-being of the children."

Implicit in Bellows's answer was the notion that the justice system should be prepared to deal differently with offending Christian Brothers, in exchange for the promise of psychiatric help for the accused, a transfer out of Newfoundland and speedy action by authorities at Mount Cashel. Richards was dumbfounded by the argument that an institution that was so well respected in the province could not survive the publication of a situation involving one Brother. He had no way of knowing that Brother Bellows had been over this ground once before in 1975 and managed at that time to keep the scandal entirely out of the public eye.

"You are saying that the publication of this one incident is going to destroy all the good reputation of Mount Cashel? It would not stand up to the one incident, the one publication?"

"I think that when you begin to knock the foundation from a building, sir, then you begin to weaken the whole structure. . . . The good name of a place, a person or an institution is beyond value. . . . I feel there's been a regrettable breach of trust and I believe that – I think the old Latin expression, and I can't quote it in Latin, but I remember the translation – 'The fall of the best is the worst.' I feel that's really what had happened. It's heartbreaking. But you know the man has done twenty-five years of extraordinary service. You don't suddenly wipe him out like that because of human weakness, and I think were the case to be heard in camera that you could go explore that particular aspect of it fully. . . ."

"So you're basically saying that the public shouldn't have knowledge that there was a breach of trust involving an individual [W.N.] who has no choice but to be there [at Mount Cashel]?" Richards asked.

"I think what you're really questioning is the ability of the Brothers at Mount Cashel to handle this matter as they've handled it. There's no doubt about it. We are taking steps to rehabilitate this particular man. We are doing it in such a way that he'll be fully returned, please God, to a fully functioning individual in the classroom. That is a key concern of ours. I really don't see what this kind of publicity will do. Will it help the individual? Will it help the institution? . . ."

"Brother, perhaps wouldn't it be of some benefit for society to know about this situation?"

"I really don't think so. I think, frankly, that in my judgment, what you're proposing is to damage children and if that's the course of action you feel [is appropriate], then I think that I would not want to be party to that."

Richards was infuriated by Bellows's smug and self-serving answers, believing as he did that the children of Mount Cashel were the last people the man in the witness box was concerned about. Nor did the Crown prosecutor appreciate the pompous and condescending manner in which the position of the Christian Brothers was being presented to the Court by Brother Bellows. Bellows's superciliousness, coupled with the high-pressure tactics of other Brothers, who asked Richards on his way into court why he was "doing this to the institution," inspired the Crown prosecutor to conduct the most aggressive cross-examination of his career.

"Of course, as you know, Brother, it is the decision of the court whether or not it is out public or not," he continued, none too gently making the point that whether he liked the idea or not, Bellows would be giving his testimony publicly if Judge Langdon so decided.

"Yes."

"And not a decision by the Crown to damage children?"

"Yes."

"If the damage, if any, was done, it was done by the individual concerned?"

"Well, I certainly am not denying that at all, but I think that the rehabilitation of the individual can be done fully and completely while at the same time preserving the emotional − what emotional balance these children have − and at the same time preserving the integrity of a long-established institution. . . ."

The next day, Judge Langdon turned down the defence application for an in camera hearing. Crown prosecutor Richards summarized the charge against Burton, chiefly by reading the accused Brother's statement. Counsel for the defence made no comment and Langdon was about to enter a conviction on the guilty plea and summary of evidence when defence counsel William English suddenly asked the judge to consider a discharge in the case. To back up his request, English called Dr. Nizar Ladha, a psychiatrist from Memorial University who also worked at Waterford Hospital, the province's mental institution.

Ladha painted the picture of a good man who had been overwhelmed on this one occasion by his biological urges − apparently forgetting that the accused had admitted to fifty sexual contacts with his fifteen-year-old charge, including buggery. Based on three and a half hours with Burton, Ladha concluded that W.N. had been his only sexual contact at Mount Cashel. He further concluded that because Burton did not have multiple sexual contacts with other youngsters, and did not have homosexual or bisexual fantasies, the Brother was not a homosexual and the case didn't involve "sexual deviation" − a flight of professional fancy that Judge Langdon found hard to swallow.

"I think it would be a pity," Dr. Ladha testified, referring to Burton's twenty-five years of sterling service to the order, "to destroy or further harm this potential . . . I think reha-bilitation, perhaps within the Order, rehabilitation to see a psychiatrist would be wise."

The judge could not have missed how remarkably similar

the good doctor's views were to the ones Brother Bellows had already espoused.

The defence then called the first of two character witnesses for Brother Burton – Raymond Lahey, Vicar General of the Archdiocese of St. John's. The future Roman Catholic bishop praised Brother Burton as an indefatigable worker in the cause of the children entrusted to him, a man who "had a tremendous talent for handling children who were tremendously disadvantaged." The Vicar General was less enthusiastic about Burton's victim, W.N.

"I think anyone who even visited there [Mount Cashel] for a short time would take note of him. He was a child who constantly demanded attention. He constantly demanded attention of someone and in particular of the accused. He would go to any lengths to gain attention. He was very aggressive in that. . . . He would demand attention by even interrupting conversation, shouting, pulling at people's arms or punching them in the arm. I even saw him bounce a ball off the wall consistently to get attention. . . ."

Lahey didn't come right out and say that W.N. had instigated the relationship with Brother Burton, but the implication of his testimony was clear; the fifteen-year-old was a problem child who relentlessly pursued the accused to satisfy his insatiable craving for affection – however that might be defined. When asked by counsel for the defence if he had noticed any change in W.N. over the past year, Lahey testified that he had.

"I think he matured over that year, very definitely. I think you could see a [visible] progress. He gained, I think, a self-esteem or self-confidence which he didn't seem to have at the beginning of my period of visiting there. He gained a certain amount of academic confidence too. He was a very slow learner academically, but he showed a very marked improvement in that respect."

Sexual abuse apparently agreed with W.N. The year in which the Vicar General noted such an improvement in the young boy was the same period of time in which he was being sexually molested by Brother Burton.

The pattern of the Vicar General's testimony – eulogizing Brother Burton and casting W.N. in a bad light – was repeated in the evidence given by the next defence witness, Brother Henry Bucher. Noting that Brother Burton was "extraordinary with children," Mount Cashel's Superintendent paid the accused glowing tribute as a favourite of the boys he looked after.

"If somebody forced me to fault the man, the only thing that I can say is that he cared too much and he loved too much. . . . From my observation of the five households, the trust and confidence and love in St. Joe's, which is the name of the group Brother Burton looks after, by far is the most distinctive. They love the man. They love him the way any one of us would love our parents. It is because of his goodness — because of his unquestion[able] goodness."

As for W.N., Brother Bucher said he was a clinging, delinquent child who had made a "marvellous turn around" under the care of Brother Burton. Mount Cashel's Superintendent warned of devastating consequences if the charges against Burton became known at the orphanage.

Crown prosecutor Richards had heard just about enough on the subject of all the people who would be hurt by publication of the facts of the Burton case. It was about time, he decided, to get the views of the Brothers on the damage done to the victim of Burton's crime, W.N.

"I haven't heard too much analysis of the individual W.N. You just gave an analysis of the effect on the other eighty-four or eighty-five back there, and a human being being destroyed never fully overcomes this. Well, what do you say in relation to this poor W.N.?"

Bucher's reply was as telling as it was callous.

"The assumption that this person has been destroyed is something that I find hard to accept and deal with. Hurt — destroyed, I question. I really wouldn't have the knowledge with me to be able to responsibly answer that question."

The defence concluded its plea for a discharge of Brother Burton by recalling Brother Gordon Bellows, whose testimony perfectly complemented the words of the preceding witnesses, as it was doubtless intended to do.

"He [Brother Burton] is an extraordinary human being who tragically fell. We weep for that fall, we weep for the fault. He is a beautiful person, and that's all I can say."

Bellows testified that he had made arrangements for Brother Burton's rehabilitation at Southdown and added a passionate plea that the accused be allowed to emerge from the tragedy without a criminal record.

"I would shudder to think that a criminal conviction would be given to a man whose twenty-five years of service to youth is so incredibly good. We can't deny the fatal flaw that has brought him down, but if he were given a criminal record, I feel it would really destroy his credibility, destroy his authenticity, make it difficult for him to continue in a teaching career, make it pretty impossible to transfer him from one Christian Brother school throughout Canada [to another]. . . . It would simply make it very difficult for him to move about. It would simply crush him as a human being. For that reason, I would find it absolutely appalling."

It was a strange logic that saw the criminal's punishment as fatally destructive, but the victim's suffering as arguable. Ronald Richards, for one, was unimpressed. He asked for a jail sentence for Burton, both to protect the public and as deterrence to other potential child molesters. He noted that Burton admitted to having sexual relations with W.N. more than fifty times – hardly what could be called an isolated failing. Although gross indecency carried a maximum penalty of five years in prison, Richards stressed that while he was looking for a period of incarceration, he didn't necessarily favour a lengthy one.

With his request for a conditional discharge of Brother Burton still before the court, William English concluded his defence by raising the example of the Father Ronald Kelly case from 1979, where the court had decided that a prison term was inappropriate despite the seriousness of his crime. He asked Judge Langdon to be guided by the Kelly case, noting that the most important thing was to get Brother Burton back into the classroom as quickly as possible. Finally, English, like the witnesses whose testimony he had called, attempted to downplay the impact of Brother Burton's crimes against W.N.

"I don't think there has been any firm evidence before you that this boy has been devastated as a result of this. One must weigh the good with the bad. I would submit that the evidence of the good outweighs the bad, despite the badness of the bad."

At 2:00 P.M. the next day, Judge Langdon made some general remarks about his feelings about the case. He began by saying that the court would not allow a conditional discharge, and that protection of the public must come before the rehabilitation of the accused. He had harsh words for the medical opinion of Dr. Ladha, which held that Brother Burton's crime didn't involve sexual deviation, homosexuality or pedophilia.

"One has to ask, how and why did the offence occur if there is no sexual deviation present in the accused and if there is no evidence of homosexuality and there is no evidence of pedophilia. Why is the accused before the court at all? . . ."

Before he pronounced sentence on Brother Burton, Judge Langdon rejected the claim made by various Christian Brother witnesses that publicity about the case would seriously damage the other boys living at Mount Cashel. He noted that "not one witness" had considered the effect on W.N., the victim. "That is certainly not consistent with logic or common sense in this court's opinion," the judge said.

Judge Langdon sentenced Brother Burton to four months in jail and three years' probation with psychiatric help.

William English filed for an appeal the next day, November 19, stating that Burton should have been discharged and that the sentence was excessive. He said the trial judge did not give weight to the mitigating circumstances, referring to "the absence of force or violence and the absence of any evidence to the effect that any injury was actually sustained to any person as a result of the offence."

Burton's appeal was heard just twelve days after his trial, speedy trip through the clogged avenues of the justice system. Ronald Richards argued that Burton's conviction and sentence should be upheld on the basis that there had been an enormous breach of trust, and that the Brother's victim had been totally vulnerable to his tormentor because he had no choice but to reside at Mount Cashel. The court, comprised of Chief Justice A. S. Mifflin, and Justices J. R. Gushue (the judge who had turned down the Crown's appeal in the Father Kelly case) and John Mahoney, preferred to focus on the high reputation of the Christian Brothers and the delinquent nature of W.N. Richards, a future Deputy Minister of Justice, later offered his recollections of the case at the Hughes Inquiry.

"What I do recall is that the court spent the majority of [its] time indicating how good and beneficial the Brotherhood and the Christian Brothers [were] and that we were only dealing with a — I forget the exact words used — but I don't think I would be totally out of line by saying 'a punk' in terms of dealing with and describing W.N.

"I can remember saying to the court 'But my Lords, this was not one but this was fifty occurrences. And I remember the court basically screaming at me, 'Don't get into the facts, Mr. Richards, don't get into the facts.' Well at that point in time I really had the feeling I had at the provincial court level when dealing with the Christian Brothers. Now I had it at the Court of Appeal that absolutely nobody really cared about W.N., the child.

"It was my feeling then and it is still my feeling today in response to the Court of Appeal hearing, that absolutely no consideration was given to the child and every consideration was given to the Christian Brothers."

The Court of Appeal upheld Burton's conviction, but reduced his sentence to time already served — twelve days. Probation remained at three years, and rehabilitation was left to the discretion of the Brother Provincial of the Christian Brothers. Brother Burton was treated at Southdown before being reassigned to teach at St. Thomas More Collegiate in Burnaby, British Columbia. The principal of the school was Brother Kevin Short, a former Mount Cashel colleague accused of sexual abuse in the suppressed 1975 Mount Cashel police probe who, under the terms of the deal struck between the Christian Brothers and the Justice Department, was not to be reassigned to the orphanage.

Once more, the Christian Brothers had closed ranks to minimize the consequences of the criminal acts of a member of their order, albeit in the Burton case, with a far less malleable cast of Justice Department players than they had dealt with in 1975. Although the trial made its way into the press, the exposure was minimal. Coverage in *The Daily News* amounted to a five-column-inch story on page twenty-one next to the crossword puzzle. Despite the publicity, Mount Cashel somehow managed to survive.

But in Newfoundland and elsewhere, these subtle manipulations of the sytem by the Roman Catholic church were getting harder and harder to accomplish. Where the system had previously dealt with religious offenders in the judicial shadows, a spectacular case in the United States would soon drag the festering problem of the sexual abuse of children by clergymen under the hard and unblinking eye of national attention.

The days of special dispensation for Roman Catholic clergy in the courts were about to come to a dramatic, and expensive, end.

Chapter *10*
An American Unmasking

> *He's a very, very unique person. He's got a sort of Dr. Jekyll and Mr. Hyde personality . . . and he certainly deceived me.* Gerard Frey, Bishop of Lafayette, commenting on Father Gilbert Gauthe, the first priest in the United States to be indicted for sex crimes against children.

THEY MAY NOT have been related, but Father Gilbert Gauthe was Jim Hickey's American cousin in crime.

From the December day in 1971 when he was ordained in St. Ann's Church at the same altar where he made his first communion, until his suspension in 1983 after molesting more than one hundred boys in four different parishes, the priest from Napoleonville, Louisiana, led a double life. On the surface, the twenty-six-year-old graduate of Notre Dame Seminary was the ideal parish priest − dedicated, charismatic, always there when needed. He even bought a powerful ham radio to intercept police calls, which allowed him to make miraculous appearances at accident scenes to minister to the spiritual needs of the injured and dying. Although his annual salary was only $7,200, it was boosted to $18,000 through financial gifts from grateful parishioners. What they most appreciated was Gauthe's remarkable interest in their children.

Like Newfoundland's priestly champion of youth, Jim Hickey, Father Gauthe couldn't do enough for his chosen constituency. He was Chaplain of the Boy Scouts in the diocese, travelled regularly with the little-league baseball and basketball teams in Abbeville, Louisiana, and took children, usually boys, on weekend camping and fishing trips to the great − and unsupervised − outdoors. When he wasn't taking them on outings in his motor camper to the enchanting cypress swamps and secluded bayous of south Louisiana, the slim, dark-haired priest encouraged the children to visit the rectory, where they had the run of the house and often stayed overnight. But as with Father Hickey, there was a price to be paid for taking Gauthe up on his hospitality: sexual co-operation with the pedophile priest who by turns coddled and coerced them.

After the sexual sessions in the rectory, which Gauthe liked to photograph with an instant camera, the priest let the boys play video games. He also let them view pornographic tapes which he surreptitiously purchased in the parking lot of an Abbeville supermarket. When rewards and entertainment didn't work, he bent the children to his will with less subtle manipulation. He told one of his victims that he would kill his father if the boy exposed the priest's secret. One way or the other, Gauthe usually got what he wanted – sex and silence. Given the ages of his victims – seven to nine – it was like taking candy from babies.

"All of the incidents had more or less the same pattern where I got to know one of the children, and, you know, they would come over to the house a few times, and then there would be just some wrestling or tickling or something like that, and then there'd be some molesting and then – from that point on – we'd get into sexual activity," the priest would later testify.

In a later civil case against Gauthe, it would be alleged that the priest seduced his victims in an initiation ring connected to the ritual installation of altar boys. Gauthe sodomized some boys before morning mass and had oral sex with others in the confessional and the sacristy. His victims were the same youngsters Gauthe had personally trained in the rituals of the mass.

But there was one important difference between Jim Hickey and Gilbert Gauthe. While Father Hickey successfully concealed his dual life from his parishioners for nearly twenty years, Gauthe's charade came to light during his very first assignment as a priest, and several times thereafter, without immediate professional or legal consequences. Senior officials of the Roman Catholic church simply chose to transfer the troubled priest to new parishes while dealing with his victims in the shadows, instead of treating his abuse of children as the serious crime that it was – an approach that would eventually cost the church $15 million in legal settlements and priceless moral collateral.

Gauthe's illicit sexual behaviour first surfaced in 1972. Several angry parents from Broussard, in the parish of Lafayette, confronted Gauthe at a church outing, with disturbing stories they had heard from their children. Gauthe freely admitted that he had molested three boys and begged the parents to help him find a good psychiatrist. Remarkably, they agreed. Without informing his church superiors, Gauthe saw a psychiatrist over the next several months and his understanding parishioners even footed the bill.

The therapist tried to shock him into curtailing his pedophilia by asking him to imagine the embarrassment of being caught. Gauthe's imagination wasn't up to the task.

The very next year, two nuns grew uneasy about Father Gauthe's activities with young boys who were frequent visitors at the rectory. Afraid to accuse Gauthe falsely, they asked Father Vincent O'Connell, a priest who regularly visited the parish to help organize sugar cane workers, if the rumours about the young priest were true. O'Connell implied that they were. The nuns shuddered, remembering a story they had been told by another Sister who had taught some of Gauthe's young charges. Father Gauthe had summoned a boy out of parochial class, who later returned to his desk with the horrifying traces of what had happened to him still stamped on his young face. The nuns made a rule never to allow young boys to leave school to go to Father Gauthe's rectory again.

In 1974, the new Bishop of Lafayette, Gerard Frey, the son of a wealthy New Orleans family, was informed that Father Gauthe had engaged in "impure touches" with a boy in Broussard the previous year. Gauthe admitted this latest deviance to the bishop, a man who hated confrontation, and promised it wouldn't happen again. The young priest was transferred to another parish in New Iberia, Louisiana, and a year later, in 1975, Bishop Frey named Father Gauthe diocesan Boy Scout Chaplain. While in New Iberia, Gauthe molested six more boys, and although he shared the rectory with six other priests, no one either confronted or reported him. That was in part, at least, understandable; it would later be revealed that one of the priests was sharing boys with Gauthe.

By 1976, Gauthe was on the move again, this time to St. Mary Magdalene parish in Abbeville, Louisiana. Not long after his arrival, Monsignor Richard Mouton received a complaint from two sets of parents that Gauthe had licked their sons' cheeks during a visit to his motor camper, a variation on Father Hickey's strange predeliction. Mouton informed Monsignor Henri Larroque, the Vicar General of Lafayette diocese, who in turn ordered Gauthe to seek psychiatric help. Gauthe attended six therapy sessions, without any interruption in his priestly duties. Mouton made no inquiries about Gauthe's treatment or progress, later explaining, "I am trained as a priest to forgive sins." He did, however, forbid Gauthe to have boys in the rectory.

Despite the worried eyes that were now watching him from within his own church, Gauthe continued to take boys on camping trips into the lush and steamy Louisiana countryside, and even travelled to Puerto Rico with Abbeville's little-league basketball team. As it turned out, little boys weren't the only people he could manipulate – a trait common to most pedophiles. As he later said under oath, "I downplayed and actually lied to both the psychiatrist and Monsignor Mouton. I made it seem like it was not as serious as it really was."

Monsignor Larroque spoke only informally to the priest about his therapy, presuming that all clinical matters had been covered by the therapist. His failure to follow up on the ethical implications of the troubled priest's behaviour clearly demonstrated that the least of the Monsignor's worries was the issue of Gauthe's moral fitness for his calling. Parishioners in Gauthe's ever-changing parishes were not informed of the tainted priest's unsavoury past. Neither was Gauthe reported to law officers by Roman Catholic church officials who knew very well what he had been doing, even though failure to do so violated Article 25 of the Louisiana Criminal Code, which defined an accessory after the fact as anyone who harboured, concealed or aided the offender of a felony.

In 1977, just before Christmas, Father Gauthe became pastor of St. John's Church in Henry, Louisiana, a small and staunchly Catholic town in the Cajun rice belt populated by the descendants of the Acadians who were expelled from Nova Scotia more than two centuries before. It was to be his last parish. For the next five and a half years he lived alone in the rectory, his solitude eased by the small boys who were regular visitors there. A little over two years later, on April 5, 1980, Bishop Gerard Frey received an anonymous letter complaining that "Father's house" had become a second home for young Abbeville boys. It was signed "Concerned Parishioners of St. John's Parish." Although Frey knew of Gauthe's past sexual assaults on young boys, he neither questioned the priest nor any of the Abbeville boys, ostensibly because he thought the letter was too vague.

Community anger began to find its voice on June 27, 1983, when a man walked into the Abbeville law office of Paul Hebert and claimed that Father Gauthe had been molesting his three sons in Henry, Louisiana, for several years. Hebert's first thought was not of the possible damages connected with the alleged assaults, but of how to get the priest out of the pulpit if the allegations against him proved true. Since the bishop was away at his summer retreat, Hebert, a Catholic, arranged a meeting with Monsignor Larroque for his new client and two of his sons. The same church official who knew of Gauthe's proclivities and who had, in fact, ordered him never to bring boys to his rectory again, expressed sympathy for the family's plight and promised action. But the boil was beginning to burst. Within days of the visit to Monsignor Larroque, Hebert had four more families to represent, all claiming that Gauthe had sexually abused their children.

Monsignor Larroque immediately set out for Bay St. Louis to inform Bishop Frey about his meeting with Paul Hebert. Two days later, the bishop summoned Father Gauthe and said, "Gil, we have a big problem. It's with little boys." Gauthe began to weep, but this time displays of remorse would not be enough; through his sobs, the slyly manipulative pedophile heard the bishop tell him that he had twenty-four hours to leave Henry. The next morning Gauthe said mass for the last time and drove to Opelousas, Louisiana, where he consulted a psychiatrist. Afterwards, he returned to his family home in Napoleonville and reportedly suffered a nervous collapse. Whatever his medical condition, Gauthe temporarily disappeared from public sight.

Since all Gauthe's victims had been altar boys, Hebert asked Monsignor Larroque to contact the families of every altar boy in Henry and nearby Esther, where Gauthe also said mass. Larroque never complied. As word of Gauthe's abuses spread, enraged parents clamoured for his arrest and jailing. Hebert explained that the boys would have to give statements to police and other legal authorities to bring that about – a process that could prove very painful for Gauthe's still-fragile victims.

Gauthe was swiftly suspended by Bishop Frey. The pastor of Abbeville, Monsignor Richard Mouton, then gave a sermon in which he told Henry's Roman Catholic parishioners that Gauthe had been sent away for "serious moral indiscretions." In a spectacular example of myopic self-interest, Mouton proposed to one parent of an abused boy that the children confess their sins as a means of remedying the pain.

In August 1983 Gauthe was interviewed and assessed at the House of Affirmation, the same church-run treatment centre in Whitinsville, Massachusetts, where Christian Brother Edward English had received treatment in 1976. After his screening, Gauthe returned to Napoleonville and lived there, essentially without supervision, for two months until a vacancy opened up at the House of Affirmation. He remained at the institution for a year, and the diocese of Lafayette picked up the bill for his stay. Under canon law, the medical expenses of priests are specifically the responsibility of the church.

Although the ostensible purpose of the House of Affirmation was to help troubled priests, the *National Catholic Reporter* would later run a story saying that the treatment centre's primary goal was to keep clergy from walking away from their ministry – an important mission given that U.S. seminary enrolment had dropped from 48,000 in 1965 to just 7,500 by 1988.

Ironically, the same year that Gauthe was sent to the House of Affirmation, staff members accused the centre's director, the Rev. Dr. Thomas A. Kane, of siphoning off funds to purchase a Florida condominium and operate a tourist inn in Maine. The board of directors of the institute took no action, and those who complained either quit or were fired. Three years later, amidst similar allegations and questions about Reverend Doctor Kane's credentials, Bishop Timothy Harrington turned over daily operations at the centre to a professional manager and ordered Kane to resign. The House of Affirmation never recovered from the scandal and closed its doors for good on December 31, 1989.

Although the church had expressed sympathy for Father Gauthe's victims, it was slow in making good on its promise to help the boys and their families. Six weeks after Gauthe's internal suspension, Bishop Frey proposed a meeting with a core group of victim-families and a psychologist, the cost to be borne by the diocese. The lengthy delay wasn't appreciated.

"This caution was necessary not simply to avoid scandal and harm to the church, but primarily to avoid any further injury or trauma to the young people and their families," the bishop lamely explained.

In fact, Bishop Frey was caught in a classic conflict of interest. The Bishop is the "father of his priests" and must forgive them when they stray. The Bishop is also the chief pastor of the diocese, and must deal with the injured flock whenever the occasion arises. Lastly, the Bishop is the chief executive officer of the diocese and must protect its interests and the interests of the church as a whole. As events unfolded in Lafayette, it became clear that of these three responsibilities, concern for the congregation was Bishop Frey's lowest priority.

The community's anger at the church's self-interested acquiescence in Gauthe's crimes was tersely expressed by Tony Fontana, an attorney and devout Catholic who eventually represented some of the victims in civil actions against Gauthe and the church.

"The damages in these cases are going to come from outrage – not that Gauthe molested kids, but that Frey knew about Gauthe in 1975 . . . I feel betrayed by Frey and Larroque."

As the church procrastinated, the anger of Hebert's clients flared. To the distraught parents, the situation was black and white – Gauthe had hideously abused their sons and ought to be arrested and put in jail. Hebert set up a meeting with the angry parents and Louisiana District Attorney Nathan Stansbury. Stansbury pointed out that the children would have to be prepared to give public testimony, and developed a plan to protect them during a process that was often traumatic for the victims of sexual abuse. While the parents were preparing their civil actions, the children would receive psychotherapy sessions that would help ready them for their ordeal in the criminal case against Gauthe – an ordeal Stansbury planned to mitigate by pre-taping their evidence and presenting the videotapes to the grand jury as a substitute for seeking an indictment through live testimony.

It was an approach that sat well with Paul Hebert. His strategy was to negotiate substantial civil settlements with the church and its insurance companies, while protecting the identities of his clients. His legal premise was that although Gauthe had perpetrated the sexual assaults, the Roman Catholic church was the "respondent superior" – an organization that could be found liable for the damages caused by one of its employees. Worried that his strong faith would colour his view of what he knew was the church's vulnerable legal position, Hebert hired an attorney to help him with the case, "someone from outside," who would be immune to the pressures that were building in the small southern community where one of Hebert's clients had already been told, "It takes a low-down son of a bitch to sue the Catholic Church."

His choice was Raul Bencomo, a New Orleans lawyer who was an aggressive specialist in damage suit litigation. More than that, Bencomo was himself a former altar boy who had once considered going into the priesthood. In addition to financial settlements, he set clear objectives for the conduct of the case: the church hierarchy had to admit they had been remiss; new procedures had to be put in place to stop abusers in their tracks; and the church had to pay for family counselling for all of the victims. Staunch Catholic though he was, he saw no conflict between the demands of his faith and those of his profession.

"I as a lawyer am distinguishing between the church as a business-like institution and the church as a religious institution. . . . My course of action, my lawsuit, my anger stems from the fact that the church, at least the Diocese in Lafayette, is a poorly managed, shoddily run operation."

Although the church had major problems with the Gauthe affair, the media at this point wasn't one of them. Only those directly involved knew that Gauthe had sexually assaulted altar boys. But when one victim's family signed settlement papers for $405,000 (15 per cent paid by the diocese, the balance by the church's seven insurance companies), a local reporter, Dee Stanley of television station KLFY, received a tip and called District Attorney Stansbury. Stansbury told him, "The problem is all worked out. The kids won't [have to] talk for the civil cases." Stansbury wouldn't discuss the pending criminal proceedings. The family's lawyer was equally cryptic with the press. "Everything has been settled," Paul Hebert told Stanley. "There really is no story."

Jim Baronet, the news director at KLFY, was frustrated. "We knew something was going on, but we were cut off. Neither party would talk, the Church for liability reasons and Hebert because he was bargaining an out-of-court, secret settlement."

The station aired a cautious story, omitting the names of the priest and his victims. Two weeks later, Paul Hebert and Raul Bencomo filed four new suits on behalf of Gauthe's victims at the Abbeville courthouse. Once again Dee Stanley received a call, but when the TV reporter arrived at the courthouse to see the filed documents in the case, the registry read, "Not available v. Not available." District Court Judge Allen Babineaux had sealed the papers and refused to discuss his seal order – just as Magistrate Seabright had in the Father Kelly case. Although another TV station had Gauthe's name, it chose not to air the story. A local paper, *The Daily Advertiser*, also had the story, as did the wire services at AP and UPI, but none of the news agencies covered the Gauthe affair, just as *The Evening Telegram* in St. John's, Newfoundland, had elected not to run the Mount Cashel orphanage story eight years earlier. As Jim Baronet observed, KLFY was "out there alone" in the beginning, a predicament that the news director candidly admitted didn't "feel good."

When the civil suits arising out of the Gauthe case were finally settled by Hebert, Bencomo and other lawyers for a record total of $15 million, it was a different matter. With the legal manoeuvring out of the way, the court-imposed seal on various cases was finally lifted on September 4, 1984 and the allegations against the priest became a matter of public record – fifteen months after Gauthe's suspension from his parish. Only then did other media report on the story, and only then did the church make a public statement on the sordid affair.

Bishop Gerard Frey's prepared statement claimed that he had helped the victims from the very beginning and admonished Catholics not to be shaken in their faith, "for we know that the spirit helps us in our weakness." As platitudes go, his words were virtually the same as the public pronouncements that would be made by Archbishop Alphonsus Penney in the aftermath of the Father Hickey scandal five years later. And as with Penney's tepid response, Frey's public remarks were swiftly denounced as hopelessly inadequate.

Paul Hebert drafted a response from his clients that was published in *The Daily Advertiser*, criticizing Bishop Frey's statement as inaccurate. Frey's prepared statement was in fact the first real response from the church to the victimized children and their families in fifteen months. Neither parents nor parishioners had been told about the extent of Gauthe's crimes, and church officials had never even visited the victims' parents to tell them what had actually happened.

"We never planned on suing," the parent of one victim said. "We just wanted help for our children, and we wanted church officials to come meet with us and tell everybody what was what. To this day they haven't done it. That's what hurts so much."

The church's popularity took another nosedive when the diocese backed out of a reconciliation retreat that had been organized for some of the victims' families and church officials after the settlement. The weekend had been arranged by the chancery with the Jesuits at Grand Coteau, Louisiana, but the bishop decided not to participate when a new wave of civil actions was filed against Gauthe and the church by other families. Bishop Frey's legal advisers didn't want the retreat to be used in pending court actions to show that the church had accepted any measure of blame for Father Gauthe's actions.

For once, the church's cheque book did not bring an end to the scandal. Instead, the culmination of the first wave of civil litigation merely cleared the way for criminal proceedings against Father Gilbert Gauthe. On October 18, 1984, the state of Louisiana returned a thirty-four-count indictment against the suspended priest, including one count of aggravated rape, eleven counts of aggravated crimes against nature, eleven counts of committing sexually immoral acts with minors and eleven counts of contributing to the deliquency of juveniles by taking pornographic pictures, marking the first time in American history that a priest had been indicted for sex crimes.

Gauthe had by this time returned from the House of Affirmation and was being held in the Lafayette parish prison, a terrifying place where other inmates so frightened him with their taunts that he curled up in a fetal position in a corner of his cell and contemplated suicide. At 9 A.M. on the morning of October 24, Gauthe entered a plea of not guilty by reason of insanity in front of Judge Lucien Bertrand in a hearing that lasted only three minutes. Gauthe's insanity defence was based on the M'Naghten Rule, which decides criminal culpability by determining whether a defendant knew the difference between right and wrong at the time of the offence. Gauthe's attorney, the flamboyant F. Ray Mouton, planned to argue that his client's pedophilia was an addictive illness, blurring his mental and moral capabilities. Mouton could be forgiven if his own powers of concentration on the issues at hand were a tad out of focus; death threats had been delivered to his law office against both the lawyer and his despised client. The pre-trial atmosphere in Lafayette was decidedly volatile and ugly.

Judge Bertrand remanded Gauthe to a secular psychiatric facility called the Institute for Living in Hartford, Connecticut. The terms of the court order stipulated a $250,000 bond, and made provision for two enforcement officers to travel with him. After being transferred to the Johns Hopkins Hospital in Baltimore, Maryland, shortly before his trial date, Gauthe received his first injection of medroxy-progesterone or Depo-Provera, a drug that diminishes the production of testosterone, which in turn represses sexual appetite. It was an experimental drug for suppressing sex offenders including pedophiles, who were otherwise capable of as many as ten orgasms per day.

The Roman Catholic church, which had the most to lose from the trial going forward, made an offer to the families of Gauthe's victims that could only be described as brazenly self-serving. If the parents would drop the charges against Gauthe, the church would bear the cost of sending him to a psychiatric facility or a church-run clinic for the rest of his life. Bad as the offer was, it had some attractive elements. The psychologists who treated Gauthe's victims were against having the boys testify at his trial; similarly the boys' parents were reluctant to subject their children to the trauma of a high-profile criminal case. But despite their protective instinct, the parents finally preferred justice to comfort. They rejected the church's offer and prepared to go to court.

One of their reasons may have been that the celebrated case had by now become public anyway through a series of courageous articles in the *The Times* of Acadiana. Starting on May 23, 1985 reporter Jason Berry delved into the Louisiana abuse case and vaulted the Gauthe story onto the national stage. Berry's painstaking work would later bring to light the pedophile activities of seven other priests in Lafayette, and a dozen similar cases in eight states.

In the end, this first jury trial of an American priest on sex-related charges didn't take place. On Friday October 11, 1985, just four days before his trial was set to begin, Gauthe's lawyer, F. Ray Mouton, agreed to an eleventh-hour deal that would send his client to prison for a lengthy term with no possibility of parole. Gauthe was sentenced later that same month. The court had the option of sending the priest to the Patuxent Institute in Jessup, Maryland, a maximum-security prison with a special program for sexual deviants. Instead, Judge Hugh Brunson consigned Gauthe to Louisiana State Penitentiary for twenty years at hard labour, his reasons as stark and uncompromising as the prison walls behind which the pedophile priest would soon find himself.

"Your crimes against your child victims have laid a terrible burden on those children, their families and society – indeed, your God and your Church as well. It may be that God in his infinite mercy may find forgiveness for your crimes, but the imperative of justice, and the inescapable need of society to protect its most defenceless and vulnerable members, the children, cannot."

The precedent-setting case had a devastating impact on the Roman Catholic church. In one of approximately twenty-one civil actions arising out of the scandal, one victim's family refused to sign a release exonerating the church from liability in the Gauthe case.

"I felt that for what Gauthe had done to my son, he had to be punished. As far as having to sign a piece of paper that was releasing the church, saying they were not liable in no kinda way and there was gonna be no further litigation, I didn't feel I was doing the right thing," Glenn Gastal said. He wanted the church publicly criticized for its part in his son's tragedy and he knew just the person for the job.

Gastal hired barrel-chested Cajun attorney J. Minos Simon to plead his case. The sixty-two-year-old Simon ran a lucrative law practice which he had built on a radical and aggressive approach to a string of high-profile, controversial cases. Working from the premise that church officials knew about Gauthe's sexual abuse of children long before the scandal finally surfaced, Simon argued that the Roman Catholic church as well as Gauthe were liable for damages. A key feature of other financial settlements with victims had been the silence of the plaintiffs and their express agreement that the church was in no way responsible for Gauthe's actions. Neither Gastal nor his lawyer was interested in playing that game.

Simon knew that Canon Code 489 of Roman Catholic church canon law said, "In the diocesan curia there is also to be a secret archive, or at least in the ordinary archive there is to be a safe or a cabinet, which is securely closed and bolted and which cannot be removed. In this archive, documents which are kept under secrecy are to be most carefully guarded. Each year documents of criminal cases concerning moral matters are to be destroyed whenever the guilty parties have died, or ten years have elapsed since a condemnatory tactic concluded the affair."

The aggressive attorney knew that the church kept a short summary of the facts of these cases and went after the private files of twenty-seven priests that he alleged would show sexual aberrations from 1970 to 1985 — aberrations that the church had tolerated. When Bishop Frey refused to hand over the documents, Simon gave television interviews in which he accused church officials of a cover-up. Robert Leake, the elegant New Orleans attorney who was lead counsel for the church's seven insurance companies, argued that disclosure of the files would compromise the separation of church and state. Behind the constitutional concern was a more practical consideration. Leake was worried that disclosure of the files would lead to more suits against the church on the basis that they might show that church officials failed to take the proper steps to stop abuse they knew was taking place.

Simon, who believed the church's tolerance of homosexuality among seminarians and priests created an atmosphere of leniency in the church hierarchy towards sexual offences, countered that there had been a violation of secular law, and

therefore church immunity didn't apply. Abbeville Judge
Bradford Ware, who had already issued an order permitting
Simon to question Bishop Frey and Monsignor Larroque
about their part in the Gauthe case, ruled that the church
had to turn over all documents in its possession relating to
the sexual abuse of children, though not those dealing with
homosexual priests.

Simon's suspicions were well founded. Files from the
secret diocesan archive brought to light the sexual crimes of
Father Lane Fontenot, including the fact that he had shared
four boys with Father Gauthe in the mid-seventies in their
New Iberia parish. Like Gauthe, the pedophile priest had
been shunted from parish to parish when reports of his
activities bubbled to the surface in the form of parental
complaints. When scandal engulfed him, the church made
quiet settlements and spirited Fontenot away to private,
church-run treatment centres, until his luck ran out in
Spokane, Washington, where he was finally convicted in
1986 of a felony count of statutory rape involving a boy.

The legal precedent that allowed Simon into the secret
files of the church in the Gauthe case opened the door for
dozens of pedophilia prosecutions across the United States,
including one in the state of Idaho where it was used to
obtain the personnel records of Father Melvin Baltazaar,
which showed a twenty-year history of sexual contacts with
youths. For two decades of molestation and sexual assault,
Baltazaar eventually received seven years in prison. The
Roman Catholic church's policy of protecting priestly
crimes was clearly in tatters – and disgrace.

In 1985, three Catholics who had reason to be worried
about this worm in the rose of their church – F. Ray
Mouton, the Louisiana attorney who acted for the church in
the Gauthe case; Rev. Thomas P. Doyle, a Dominican canon
lawyer; and Rev. Michael Peterson, a psychiatrist who
specialized in treating troubled priests – prepared a
one-hundred-page confidential report which they sent to
every bishop in the United States. They wanted to discard
the policy of denial, secret settlements and strategic transfers
of suspected pedophiles. They advocated a more responsible
approach based on immediate church intervention with the

victim's family, and the swift suspension and hospitalization of the priest in question. In making their case, the authors sounded a note of profound financial caution: they predicted that Catholic dioceses could soon be facing up to $1 billion in claims if the policy of cover-ups continued – no mean consideration when it was remembered that after the Gauthe case, it was nearly impossible for the church to obtain liability insurance.

But the report was never adopted as policy because America's Catholic bishops would then have had to publicly acknowledge that the problem existed. Then in 1989, the problem was unceremoniously dropped in their collective lap. While the National Conference of Catholic Bishops was meeting in Baltimore, Maryland, a young man accused Joseph A. Ferraro, the Bishop of Honolulu, of having sexually molested him on a regular basis from the time the complainant had been a grade eight student. Bishop Ferraro held a press conference to deny the allegations, but admitted that he had given the young man money. He also said he had no intentions of launching a defamation suit against his accuser. U.S. Catholic Conference media officers later issued a statement claiming that the allegations "have been examined by Church authorities and ... determined to lack substance."

In an article in an Ohio newspaper outlining the scandal, Jason Berry quoted a Washington priest familiar with Vatican procedures in such matters.

"They'll say there's no substance [to the charges] but that doesn't mean anything. With a Bishop, they circle the wagons. The question is, what's going on inside the circle?"

From a policy point of view the answer was, very little. Despite mounting public criticism and more and more scandals, the church clung to its policy of transferring suspected pedophile priests and silencing their victims with its money and power. The policy of strategic acquiescence was too much for Rev. Thomas Doyle, one of the authors of the controversial policy report, who resigned his position at the Vatican Embassy in Washington after the report was rejected. He later told the San Jose *Mercury News* that as many as 5 per cent of U.S. Catholic clergy could be pedophiles – approximately 3,000 out of a clergy population of 57,000.

It was a shocking number and Reverend Doyle used it to draw a forbidding conclusion in a 1987 newspaper interview. Pedophilia was "the most serious problem that we in the church have faced in centuries."

Two years later, events in Newfoundland would graphically demonstrate what could happen to a Catholic order when, instead of coming to grips with that problem, they chose to bury it.

Chapter 11
The Scandal Declared

> *You can't erase what happened and that's not what I'm looking for. I'm just looking for a lot of answers. Why this went on? Why nothing was said? Why there was no counselling? And why there was no guidance? Mount Cashel was supposed to be the place for boys. But it turned out to be hell on earth.* Shane Earle, March 26, 1989.

EVERY WEEKDAY MORNING just after the nine o'clock news, George MacLaren makes a stabbing motion with his right hand at the compact figure seated behind the glass in the cramped radio studio in front of him. Cued, the dark-haired man in the headset leans towards his live microphone and begins a Newfoundland ritual – VOCM's morning talk show, "Open Line." The show's host, Bill Rowe, begins the program with unabashed hucksterism, listing the provocative events in the news and cajoling his listeners to call in and say their piece. There is not much of the Oxford-trained lawyer, author or Rhodes Scholar to be found in this media barker's spiel, but Rowe, who is all three, has a gift for creating a communicative itch that his listeners can't resist scratching on the air.

Most mornings, the switchboard lights up gradually, at about the same pace as listeners shake off a night's sleep over their first cup of coffee. The ice-breaker calls come from people like "Kay," "Captain Corruption" and the "Million-Dollar Man" – regulars Rowe knows well enough to inquire about their health problems and relatives. Once the conversational ball gets rolling, the people of St. John's, and Newfoundlanders from all over the province, get in on the act, giving their views on everything from the state of the cod stock to the Prime Minister's collection of Italian shoes. Although the show has its highbrow detractors, most public figures in Newfoundland honour the political axiom that there is wisdom in the masses; accordingly, more than one radio in Confederation Building is tuned in to Bill Rowe's daily reading of the public pulse.

On Monday, February 13, 1989, the talk-show host received a call early in the program from a man he had reason to know very well. Steve Neary, a silver-haired, Smallwood-style Grit from Bell Island, had contested the leadership of the provincial Liberal Party with Rowe in 1977. After his defeat, Neary became the elegant lawyer's blue-collar lieutenant, cultivating the raw working-class precincts for his patrician chief until Rowe's political career was abruptly ended just two years after winning the party leadership. Ironically, Neary was calling about the very controversy that was inadvertently brought to light by Rowe's actions following the 1978 fire in the apartment of Dr. Tom Farrell – a scandal that cost Rowe his chance of becoming the first Liberal Premier of Newfoundland since Joey Smallwood.

Neary's call to his former political chief had been prompted by a television documentary about the spate of Roman Catholic priests and Brothers who had been charged with sexual offences against children. The political war-horse decided the time was right to do something about a subject that had been bothering him ever since Patrol Sgt. Art Pike's testimony at the Soper Inquiry – the official handling of the 1975 police report into physical and sexual abuse at Mount Cashel Orphanage.

Neary had always believed Pike's sworn statements about official interference in the 1975 police investigation at Mount Cashel, and was appalled that the Director of Public Prosecutions of the day, John Kelly, had testified that the Mount Cashel affair had been handled according to routine procedures, including the prosecutorial discretion that had agreed to send two Brothers out of Newfoundland for medical treatment rather than charging them. Neary claimed that there had been an official cover-up of the 1975 scandal and read over the air from a transcript of the in camera evidence from the Soper Inquiry to make his point.

"Little did I realize when I made the call that it was going to set off such a chain reaction, and in my wildest imagination I did not think that there were such goings-on, that it was so deep-rooted at Mount Cashel as we've heard about . . . I was completely shocked, the same as everybody else in Newfoundland," Neary would later say in an interview. However inadvertently, the champion of the working class was about to make his biggest contribution to the constituency that had sustained him over a twenty-year political career.

Although the Mount Cashel scandal was destined to generate the largest public reaction of any subject ever aired on "Open Line," Rowe did not have a strong personal reaction at the time of Neary's call. The story of stale testimony from a ten-year-old inquiry was "too general, too wishy-washy" to prompt a groundswell of burning public interest or righteous indignation. Having lived through the whole affair, which he candidly admitted he had handled "stupidly and clumsily" as Liberal leader, Rowe, like a lot of other people, assumed that there had been no wrong-doing at Mount Cashel because Judge Lloyd Soper found in 1979 that the matter had been properly handled by the Justice Department.

But at least one of his listeners that morning took a very different view. The same day Steve Neary made his charges about Mount Cashel on "Open Line," Mrs. Catherine Caddigan called Robert Hyslop in the Justice Department and demanded a public inquiry into the cover-up at the orphanage. The startled Assistant Deputy Minister of Justice, who only vaguely remembered the case, told his caller that the incident had involved the strapping of children and that no charges had been laid. He also told her that he wasn't the person to decide whether an inquiry should be called and advised her to contact her member of the House of Assembly.

The next day, Hyslop received the call that broke the dam of official silence on Mount Cashel that had lasted for fourteen years. Mr. Justice John Mahoney of the Newfoundland Supreme Court of Appeal telephoned to inquire about allegations of a cover-up of crimes at the orphanage that his wife, Carmel, had heard about on the radio the day before.

The judge, a staunch Catholic and Honorary Life Member of the Benevolent Irish Society, wanted to know if there was anything to the allegations. Mahoney had also been involved in a defamation action brought by Dr. Tom Farrell against *The Evening Telegram*, and since he had no recollection of anything arising at the time connecting the Farrell fire to Mount Cashel, the eminent jurist wondered if he were going senile.

Hyslop assured Mahoney that his wits were intact; the connection between the Farrell fire and Mount Cashel had been made at the Soper Inquiry, not during Farrell's defamation suit against the newspaper. "Well, Robert," Hyslop remembered the judge asking, "was there anything sexual involved?" Hyslop repeated what he had already told Catherine Caddigan, that the incident involved physical abuse in the form of over-zealous strapping and that it had been personally handled by the Deputy Minister of the day, Vincent McCarthy. Hyslop admitted that he had never actually seen the police reports into the matter and told the judge he couldn't be certain that his sense of the case was accurate until he had read them. Mahoney asked Hyslop to keep him informed.

After talking to the judge, Hyslop immediately called Superintendent Len Power of the CID and asked him to find whatever the police had on file about the Mount Cashel incident of 1975, a simple request that could have blown the story wide open at any time during the fourteen years the case had remained dormant. "You find out what you've got," Hyslop said, "and I'll find out what we've got and we'll marry them up."

Power, who knew about the allegations on "Open Line," had been half-expecting Hyslop's call. He contacted Sgt. Leonard Clowe and told him what he wanted. Fifteen minutes later, Sergeant Clowe walked into the Superintendent's office with a single brown file folder containing Hillier's police reports from 1975–76. There was no other communication or correspondence in the file. Power called the Justice Department with ominous news. "We've got a problem here," he reported, explaining that the police had the explosive reports, but there was no indication that they had either been seen or acted upon by the Department of Justice. Vincent McCarthy's covering letter to former Chief of Police Browne, which had accompanied Detective Hillier's two reports back in 1977, had apparently disappeared.

When Power explained what was contained in the reports, Hyslop ordered that they be sent over to the Justice Department immediately. Copies of the two reports were hand-delivered to Hyslop at 12:25 P.M. by Lt. Alexander Kielly of the CID. Just as Power had warned, there was no correspondence from the Justice Department with the reports. With a sickening feeling in the pit of his stomach, Hyslop alerted Ronald Richards, the Deputy Minister of Justice, and his Director of Public Prosecutions, Colin Flynn.

Hyslop and Flynn quickly reviewed the files, with the Deputy Minister of Justice, Ronald Richards, and the head of the Special Prosecutions Unit, Bernard Coffey, in attendance. The room was electric with a sense of collective shock. Within a few moments everyone realized that Staff Sgt. Arthur Pike had been right – the Mount Cashel investigation had indeed uncovered gross sexual abuse of boys at Mount Cashel by their guardians, substantiated by the confessions of at least two Christian Brothers.

Based on exactly the same information that Vincent McCarthy had looked at on December 18, 1975, the most senior Justice officials in Newfoundland, including the Minister of Justice, reopened the Mount Cashel case with a view to laying criminal charges in those matters which did not have a statute of limitations.

On the afternoon of February 14, Hyslop made an informal call to the Chief of Police, with instructions to reopen the Mount Cashel case. From the outset, there were two issues to be resolved: the apparent criminal acts of Christian Brothers against their former charges at the orphanage, and the reason charges weren't brought against them in the first place. Lieutenant Kielly, who had remained at Justice for the two-hour general discussion of the case by senior departmental officials, left the building that day with the distinct impression that the RNC would soon be officially asked to reopen the investigation.

After leaving his office, Robert Hyslop spent the evening of Valentine's Day reading the Mount Cashel file. He was so revolted by what the reports contained that he couldn't sleep that night. Hyslop was feeling particularly sheepish since he had advised two people during the previous forty-eight hours that the Mount Cashel case had been about non-serious physical abuse of boys at the institution – assurances he had offered without benefit of personal knowledge of the facts. He may also have been troubled by memories of how he had handled the 1982 investigation into sexual abuse at Mount Cashel, and his apparent failure to read the in camera testimony from the 1979 Soper Inquiry in which Art Pike had clearly referred to sexual abuse at Mount Cashel.

Appalled by Hillier's reports, Hyslop dictated a letter to the Chief of Police, Ed Coady, laying out how he wanted the police to proceed in the matter. Keenly aware of the fact that Det. Robert Hillier had been pulled off the case before he had finished his work, Hyslop's instructions were unequivocal: complete the investigation into sexual abuse of children at Mount Cashel and determine why these individuals were never brought to justice.

Hyslop made it very clear that he wanted to know if there was "criminal liability on the part of any person(s) responsible for the termination of this investigation." He stressed the need for the police to take urgent action in the requested investigation, a spectacular irony, given that it had taken fourteen years for the Justice Department to act on the police work that sparked Hyslop's demand for expeditious action on the same case. But the Justice official had little choice. After reading Hillier's December 1975 report, Hyslop was faced with the numbing reality "that at least one person had committed over one hundred individual indecent acts on at least fifteen boys." Even worse, absolutely nothing had been done about it by the Justice Department.

That same night, Hyslop dictated a letter to Justice Minister Lynn Verge saying, with reference to Hillier's reports, that the cases of "excessive discipline on the part of the Brothers might have been dealt with properly by prosecutorial discretion." In any event, they were statute-barred. But Detective Hillier's first report was an entirely different matter; "A review of an earlier report, however, dated December 18, 1975, which has come to my attention for the first time today, reveals sexual abuse by at least three Brother on a horrifying scale."

Hyslop was worried about where the alleged offenders were now and whether other children were at risk under their care. He also wondered if they were the only offenders, given that other Christian Brothers were mentioned in Hillier's reports — individuals the detective hadn't yet interviewed when then Police Chief John Lawlor had closed the case, on instructions from the Justice Department. Wondering where the childhood victims were now and whether they would be prepared to testify, Hyslop instructed Department of Justice secretary Joyce King to "have absolutely every stone turned over" to locate the file he remembered being shown by Mary Noonan in 1979 at the time of the Soper Inquiry.

King scoured the criminal files in the department but was unable to find the documents requested by Hyslop. Two days after the search began, the slim file was located in Box V – #77 in the dead files of the Crown Attorney's Office, which were stored in Mount Scio House, the former official residence of the premier of Newfoundland, which Brian Peckford had vacated and handed over to the civil service as additional office space. Hyslop and the Chief of Police personally picked up the file around noon. Hyslop gave a copy to the Minister of Justice and kept the original under lock and key in his office. It contained Vincent McCarthy's January 26, 1979, letter to Chief of Police Browne, Gabriel McHugh's January 23, 1976, letter to McCarthy, and Rev. Dr. Thomas Kane's January 15, 1976, letter to Brother McHugh.

After reviewing boxes of material from the Soper Inquiry, Hyslop realized that the Justice Department had only volumes one and two of Judge Soper's report. He asked Joyce King to get the rest of the report directly from the judge, who couriered a complete transcript of the proceedings, including the in camera portions of Pike's testimony about Mount Cashel, to Hyslop on February 20, 1989. Two days later, after reviewing the material, the Justice Department official turned the transcript over to Superintendent Power of the CID to assist him in the RNC's re-investigation. Hyslop also gave the policeman a written statement of his previous involvement in the case, both to assist in the re-investigation and as an *aide-mémoire* in the event he was called to testify before any future judicial proceedings. Robert Hyslop had been around too long not to sense where the case was headed.

The system had finally reacted. All it could do now was brace for the jolt it would soon be receiving when the full details of the Mount Cashel affair became public, as inevitably they would.

Shane Earle left Mount Cashel Orphanage for good at 11:30 P.M. on the evening of September 7, 1987, fourteen years after he and his two brothers had climbed the broad front steps and been put in the care of Brother Douglas Kenny. He was twenty-one years old. After taking on various part-time jobs in St. John's, the unassuming young man with the trim moustache and the dreamy hazel eyes had enrolled in a waiter's course at the Cabot Institute. On graduating, he got a full-time job at the Hotel Newfoundland where his cousin was the Food and Beverages manager.

But Shane soon discovered that memories could not be vacated as easily as an address. He could not shake off the inexplicable crying spells and flat depressions that had dogged his later school career and landed him first in Brother Rice monastery, in the hope that reflective seclusion might ease his troubled mind, and, later, in the psychiatric ward of the Health Sciences Complex after an unsuccessful suicide attempt in 1983 in the presbytery of St. Peter's parish in Mount Pearl.

Following his hospital treatment, things seemed to get a little better. Perhaps it was an illusion partially fostered by the strong medication he was given after Father Raymond Lahey, in whose quarters Shane had swallowed two handfuls of Centrum multi-vitamins in his thwarted suicide attempt, arranged for him to see Dr. John Angel, a local psychiatrist.

Feeling more optimistic, Shane returned to Mount Cashel, though not to the dorm where he had had most of his sexual encounters, and enrolled in a youth employment-readiness school offered at the orphanage. Although he was doing well with his courses, he soon got "sick and tired" of this newest form of therapy and decided he needed a vacation. He approached Brother John Buckingham, who was in charge of spiritual retreats, and arrangements were made for Shane to spend a month in Antigua. Before he left, he was informed by Brother Buckingham that one of the people he would see on the retreat was Brother Alan Ralph, who taught in St. Joseph's Academy on the tropical island.

"I said to myself 'Now this is a way for me to see if I'm over this.' So I went there and met Brother Ralph. I remember on the night I got there the power was out in the province, in the country. I walked into the living room with all candles and the Brothers were sitting around talking and I shook hands, I was going to meet every one of them, some of which I knew from previous years. And I met Brother Ralph for the first time since '75 and he knew me and I knew him and . . . he never did have a conversation with me down there, even when we were one on one in the dining room, eating breakfast or in the living room watching TV or out in the car for the day."

After returning from Antigua Shane realized that his recovery wasn't as solid as he'd thought and he made the decision to leave Mount Cashel.

"Whatever I could salvage of my life – I wanted to start over, and that involved leaving what happened to me in Mount Cashel, leaving the memories there, and I'd done that for a period of time until I kept hearing about the Jim Hickey case . . . and the Corrigan case."

For months Shane had been watching news stories unfold about priests being brought to justice for molesting young boys. Every day he bought the newspapers to follow the progress of events. The more he read, the more the marl of his own buried past was churned up inside him, ghostly memories that couldn't be exorcised by pills or pilgrimages. Sometimes it was the physical and sexual nightmares, the constant groping and probing by the Brothers who put their charges to bed each night; occasionally, it was the savage beatings he had witnessed the Brothers administering to other residents of Mount Cashel. Intensifying Shane's torment was the fact that absolutely nothing had been done about the ink that certain Brothers had dropped into the spring water of his innocence, clouding his life forever.

"You know, here was Father Hickey going through a trial and he's being punished for it and why the hell were the doors shut on us back in 1975?"

On the night of February 16, 1979, Shane returned to his home at 65 Freshwater Road just in time to hear the last segment of a television newscast which reported that the investigation into alleged physical and sexual abuse of children at Mount Cashel was being reopened. It was as if someone had kicked him in the stomach. With his head spinning, he sat down on the couch and wondered if this was the opportunity he had been waiting for. Struggling to compose himself, Shane got into his car and drove to the police station two or three minutes away, where he asked to speak to the person in charge of the Mount Cashel case.

Fifteen minutes later, two CID officers arrived to take down Shane's story. Ironically, one of them was Supt. Len Power, who had tried unsuccessfully to interview Shane in 1982 in connection with Brother Henry Bucher's complaint that older boys at the orphanage were sexually abusing some of the younger residents. Shane was escorted to Power's office where, at 9:50 P.M., he began giving his official statement to police – the first by a Mount Cashel boy since the investigation was reopened. With the two policemen listening in disbelief, Shane Earle outlined how four Christian Brothers had physically and sexually abused him from the time he entered the orphanage as a six-year-old.

"Often when going to bed, Brother English would have me say my prayers, then he would kiss me, put the sign of the cross on my forehead and touch my private parts all over. He used to start at my neck and work right down. This was an ongoing thing, very frequent, and was taking place when I was between six and up until the time he left around 1975."

By 1 A.M. the distraught young man had filled seven

legal-size sheets with his nightmarish recollections of Mount
Cashel. Weeping uncontrollably at times, he articulated the
sense of betrayal he felt at the way the Mount Cashel affair
had been covered up in 1975, telling the detectives that
society had "shut the door on us, and society didn't really
care about what happened to the kids at Mount Cashel."

Before he left Fort Townshend, Shane was assured by the
detectives that he was doing "the best thing" possible by
coming forward, given their cards and advised to seek
counselling. Shane felt relieved after talking to the police,
but after five days passed without word on the progress of
their investigation, Shane Earle sought help from another
and more familiar quarter.

Worried that he might once again be ignored, but at the
same time wracked by guilt that his story to police had
"jeopardized a lot of people," Shane decided to visit Father
Kevin Molloy at Holy Rosary Parish in Portugal Cove –
Father Jim Hickey's former parish. Anxious as he was for
retroactive justice, he also wanted reassurance that he had
done the right thing. The fifty-six-year-old priest and former
Christian Brother had just returned from a meeting on the
afternoon of Wednesday, February 22, 1989 and was
checking his calls and mail when the doorbell rang. Before
his housekeeper could answer it, the priest himself opened
the door to a young stranger who softly asked him, "Do you
remember me?" Shane explained that he used to serve
Father Molloy's mass at Mount Cashel's chapel. Although
he recognized Shane's face, the priest couldn't remember his
name. Half an hour later, Molloy would never forget it.

After calming Shane down, the startled priest listened to
the same story his visitor had already told police, including
the fact that he hadn't heard back from authorities since
giving a formal statement several days before. Father
Molloy told Shane of his earlier involvement in the 1975
incident after a woman had told him about Chesley Riche's
tale of sexual misdeeds at Mount Cashel. Shane informed
the priest that the woman was Kathryn Burry, his aunt.
Father Molloy assured the young man that he would check
into the situation and get back to him in a day or two. Molloy
subsequently visited Mount Cashel and urged the Brothers

to arrange for counselling for the victims of 1975. But when Shane didn't hear back from the priest, he once more grew suspicious that no one was listening. It was time, he concluded, to go to the media.

He chose the St. John's weekly, *The Sunday Express*. On Sunday, March 12 Shane read a column by the newspaper's publisher and editor-in-chief Michael Harris under a headline "Miscarriage at Mount Cashel: Where was the rule of law?" Part of the column touched a nerve in the frustrated young man, who was tired of waiting for someone in authority to do something about the long festering scandal:

> The rule of law — the absolutely vital principle that everyone gets equal treatment in our justice system — was not followed in this case. Orphans were simply shuffled off to one side. Beyond the pitiful degradation so many boys may have been exposed to because of that deviation, we must now find out why. Justice Minister Lynn Verge says there is no need for such an inquiry. Even for a minister who acts as though she is a permanent resident of Disneyland, a more complete abdication of responsibility to the public could scarcely be imagined. We must find out if there was prima facie evidence to support the laying of charges against the three Brothers who were reportedly sent out of the country. We must find out who in the church and who in the justice system sanctioned the deal. We must find out when officials of the Roman Catholic church learned of abuses at Mount Cashel. We must find out if justice was obstructed and by whom. And because both the church and the justice system are at the centre of this debacle, they cannot be the factfinders. . . .

Harris had written the column in reaction to a story by reporter Philip Lee that had appeared in *The Sunday Express* on February 19. Lee's story, leaked to him by an anonymous source the day before the Mount Cashel investigation was officially reopened, outlined how the provincial Justice Department had agreed to let the church deal with a sexual abuse case at Mount Cashel in lieu of laying charges against three Christian Brother suspects. The story, the first of many by the persistent reporter, also quoted former Director of Public Prosecutions John Kelly's testimony from the Soper Inquiry, saying that it was a decision that prosecutors often made in similar circumstances.

Shane read and re-read Harris's column and finally decided to contact the newspaper. As he would later explain to the Hughes Inquiry, "I said to myself, my God, finally somebody knows what they're talking about, finally somebody's not talking in circles any more."

The next morning he called *The Sunday Express* from work, and at 4 P.M. that afternoon Harris returned his call. On Tuesday the two met at the Radisson Hotel, and while Harris nursed a cup of coffee and Shane picked at his dinner, the young man related his story. The journalist was sickened and angered by what Shane had to say, but he knew the enormous personal risks the other man would be running if he decided to go public. Harris asked him to think about it that night, and they agreed to meet again.

Two days later, Harris wrote a letter, which he gave to Shane at their third meeting. He didn't want the young man to pry the lid off Pandora's box and expect a welcoming committee; nor did he want anyone to later charge that the newspaper had taken advantage of an emotionally over-wrought victim of child abuse. The cards had to be laid squarely on the table and Shane had to decide how he wanted to play them.

The Sunday Express   March 16, 1989
Office of the Publisher
Editor in Chief

Dear Shane,

I told you yesterday that if you came forward with your story through *The Sunday Express*, there were a number of things you would have to clearly understand.

The first is that you would very likely find yourself in the eye of a media storm. Many people may want you to tell your story publicly and not all of them will have the sensitivity to make that an easy thing to do.

Secondly, with all of the publicity, you must expect that your personal life will also be affected. Once people know who you are, your ordeal will become the focus for their curiosity.

Thirdly, if, as I suspect, charges arise out of the nightmare that you and others experienced at Mount Cashel, there will be the added ordeal of a public trial. As part of that process you should expect lawyers for the defence to delve into your present day personal life, as a means of defending their client or clients.

I do not mention these matters to frighten you, I just think it is vitally important for you to understand the consequences of going public with such a tragic and powerful story. As I told you yesterday, should you decide to proceed I will do my best to get the truth out.

One other thing; there are powerful forces involved in this story, for whom the last thing that is wanted is the truth. I don't believe that many people will be congratulating either you or me for bringing this sordid affair into the public eye. Given the enormity of the public interest involved, it is my job to do that. But it is your choice.

Yours Truly,
Michael Harris

After considering the letter, Shane decided to go public. Before the journalist and the waiter began the intensive interview process that would result in two feature articles on Mount Cashel in successive issues of *The Sunday Express*, Harris asked Shane what, in addition to informing the public about the dark events of 1975, he hoped the stories would achieve. The young man replied that he wanted the responsible parties brought to justice and, beyond that, an inquiry to delve into how the cover-up had occurred in the first place. It was a tall order, but one the journalist believed that Shane was perfectly entitled to place, given what he had been through. Whether his hopes would be realized was another matter.

For the rest of that week, elaborate and unusual preparations were made for the publication of the first article. When someone realized that part one of the series would be appearing on Easter Sunday, the suggestion was made to delay publication for a week so that Catholics wouldn't feel they were being attacked on one of their holiest days. Although he acknowledged the potential for such a backlash, Harris decided to go ahead as planned on Sunday, March 19, explaining to his staff that the world of appearances was best inhabited by politicians, not journalists. No one had plotted to have the story come out on Easter Sunday, and no one was going to plot to see that it didn't either.

By Saturday evening the first piece was finally ready to go. In a very unusual move, Harris handed it to Shane Earle for final approval. Given the explosive nature of the article, Harris wanted to be absolutely sure that the story fairly and accurately reflected the facts as Shane had related them. He had also given the nervous young man the option, up to the very last moment, to change his mind about going public. After Shane read and approved the story – a procedure that would be repeated the following Saturday night for part two – Harris contacted the newspaper's lawyer, Edward Roberts, who then privately discussed with Shane any personal legal consequences that might flow from the publication of his story. Satisfied with the answers Roberts gave him, Shane Earle gave his final approval to run the Mount Cashel story at 11:15 P.M. on Saturday, March 18. Emotionally exhausted, everyone at the paper had a last cup of coffee and headed home, wondering what Easter Sunday would bring.

The article went off like a bomb. Shane's father, who had been taught by the Christian Brothers that it was a good Roman Catholic's duty to bring children into the world, was horrified by the terrifying account of physical and sexual abuse of youngsters at the orphanage. "It just tore me to pieces," he would later testify. Alice (Walters) Crewe, the social worker who had dealt with Shane's case so many years before, instantly recalled the genesis of the story. "When I saw Shane's article in the *Express* in March, I knew immediately that was the child I had brought to the Janeway."

Graphic and disturbing in its portrayal of the sexual abuse the children were subjected to at Mount Cashel, the initial story and the one that followed it a week later put a human face on the scandal that transformed the incident from a distant institutional malfunction into a living human tragedy. As the switchboard at VOCM's "Open Line" lit up the next day, Bill Rowe had his own ideas about why an article that appeared a month after news of the Mount Cashel story first broke so captured the public's attention.

"It was those stories about Shane Earle and the commentary on it that indicates why something was finally done about it. It's one thing to hear Brothers doing something to the boys and that the bad apples were shipped out. It's quite another for a boy to talk about when he was six or seven years of age and graphically describe how a grown man grabbed him and sexually abused him. That's why there's no doubt that *The Sunday Express* stories about Shane really got people going . . ."

Some, like the author of an anonymous letter that arrived at the paper the day after the apperance of the second Shane Earle piece, attacked the editor of the *Express* as "a dirty old man who loves to wallow in filth."

Hate mail, however, was not the order of the day. The vast majority of Newfoundlanders, including the Roman Catholic community, felt shocked and soiled by Shane's revelations, but welcomed the painful liberation of the truth. If hearts groaned around the breakfast table at a small boy's dark chronicle, Shane Earle's eloquent and haunting commentary on his ruined childhood set the agenda for things to come. Beyond the tragedy of Mount Cashel, as he knew better than anyone, was a burning need for answers.

"You can't erase what happened and that's not what I'm looking for," Earle said in the second article. "I'm just looking for a lot of answers. Why this went on? Why nothing was said? Why there was no counselling? And why there was no guidance? Mount Cashel was supposed to be the place for boys. But it turned out to be hell on earth."

Determined to follow through on his drive for a belated accounting, Shane met with Newfoundland's Justice

Minister, Lynn Verge, and Opposition Leader Clyde Wells, to press his demand for a public inquiry headed up by a judge from outside the province. Verge was receptive but talked about a general inquiry into the whole area of child abuse in Newfoundland. Unimpressed, the young man urged her to focus instead on Mount Cashel, where so much sexual abuse had taken place with such devastating consequences for its now grown victims.

Shane was just as skeptical of what Clyde Wells thought should be done. Critical of what he considered to be Verge's transparent attempt to conceal serious faults in the criminal justice system by establishing an unfocused or hobbled inquiry, the Liberal Opposition leader promised to establish a full public commission of inquiry into the failure of Newfoundland's criminal justice system, headed up by a person who had never played a role in it. Such an inquiry would deal with Mount Cashel, but also look at other cases where the system had failed to respond to complaints of sexual or physical abuse. After reading John Kelly's Soper Inquiry testimony in *The Sunday Express*, Wells had nothing but contempt for the former Director of Public Prosecution's stated view that the decision to send two Christian Brothers out of the province in 1975 rather than charge them was a normal exercise of prosecutorial discretion.

"Having practised law for twenty-five years, I can state categorically that such a position is totally contrary to our system of law. We operate on the basis of 'the rule of law,' that is, all persons are equal before the law. No matter who you are, or what position you hold, if you break the law you must answer to the law. Prosecutors do not have the discretion to choose not to prosecute any individual because of the nature of the offence or because of who he or she is or to what group in society they belong."

With the provincial election that would make him premier less than a month away, the man with the cornflower blue eyes would soon be getting the chance to follow through on his plan to deal exhaustively with the towering failures of the justice system that cast a shadow all the way back to 1975.

While the police, the Justice Department and the politicians scrambled to deal with what was now openly being referred to as the cover-up at Mount Cashel, the Christian Brothers in Newfoundland struggled to cope with an aggressive press and an increasingly angry public. Although Brother Francis Hepditch, the Brother Provincial of the order, was in St. John's shortly after the story broke, he refused to return calls from *The Sunday Express*. Even former superintendents of Mount Cashel were close-mouthed and elusive. Former Brother John Barron, who had been head of the orphanage from 1968 to 1971, and who was "upset" by the re-investigation, refused to say whether he had ever received complaints of sexual abuse about any of the Brothers during his tenure as Superintendent. Just how far the siege mentality had settled in was captured in a response to Philip Lee of *The Sunday Express* when he called Brother Henry Bucher and asked him to confirm that he had once been Superintendent of Mount Cashel.

"Why would you be asking me that? What business is that of yours? Not everybody has full and complete right to ask whomever they want whatever they want.... I'm not answering any questions."

It was a very different world from 1975, and the Brothers were having a hard time adjusting to it. A little more than a week after the Justice Department ordered the reopening of the Mount Cashel case, the Christian Brothers announced a new policy which they insisted had nothing to do with the renewed police investigation. Senior officials of the order told *The Sunday Express* that Brothers convicted of sexual misconduct would never be allowed to hold teaching posts again, even if they received psychiatric treatment and were given a clean bill of health.

One of the first casualties of the policy was Brother David Burton, the former Mount Cashel Supervisor who had been convicted of gross indecency in 1982, and who had been given a suspended sentence over the strenuous objections of Crown attorney Ronald Richards. Brother Burton was removed from his teaching position at St. Thomas More Collegiate in Burnaby, British Columbia. The school's Director, Brother Kevin Short, who would soon be arrested in connection with the Mount Cashel investigation, refused to comment on the reasons behind Brother Burton's hasty departure from the classroom. Another of the Brothers who lost his teaching post was one of two men at the heart of the Mount Cashel affair, Brother Alan Ralph, who was hastily removed from St. Joseph's Academy in Antigua in the wake of the reinvestigation.

When asked about the reasons behind the new policy, Mount Cashel's Superintendent, Brother Barry Lynch, replied, "I feel that it's important for people in responsibility to admit . . . that [reassigning offenders] was a mistaken way to approach things in the light of what we know today."

The Brothers also arranged a meeting with Sheila Devine, the Assistant Director of Child Welfare, to discuss institutional supports for the staff and boys of Mount Cashel in light of the worsening controversy. Having been informed by Father Molloy of Shane Earle's dreadful experiences, Brother Timothy Turner followed up the meeting with a letter to Devine in which he asked for help "to assist the adult survivors" of the Mount Cashel affair – assistance the Department of Social Services never ultimately provided. Turner also asked for a full-time social worker for Mount Cashel. Before Devine could answer his March 9 letter, the first of eight Christian Brothers, Richard Thorne, was arrested on four counts of sexual offences, including buggery and gross indecency. Although the charges arose out of the police reinvestigation of the Mount Cashel affair, Thorne's alleged offences were not related to the original 1975 investigation.

On St. Patrick's Day, Sheila Devine advised Brother Turner that the Department would assign a full-time social worker to Mount Cashel for a trial period of six months. For fourteen years, the Christian Brothers and the government had been unable to agree on the duties and reporting line of an outside social worker for Mount Cashel; within a month of the scandal becoming public in 1987, the arrangement was confirmed in a simple exchange of letters. Two months later Patricia Croke would take up her new duties, reporting to the department of Social Services rather than the Superintendent of Mount Cashel.

Although Brother Lynch tried valiantly to portray Mount Cashel as an institution worth saving, a place where corporal punishment and sexual abuse were relics from an aberrant past, the pressure of events was beginning to show. Plans for a $7.5 million expansion to the institution were put on hold, and the orphanage's enrolment continued to plummet. There were now only thirty-seven boys in the residential facility and another five in a special assessment centre for severe problem cases. The year before, there had been fifty-five residents, and in 1975, ninety-one. Although the Brothers insisted that the decline was not necessarily related to sex crimes at the orphanage, Brother Lynch admitted that the scandal was "possibly one of the factors." Mount Cashel residents were now being teased at school, but Brother Lynch insisted the boys hadn't lost faith in the Christian Brothers. Rather, they resented the media because, as Brother Lynch put it, the media had "painted them with history."

At least a few people directed their wrath in another direction. Late one spring night, someone vandalized two cars belonging to the order and hurled a beer bottle through the front window of the house where some of the Brothers lived in Buckmaster's Circle, a tough, city-core neighbourhood in St. John's. Shortly afterwards, the Brothers moved from the place where they had lived without incident for the past four years. Brother Lynch denied that their decision to leave had anything to do with smashed windshields or well-aimed beer bottles.

Official denials to one side, there was little doubt that the fate of Mount Cashel was hanging by a thread that quivered in the approach of that irresistible Atropos known as public opinion.

The reopening of the Mount Cashel case touched off the biggest, though hardly the best, investigation in the history of the Royal Newfoundland Constabulary.

CID Supt. Len Power, who was put in charge of the *cause célèbre*, failed to request extra resources from RNC Chief Ed Coady to conduct the mammoth reinvestigation – a logistical error that would move the work ahead at a snail's pace until additional officers were assigned. Nor did it occur to him to contact RNC members Robert Hillier or Ralph Pitcher, even though the original investigators were intimately familiar with the file. Strangest of all, Power decided that the RNC should contact only the boys mentioned in Hillier's 1975 report who had already been interviewed – a strategy doomed to repeat rather than complete the detective's original work. In accounting for this inane strategy, Chief Coady would later explain that the police had at first decided that it would be unethical to intrude into the lives of young men who were not interviewed in 1975 – a judgment call that completely ignored the possibility that other offenders, who did not come to light in Det. Robert Hillier's truncated investigation, could still be in positions of trust working with children.

Although he was in charge of all aspects of the reinvestigation, Power would be primarily focused on obstruction of justice, while Staff Sergeant Freeman Twyne, who headed up the Morals Section of the RNC, would be detailed to look into allegations of sexual abuse. Twyne's experience in missing-persons investigations would prove a valuable asset in the impending investigation. Power and Twyne, who were neighbours as well as colleagues, were expected to continue with their other duties while conducting the Mount Cashel investigation – an unreasonable demand that in part explained the appearance at times of a lackadaisical and insensitive performance by the RNC. By November 1989, the police and the Justice Department would realize how untenable such an arrangement was and a Special Investigative Unit comprised of four full-time officers would be set up to deal with Mount Cashel and related complaints that went back to the 1960s.

The agenda for the parallel police investigations was clearly driven by the politics of the imminent provincial election. In total disagreement with the way the Mount Cashel investigation had been handled by the Justice Department in 1975, and sensing how political the issue had become, the Leader of the Opposition, Clyde Wells, called for a full judicial inquiry into the failures of the criminal justice system in Newfoundland. In the wake of Wells's announcement, Robert Hyslop immediately asked Len Power to submit a report on possible obstruction of justice charges arising out of the Mount Cashel affair. The same day, Justice Minister Lynn Verge announced that criminal charges for obstruction might be laid as a result of the reopening of the orphange investigation. For reasons of short-term political expediency, the government appeared to be more concerned about the allegation of a cover-up in the Justice Department than about what had gone on at Mount Cashel so many years before. Verge, who was the co-chairman of Fisheries Minister Tom Rideout's successful campaign for the Tory leadership, also said that the government was considering a public inquiry into the whole affair to be presided over by a judge.

On March 11, 1989, Rideout became leader of the Progressive Conservative Party, replacing Brian Peckford. Peckford had resigned shortly after the New Year, disgraced by the Sprung greenhouse fiasco in which his government squandered $22 million on a doomed plan to grow high-tech cucumbers in St. John's at an eight-acre complex of plastic pods. Although Rideout had intended to govern for at least six months before calling an election, the timing of Peckford's resignation painted the new PC leader into a corner.

Originally intending to go to work for Newfoundland aviation czar Craig Dobbin in 1988, Peckford changed his agenda when *The Sunday Express* published a story about his planned departure from public life. By the time Peckford's hollow denials that he was about to resign subsided and he finally quit in 1989, his party was in the fifth year of its mandate, and its seventeenth year in power. Worse, the tired Conservatives were facing a harsh federal budget from their political cousins in Ottawa, chronically stalled Hibernia talks and a crisis in the fishery that could only worsen by the fall.

The one bright spot was Rideout himself. Conciliatory and open, he represented a clear alternative to the petty despotism that marred Brian Peckford's last years in power. Newfoundlanders seemed to respond. Buoyed by favourable polls and urged by his local political brain trust to seize the day, the youthful Rideout called an election for April 20, a decision that would make him the shortest-lived premier in Newfoundland history.

A week before Rideout's March 29 provincial election call, Robert Hyslop called Superintendent Power and made a second request for the CID's report into possible obstruction of justice, explaining that he needed it by March 30. (The subjects of that investigation included a number of people in Social Services, the Department of Justice and retired RNC officers.) That was the day that cabinet would approve an inquiry into Mount Cashel under the Public Inquiries Act; Justice Minister Verge would announce the inquiry on March 31. Three weeks later, a beleaguered Archbishop Alphonsus Penney established the church's commission of inquiry into sex abuse amongst the clergy, headed by former Lieutenant-Governor Gordon Winter.

On March 30, Power submitted his 162-page report on possible obstruction of justice in the Mount Cashel case to the Justice Minister, including a statement by Det. Robert Hillier that he had been ordered to change his original report. Power was then contacted by the Director of Public Prosecutions, Colin Flynn. Flynn informed him that the department was in the process of obtaining an independent legal opinion as to whether the facts as gathered by Power supported the laying of charges.

Power subsequently held a meeting at the Hotel Newfoundland with Rod McLeod, a former Deputy Solicitor-General of Ontario who was hired as an outside legal consultant by the Newfoundland Justice Department. The two men, in turn, held a meeting with Director of Public Prosecutions Colin Flynn, where it was agreed that Power should gather more facts. After receiving Power's second report, McLeod submitted his views on the case, together with the advice that the province put any obstruction of justice charges on hold until the royal commission into Mount Cashel had finished its deliberations. Long after Sam Hughes had heard his last witness, the Justice Department remained stubbornly silent about how it intended to handle McLeod's secret recommendations.

Meanwhile, Freeman Twyne's investigation into alleged sexual abuse at Mount Cashel dating from 1975 had struck pay dirt, although the assignment had not been easy for the sandy-haired detective with the rakish smile. In addition to Shane Earle, another Mount Cashel victim, hungry for justice, went to police shortly after the orphanage investigation was reopened. On February 17, Johnny Williams told his story of sexual abuse at the hands of the Brothers to Lt. Alexander Kielly of the CID. A little over a month later, Williams returned to give a second statement regarding physical abuse he had suffered at Mount Cashel. Apart from Earle and Williams, very few of the now grown victims of physical and sexual abuse at the orphanage were anxious to volunteer information. New lives had been established and people had made peace with the past as best they could. Suddenly demons were coming out of the ground and former victims had to balance the acute embarrassment of going public with whatever good might come of telling their stories. Faced with added legal uncertainties, many opted for simply keeping their heads down. One former Mount Cashel victim living in Toronto moved five times, without informing Twyne of a single change of address.

Some of Twyne's problems with the investigation were of his own making. An array of witnesses who were contacted by the investigator later complained of his crude overtures to obtain information from them — a deadly shortcoming in so sensitive a case. John McIsaac, Frankie Baird, Malcolm Baird, Ronald O'Brien, Gregory Connors and Darren Connors were all put off by Twyne's offensive abruptness and requests that they pass along their recollections to him in writing rather than in face-to-face interviews.

Twyne's mail-order police work was particularly upsetting to John McIsaac, who returned home from work one day to be told by a church worker visiting the elderly couple he lived with that the RNC had called and wanted to talk to him about physical beatings and sexual abuse he had suffered as a boy at Mount Cashel. He couldn't believe that the most carefully guarded secret of his life had been revealed to third parties without the slightest concern for his feelings. The outraged young man called CID Superintendent Power from Toronto and asked the officer "what kind of bullshit operation" he was running. Power apologized profusely to McIsaac and then asked him to mail in his statement to Freeman Twyne!

Failures in diplomacy to one side, Twyne's investigation had progressed far enough by April 10, 1989 to seek warrants for the arrest of various Brothers who had been named in Det. Robert Hillier's original report. Cathy Knox, the Crown prosecutor assigned to the case by Colin Flynn, helped draft the charges. Brother Francis Hepditch, the head of the Canada–West Indies Province of the Christian Brothers, provided authorities with the addresses of the first five suspects.

The police action hadn't come quickly enough for Shane Earle. On April 5, 1989 his lawyer prepared a Notice of Claim, the first formal step in a civil lawsuit, and served it on the Deputy Minister of Justice. John Harris advised Shane that Ronald Richards had agreed that the granting of the Notice, or commencement of civil proceedings against the Crown, public officials or the Christian Brothers for $2 million would not affect the laying of criminal charges against anyone the Department of Justice might be investigating for obstruction of justice or physical or sexual assault. By summer, Shane would have a new lawyer who would be pressing a joint lawsuit representing nine former Mount Cashel boys looking for a total of $18 million, on the ground that the police, the Justice Department and Social Services knew about the alleged assaults and did nothing to protect the children from an abusive and dangerous environment.

Armed with warrants empowering them to make arrests outside Newfoundland, Staff Sergeant Twyne and Lt. Alexander Kielly apprehended former Christian Brother Stephen Rooney, thirty-six, and Brother Joseph Burke, forty, in British Columbia and escorted them back to St. John's. Rooney was charged with three counts of gross indecency and two counts of assault, Burke with one count of indecent assault, one count of gross indecency, and one count of assault causing bodily harm. At the time of his arrest, Burke was vice-principal of Vancouver College, a private boys' school operated by the Catholic church.

Brother Hepditch informed Superintendent Power that two other Brothers would shortly be coming to Newfoundland from Toronto. Alan Ralph and Edward English, the two men at the eye of the Mount Cashel storm in 1975, were arrested in St. John's on April 17. The next day Douglas Kenny, who also arrived from Toronto, was taken into custody. Kenny had been removed as vice-principal of Michael Power–St. Joseph School when the Mount Cashel investigation was reopened, and assigned duties at the central office of the Metropolitan Toronto Separate School Board, which had hired him in 1979 without knowing of Kenny's involvement in the 1975 incident at Mount Cashel. The arrests of Brother Kevin Short and Brother Edward French would follow six weeks later.

Before the police investigation was finished, a total of fourteen people – nine Christian Brothers, and five civilians would be arrested on eighty-eight counts of alleged sexual and physical abuse, with more charges expected.

More than six weeks before the new government of premier-designate Tom Rideout publicly called its royal commission, and three weeks before anyone was arrested in relation to the Mount Cashel affair, public pressure had been building to get to the bottom of the most disturbing scandal Newfoundlanders had ever seen.

On February 22, 1989, the St. John's Status of Women's Council was already calling for an independent public inquiry into the sexual assault of children by members of the Roman Catholic clergy in Newfoundland – a demand that was being echoed by the political opposition, the press and concerned clergy. Although she would not initially commit to a public inquiry, Justice Minister Lynn Verge pledged to provide the public with an explanation of what went wrong in the justice system in 1975, regardless of which vehicle was chosen to do it.

One person who was very concerned about the kind of inquiry the Conservatives would call was Arthur Pike.

Having lived under a cloud for the ten years following the Soper Inquiry, he wanted government to conduct a wide-ranging inquiry into Newfoundland's criminal justice system that would delve into Mount Cashel, but not to the exclusion of other travesties he believed an unrestrained commission would uncover. Pike also worried about any of the Justice Department players in 1979 having a hand in determining the kind of inquiry that would be held in 1989. Convinced that all of them had read his evidence in the Soper Report, he was appalled that nothing had been done about it.

"What bothers me now," he told *The Sunday Express*, "is that there may be a conflict now because of the fact that Hyslop reopens the investigation when he himself, nine chances out of ten, read my evidence and knew about it in 1979 and never did anything about it. The report in 1979 would have gone back to the Minister. Certainly he didn't take the report and lay it on the shelf without reading it."

(In fact, the Justice Minister of the day, T. Alex Hickman, was recuperating from an operation for lung cancer after May 21, 1979, and only performed token official duties until he left politics in July of the same year.)

On April 14, 1989, just six days before Newfoundlanders went to the polls to elect a new government, and with the results of the RNC's reinvestigation in her briefcase, Lynn Verge announced the appointment of the Honourable Samuel H. S. Hughes, a seventy-six-year-old retired Justice of the Supreme Court of Ontario, as commissioner to head a public inquiry into the Mount Cashel affair. The PCs clearly wanted to feature the announcement of a public inquiry into the Mount Cashel affair as a central plank in their bid for re-election, a visible sign that they were no longer the secretive and arrogant crowd who had swept the Sprung scandal under the rug. With the city still buzzing over Shane Earle's heartbreaking revelations, no one in the backrooms of the party was discounting the potency of the Mount Cashel affair to affect the outcome of the vote.

Despite the political orchestration, the electoral symphony turned sour for the PCs. Less than a week after Lynn Verge made her announcement, the governing Tories were ousted by Clyde Wells and the Liberals, who captured thirty-one of the legislature's fifty-two seats. Unfortunately for the Grits, the new Premier's electoral triumph was spoiled by Justice Minister Verge who narrowly defeated Wells in the riding of Humber East in Corner Brook. Two days after winning Newfoundland's forty-first general election, Wells promised to proceed with the inquiry called by the Conservatives, but with a greatly expanded mandate for Samuel Hughes and his co-counsel, David Day of St. John's and Clay Powell of Toronto. Once the televised hearings got underway later that summer, the three men would quickly become the best-known faces in Newfoundland.

Reflecting on the PC defeat in St. John's, the most senior Conservative organizer in Newfoundland, Frank Ryan, laid the blame squarely on the Mount Cashel scandal.

"It was the last straw. The public couldn't handle the Mount Cashel revelations and turned their discontent with the church establishment against the political establishment."

While the ruling Conservatives may have been hit by the first wave of public anger over Mount Cashel and priestly sex crimes, the day of reckoning for the Roman Catholic church was just over the horizon.

Chapter *12*
██████ *Dark Shadows, Bright Lights*

You can never solve the problems of what happened, but if one person turns on their TV set this evening and sees anyone on the news or hears anything and it stops them from going out and molesting a child . . . even one child once, then I believe everything is worthwhile no matter what. . . . It's the future for the children, not for myself, not for the rest of these young men who came here before you. . . . It's for the children now. Frankie Baird, former Mount Cashel victim, in testimony at the Hughes Inquiry, November 14, 1989.

THE DARK SHADOWS of Mount Cashel went under the bright lights of television on June 28, 1989.

It seemed somehow appropriate that the Hughes Inquiry hearings were held in Exon House, a former group home for mentally disabled children, now used for day therapy. Every morning on their way to the hearing room, lawyers, witnesses and members of the press shared the lobby with children in wheelchairs—contemporary symbols of the same dependent innocence that was at the heart of the Hughes Inquiry. From Exon House you could also see Confederation Building, high on its hill looking out over the city towards the sea, home of the Justice and Social Services Departments, whose actions in the Mount Cashel affair would so dominate the proceedings in the coming months.

In his opening remarks, commission co-counsel David Day said that the primary focus of the inquiry would be the "lack of response to complaints, rather than the sinuosities of the complaints themselves," a qualification that signalled from the beginning the tension between bringing out the sordid facts of the Mount Cashel affair in order to assess the official reaction to them, while minimizing the crushing burden that the process would place on witnesses, the criminal justice system and the inquiry's large television audience. For some, the televised proceedings would become a daily addiction. In Conrad's dread phrase, "the fascination of the abomination" was the flame that drew the moth.

Discerning the difference between necessary evidence and tawdry theatre was not the only consideration in the business at hand. Since no court of law had yet found anyone criminally or civilly responsible for the allegations that gave rise to the inquiry, Day stressed that there would be no interference in the constitutional or legal rights of people already charged with offences related to the Mount Cashel reinvestigation. Admirable in principle, it was a promise that in practice would make it impossible for the commission to get to the bottom of what happened in 1975—a dilemma brought on by the Justice Department's decision to proceed with charges against certain Christian Brothers as if the Hughes Inquiry didn't exist. As Newfoundland's Justice Minister, Paul Dicks, put it: "This inquiry is not operating as a stay of police proceedings. Our instructions to the police are clear; to proceed in the normal course of things."

In scrutinizing its own part in the Mount Cashel affair, the Justice Department followed a different course, opting to wait until after the royal commission had heard its last witness before proceeding with any charges of obstruction of justice. Ironically, it would be the belated operation of the criminal justice system that hobbled the inquiry rather than the inquiry interfering with due process, since the commission ultimately decided not to call witnesses who were either charged or likely to be charged with matters arising out of the 1989 police reinvestigation of the Mount Cashel affair.

Day also explained the mandate of the commission, and the four phases it would encompass—complaints of child abuse at Mount Cashel, complaints of abuse elsewhere in Newfoundland and Labrador, complaints about the response of the justice system in cases not involving child abuse, and the need for corrective measures. As the catalyst for the inquiry, Mount Cashel was the first phase.

When Day finished speaking, Shane Earle got to his feet and read a letter into the record which pressed the case for the commission to supply legal counsel to the now adult victims of the Christian Brothers. Shane's appeal was passionate, with pain behind the emotion, simplistic, with hope underlying the naïveté.

> We are the victims of Mount Cashel Orphanage. We were the ones that were treated with disdain when we raised our voices to protest against the brutalization of our bodies in 1975 and '76. We are the ones who were ignored by the Royal Newfoundland Constabulary when we told the truth. We were the ones who were abandoned by the Department of Social Services which had the obligation to ensure our welfare. We are the ones who were deserted in an institution by the Director of Child Welfare who shut his eyes to our fates. We are the ones who were ignored, lied to, abandoned, deceived, frustrated, brutalized, sodomized, tortured and treated with less respect than some people treat their pets. . . .
>
> We are not just another interested party. We are the persons whose lives have been destroyed. We are the persons whose means of earning a living has been curtailed by systematic abuse. None of us is wealthy. None of us has the means of paying for a lawyer. If this commission is to begin to rebuild the trust which has to exist between adults and child, between forces of the law and victims of the law . . . then it is essential that the commission begin by providing us effective participation now.

The response from Mr. Justice Samuel Hughes gave the public its first insight into the mind of the man who was in charge of the inquiry. When Shane had finished reading, Judge Hughes put a single question: Who had written the letter? After he was informed that Shane and Ontario lawyer Harry Kopyto were the authors, Hughes replied that he "would hardly credit a professional man issuing or being responsible for" such patently rhetorical words. Dispassionate and trenchant, here was a heart that wasn't about to hemorrhage for the dark deeds he was charged with exploring.

As for the then forty-four-year-old Jewish lawyer who had been fighting the establishment since the day he was born in a German refugee camp back in 1946, Kopyto didn't mince words when it came to his description of what the boys required.

"This case needs somebody who is a shit-disturber. This case needs somebody who doesn't mind raising hell. This case needs somebody who is dedicated to only one idea . . . and believes in only one thing and that is justice with a capital 'J,' real justice. . . . I'm not looking for money, I'm not looking for the work, I'm doing what I have to do."

For better or worse, Kopyto and Hughes were to have but a single dealing during the course of the commission. In a second organizational meeting held under the cameras on August 14, Commissioner Hughes refused to permit Kopyto to act for former Mount Cashel residents, insisting that the boys either had to represent themselves or be represented by counsel in good standing with the Newfoundland bar. The latter qualification ruled out Kopyto since he would be refused a temporary appearance certificate by the benchers of the Newfoundland Law Society. Finally, Hughes also decided that the commission wouldn't pick up the legal tab of those who received standing at the proceedings. Kopyto branded the judge's ruling the beginning of a second cover-up of the Mount Cashel affair.

"Are they afraid I may end up asking too many questions? Are they afraid that I may end up pointing . . . at the legal profession who didn't behave in the perfect way in the 1970s? . . . Frankly, it doesn't smell too well to me."

But the odour he detected from Mr. Justice Hughes's ruling was not nearly as pungent as the one wafting from Harry Kopyto's bill to the Ontario Legal Aid plan between 1984 and 1986. Having already twice reprimanded Kopyto for dishonesty—once for cheating on his bar exams and again for making false statements in court—the Law Society of Upper Canada recommended disbarring Kopyto for overbilling provincial legal aid to the tune of 2,000 hours.

Rejecting Kopyto's claim that he was simply a bad bookkeeper, a disciplinary panel of the Law Society concluded that he "was dishonest and was dishonest with the intention that he would profit from that dishonesty." By the time the Hughes Inquiry had begun in earnest, the lawyer who claimed to "eat RCMP officers for breakfast . . . to get me going in the morning" was disbarred and the Mount Cashel boys were looking for new counsel.

They eventually settled on John Harris, a local lawyer and former NDP Member of Parliament who was defeated in the Conservative sweep during the 1988 election. For Harris, the affair was no local story but a legal case of international importance, dealing as it did with the issue of how church and state ought to compensate victims of physical and sexual abuse.

Although Lynn Verge was firmly, if a little uncomfortably ensconced in her tiny Opposition office by the time the royal commission got down to work, decisions made while she still occupied the sumptuous quarters of the Justice Minister would have a profound effect on the investigation into Mount Cashel. Clyde Wells may have broadened the terms of reference of the commission, adding the pinched, and ultimately untenable, requirement that it report within ninety days, but it was still Verge's appointees who would conduct the inquiry.

Verge's most crucial decision was the one that put the gavel in the hand of Samuel Hughes. When the Newfoundland government began planning the inquiry in 1989, Verge contacted Ontario's Attorney-General, Ian Scott, to find out what senior Ontario justices expert in the criminal law might be available to conduct the royal commission. After consulting with Ontario's Chief Justice, Scott recommended Hughes as a person who was both eminently qualified and available. After talking to Verge, the retired Supreme Court judge accepted the appointment.

There was no disputing that Mr. Justice Samuel Harvey Shirecliffe Hughes came with impressive credentials. Educated in a succession of private schools—Stowe in

England, Upper Canada and Ridley Colleges in Ontario—
Hughes later graduated from Oxford University and
Osgoode Hall Law School.

During World War II he served as a staff officer in the
Canadian Intelligence Corps, ultimately helping to write the
Armed Forces' official history of the war. Having been
raised on war stories about his grandfather and namesake,
Sir Samuel Hughes, who had created a controversy by
dispatching Methodist ministers to Quebec to recruit troops
when he was Minister of Militia and Defence in the Tory
government of Robert Borden, Sam Hughes had a natural
bent for the work.

After the war, he continued his legal studies and was
called to the bar in 1947, later practising with the Welland,
Ontario, firm of Raymond, Spencer, Law & MacInnes,
where amongst his other notable accomplishments he
managed to marry the boss's daughter. In the late forties and
early fifties Hughes twice ran for the provincial PCs, failing
both times to make it to Queen's Park. At forty-five he was
appointed to the Supreme Court of Ontario, but temporarily
left the bench the following year when Prime Minister John
Diefenbaker appointed him Chairman of the Civil Service
Commission of Canada. Three years later, Hughes, his wife,
Helen, and their two children left Ottawa when he was
reappointed to the Ontario high court.

By the time the bald, witty and occasionally esoteric judge
began his deliberations into Mount Cashel, he had already
conducted two royal commissions—both at the behest of
Ontario's Conservative government. The first was a complex
and long-running inquiry into the collapse of the Ontario-based financial institution, Atlantic Acceptance Corporation. A notoriously ponderous writer, Hughes referred to
the four years between the commission's appointment and
the submission of its final report as "my own Third World
War." Hughes's second royal commission, which lasted just
one year, was created in 1977 to determine the propriety
of a $35,000 donation to the Progressive Conservative
Party of Ontario by Waste Management Incorporated—
a transaction that he ultimately found neither illegal
nor improper.

Mount Cashel wasn't the first professional encounter with religious matters for Mr. Justice Hughes. While sitting on the Ontario bench, he presided over two well-publicized cases involving splinter religious groups. In one of many judgments that showed him to be a stickler on procedural matters, Hughes upheld the right of the Church of Scientology to protect the confidentiality of church documents seized in a 1983 police raid of the church's Toronto headquarters. Hughes, a lapsed Presbyterian, ruled that the church had not been properly notified of an Ontario civil servant's application for access to the documents.

In 1982, Hughes dealt with the bizarre case of Brother Michael Baldasaro, a devotee of the Church of the Universe, who argued that the marijuana possession charges against him should be dropped because his church believed that the substance at issue was not an illegal drug but a sacrament. Allen Ginsberg might have been impressed with the notion of "holy smoke," but not Mr. Justice Hughes.

"I can see we're going to have difficulty listening to any rational arguments, but if you have any, proceed," Hughes told the T-shirted defendant of his faith. Brother Michael's debut as a barrister was inauspicious; half an hour later, the judge upheld his conviction by the lower court. With his tongue planted solemnly in his cheek, Hughes quipped, "This is a proposition of some novelty . . . I don't want to delay you on your way to the Supreme Court of Canada."

Over the coming months, Newfoundlanders would be treated to more than a few examples of "Old Sam's" withering wit.

One condition Mr. Justice Hughes set before taking on the Mount Cashel inquiry was that Lynn Verge abandon her original plan to hire Toronto lawyers as commission counsel and appoint instead at least one experienced criminal practitioner based in St. John's. There were few better choices than David Day, the rangy, introverted lawyer with the drooping moustache who resembled a frontier marshal without the guns rather than a man who made his living reading through documents word by word. Moody by temperament, Day was a pessimist who lived in hope.

At forty-six, the former federal drug prosecutor knew his

way around a courtroom. He had an almost perfect record in the 4,000 drug prosecutions he handled between 1970 and 1985, including a celebrated 1974 case in which a medical doctor and a gang of dashing young smugglers tried to import two and a half tonnes of marijuana into Tors Cove, Newfoundland.

As a political science student at Memorial University, Day worked on a six-year study on divorce reform in Newfoundland headed up by Raymond Gushue, a prominent St. John's lawyer. Implementation of one of the report's recommendations led to the hearing of divorce cases in the Supreme Court of Newfoundland for the first time as of July 1968. (Up until that date, it required a private act of Parliament for Newfoundlanders to obtain a divorce.) His interest in family law piqued, Day went to Dalhousie Law School and after graduation acted in nearly 3,000 divorce cases between 1968 and 1989. The vicarious trauma of seeing so many couples stray over the continental shelf of the emotions as their marriages went to the bottom left him a confirmed bachelor who lived quietly with his parents in St. John's.

A prodigious worker, Day busied two secretarial staffs at his law firm — one from 9 A.M. until 5 P.M., and another from 7 P.M. until midnight. He would bring the same indefatigable work ethic to the Hughes Inquiry, occasionally pushing secretaries Margaret Linehan and Patricia Devereaux, "Davy's Angels," around the clock in order to prepare for the next day's testimony. One morning, when Mr. Justice Hughes remarked that Miss Devereaux had clearly been the first person to work that morning because her car was covered with the most snow, David Day promptly stood up and informed the Commissioner that she hadn't gone home yet after an all-night session to prepare an exhibit.

Day's predisposition to bring back slavery, in however benign a form, was heightened by the challenge he felt in signing on as co-counsel with the Mount Cashel inquiry — a challenge that put him on a collision course with the very establishment of which he was so prominent a member.

"It was a challenge unlike others in that ... it might ultimately involve me stating publicly my views as a lawyer about the deportment in office of justices, ministers of the Crown, members of the Justice Department, lawyers in private practice. . . . Yet I felt that . . . if you're a member of the bar, you have ethics and principles. And while many people doubt, mistrust the legal profession, mistrust the whole administration of justice, we do have ethics, we do have principles and I felt this was a challenge that I could not turn my back on."

David Day's co-counsel would be an old acquaintance from criminal law seminars, Clay Powell. When contacted by the Newfoundland government to take part in the Mount Cashel inquiry, the fifty-three-year-old criminal lawyer from Toronto was working in Windsor, Ontario, on an inquest involving a fatal shooting by the tactical unit of the Ontario Provincial Police. After being briefed by Newfoundland's then Deputy Attorney-General, Ronald Richards, Powell decided "this was an important inquiry and probably my background fit as well as, perhaps better than, anybody else's in Canada."

Although he mastered the rudiments of the story before accepting the assignment, it wasn't until he drove past the orphanage on his way into St. John's from Torbay Airport that he grasped the dimension of what was at stake.

"I had no idea what Mount Cashel Orphanage was. I thought it would be some little house off in some wooded area somewhere . . . [I] realized that this had to be a very major institution in St. John's, just by its imposing structure."

Despite his stature in the profession, Powell's first love had been journalism rather than law. During his student years at the University of Western Ontario he had worked nights and summers as a reporter with the old *Toronto Telegram*.

"It was a crazy time. It was a terrific time. I dealt mainly with crime stories, murders, or whatever was happening, which led me to have an interest in, I suppose, the criminal sub-culture of Toronto. I didn't intend to practise law. I was going to continue as a journalist, but I found that the criminal law intrigued me."

The law's spell was woven in part by the man Powell

articled with after graduating from Osgoode Hall in 1958, G. Arthur Martin, arguably the greatest criminal lawyer in Canadian history, a cerebral courtroom presence who seduced generations of judges and juries with sweet reason. At Martin's urging, Powell got a job with the Attorney-General's Office in the spring of 1963, intending to leave after a year's seasoning. Three years later, he was head of the Attorney-General's Special Prosecutions Branch, a post charged with looking into commercial and organized crime in Ontario. It was the perfect assignment to get an old police reporter's heart pounding.

In June 1965, Atlantic Acceptance Corporation collapsed, with losses of more than $100 million. While Mr. Justice Samuel Hughes of the Ontario Supreme Court conducted a painstaking investigation of the affair, Powell monitored the evidence from the Attorney-General's Office and laid charges where they were warranted—mostly against lawyers and accountants. He was deeply impressed with the way Hughes handled "the mammoth inquiry" and on that account relished all the more the idea of working with him on the Mount Cashel affair when the opportunity later arose.

Another of Powell's high profile cases as a prosecutor involved the now deceased owner of the Toronto Maple Leafs, Harold Ballard, who was convicted of theft and fraud and sentenced to three years in jail after a trial that attracted wide media attention. Powell also handled a number of prosecutions of corporate and organized crime figures in Ontario, earning the reputation of being a tough interrogator – an aspect of his talent that wouldn't overpower observers of his performance at the Hughes Inquiry.

The co-counsels were as different in temperament as they were physically—the Sparta and Athens of their profession. The tall, austere Day was a soldier of the law, a blinkered professional who readily admitted that his life was his work. For the duration of the commission, his camp was the walls and roof of Exon House and there was no such thing as a missed watch. Small and animated, Powell experienced life on a broader plane—a cosmopolitan with a wife and family, who practised law, wrote, lectured and travelled. Involved in

Mount Cashel but not obsessed by it, Powell was not a proponent of the nineteen-hour day, as was his ascetic co-counsel. Although Day would be the first to admit that Powell was more "work-efficient" than he was, it was an observation that may have had more to do with diplomacy than accurate reporting. Powell and his wife, Joan, found time to go to the Bahamas during the Christmas break of the inquiry, returning tanned, relaxed and, in the opinion of some observers, not nearly as prepared as Day for the resumption of the hearings in January.

The Powells also tried to surround themselves with a few of the comforts of home, while chipping away at the layers of social and cultural sediment that encased the buried mysteries of Mount Cashel. They flew their two standard poodles to Newfoundland to stay with them in a rented house on Hogan's Pond, just outside the city, where a number of prominent Newfoundlanders, including federal Cabinet minister John Crosbie had their summer homes. (One of the poodles ended up back in Ontario, Powell explained, after "a big Newfie dog beat him up.") Home in Ontario was a century farmhouse the Powells were renovating. Ironically, it was a scant five miles from the former headquarters of the Christian Brothers in Mono Mills.

For the urbane and accomplished Powell, there was a rich life beyond the forbidding events of the courtroom; for David Day, only sombre echoes from the pitiless forum in which he doggedly campaigned. Before the inquiry was over, the friction between Sparta and Athens would break out into a minor skirmish in the press, as the cruel grind of the proceedings took its toll. The relationship wouldn't be helped any by Powell's refusal to handle Day's witnesses while Day conducted a planned interview with an ailing Christian Brother in Antigua, a lack of co-operation that forced the postponement of the trip.

Day and Powell would be supported in their work by Weldon "Buck" Orser and G. Fred Horne, a pair of recently retired RCMP officers who were hired as the inquiry's investigators in the summer of 1989. The two had worked together in the General Investigation Section of the RCMP in the early seventies, until Orser, a New Brunswicker, was put in charge of St. John's two-man drug section in 1973.

The tall, lean investigator had handled his share of intriguing investigations. Without the aid of electronic or manual surveillance, Orser and fellow officer William Parker broke the Tors Cove smuggling case, in which Dr. Michael Carr and a band of young men were eventually arrested for importing two and a half tonnes of marijuana into Newfoundland on the luxury yacht *Carrero*. The case would involve Orser in travel to the United Kingdom, extradition proceedings in Jamaica and the United States, and ultimately a second huge drug bust in British Columbia in 1977 where many of the principals of the foiled Tors Cove importation who escaped in 1974 were finally arrested for smuggling twenty-two tonnes of marijuana into Canada. The Tors Cove case was prosecuted by David Day, a man the forty-eight-year-old former RCMP officer had learned to admire during their years of working together on hundreds of drug cases. As for the job at hand, the soft-spoken Orser was characteristically laconic.

"I don't see it as being an adrenalin-building process. If the system is wrong or the system can be better, then great, we do something that is going to benefit the system. You know, to me, it's not a fault-finding process as much as it is corrective criticism."

Orser's partner in the Mount Cashel investigation, fellow maritimer G. Fred Horne, was a Nova Scotian who spent most of his RCMP career in Newfoundland. Despite his large frame, the fifty-four-year-old former policeman was woefully overweight and had once been ordered to go on a diet by his RCMP superiors. But while they may have had second thoughts about his appearance, no one in the force doubted Horne's capabilities as a shrewd investigator of major crimes, including homicide. His forte was arson investigation, a specialty perfectly suited to a mind that circled and sifted the evidence until proof of a crime emerged from tell-tale ashes. In one case, the burning of the Blue Fin service station in Holyrood, Newfoundland, Horne made an arrest more than a year after others had decided there had been no crime.

In 1987, two years after retiring from the RCMP, Horne had his entire sense of the justice system turned on its ear by his involvement in the royal commission into the Donald Marshall case, the nationally celebrated story of a seventeen-year-old Micmac Indian who spent eleven years in prison for a murder he didn't commit. Along with Jim Maloney, a Micmac martial arts specialist, Horne became an investigator for the royal commission looking into how the justice system failed Donald Marshall in 1971. Ironically, he was hired by the Commissioner of the Marshall Inquiry, T. Alex Hickman, Newfoundland's Chief Justice—a man whose role in the Mount Cashel affair Horne would now be probing. But if the Marshall story had taught Horne anything, it was that a good investigator looked at every case from both sides. The object was to get the truth, not a conviction, and it didn't matter where the finger eventually pointed.

Fred Horne's RCMP bosses would have been impressed; their former colleague was finally on a steady diet, albeit of hard work. In Orser and Horne, the commission had a pair of seasoned hounds with good noses, the perfect pair to follow a trail that had been cold for fourteen years.

After the public organizational meetings, in the weeks before the first witness testified at the Hughes Inquiry, commission lawyers and investigators laid a plan for dealing with the enormous task that confronted them. It was decided that Clay Powell would deal with the Justice Department witnesses, including the cast of senior judges who would be called to give evidence. The reason was obvious; the judges to be examined were the same people Day argued in front of as a practising lawyer in St. John's. For his part, Day would handle police and Social Services witnesses, based on his previous work as a drug prosecutor and practitioner of family law.

In early summer, Orser and Horne went to work with a vengeance on the first phase of their assignment, gathering up the mountain of government documents, including court transcripts, medical records, Social Services and police reports from which commission staff would compile a master witness list. Once that was done, a plan was developed to locate each prospective witness, including the ninety-one boys who had lived at Mount Cashel in 1975.

Between missing and misfiled material, the investigators often discovered they needed long stretches of time to search through thousands of files in any given government department to find what they needed. On more than one occasion, the investigators watched the sun come up on their way home from work. In their first eight months on the commission, Orser and Horne had six days off—a grind neither former policeman complained about.

"That goes with the territory, doesn't it? You know, if you're not prepared to commit yourself to it, then don't do it," Buck Orser observed.

Once the documents were compiled and processed, Fred Horne began the toughest duty he had ever pulled—expeditiously locating the boys of Mount Cashel who had now grown to manhood, started families and moved to other parts of North America. Things got even tougher when he travelled to various cities in Canada and the United States to interview potential witnesses. Nothing in Horne's previous police work prepared him for the emotional roller-coaster he would be riding non-stop for the rest of the summer.

"In the police force, you might have a serious sex offence, sex case where the victim might break down and cry or become very upset. But you probably wouldn't have another one like that for six months or a year. But here you have the impact of day after day after day of the same thing. I found it very draining, very unsettling."

But if Horne found the exercise stressful, it was flatly traumatic for the victims. It was remarkable that the two investigators were able to convince so many former Mount Cashel boys to recount the sickening details of the past under the glare of television lights on a subject most of them had religiously kept from their wives and families for years. In some cases, it was simply too much to ask.

"One said that if his name came out or he was forced to give evidence, don't expect to see him. Come by the funeral home and look at him. And I believed him," Clay Powell recalled. "There was no doubt about it. Fred Horne talked to him and he was of the same view. He was really, really on the line."

Former Mount Cashel boys willing to come forward were handled sensitively by the investigators and treated with respect by commission counsel. Two members of the team who provided support and encouragement for the distressed witnesses, Margaret Linehan and Patricia Devereaux, welcomed them with simple and generous compassion.

"We can have all the social workers, psychiatrists, psychologists, experts running around wanting to deliver service to the former residents of Mount Cashel. I don't think all of them put together could have done what those girls did for so many of those guys who still come back. . . . They've just been incredible," Clay Powell observed.

By September, the commission team was ready to begin unfolding the tragedy of Mount Cashel to the province and the country, poised to work through the allegations, the embryonic police investigation of 1975 and the subsequent and almost unpunctuated silence of the next fourteen years. But as they would soon find out, no amount of hard work or painstaking analysis could fill in the gaps created by deceased players, lost documents and the memories of key witnesses that proved to be fuzzier than a television screen at three in the morning.

By the time the first national journalists covering the event checked into their hotels, the staff of the Hughes Inquiry were already banking on a big break to help them unravel the mystery of Mount Cashel, a *deus ex machina* that never appeared.

Between September 11 and mid-December 1989, a ghostly parade of former residents of Mount Cashel Orphanage appeared at the Hughes Inquiry to tell stories of sexual abuse that had been officially covered up or stifled by their own fears as children. Unlike the bloodless words contained in official reports about Mount Cashel, the physical presence of the young men who had been orphaned or abandoned early in life and then abused by their guardians showed that the tragedy had a long reach.

Their testimony kept thousands of horrified Newfound-landers riveted to their television sets as the hearings unfolded, day after painful day. The commission was so popular, in fact, that the cable company providing gavel-to-gavel live coverage added a new channel to its basic service roster to replay each day's testimony in full every night. An astonishing 15 per cent of the viewing audience in Newfoundland was tuning in to the Hughes Inquiry on a regular basis!

One of the first spectacles they were treated to was an attempt by the Hughes Inquiry to satisfy both a witness's need for privacy and the media's demand for information, which went desperately wrong. Reporters were permitted to hear the testimony of forty-four-year-old Chesley Riche on the condition that no one film or photograph Mount Cashel's former maintenance man who had come close to blowing the story wide open in 1975.

The burly, straight-talking Riche, who now worked as a mechanic, testified that he saw boys physically abused and heard their stories about sexual molestation by the Brothers during his brief tenure at the orphanage in 1975. Under cross-examination, Riche was asked by lawyers representing Brother Douglas Kenny about Kenny's statement to him in 1975 that the boys had only made their allegations to get attention. Riche had a trenchant reply: "A child looking for attention don't go to bed with a man. That's my opinion."

Riche explained that he took his complaints to the Director of Child Welfare, Frank Simms, after Shane Earle was allegedly beaten by Brother Joseph Burke in December 1975.

"The man [Simms] told me, 'The Catholic church is on a pedestal. We can't touch them.' I said, 'You do something or I'll put your pedestal on the front page of *The Telegram.*'"

Following his testimony, Riche had a bizarre run-in with the media as he left Exon House after giving his testimony. Television cameramen on the run recorded the scene as Riche charged after the group with curses, threats and clenched fists. He attacked one of them, breaking his camera. Then he chased a photographer into the building, got the unfortunate man in a bear-hug and demanded that he turn over the film in his camera.

"Give me that film, give me it," he shouted. "It's my life we're talking about."

After emerging from Exon House, Riche chased another cameraman out of the parking lot and along the sidewalk. The dispute ended when the police arrived. Before leaving the parking lot, Riche threatened to get a gun and do his impression of Clint Eastwood at any media outlet that used his picture.

When several media agencies unsuccessfully challenged a later decision by the Hughes Inquiry to allow one of the Mount Cashel victims to offer his evidence in camera, Commissioner Hughes pointed out that a similar arrangement in the case of Chesley Riche had ended in chaos.

"It ended in a small riot on these premises and outside them. . . . A camera was seized and smashed as I understand and the riot went roaring down the hill and left us here in a state of some doubt as to whether any such procedure should be repeated in the course of the inquiry."

Understandably, emotions were running high. Just a week after proceedings got under way, at 3:20 in the afternoon, an anonymous caller to *The Evening Telegram* claimed that "a small plastic explosive" had been placed inside the hearing room and was set to detonate at 4 P.M. At 3:25 P.M. David Day calmly but firmly advised the commission that it was necessary to vacate the building in the interests of public safety. After fifty or so people filed out of Exon House, a dozen police officers and a single bomb expert combed the hearing room without finding any explosive device.

But security measures couldn't protect the public from the bombs that were about to go off in the witness box.

Robert Connors, a tall twenty-six-year-old who occasionally bit his lower lip as he testified, explained how he had been sexually abused by three Brothers and physically abused by many more during his thirteen years at the orphanage. Hiding his eyes behind his hands as he described the nightly gropings by Brother Alan Ralph, the witness, who had been placed in Mount Cashel at age eight along with his two brothers, choked out, "Time-wise it seemed like forever, but I guess it was fifteen or twenty minutes."

Connors explained that the boys at Mount Cashel were too terrified to tell anyone, including their own peers, about what was happening.

"I'll tell you how secretive it was . . . I didn't even know about my own two brothers . . . about my own brothers being sexually molested."

As a boy, Connors knew that his social worker was a woman named Peggy Gosine, but he never got the opportunity to tell her about conditions at the institution. During his thirteen years at Mount Cashel, he had only one chance meeting with her and by that time his terrifying relationship with the Brothers had poisoned his view of all grown-ups.

"At the time I had no respect for adults at all, whether they were Christian Brothers or whatever because of what was happening to me. Anytime somebody talked to me adult-wise, I was scared no matter if it was a Christian Brother or a teacher, whether it would be a man or a woman, I was scared. So I more or less shied off and my only responses would be yes, no. I wouldn't engage in conversation," Connors testified.

The notable exception to the former Mount Cashel resident's rule about grown-ups was the visit he and Billy Earle, Shane's older brother, paid to Social Services in September 1975 when the two boys told social worker Robert Bradbury what was going on at the orphanage, oblivious to the bitter irony that their report would be handed over to Brother Douglas Kenny for investigation, and subsequently die at the desk of the Director of Child Welfare, Frank Simms. A few months later, when Shane Earle's beating sparked an investigation, Connors quickly paid the price for talking to the police about the abuse he and his friends were suffering at the hands of certain Christian Brothers. Returning to Mount Cashel from the police station, Connors and the others had a late supper. As he was leaving the dining hall, another boy told him that Brother Kenny wanted to see him in the Quiet Room. Connors found

Mount Cashel's Superintendent waiting for him at the far end of the room. Kenny, on crutches from a hockey injury, accused Connors of denouncing him to the police. The terrified boy denied it.

"With that, he looked at me and he called me a liar. And up with the crutch and he made a swing with the crutch and he just managed to . . . [catch] me on the shoulder with the crutch and he broke the top of his crutch off on my shoulder."

After leaving Mount Cashel in 1984, Connors was unable to find another place to live. A few nights a week, he would creep back into the orphanage to sleep in a bed. His life became a phantasmagoria of drugs, petty theft and alcoholism until the night he tried to slash his wrists with a piece of glass. Eventually he left Newfoundland and moved to Ontario, where he married and settled down in Kitchener, keeping his painful secrets to himself until the day the commission investigators called him.

Billy Earle, who had gone with Connors to Social Services in 1975, also tried to commit suicide after leaving Mount Cashel. His life on the street, while he was still a permanent ward of the state, was a whirlpool sucking him down into drug abuse and a pathetic vagrancy in which he would admit to crimes he hadn't committed just to get in out of the cold. At fifteen, he was placed back in school, but one day his world simply collapsed, "because there was that much built up inside me about what went on in there. . . ."

"I was in school. . . . We were doing a test and everything flashed back on me about what I had experienced in life and I wasn't getting nowhere . . . I said, 'Fuck it.' . . . I was seeing somebody for the longest time and they gave me a refill on the narcotic to relax me and I took whatever was in the bottle. And I jumped up in school . . . I didn't know what I was doing. I got up and tipped over a desk and I ploughed everything out from under me. And I remembers I ended up in the office, and I went wild up there, and they were trying to keep me there because the cops were coming to take me, and I batted out of there and the last place I came to, I was up on the back of the Battery Motel, lit in a field. And I didn't know if it was day or night . . . I didn't know what I was doing. I took everything in sight, I stole everything, I just run. I didn't know any other way to survive."

Billy testified that Brother Ralph had sexually abused him and that another boy (Gerard Brinston) warned him against reporting the incident to Brother Kenny. He also testified that he told social workers at the Harvey Road Office of the Child Welfare Division about the physical and sexual assaults that were taking place at Mount Cashel, referring to the Brothers as "gearboxes" and claiming that there was "a lot of it on the go in there." When asked by David Day whether he was recounting what he had actually seen or merely heard about, Billy quickly replied, "I was speaking about what I saw."

Fearing for Shane, who was still at the orphanage, Billy and his elder brother Rick broke into Mount Cashel at 3 A.M. one morning, determined to spirit their younger brother away. Although Shane appeared to be very nervous, he refused to come with them or tell his brothers what, if anything, was happening to him.

After listening to the heartbreaking testimony of Billy Earle, Dereck O'Brien and Johnny Williams, Premier Clyde Wells said that he had heard enough evidence to be "very concerned" about the reaction by authorities to the Mount Cashel affair in 1975 and suggested that government might move to establish a police commission, where complaints about interference in legitimate investigations, as well as shoddy practice, could be aired.

Fourteen years after his initial complaint to police, Shane Earle came to Exon House in search of retroactive justice. Dressed neatly in a shirt, jacket and tie, Shane elaborated on allegations of sexual and physical abuse he had already made in *The Sunday Express* and on the "Oprah Winfrey Show" in front of fourteen million television viewers. Looking nervous and agitated, he described how Brother Kenny had fondled him the very day he entered Mount Cashel and later sexually assaulted him during an outing to the beach.

"He'd get me to rub lotion on his back and on his stomach and on his arms and his legs and his neck. An↑ when he was laying down on the blanket, he was lying on his back. I would be sitting by him. He would not pick me up, but he would haul me against him and get me to lie on his stomach. And he'd hug me and then he started undoing my shirt and opened it up. He didn't take it off me. And then he reached, put his hands down by my private area and undid my pants and hauled my pants down. And next thing I know he was making gestures with my bare private area against his groin area. And he, he'd have an erection. He would try to stick it up my bum. Then I said, 'It hurts,' and I started to cry. And he rolled me off his body, told me to go down to the beach and send this other guy up. . . ."

Shane testified that Brother Edward English first molested him while making the rounds in the dormitory one night. He also described how English liked to relax back at the orphanage after taking the boys skating at St. Bonaventure's Forum on Saturday afternoons.

"He would have a number of the boys gather around him and he would talk, chat about different things, you know, probably start telling a story. He would get us to scratch his head, scratch his back. And by this time he was probably after loosening up his belt . . . and get us to put our hands down in his pants to scratch his, his private area. . . ."

Shane also testified to sexual encounters with Brother Alan Ralph and Brother Joseph Burke, the man whose beating of Shane in 1975 touched off the abortive investigation by Det. Robert Hillier. Shane explained how Brother Burke once climbed on top of him in his temporary bed in the women's quarters when Mount Cashel was being renovated.

"He'd haul down his zipper and he'd get me to touch his penis. And I'd touch it. And I remember telling him I couldn't breathe. And he'd stay there briefly and then get off of me and he'd haul up my pyjama pants, tell me to put my shirt back on. . . ."

One of the most poignant parts of his testimony outlined how Brother Kenny discouraged John and Elizabeth Scurry from adopting Shane as a small boy. When they approached Brother Kenny about Shane in 1975, the couple was told that the boy's parents were on the verge of a reconciliation and that he faced a bright, happy future. Brother Kenny advised the Scurrys that they were getting too close to Shane. They never tried to contact him again and John Scurry, who worked at Exon House, started bringing home a boy from that institution. According to Shane's testimony about the episode, Brother Kenny gave the puzzled little boy a very different reason to account for the sudden end to the visits from the friendly couple that had once shared Christmas with him.

"He said, 'Well, you won't be visiting that family no more. They said you got out of hand, that you were disturbing their household.' They were just after going to the pet store and buying me a bowl of goldfish. He [Brother Kenny] was taking me upstairs to the dorm and when we got to the top flat, we were in the basin area. . . . He took the bowl and said, 'Well, you won't be needing them any more,' and he threw the fish down into the sink."

In March 1989, the Scurrys finally found out what happened to Shane when they saw the story in *The Sunday Express*.

"John was working the night shift and he brought the paper home. I saw the picture and I said, 'That's Shane.' When I read the story, I fell to pieces. . . . I wouldn't believe a Brother would tell us a lie. We were always taught to respect the Brothers and the priests. But how can you have any respect for those people today? . . . Shane was deprived of a good home," Mrs. Scurry said.

The same day that Shane gave his emotional testimony officials in the Department of Health began organizing volunteers to counsel Mount Cashel victims testifying at the Hughes Inquiry.

Short, slight and well-dressed, twenty-four-year-old Gregory Connors reminded the inquiry that sexual abuse wasn't the only peril young boys faced at Mount Cashel in the mid-seventies. During an outing to a Christian Brother summer camp, Connors cut a hole in a tent with a small knife and was caught and brutally punished by a volunteer worker.

"He dragged me into the tent and he pulled down my pants and he threw me down on a mattress and he put one foot on the back of my neck to keep me pinned down. . . . And he beat me across the backside with a stick. I don't know how many times he hit me. When the stick broke, he dropped to his knees and he had a motorcycle glove that he used to wear and he beat me with that. It was a black motorcycle glove and it had the studs around the cuffs and on back where each knuckle would be. And he beat me with that on the bare bottom."

In excruciating pain, Gregory went to Brother Richard Thorne to complain of the savage beating. The Christian Brother had trouble getting the boy's pants down because the blood on his buttocks had dried on his clothing. While he was examining Gregory's wounds, Thorne noticed a boil on the boy's backside and told him that was what was causing his pain. The Christian Brother called the cook and had him make a bread poultice to treat the boil.

"So while the cook was preparing this, Brother Thorne had seen the marks and everything on my backside and he started making jokes about how he could play checkers on my behind. And he got the Mercurochrome or iodine out and he said he was playing connect the dots. . . ."

Like a lot of other Mount Cashel boys, Gregory Connors learned to take unspeakable abuse from adults without uttering a word to anyone in authority, because, as he testified, "We [Mount Cashel boys] were treated a lot different than normal students." The ingrained lesson of expecting nothing from the system could be carried to tragic lengths. One day on his way back to the orphanage from school, Connors stopped to play with a dog that was chained on the front lawn of a nearby house. A man came out and asked the nine-year-old if he wanted something cold to drink.

". . . He told me to come into the kitchen and he picked me up and sat me up on the counter and poured me some Pepsi. I drank a bit of it. And he grabbed me by the face and he kissed me full on the mouth. Then he lifted me down off the counter and he took me by the wrist and dragged me into the bedroom and closed the bedroom door and he raped me."

The hitherto stoically composed witness winced as he

finished his story, his small hands clasped in front of his mouth as though he were trying to catch the words that had finally escaped from him into a roomful of strangers. For a few moments he was slightly breathless, as though he were going to faint. A dread hush came over the hearing room, the apprehensive silence of a boxing crowd when a downed fighter remains motionless for too long. After a few painful moments, the witness regained his composure. But through Connors's pathetic testimony, longstanding pain had suddenly opened over vistas of a terrible and enduring damage to the former residents of Mount Cashel.

The courage it took for so many former Mount Cashel boys to exhume their past in front of thousands of strangers did not go unnoticed by Newfoundlanders. Christopher Hatch, a forty-one-year-old teacher, voluntarily came forward to substantiate Johnny Williams's story that an alleged beating from Brother Edward English had left his small body tattooed with bruises. Hatch, who had worked at Johnny's former school, testified that he had been naïve in his treatment of Williams at the time.

"It has been a thorn in my side ever since to realize what I had seen and done nothing about. Basically, I felt inadequate because I didn't know what to do."

Lawyer Raymond Fahey, a former teacher at various Christian Brother schools, also came forward to detail his personal observations of how violent the Catholic order could be in the course of disciplining students. On one occasion, the teacher was called to the principal's office to witness a strapping that became so abusive that he reported the man to the school board.

"The Brother, during the administration of the strapping, I guess he felt that he wasn't making enough of an impression on the young fellow and he literally jumped off of his feet to apply pressure on the strap on the downstroke to the young fellow. And the Brother himself turned red. He was actually, obviously, very, very angry," Fahey testified.

At the conclusion of his testimony, the practising Catholic summed up his experiences teaching in schools operated by the Christian Brothers.

"I have categorized my stay there in the following manner,

that there was nothing very Christian about the Christian Brothers."

Appalled by what they were hearing, one hundred people assembled in a St. John's park on Thanksgiving Day to demonstrate their support for the child victims of physical and sexual abuse. Following a rally and a short march through city streets, the demonstrators planted crocus bulbs behind the bandstand in Bannerman Park, explaining that the crocus was their chosen symbol of courage for the young people whose stories had so moved everyone.

"Because of each and every one of them, this community is going to be a safer place for my children and yours," said Bobbie Boland of the Social Action Committee of the Roman Catholic church.

Gregory Connors was followed to the stand by Gerard Brinston, a frail twenty-eight-year-old from St. Lawrence who recounted his experiences at Mount Cashel like a prisoner of war telling the tale of his heartless captivity. In a voice shaking with emotion, he described how he had been assaulted by Brother Edward English within a week of his arrival at Mount Cashel.

"I was showering after swimming and I was the last one to leave the pool area. Brother English grabbed me by the privates and he started pushing his penis towards my backside. I was scared and I ran and caught up with the rest of the guys."

On another occasion, at a lonely cabin in the Goulds, there was no escaping his determined tormentor.

"He [English] pushed me up on the bed. He tore my clothes off and he got up on top of me, and he came all over my stomach. He said it would put hairs on my chest."

Brinston also told the commission how another Brother had punished him by holding him under a running hot-water tap.

"It was enough to scald my shoulder. He told me to go to bed, so I went to the dormitory and my back started bubbling up. I got big blisters."

Brinston was admitted to the psychiatric unit of St. Clare's Hospital when he left Mount Cashel. Lost and without hope, he tried to take the only way out that promised relief.

"I took an overdose at fifteen years old and slashed my wrists around the same time. I went to drugs and alcohol. I worked the streets for money. I didn't know who to trust. I didn't get any education. I lost all moral values. I had no respect for my family for letting it happen, but it wasn't their fault. I lost all respect for authority."

In 1977, Brinston went to Holy Cross monastery in St. John's to get help for his drug problem and to talk to someone about what had happened to him at the orphanage. Brother John McHugh, the brother of the order's leader, Gabriel McHugh, invited the teenager to his bedroom, where Brinston detailed the horrors of his past at the orphanage, totally unprepared for what he claimed happened next.

"He was not one bit surprised. . . . He was very calm. He just said, 'Who did this?' And I told him and he turned around and did the same, only it wasn't violent like at the orphanage. It basically had my own consent, I guess. . . . And I was getting paid for it," Brinston recounted in an interview with *The Sunday Express.*

The teenager was well launched in the profession that would sustain him in a world of threatening shadows from which he still obviously cowered. Over the next several years, Brinston claimed to have received $10,000 in airline tickets, meals, clothing and cash from the man he said arranged an apartment for him and paid him for sex. Just before Brother McHugh died in July 1989, he would make a dying declaration that Brinston's allegations were untrue, a declaration that was released by the Christian Brothers.

"The charges which are made against me and the motivations for these charges leave me dumbfounded . . . I am absolutely innocent of the accusations."

Brinston stuck by his story and remained philosophical.

"Deep down inside he was a caring, giving kind of person. He just went about it all the wrong way. . . . He could have helped somebody in a different way. He figured, I guess, money would make anything work. . . ."

Like Gerard Brinston, John MacIsaac was very much a survivor. Testimony from the small, thin man in the grey pinstriped suit had the sharp and unembellished edge of a military report – hardly surprising since he had spent time in the army after leaving Mount Cashel. According to MacIsaac, the harsh disciplines of Canadian Forces Base Cornwallis were no match for the draconian regimen of life amongst the Brothers. The word "sir" often punctuated his staccato evidence and there was a sense of vulnerable brittleness to his tough-guy exterior. He was the only Mount Cashel boy who affirmed rather than swore an oath at the outset of his testimony; God, apparently, was another casualty of John MacIsaac's years at the orphanage.

Unlike most of the other witnesses, MacIsaac wasn't interviewed by the Newfoundland Constabulary in 1975, and in fact had denied any mistreatment by the Brothers when police questioned him in an earlier theft investigation at Mount Cashel. MacIsaac had simply lied to protect himself from the rage of the Brothers.

"I denied it. But of course the Christian Brother that was standing behind me had his hand on my neck and my shoulder. With a Christian Brother in the room, it was naïve to assume I would admit that I was being punished or sexually abused at that point. So I flatly denied it . . . I was petrified of the Christian Brothers. In no way, shape or form would I have told anybody out of my fear of them. I watched that many beatings and I knew, I had been beaten and I knew what would happen to me. . . . Preservation of my life was of the utmost importance to me," he testified.

When he entered Mount Cashel at the age of six, MacIsaac was exceptionally small for his age and one of the youngest residents of the orphanage, characteristics that made him the target of frequent beatings. One particular Christian Brother took an instant dislike to his tiny charge and singled him out for a variety of painful and degrading attention.

"This man from the day I met him called me a slob. . . . This man would issue me clothes that were too large for me, shirts that wouldn't fit me. When I put them on the next day, he would grab me by the shoulder and lift the shirt up to show how big it was. And he would slap me in the face and he would say, 'You can dress you up but you can't take you anywhere. You're a slob.' Smack me in the head and say, 'Get out of my sight,' " MacIsaac testified.

The same Brother would also incite the other boys to torment their pint-sized confrère, sometimes to the point where he believed his life was at risk. It was not unusual to hear the Brother cry, "Everybody get John MacIsaac." The next thing the unfortunate boy knew there were twenty boys jumping on top of him, kicking, kneeing and punching him in an orchestrated but unprovoked frenzy.

"I was in the swimming pool doing laps. And this particular Brother asked everyone to get out of the pool. And he told me to stay there. He said, 'MacIsaac, stay put.' He said, 'Continue your laps.' I w⁻⁻ going from side to side doing laps and I was tired som̲ ̲re in the middle. And he said, 'Everybody get ...' and froze. And I remember looking back at all the boys lined up on the pool and I knew what was about to come. And he said, 'John MacIsaac.' And then everybody jumped in the pool on top of me. I felt I was going to drown. I went under. I gasped for air when I came back up. I was crying. It was terrifying."

On another occasion, MacIsaac and another Mount Cashel resident were caught smoking by a Christian Brother. At the last moment, the ten-year-old glimpsed the approaching Brother and thrust the still-lit cigarette in his pocket.

"It was actually quite funny," MacIsaac testified. "He knew I was smoking and I knew he knew. And he just stood there and waited for my coat to catch on fire."

Afterwards, MacIsaac was taken to the office and "smacked around" for his offence. The next day, he was called down to the office by a second Brother and asked to confirm or deny the report that he had been smoking. When the terrified boy denied the story, the Brother slapped his face. A second denial brought a second slap.

"So I figured if I admitted it, I would be O.K. But when I admitted it, he punched me in the face and he knocked me over a chair that was sitting in his office. There were many times when they touched me or they grabbed me by the arm, they would squeeze. Or they would put their finger on my chest up against a wall and dig it right into my [chest]. I felt that finger was going to go right through me. . . . There was so much physical beatings . . . I was very frightened for my life."

MacIsaac testified that he was sexually abused by Brother Alan Ralph seven or eight times in the course of one year.

"When it was initiated and he asked me to join him on the bed with another boy, he was a paternal figure to me and I more than wanted to jump up next to him and snuggle into him as a father figure. There was no real problem with me doing that because this sexual act had never happened before."

MacIsaac further testified that even his chief tormentor, the Brother who had beaten and humiliated the little boy on so many occasions, had once sexually molested him in the basement workshop at Mount Cashel.

"He closed the door. After a minute or so he had his arm around me and his hand was placed on my crotch. He felt my genitals from the outside of my clothing and I squirmed away from him."

Escape was not so easy from some of MacIsaac's bullying peers who demanded sexual favours which he grudgingly dispensed to avoid their furious beatings. "The general consensus was that if you went along with the sexual acts, the physical beatings weren't going to happen as much."

When asked by David Day to summarize his sense of Mount Cashel, John MacIsaac drew a picture that symbolized the experience of many of the orphanage's former residents.

"I personally felt, sir, that my eleven years at Mount Cashel were filled with psychological cruelty towards me, sexual assaults, physical assaults, and something that once this commission is over with and everyone goes home, that is something I will have to live with for the rest of my life. . . ."

Like John MacIsaac, Malcolm Baird hadn't given a statement to police during the 1975 Mount Cashel investigation, although he and his brothers had spoken to Det. Robert Hillier at their mother's home in Mount Pearl.

The twenty-eight-year-old roofer, who was now married with two children and living in Calgary, testified that he was sexually assaulted by Brother Edward English a little over a week after he entered the orphanage in October 1975. Malcolm had been standing in a group of boys in Mount Cashel's main hallway when Brother English came up behind him and put his arms around Malcolm's neck. Holding the boy close to him, Brother English pulled the fourteen-year-old's hands behind his back and pressed his own groin against them.

Approximately three weeks later, Brother English took Malcolm to pick up communion bread at a local church. When English got back in the car, he gave Malcolm a piece of the "holy bread." English then undid his zipper, took out his penis and began masturbating until he ejaculated. After-wards, he reached over and pulled out Malcolm's penis and began to masturbate the frightened boy. English then put his hand on the back of Malcolm's head and pushed the boy's face towards the Brother's penis. Malcolm refused to perform fellatio and English quickly relented. Instead, he masturbated again, and then reached under the car seat for some napkins. After attending to himself, he started the car and drove back to the orphanage.

Spurred by several incidents of sexual abuse, Malcolm repeatedly ran away from Mount Cashel in the few short months he was there. When Detective Hillier later came to his mother's house during the Shane Earle investigation, Malcolm described how he had been fondled by Brother English at bedtime. But that was all he told the tall detective; he was still too frightened and humiliated to reveal what had happened in the church parking lot.

Malcolm Baird's testimony marked the end of an October filled with shock and pain for everyone who watched the proceedings. It was now obvious that the work of the commission couldn't be completed in the ninety days Premier Wells had stipulated, and the government allotted another $535,000 to the Hughes Inquiry, bringing the total funding to just over $1 million. The welcome extension allowed commission counsel and the investigators to bring prospective witnesses around at their own pace and to work carefully with the former Mount Cashel boys who had already agreed to testify.

One former Mount Cashel resident who came forward voluntarily was James Ghaney — the boy who had been stripped of his clothes, handed his suitcase, and told as a joke by Brother Alan Ralph that he had to leave the orphanage because of persistent bedwetting. Ghaney, who had entered Mount Cashel at the age of five, testified that he had been physically, sexually and emotionally abused at the orphanage. He was not interviewed by police in 1975 but remembered seeing other boys going to the police station and thinking that Mount Cashel would be closed.

"The abuse that went on at Mount Cashel was very severe. . . . We knew that if the police were investigating at this time and if they knew the things we knew, the orphanage would surely be closed down," he testified.

Ghaney developed a drinking problem at Mount Cashel, which he claimed the Brothers reacted to with "pure ignorance and brute violence." At sixteen, he was removed from the orphanage and placed in a series of increasingly seedy boarding houses. The last one was a rundown facility for alcoholics at 93 Bond Street in St. John's. It was already occupied by two hardened adults who transformed the tiny room into a twelve-by-twelve-foot hell for the troubled grade ten student.

"I was in a room . . . with two men much older than myself. One was a reformed alcoholic and one was an alcoholic. They constantly fought at night. One . . . I was scared to death of because he was always drunk. The other one I didn't worry about because he only had one leg anyway."

The young boy begged to be moved to more congenial quarters while he studied for his final exams, but his social worker advised him to stick it out to the end of the school year. After exams, James began drinking again and sleeping on neighbourhood lawns rather than return to the boarding house. Fastidious about his appearance, he was particularly upset by the fact that he had no money for clothes and bitterly complained to his social worker, Stead Crawford.

"I don't look like everybody else," he pleaded. "Look at

me!" The distraught teenager was given sixty dollars with which he bought shoes, food and liquor. In a matter of weeks he was picked up dead drunk in a meadow and taken by police to the General Hospital. His hospital record stated that the patient "claims his life is all mixed up and he wants to sort it out." He was diagnosed as suffering from acute alcoholic intoxication, adolescent maladjustment and depression. He was sent to Talbot House, a reform home for alcoholics, where he turned seventeen.

One of the most unlikely witnesses to take the stand at the inquiry was Frankie Baird, Malcolm's brother. After leaving Mount Cashel in December 1975, Frankie was shuffled through a string of foster homes, including a brief stay in Dunnville, Ontario, on the edge of Lake Erie. Poisoned by the memory of how police had handled his boyhood effort to reveal the horrors of the orphanage, he at first coldly denied he had been abused at Mount Cashel when RNC investigators telephoned him in 1989. Not long afterwards, his foster mother in Mainland, Port au Port, told him that a Mr. Horne from the royal commission wanted to talk to him. Frankie brushed the request aside, remarking that the inquiry investigators would never really do anything about the sexual and physical abuse that had gone on. Besides, no commission could change what had happened to him and the others in 1975.

But a short time later, one Saturday afternoon when Frankie was sitting in his apartment watching television with his girlfriend, he suddenly decided to call Fred Horne. The experienced investigator told Frankie that he didn't want to talk about anything over the phone and didn't ask him "any bad questions" as the RNC investigator had. Instead, Horne offered to meet with Frankie at a time and place of his choosing. The investigator told him there would be no pressure to talk about anything he didn't want to discuss. After considering the offer for a few days, Frankie agreed. A week later, Orser and Horne flew to Ontario and interviewed Frankie Baird.

"It was after work and we sat in my van and it was a horribly cold night up there. And we sat in the van in the cold where I wanted to speak," Frankie said.

The care with which he was treated convinced Frankie that there was a point to telling his story in front of the commission after all; by coming forward, future child abuse might well be stopped in its tracks. Among other things, his testimony exposed the profound influence that events at Mount Cashel had on former residents — even after they were thousands of miles away from the silent walls that had absorbed their screams and sobs so many years before. He testified that one night in Ontario he had been watching a movie in which a man witnessed a murder. The murderer eventually decided to hunt the witness down and kill him to prevent him from exposing his crime. For the eleven-year-old, fiction carried him all the way back to the brutal fact of Mount Cashel.

"That movie, I mean, brought back a lot of memories, a lot of memories," Frankie testified. "I started thinking maybe this could happen to me because I witnessed and I was near, you know, a horrible crime.

"And at that point, after I had watched the movie, I made a sort of last will . . . in that last will, I had mentioned all the names, the people, the children, what I had seen, what had happened . . . the events from where I went in, in October to where I left in December, everything that happened at Mount Cashel."

Unfortunately for Orser and Horne, Frankie's diary of horrors was the casualty of one too many moves.

The scars of the past were just as clearly etched on Darren Connors, brother of Robert Connors and one of the bitterest of former Mount Cashel boys to take the stand. Dark and brooding, the angry twenty-three-year-old left behind his job, apartment and even his extra clothes to travel from Kitchener, Ontario, to appear at the inquiry. Like his brothers, Darren's memory of Mount Cashel was like a chancre that wouldn't heal. After an outbreak of measles during the mid-seventies, staff checking for spots on the boys noticed that Darren had a different rash on his legs. He was taken to the Janeway Hospital, examined and given a prescription ointment.

Back at the orphanage, Brother Joseph Burke took the cream away from the nine-year-old and later that night escorted Darren into a large linen closet adjacent to his dorm where he told the boy to take off all his clothes. Naked, Darren was ordered to stand on a chair.

"I did as I was told. I stood on the chair and he would rub this cream on me. . . . He did rub cream on my legs. He also rubbed it on my buttocks and my penis and my genitals. He also would insert his finger into, up my backside and he would say to me that he had to do it because he was afraid that the rash would spread."

Darren wouldn't tell anyone, including the other boys, about incidents of sexual abuse; the Brothers had their "pets" and there was no telling when a fellow resident might denounce you to the abusers.

Ironically, the chance he thought he was finally going to get to tell his story never materialized. When one of the lawyers for the boys asked Connors to describe the abuse inflicted on him at Mount Cashel, commission counsel David Day objected on the grounds that Darren hadn't been interviewed by police in their 1975 investigation.

Since the royal commission had been set up to determine the response of the justice system to past complaints of physical and sexual abuse, and since Darren had never made an earlier complaint, Commissioner Hughes supported Day's objection, concluding, "I think it is irrelevant to pursue it. . . . I rule that it is irrelevant and therefore forbidden in fact to pursue examples of sexual abuse any further."

When Connors protested, Hughes tried to explain that he didn't mean that the young man's painful past was trivial, only out of context given the mandate of the inquiry. But Connors, who had also tried to kill himself after leaving Mount Cashel, hadn't travelled to St. John's to be silenced by what he saw as an empty technicality – particularly when he had heard other boys who hadn't been interviewed by police in 1975 describe their brutal treatment at the hands of the Brothers. Outside the hearing room he told reporters that his faith in the justice system had been destroyed for the second time.

"I felt that I had the right to tell my story. They said that what I had to say was irrelevant. I felt that it was relevant.

I felt I had to tell my story in order to get it off my chest and this was the only chance I had to tell it."

The decision to prohibit Darren Connors from giving his evidence on November 16 stemmed from a controversy that had been brewing since late September. At that time, the lawyer for the Congregation of Christian Brothers, Francis O'Dea, had registered his strong exception to the way in which commission counsel were leading evidence. In particular, O'Dea objected to witnesses accusing by name Christian Brothers who had never been the subject of an investigation by either the police or the Department of Social Services.

"Simply," O'Dea argued, "a witness comes forward and in the process of his evidence presents a name and connects it with a wrongdoing. In that case, the individual has no redress whatever. The world has been told that he did this. And human nature being what it is, many people will believe it even though no proof has been laid before the commission and the commission is unable to make a finding. So he stands naked with nowhere to go and that is why I would suggest, Mr. Chairman, that consideration be given to some bounds or restrictions set by you to protect the reputation of individuals from being smeared for life."

O'Dea's objections were supported by one of the lawyers representing Brother Douglas Kenny. Jack Lavers, a former policeman, accused the commission of permitting witnesses to introduce hearsay evidence that could have a detrimental effect on the trials of those Brothers already charged with offences dating back to 1975. According to Lavers, commission counsel wasn't exercising the "neutrality we would expect to see." Rather, they were behaving as "thorough prosecutors in the extreme in the way they present their evidence." Lavers requested that commission counsel should restrict their line of questioning with former Mount Cashel residents to questions about information contained in their 1975 police statements.

Mr. Justice Hughes rejected the request and two days later Brother Kenny's lawyers, Derek Green and Jack Lavers, announced their partial withdrawal from the inquiry, hinting that they might ask the Newfoundland courts to limit evidence given at the hearings. Green complained that the inquiry had put Kenny's lawyers in a "Catch-22" dilemma: any attempt to protect their client's reputation on cross-examination about specific allegations would tip off Crown prosecutors to Kenny's defence at his pending criminal trial, but the failure to cross-examine would leave the public with the impression that the allegations were well founded. "My client must therefore sit here and take it on the chin without really being in a position to try the validity of these allegations."

Mr. Green did not mention that his client had another option: to appear at the royal commission to deny the allegations against him, as other people named in the boys' testimony had decided to do in defence of their reputations.

A little over a week later, the Department of Justice sent a controversial letter to commission counsel reminding them of fundamental legal principles that would scarcely need to be brought to the attention of a law student, let alone eminent members of the bar. Despite the almost fawning diplomatic terms in which his letter was couched, the Deputy Minister of Justice, James L. Thistle, was sending a clear shot across the bow of the Hughes Inquiry, echoing the feeling that the commission was going too far in bringing out detailed sexual allegations against named individuals: "I again ask you to be cognizant of these concerns with respect to pending criminal charges when planning the direction of Inquiry testimony."

Thistle pointed out in his letter that it had been his understanding from a meeting held on August 15 with Mr. Justice Hughes, commission counsel and the two police forces involved (the RNC and the RCMP) that the commission did not intend to lead detailed evidence of alleged sexual assaults. Rather, it was his impression that the inquiry would be concentrating on the process by which the investigation was commenced and how and why it had ended.

The letter to David Day and Clay Powell touched off a fiery confrontation in the House of Assembly between former Justice Minister Lynn Verge and Premier Clyde Wells. Verge charged that the government had acted improperly in sending a letter of caution to commission counsel. Verge said the letter "raised doubts about the government or the Justice Department trying to intimidate the commission and its counsel and calls into question whether the government was trying to influence the commission counsel in their work."

Premier Wells defended the Thistle letter as a legitimate attempt to ensure that "nothing, the conduct of commissions or anything else, impairs the proper administration of the criminal law in this province." Commission counsel, he said, must balance their interest in conducting a full and open investigation "with the interest of ensuring that there would be nothing interfering with the proper prosecution of persons alleged to have committed crimes."

Since David Day had already made a specific commitment to safeguard the right of accused persons on June 28 when the inquiry held its first public session, it could hardly be argued that Premier Wells was telling commission counsel something they didn't already know. Rhetoric to one side, the premier was simply putting the Hughes Inquiry on notice that, in government's opinion, it wasn't living up to its promise to safeguard the rights of the accused. The tacit but pervasive sense in Newfoundland's legal community that the Hughes Inquiry had gone too far had reached all the way to the premier's office.

When *The Evening Telegram* picked up on Thistle's line that the inquiry had somehow gone back on its undertaking given in the August meeting to limit testimony on sexual and physical abuse, Mr. Justice Sam Hughes wrote a stinging rebuttal to the newspaper's editorial, claiming that it was "essential to address these falsehoods head on. . . . I say categorically I gave no such undertaking to the Department of Justice and that no such undertaking was asked for. It would have been improper to have given it as commissioner under my terms of reference and it would have been improper for any officer of the Department of Justice to ask for it."

Hughes explained that in order to "measure the response

[of the justice system] we have to indicate what the challenge was, what evidence was available and what evidence might have been available if the investigation had been prolonged."

The justice's spirited defence of the independence of his commission was exactly what those people whose main interest in the proceedings was getting to the bottom of the Mount Cashel tragedy wanted to hear. But Hughes' statement of principle and his November 16 ruling not to hear evidence from Darren Connors on the physical and sexual abuse he suffered at Mount Cashel did not square. After all, if the police investigation had been prolonged in 1975 and the Newfoundland Constabulary had followed through on its plan to interview every resident of Mount Cashel, Connors may well have made his evidence available at the time. It was left to others to puzzle over why Darren Connors was denied the opportunity to tell his story on the basis that his testimony was "irrelevant," when several others, including John MacIsaac and James Ghaney, had been given that chance, even though they hadn't given police statements during the 1975 investigation.

In subsequent weeks, some observers would discern a dramatic softening in the will of the commission to confront witnesses or to vigorously press forward with all the powers at its disposal. The greatest zeal was reserved for the marginally relevant, and crucial witnesses were postponed or spectacularly ignored. But it would not be until after a remarkable reversal of strategy by commission counsel early in the New Year that even the strongest supporters of the royal commission would realize that the Hughes Inquiry had somehow lost its zest for the task at hand, possibly out of an exaggerated and dubiously reasoned concern for due process, or, perhaps, because of increasingly ominous rumblings from the backrooms of the St. John's Establishment.

Chapter *13*

 ■■■■■■■ *The Establishment Quartet*

*That [the order to halt the 1975 investigation]
was on the instructions of the Justice Department. I wouldn't do that.* John Lawlor, the
Chief of Police of the Newfoundland Constabulary in 1975.

*I assumed that the matter had been satisfacto-
rily dealt with at both the Justice level and the
Social Services level. I had no reason to be
concerned.* Madam Justice Mary Noonan,
former Justice Department adviser to the
Director of Child Welfare in 1975.

*We did what we could . . . and that was to report
the matter to the Director, since it was very well
understood by myself and by the staff at the
office that the boundaries of Mount Cashel were
off-limits to us.* Sharron Callahan, Director
of Youth Corrections and former Supervisor
of Child Welfare and Corrections at City
Welfare in 1975.

*I sincerely was not aware of the terrible impact
this kind of abuse has on individuals, on the
victims.* Gabriel McHugh, Superior General
of the Congregation of Christian Brothers
Worldwide and former Brother Provincial of
the Canada–West Indies Province in 1975.

THE ONLY THING at the Hughes Inquiry more pathetic than
the testimony from abused Mount Cashel boys was the
evidence from key members of the system, almost all of
whom failed utterly to protect the children who were at the
mercy of the state in 1975.

One after another, representatives of the police, the justice and social service establishments and the Christian Brothers trooped to the stand to tell their sorry tale as Newfoundland's raw and misty autumn slipped into the dreary grip of winter. Some rationalized their failure to act by a narrow and conveniently self-serving interpretation of their official duties; others blamed more senior players or different government departments for the heartbreaking course of events that had scarred so many lives; many claimed that they were never aware of the Mount Cashel affair; and a few blithely protested that they simply couldn't remember what part they had played in one of the sorriest scandals Newfoundland had ever seen.

Individual responsibility to one side, the children of Mount Cashel were the victims of a stunning moral entropy that had immobilized the entire system and allowed the authorities of the day to sleepwalk through the sordid affair as though it were a dream.

The Royal Newfoundland Constabulary was confronted by devastating evidence from within its own ranks. Det. Robert Hillier, who had taken early retirement from the force and now ran a hardware store in Torbay just outside St. John's, testified that he had been ordered to halt the Mount Cashel investigation and to alter his police report by then Chief of Police, John Lawlor. Hillier also testified that although he had the evidence to arrest Brothers Alan Ralph and Edward English after their interviews in December 1975, he had been ordered not to do so by the Chief and Assistant Chief of Police.

Showing the emotional strain of reliving the darkest episode of his police career, Hillier described how he had told the new Justice Minister, Gerald Ottenheimer, and Associate Deputy Minister Cyril Goodyear about the Mount Cashel cover-up while the three men were on an airplane heading for a police graduation in Prince Edward Island in 1979. In a parting shot aimed at the system in which he had finally lost faith, Hillier said, "The Chief of Police is not running the police force, government is. I don't see it as being any different today, nor do I see it being any different in the future."

When Supt. Len Power testified, he confirmed Hillier's observation with the shocking revelation that there was still a two-tiered system of justice operating at the police level based on a tacit reluctance to charge well-known citizens without prior approval from more senior police or justice officials.

"In certain cases dealing with prominent . . . people who have certain positions affecting public policy and affecting society generally, my perception was that the decisions to take action, like laying of a criminal charge, in dealing with situations like that, that it was wise to get a decision from people in authority at the higher level of authority."

When David Day asked if that meant that police would be more willing to charge an unemployed labourer than an influential citizen, Superintendent Power replied, "That would be correct. . . ."

As he would on so many occasions, Mr. Justice Hughes hunched over his desk and made deliberate jottings with a black Sheaffer pen, his immobile face giving no indication of how he felt about the remarkable disclosure he had just heard.

Senior CID officer Austin LeDrew testified that the Mount Cashel investigation had been handled with unusual secrecy. Neither he nor the head of the CID, Chesley Yetman, knew anything about the details of the police work, although under normal circumstances they would have been fully briefed. LeDrew, who had been the officer in charge of recording all complaints, said he never received a copy of either of Detective Hillier's two reports on the Mount Cashel investigation.

"The only thing I had in my record was the number that was assigned to that investigation and the date it was received . . . just the one complaint [from Carol Earle]."

The first time LeDrew saw Hillier's 1975 report was in David Day's office on Sunday, November 26, 1989.

Two other senior RNC members, former Police Chief Donald Randell and former CID head Arthur Pike, both testified that they had discussed the Mount Cashel case with senior members of the Justice Department. Randell said the case came up during two meetings with Justice Department lawyer Robert Hyslop. One meeting occurred while Gerald Ottenheimer was Justice Minister (1979–1985) and the other when Lynn Verge (1985–1989) filled the post. Arthur Pike claimed that he was always bringing up the Mount Cashel affair with anyone in authority who would listen to him.

"Mr. Hyslop had to know. Mr. Kelly had to know. Everybody in there [the Department of Justice] had to know. But nobody made an attempt to do anything," Pike testified.

When John Lawlor's turn came to take the stand, the hearing room was charged with a sense of electric anticipation. As the tall, silver-haired former Chief of Police took the oath, there was a feeling that the inner workings of the deal that had allowed two-self confessed child molesters to escape justice would be laid bare. Instead, for the next two days observers were treated to the jumbled meanderings of a man who remembered virtually nothing. As one pundit put it, "The evidence of former Police Chief John Lawlor was the intellectual equivalent of a few revolutions in the family dryer: disorienting, nonsensical and hard on the head."

The retired policeman flatly denied ordering Robert Hillier off the case, denied telling him to change his report and denied asking the detective to prepare a second report for the Minister – despite the fact that Hillier's evidence was backed up by two fellow police officers. Lawlor admitted to only vague recollections of Brother Gabriel McHugh paying him a visit at the police station a little more than a week before the two Christian Brothers were sent out of Newfoundland. With his eyes averted from his inquisitor, he claimed that he couldn't even remember talking about the Mount Cashel case with any detectives of the CID. In fact, Lawlor, who retired in 1976, had even apparently forgotten that he had been Chief of Police at the time of the orphanage investigation.

"So all I can say, that at the time Superintendent Power came to see me [in 1989], in fact, I was at a loss because I thought at the time, I was sure, that I had been retired when all of this came to light. I had a vague recollection of that, seeing it in the newspaper and radio and everything else. But all of this, of course, I really couldn't believe it when he said, 'No sir, you were working at that time.' "

Lawlor's explanation that his memory had been affected by an operation he had undergone two years earlier did not ease the exasperation of lawyers who tried to cross-examine him. One of the lawyers, Brian Casey, expressed the sense of incredulity that many people experienced listening to Lawlor's repeated protestations that he had completely forgotten most of the details of what must have been one of the most memorable cases during his four-year tenure as Chief of Police.

"I am going to suggest to you again, sir, that of all the investigations that took place while you were Chief of Police, if there was ever an investigation that you ought to be able to recall fairly clearly fifteen years later that this surely would be it. This is the one matter you would have had the most interest in, this is the one matter that would have been the most sensitive during your four years as Chief of Police and this should be the one matter that you should recall till your dying day."

But nothing was about to change the homage to amnesia that was John Lawlor's testimony. Though he purported to remember nothing, he opined that the directive to kill the Mount Cashel investigation had come from the Justice Department and may have been communicated to the investigators by the Assistant Chief of Police, John Norman. (Richard Roche, who served as Chief of Police from 1980 to 1984 subsequently testified that he never received orders from the Justice Department to slow or halt a criminal investigation. And he also made a point that seemed to escape former Chief Lawlor: "That never occurred," he said. "I just wouldn't entertain that suggestion at all. If I was ordered to do it, I would have to resign.")

Although several former police officers would contradict his testimony about police procedures and past events as fundamentally inaccurate, Lawlor's essential evidence was as incontestable as it was unbelievable; both his former Assistant Chief of Police, John Norman, and the Deputy Minister of Justice of the day, Vincent McCarthy, the men he was suggesting had done all the things others had attributed to him, were long since dead.

When asked if his strong and longstanding ties to the Roman Catholic Church may have influenced his handling of the Mount Cashel affair, Lawlor insisted that he would never let religious bias invade his work. The man who admitted that he had blindly deferred to a Justice Department directive to halt a criminal investigation that had turned up prima facie evidence of serious crimes proudly claimed he was a "police officer first and foremost."

The police force under John Lawlor had simply been following orders.

It didn't take very many witnesses to establish that Newfoundland's social service system failed the children of Mount Cashel at every step of the way, both in 1975 and for a long time afterwards.

Like a weaver meticulously working a vast oriental carpet, David Day revealed in minute detail how critical information about allegations of abuse often failed to reach the most senior child welfare officials, and when it did how the end result was bureaucratic paralysis. Testimony showed that provincial government policy and departmental procedures resulted in Social Services officials abdicating their responsibility for public wards while permitting the Christian Brothers to run Mount Cashel as a kind of private fiefdom, and, occasionally, a torture chamber.

But the most disturbing aspect of the role played by the Department of Social Services in the tragedy of Mount Cashel was the inescapable impression that so many senior social workers seemed to lack any strong human concern for the welfare of abandoned children who relied totally on the state for protection. Although some officials made a limited effort to investigate and rectify the abuse at Mount Cashel, virtually every attempt failed. From start to finish, everyone in the department seemed blinkered and bureaucratic, stupefied by the deadly opiates of job description and the policy manual.

Robert Bradbury, who was district liaison officer between the Social Services Department and Mount Cashel Orphanage between 1974 and 1977, presented the dilemma in its most naked and ludicrous form. He testified that provincial social service workers had no authority to investigate complaints of child abuse at Mount Cashel during the mid-seventies – a declaration rooted in custom rather than the dicta of the Child Welfare Act. Bradbury told the inquiry that his duties in connection with Mount Cashel were strictly administrative – providing clothes, school books and medical cards for the boys. He never had personal contact with the Mount Cashel boys and had absolutely no responsibility for supervising their care, even though they were wards of the provincial government. During the three years he acted as liaison officer, he never so much as toured the Christian Brother facility that was home to as many as one hundred wards of the state.

In a voice that at times dropped to a whisper, the bearded former social worker turned guidance counsellor explained that Mount Cashel was treated differently from foster homes where professional social workers made regular visits and compiled reports on children at least twice a year for the Director of Child Welfare.

"We had no authority to visit a child at Mount Cashel," he testified.

In a second appearance before the Hughes Inquiry, Bradbury testified that he obtained vague information through office chatter about the 1975 police investigation and the subsequent transfer of several Christian Brothers out of Newfoundland. But the Social Services Department's official liaison officer was never formally advised about either the abuse allegations or the resolution of the police investigation by the Newfoundland Constabulary.

"I knew perhaps no more than the man on the street, nothing from my department, nothing from the police department, nothing other than a scattered rumour."

The strength or weakness of his information notwithstanding, Bradbury didn't make any independent efforts to get to the bottom of the allegations involving boys under the department's care.

Neil Hamilton, a career civil servant who was the longest serving liaison officer between the Social Services Department and Mount Cashel at the headquarters level, echoed

Robert Bradbury's testimony that there had been a persistent buzz amongst social workers of something being amiss at the orphanage long before the scandal of 1975.

"The rumour mill was very busy . . . and social workers in the field talked and whispered that there were problems at Mount Cashel," he testified. "It was one big, dark kind of secret that something was going on."

According to Hamilton, the department wasn't getting much help from the Christian Brothers when it came to getting detailed information about life at Mount Cashel. He testified that the Christian Brothers repeatedly resisted efforts to post a professional social worker at the orphanage who would report to Social Services, a reluctance that caused him concern.

"Their resistance was certainly remarkable. I thought it was extremely inappropriate. I have had concerns for a long time," he testified. "What was being said to me was that 'Mount Cashel is our home by way of the Congregation' and they would look upon a social worker, especially employed by the Department of Social Services, as an outsider. In fact, last spring [1989], when we finally agreed to get a social worker in Mount Cashel, it was even said to me then, 'This is our home.' And the Superintendent at the time was resisting."

Hamilton told the inquiry that Frank Simms, then Director of Child Welfare, had in fact ordered an investigation into allegations of child neglect at Mount Cashel in August of 1975. But the district administrator responsible for handling complaints of child abuse at the time, Terrence Haire, had no recollection of receiving a request from Simms to conduct such an investigation into Ruth Williams's complaint about the treatment of eight-year-old Dino Santuccioni, and no idea whether, in fact, it was ever carried out.

"It bothers me because I cannot recall the issue . . . and to my knowledge it was the first formal letter we had expressing concern over the quality of care of boys in Mount Cashel," Haire told the inquiry. He would not be the last departmental official to look back on the events of 1975 as though they had occurred in the Pleistocene period.

Sheila Devine, who was Assistant Director of Child Welfare in 1975, described how Social Services made unsuccessful attempts to get information about the December police investigation at Mount Cashel from the Justice Department. Frank Simms, she recalled, tried repeatedly to access the police report through Mary Noonan, the Crown attorney who was legal adviser to the Director of Child Welfare. When those efforts failed, Simms told his Assistant Director that he would have to involve the executive of the Department of Social Services in the quest for the Mount Cashel police report.

Devine also testified that in January 1976, Brothers Gabriel McHugh and Dermod Nash met with Social Services officials, in part to discuss Mount Cashel's problems with excessive discipline. Devine testified that no mention was made of any allegations of sexual abuse. At that meeting, the Brothers refused to provide Devine with the names of boys involved in the police investigation and reported that there were no grounds for criminal charges arising out of the incident. Devine testified that following the events of 1975–76, she became informally aware of the allegations of sexual abuse that would surface so dramatically in 1982 and again in 1989.

"There were rumours later on which circulated in later years, but the full confirmation that there had indeed been alleged sexual abuse was really only known to me recently through these hearings and through the police investigation. When the police investigation began [in 1989] . . . a police official offered me a copy of the police report to read, however, that was fifteen years too late."

When asked about Robert Bradbury's ominous report of alleged sexual abuse at Mount Cashel that pre-dated the Shane Earle incident by more than two months, she conceded that it had indeed alerted Social Services to the possibility that boys were being physically mistreated and Brothers were making homosexual advances to the children under their control. But having admitted that, she added a curious rider.

"Again, taking that in the context of 1975, I would not have picked up as quickly on the mention of homosexual

activity or advances. During the mid-1970s, we were dis-
inclined really to even believe sexual abuse occurred. . . .
At that time in 1975, we were just grappling with the reality
of physical abuse and trying to train staff and educate
ourselves around the fact that there was physical abuse and
it happened in all sections of society and so on. We had not
yet begun to even begin to grapple with the problem of
sexual abuse."

The Social Services Department, it appeared, followed the
novel policy of dealing with only those problems it was
trained to handle; outside the realm of the familiar, the rule
was apparently to discount or ignore. Astonishingly, sexual
abuse was something in which social work professionals like
Sheila Devine simply did not believe.

The most crucial witness from the Department of Social
Services was Newfoundland's Director of Child Welfare,
Frank Simms, the man who was the "father" of all wards of
the province. He was all the more important a witness
because every complaint about Mount Cashel bypassed
normal channels within Social Services and had to be
forwarded directly to him and him alone for action. But like
John Lawlor before him, the moon-faced thirty-year veteran
of the provincial civil service was hazy, changeable and
self-contradictory during his repeated trips to the stand. His
testimony was further clouded when other senior departmental officials gave evidence repudiating many of the key
details he purported to remember.

Simms initially presented himself as a man who had not
been fully informed about events that he was entitled to
know about as the Director of Child Welfare. He recalled his
surprise that both Mary Noonan and Brother Dermod Nash
had already known about allegations of abuse at Mount
Cashel when he contacted them in 1975, a claim that did not
square with the recollections of the people directly involved.
He testified that the police, too, already knew about the
situation at the time he called them.

"I share this with you because here was the Director of
Child Welfare—the one official in the Department of Social
Services [who] ought to know what is going on in terms of
child abuse—here I had called two people who had known

something and I didn't. . . . It has stuck in my mind that
normally the Director of Child Welfare would be aware of
that kind of situation and I wasn't."

Having implied that officials in the Justice Department
had failed to keep him fully informed about a situation
clearly within his mandate, Simms testified that he was
relieved when the police launched the Mount Cashel
investigation following Chesley Riche's complaints about
Shane Earle's beating in December 1975.

"That particular complaint had been the second complaint in about, well, a space of three months, maybe in a
space of two months. It caused a lot of concern, sir, in the
Department of Social Services. . . . So when I became aware
that a police investigation was going ahead, then I felt very
relieved by it."

But Simms's recollection of events surrounding the
Mount Cashel investigation quickly proved to be vague and
incomplete. Mr. Justice Samuel Hughes became so impa-
tient with the professional bureaucrat's habit of describing
what he would have done rather than what he actually
did that the commissioner expressed disbelief that Simms
could have so completely forgotten how he had handled the
unique crisis.

"Surely this—you have already agreed with counsel that
this was a very serious matter. Unless you were accustomed
to receiving complaints about sexual malpractice at Mount
Cashel almost every week, it must have hit you like a tonne of
bricks, to use vulgar speech."

Apparently it had not. The ex-bureaucrat droned on
comfortably when it came to matters of policy and
procedure, but protested to lapses of memory when it came
to detailing what had happened from the perspective of
Social Services in 1975. At one point, the pedantic and at
times self-serving Mr. Simms even managed to provoke the
unflappable David Day while recounting how he had
handled the Bradbury report and its allegations of physical
and sexual abuse at Mount Cashel. The report included the
charge that a Christian Brother had twice punched Billy
Earle in the face. Noting that there was a fine line between
excessive discipline and physical abuse, Simms added,

"And I would suggest to you, sir, that line was even finer in 1975."

When David Day in turn suggested that the Director of Child Welfare should have considerable experience in differentiating between discipline and abuse, Simms replied, "But identifying child abuse, particularly physical abuse, and trying to distinguish between what is excessive discipline and what is actual abuse is not an easy thing to do even today and it certainly wasn't in those days. But I recognized this complaint as a case of alleged physical abuse."

At the end of his patience, Day asked, "Did you have to reflect for any length of time on the contents of this letter before you decided it was physical abuse or alleged physical abuse? Or are you suggesting that there was a period after you got this letter [the Bradbury memo] when you weren't really certain whether blows to the face with a fist, marks on the body of an individual and allegations of sexual advances might have constituted excessive discipline of one form or another?"

Sounding like Polonius resurrected, Simms replied by way of a history lesson to the inquiry that raised echoes of Sheila Devine's view that sexual abuse was somehow an invisible offence because social workers didn't quite believe in it at the time of the Mount Cashel investigation. The only difference was that Simms was applying a variation of the same argument to physical abuse.

"Well, we have to reflect back to 1975, sir, and how we perceived situations then. And you know, I had experiences before I came with the Department of Social Services when I saw children being disciplined. It was certainly called discipline, but it wouldn't be called discipline today. . . . Physical abuse, Mr. Day, was in the 1950s and the 1960s, sir, was perceived quite differently from the way we perceive it now. And if a parent decided that a child, one of their children, had done something that required disciplining, their methods of doing it in those days would not be accceptable today, but were acceptable in those days."

Simms's astonishing answer prompted Day to ask what type of discipline parents meted out in the fifties and sixties, to which the former Director of Child Welfare smugly replied, "Whatever was nearest to hand."

Samuel Hughes had heard enough.

"That is a reaction of anger. It's not discipline in any sense of the word. . . . I am suggesting that there is no fine line which would make a blow to the face with a fist acceptable. And certainly it would appear that Mr. Bradbury didn't think that . . . there was any doubt about what the nature of this was. He said it would be neglect on our part . . . if some action were not taken."

At another point, David Day became obviously annoyed when Simms explained that he handled the 1975 and 1982 investigations at Mount Cashel according to standard departmental policy. While discussing the 1975 investigation Day asked, "You agreed that you had a duty to follow up with the police. You did telephone the police, but after you did that on December 8, 1975, for whatever reason, you had no further contact with the police as Director of Child Welfare to get the names of the boys when you couldn't get them anywhere else?"

Simms wasn't about to acknowledge that he might have lacked the moral energy to pursue the matter in the interests of protecting the children under his care, claiming that it "was not the practice" to go directly to the police. When Day asked Simms if he recalled having discussions with Justice officials about the contents of social worker Stead Crawford's explosive report into homosexual abuse amongst the boys at Mount Cashel in 1982, Simms replied that he could not remember any conversations, and besides, it was "not a procedure that we normally would have followed."

In a rare display of temper, Day shot back, "I don't for a moment question that answer, but what I do have, and have been having considerable difficulty . . . with is the fact that do procedures really matter a damn when the ultimate goal of you as a professional, your advisers as professionals, your executive professionals, is the protection of children? Don't procedures take a back seat to the protection of children, particularly where some of the allegations that you were hearing, certainly in 1982, were very serious?"

During cross-examination, a number of verbal sparring

matches erupted between Simms and Crown counsel George Horan, who was representing the Justice Department and government generally at the Hughes Inquiry. The bearded and soft-spoken Horan bluntly challenged Simms's handling of the Bradbury report, noting that the Director of Child Welfare only spoke to the Assistant Deputy Minister of Social Services, George Pope, two weeks after receiving the report.

"What concerns me is, I suppose, that you as an independent statutorally empowered official would feel that it was necessary on a matter of child welfare concern to seek the approbation of the Assistant Deputy Minister. I would think that you would have a responsibility which you could defend in terms of the Act to act independently of whatever the Assistant Deputy Minister may have thought of the matter."

In fact, George Pope testified that he was never told about the Bradbury report or consulted about Simms's decision to have Brother Douglas Kenny investigate the allegations of physical and sexual abuse it contained.

Horan then noted that Simms insisted three times, once during an interview with RNC Supt. Len Power and twice at the Hughes Inquiry, that he never received any report from Brother Douglas Kenny about his investigation into alleged child abuse at Mount Cashel. Yet on February 19, Simms reversed his field and told the commission that Kenny had, in fact, reported back. When confronted by the contradiction, Simms said his previous testimony related only to written reports, and that Kenny's follow-up had been verbal. The creative revisionism incensed Horan.

"I don't believe we are dealing here with questions of semantics. I would ask you to please have more regard for the questions that are asked and the answers which you give."

Horan also pointed out that the commission had heard no evidence to corroborate Simms's contention that Mary Noonan and the RNC already knew about the Mount Cashel situation when he contacted them on December 8, 1975. Once more, Simms backed away from his earlier testimony, protesting that he could not clearly recall the

timing of his various phone calls. This time it was the turn of
Sam Hughes to lower the judicial boom on the bureaucrat's
frustrating doubletalk.

"Mr. Simms, you are sworn to tell the truth and if there is
any doubt about your recollection you should express it. But
these assertions that are made and then retracted are very
disturbing."

When former Deputy Minister of Social Services Vernon
Hollett took the stand, he testified that he had never heard
anything about the 1975 Mount Cashel affair. Although
Hollett did remember attending a January 1976 meeting
between senior members of his own department and
top-ranking members of the Christian Brothers, he could not
recall what was discussed at the meeting. Accordingly, no
information tainted what he called his "rosy picture" of life
at the orphanage in the mid-seventies.

In fact, Hollett's Assistant Deputy Minister, George
Pope, testified that he had been notified by Frank Simms of
the 1975 Mount Cashel investigation. But since he
understood that the allegations involved nothing more than
two or three over-zealous Brothers who went too far with
acts of discipline and no criminal charges were laid, Pope
assumed that police and Justice officials had found no
grounds to prosecute. The Mount Cashel affair did not,
therefore, constitute a "serious problem" for Social Services
and he decided not to brief the Deputy Minister.

"We felt that any ruling from the Department of Justice to
Social Services was a ruling from the government," Pope
testified, inadvertently suggesting how far down the
bureaucratic pecking order the Department of Social
Services was in 1975 – or how close the relationship was
between the Justice Department and the government of
the day.

Judging from the rest of Vernon Hollett's testimony, it
wouldn't have mattered very much if he had been briefed
about physical abuse at the state-financed orphanage.
Admitting that it was at least conceivable that he had been
told about beatings at Mount Cashel, Hollett noted that
such a report would not have been unduly alarming.

"It is possible that I could have heard that somebody got a

physical trimming. But it wouldn't have registered with me because I thought, 'Well, so what?'. . . . You also have to take into consideration here, Mr. Day, that the interpretation of what constituted abuse had, I think, changed over time because, personally having grown up in St. John's, I often heard my friends on the street talk about, indeed brag about, being beaten up in school by the Brothers, or a teacher gave them a terrific caning and of a pupil and teacher engaging in fisticuffs. And while I don't recall this as being common-place, it was something that was generally understood to occur. . . ."

Getting an education also meant getting the occasional beating, the former Deputy Minister clearly implied, and more than that, in 1975 Social Services professionals, like the victims themselves, were not at serious odds with this alleged community standard. Billy Earle's beating was just part of growing up in St. John's, or at least it was in the opinion of the official to whom the Director of Child Welfare reported.

But when it came to the allegations of sexual abuse at the orphanage in 1975, Vernon Hollett laid the blame for his department's failure to look after the interests of Mount Cashel boys at the feet of the Justice Department in general and Vincent McCarthy in particular.

"I have the most annoying perspective on it now. To put it in the vernacular, I think we were let down. . . . Our trust in them [the Justice Department] was betrayed. That's how I feel frankly. They apparently had information that would have been absolutely vital to us in terms of our program at Mount Cashel. It comes to light that twenty-five of the seventy-five or eighty boys in there, one-third, were sexually abused allegedly. . . . My reaction then, to keep it in the vernacular, is, well, this place is a den of iniquity. It was not a panacea as I said yesterday for child-caring institutions. It would have ripped me out of my seat if I knew that. I wouldn't stand for it. I would go to the Minister immediately and say, 'Look, we've got to close this place and get the kids out of there.'

"I'm sorry, I am a little emotional about that and it bothers me because we were the fall guys in this. A department that was trying to do its best is discredited now in the eyes of the public because information that we needed was kept from us. I don't like it."

Hollett described the decision not to share information about Mount Cashel with Social Services as "sinful" and accused his counterpart in the Justice Department, Vincent McCarthy, of betraying a trust.

"I hold him responsible," Hollett testified. "I had a working relationship with Mr. McCarthy and I had an expectation, an understanding. And . . . over the years we got the kind of service, as I said, the promptness and adequacy of his responses were second to none. So there is something wrong here in this situation. . . .

"If he had the information that we have now in the police reports, then while he might not appreciate all the professional social dynamics of the implications because he was a lawyer . . . I think that he must have seen some of the inherent problems from a social point of view and should have apprised us. Or he was put in the dilemma of ruining the reputation of Mount Cashel and the Roman Catholic Church—one organization and indivisible to me and the public."

Uninformed as many of the senior officials in the department claimed to be on the subject of physical and sexual abuse at Mount Cashel, the three blind mice of Social Services turned out to be the men who acted as Minister from 1974 to 1982—Ank Murphy, Charles Brett and Thomas Hickey.

Under questioning, Mr. Murphy not only insisted that he never heard "a whisper" about the 1975 child abuse scandal but that he wasn't even aware that his own department was so closely tied to the orphanage.

"My opinion always was that Mount Cashel was supported entirely by the Catholic population of Newfoundland. There used to be a garden party. There was a raffle. They had a band and the whole works. And I always understood that only orphans went to Mount Cashel," the diminutive ex-minister testified, apparently forgetting about the huge government grants and interest write-downs he championed for Mount Cashel during his last year in the Social Services portfolio.

"It took a great burden off the department to have an outfit like Mount Cashel to train and educate the whole works of these boys ... I thought if we had eight or ten Mount Cashels what a wonderful place it would have been for the orphans and the type of youth that they looked after. .... Mount Cashel was always considered the apple of the eye, if you like, of the Department of Welfare and I saw no reason to destroy a good thing. And for that reason I didn't try any innovations as far as Mount Cashel was concerned."

Although he didn't say so, the former Social Services Minister may well have had another reason for not wanting to look too closely at the shortcomings of Mount Cashel. After the closure of the United and Anglican orphanages in St. John's, Mount Cashel was by far the cheapest place to accommodate needy children within an overburdened social services system.

Interestingly, Murphy took the trouble to note what he would have done had he been informed in 1975 about alleged child abuse at Mount Cashel. The obvious course of action would have been to protect the boys who were allegedly being abused, and then to turn the matter over to the police to investigate for possible criminal wrongdoing. But Ank Murphy outlined a different approach, a response that betrayed how deeply political an issue a possible sex scandal at Mount Cashel really was; Murphy told the inquiry he would have taken the matter straight to Premier Moores.

But despite the fact that the former minister knew 95 per cent of the Brothers in St. John's, was an old chum of Police Chief Jack Lawlor and worked closely with him on preparations for the centenary of the Christian Brothers in Newfoundland, and drove Vincent McCarthy home from Confederation Building "pretty well every afternoon," Murphy insisted that he never heard a peep about the scandal at the orphanage. He himself confessed surprise that the issue had never come up on the radio talk shows he regularly participated in as a politician.

"You know, it's an amazing thing, if I may add at this time, that I made myself available for every open line that was on in St. John's, Grand Falls and Corner Brook and I was on two or three times every month and over those two and a half years that I served, I never heard one whisper about any scandal. . . ."

In 1979, when the scandal resurfaced at the Soper Inquiry, Murphy didn't read any of the press coverage surrounding Mount Cashel, possibly because he was away in Florida—or so he testified.

Charlie Brett, the silver-haired and distinguished-looking man who was appointed to the Social Services portfolio after the provincial election of September 1975 and who was actually in office during Det. Robert Hillier's investigation into Mount Cashel, also testified that he knew nothing about allegations of child abuse at the orphanage, the brief police investigation or the meeting between senior officials of his department and members of the Christian Brothers in January 1976.

Clearly baffled by the ex-minister's complete lack of information, David Day asked, "Can you offer any view, any helpful view, on how for three years you were the Minister and during that period what is safely said to be the largest single police investigation involving alleged mistreatment of wards probably anywhere in Canada at any time, based on my research, was taking place over at Mount Cashel involving police, twenty-six boys, certainly some parents were aware, there were some people in Justice at the lower levels that were aware, can you offer any helpful explanation as to how all of that could be taking place and you as the Minister of the day would not have even a smidgen of knowledge that it was going on?"

"No, it's most unusual. The only answer is that the people who would normally brief me on that sort of thing didn't know. . . ," Brett replied.

"Were you aware," Day continued, "that within twenty feet of your office on a date in late December of 1975 or early January of 1976, it appears that your Deputy Minister, your Assistant Deputy Minister—although both of them are rather cloudy on the subject in terms of recollection—your

Director of Child Welfare and your Assistant Director of Child Welfare met with two senior Brothers within the Congregation of Christian Brothers at which they were told of allegations of physical and sexual abuse at Mount Cashel and the involvement of the police?"

Somewhat sheepishly, Brett replied that he had not known about the meeting. After completing his questions, David Day slumped down into his chair and put one hand across his eyes, exasperated by the emptiness of the retired politician's testimony. Sam Hughes, too, appeared unimpressed with Brett's answers. Noting that the Mount Cashel affair was surrounded by "a good deal of silence bordering on concealment," the Commissioner remarked on the social attitude that might possibly account for such a reaction.

"I would have expected that any report of the sort of physical and sexual abuse which we are now advised of would have been so startling and unacceptable that silence or concealment would have been impossible unless there was a feeling that in an institution like the orphanage excessive discipline as it's been described or sexual approaches were taken for granted."

Although he didn't have a comment on Mr. Justice Hughes's theory, the ex-minister did offer his personal view of the orphanage. Unlike Ank Murphy, Charlie Brett was not a fan of Mount Cashel, and, in fact, had an inkling that all might not be well at the government institution.

"There was something intangible, something that you couldn't feel, that you couldn't touch. There was an air about it. Whenever you talked about Mount Cashel there was something that you couldn't really put your finger on. . . . I always had the feeling that probably things weren't right or didn't go right. But I never knew what it was."

If he didn't know, Charlie Brett didn't try very hard to find out. In the three years he was Social Services Minister, he never so much as visited the institution that filled him with such nagging, if vague, foreboding.

The last former Social Services Minister it was hoped might have valuable information about Mount Cashel was Thomas Valentine Hickey, the ruggedly handsome retired Tory politician who had held office during the 1982 police investigation of the orphanage that led to charges against Brother David Burton. Despite previous testimony from his former Deputy Minister, Gilbert Pike, that the Minister had been orally briefed and copied on all reports concerning the 1982 investigations at Mount Cashel, Hickey denied any knowledge of what was going on at the orphanage.

"I've absolutely no knowledge of any activity at Mount Cashel. I am still reeling from reading the reports. I have never seen them before. I am astounded to find that I presided over the department and this could go on under my nose—not only that, but my senior officials knowledgeable in it! I don't mind telling you, sir, I feel betrayed. I feel let down. And further to that I am astounded by the evidence that is given to this inquiry in relation to that [which] I am supposed to have known."

Hickey attributed the alleged failure of his senior officials to fully inform him about the known details of the 1982 Mount Cashel affair to the fact that they had become "case hardened" and knew what he would have done had he received a complete briefing.

"Mr. Pike and Mr. Pope and Mr. Compton, the other Assistant Deputy Minister in the department, had discussed the issue of homosexual activity in other institutions. My views on this matter, strongly held as they are today, were extremely well known by those people. There could be no doubt in the minds of my officials in the department that being made aware of the situation at Mount Cashel, I would have acted . . . in a manner that would have been permanent. . . . If I had known about this situation, Mount Cashel would have been closed, the boys removed. . . ," he testified.

When it was pointed out that Gilbert Pike had indeed forwarded a report to Hickey on the 1982 police investigation into Mount Cashel, the ex-Minister complained that the bureaucrat should have personally impressed on his boss that the document was to be set aside from the mountain of official reports that passed over Hickey's desk but that were routinely dealt with by others.

If Ministers weren't informed by their senior officials and senior officials weren't informed by their subordinates, the argument from the Social Services department was that the subordinates in turn weren't briefed on the true facts of the Mount Cashel affair by Vincent McCarthy. The effort that went into demanding those facts was a subject few witnesses from the department were interested in pursuing. Not knowing about Mount Cashel was equal to not being responsible—a comfortable out that tended to obscure the fact that when Social Services had been fully apprised of a major sex scandal at the orphanage in 1982, absolutely nothing was done about it.

Like the police before them, former Social Services employees preferred to lay the blame for what happened in 1975 squarely in the lap of the Justice Department.

The last finger pointed at the Justice Department over the Mount Cashel affair of 1975 belonged to the Congregation of Irish Christian Brothers.

Brother Gabriel McHugh, who became Superior General of the Congregation of Christian Brothers worldwide in 1978, told the Hughes Inquiry that the arrangement that led to the expulsion of Brothers English and Ralph from Newfoundland had been ordered by former Deputy Minister of Justice, now deceased, Vincent McCarthy.

Claiming to be a novice in such matters and without consulting a lawyer or questioning McCarthy's alleged—and bizarre—dictum, Brother McHugh meekly complied. He said he had the impression that the case was somehow in limbo after the December 18, 1975 meeting with McCarthy and that charges could still be laid at a future time—testimony in direct conflict with that of Newfoundland's former Assistant Director of Child Welfare, Sheila Devine. Devine clearly recalled that Brother McHugh had assured Social Services officials in a January 1976 meeting that the police had investigated the Mount Cashel situation and found no grounds for laying charges. McHugh also testified that Social Services was made "aware" of the allegations of sexual abuse in the same January meeting, a contention at loggerheads with Devine's recollection that the Brothers hadn't mentioned anything about allegations of sexual abuse.

Like various witnesses from the Department of Social Services, Brother McHugh admitted to a woeful ignorance on the subject of the sexual abuse of children – a pathetically hollow explanation for the fact that he hadn't so much as talked to any of the victims of Brothers English and Ralph during his December 1975 visit to Mount Cashel, let alone arranged counselling or psychiatric help for them.

"I sincerely was not aware of the terrible impact this kind of abuse has on individuals, on the victims. . . . Lacking the knowledge of the harm and damage that can be done to individuals as a result of this behaviour, the best procedure was thought to be to try and rehabilitate the perpetrators so that this kind of thing can be minimized or prevented from happening in the future," he testified.

Brother Gordon Bellows, who personally heard Brother Edward English's confession that allegations of sexual abuse brought against him by various Mount Cashel boys were largely true, testified that he received very little additional information about the Mount Cashel affair after his initial conversations with Gabriel McHugh, Dermod Nash and the two Brothers who were accused of sexually abusing some of the boys in their care. Even though Brother McHugh testified that the Canada–West Indies Council of the order had discussed the March 1976 memorandum sent by Brother Nash to Christian Brother headquarters outlining the need to deal with three other Brothers facing similar allegations of physical and sexual misconduct at Mount Cashel, Bellows insisted that he was never made aware of the new allegations.

"Up to this present time, my information is that there were only two people involved and two people only."

Brother Bellows had apparently forgotten about the March 20, 1976 meeting he attended at Mono Mills, where the wider allegations against other Christian Brothers at Mount Cashel were discussed. He had also forgotten about his 1979 memo to Gabriel McHugh in Rome, where he noted that the 1975 incident had involved "three monks."

Although Brother Dermod Nash played an important part in handling the 1975 crisis at Mount Cashel, the elderly Brother was unable to testify at the Hughes Inquiry, or even to meet with commission investigators at his bedside because, as the Brotherhood put it, he was "terribly unwell." Nash was reported to be in a Vancouver hospital recovering from an operation to correct an aneurism. But sometime between February 15 and 18, the patient flew from British Columbia to Toronto, went on a shopping junket at Yorkdale Plaza and departed again on February 23 for the Caribbean island of Antigua.

The Congregation's lawyer, Francis O'Dea, solemnly explained that although Brother Nash was strong enough for travel, he was not yet healthy enough to face the stress of questioning at the royal commission.

"The fact that he went there," O'Dea protested, "doesn't mean he went to avoid [testifying] or anything like that. . . . The whole idea was to get him fit to provide some evidence to the commission. At the moment, he is residing with the community down in Antigua and I think that will help speed his recovery. . . ."

A sworn deposition was eventually taken from the ailing Christian Brother in the Anchorage Hotel in Antigua, with David Day personally administering the oath on a copy of the New Testament. The elderly Brother with the receding hairline took questions from four lawyers in the sweltering West Indian heat, speaking in a faint voice that grew fainter by the answer. By the time he had mopped his brow with his handkerchief for the last time and the five-and-a-half-hour interview was over, the evidence of this long-delayed witness had only marginally illuminated the dark saga of Mount Cashel.

Beyond Brothers Gabriel McHugh and Gordon Bellows, the Hughes Inquiry heard from a string of Christian Brothers whose testimony dealt primarily with administrative details of the Brotherhood rather than the events of 1975. What everyone was waiting for was the appearance of the people at the very centre of the Mount Cashel storm, Brothers English, Ralph and Kenny, the only people who could unravel many of the mysteries surrounding the chain of events set in motion by Shane Earle's 1975 physical abuse complaint to police.

Brother Alan Ralph was the first of these key witnesses

scheduled to give evidence at the royal commission. On November 27, 1989 commission counsel issued a summons to Brother Ralph to appear at the Hughes Inquiry on January 15, 1990. The summons had been drafted by Clay Powell and authorized by Commissioner Hughes. Because Ralph stood charged with sexual assault, commission counsel had decided to limit their questioning to the Brother's knowledge of the 1975 deal that led to his expulsion from Newfoundland in 1975 and subsequent psychiatric treatment at Southdown.

But on January 9, Ralph's lawyer, David Hurley, brought a motion before the Supreme Court of Newfoundland seeking a prohibition order restraining the commission from compelling Ralph's attendance at the inquiry. It was the second time Brother Ralph's lawyer had appealed to the Supreme Court of Newfoundland for relief for his client. An earlier application for a stay of proceedings against Ralph and four other Christian Brothers—Edward English, Douglas Kenny, Edward French and Kevin Short— because of inordinate pre-trial delay had been dismissed. In rendering his judgment, Mr. Justice Nathaniel Noel rejected the argument that there had been any abuse of process under the provisions of Section 7 and 11 of the Canadian Charter of Rights and Freedoms in laying charges against the Brothers.

"A fair assessment of the facts stated leads to the conclusion that the inordinately long delay in laying the informations resulted from arrangements made between the Provincial Superior and the Deputy Minister, and that the decision to terminate the investigation and to take no further actions was not made in good faith, without fear, favour or affection in the administration of justice but for other reasons. It is also fair to find that these arrangements were acquiesced in by the Chiefs of Police and that the applicants were aware of the investigation, their involvement in it, and the arrangements made for their benefit. . . . It was not an abuse of process."

But this time, Brother Ralph would not have to wait for the Supreme Court to decide his fate. On January 29, just four days before Ralph's application was scheduled to be heard, Clay Powell explained at the outset of the day's hearings at the inquiry that the commission had reversed its earlier decision to call accused Brothers to testify.

"It seems to me . . . it could possibly be helpful to the commission to have whatever evidence the Brothers might be able to give us in relation to their knowledge of any bargain, if there was a bargain, and it certainly appears from the evidence that there was," Powell said. "But that has to be balanced with the actual or certainly the perceived perception on their part expressed through counsel in the motion that this could affect their right to a fair trial. . . . I think that there is no question of our legal right, if you will, subject to an order of the court to stop us from issuing summonses. But in balancing the matter, it seems to me that we should come down on the side of not pursuing the matter."

Richard Rogers, a lawyer representing some of the former residents of Mount Cashel, registered his strong disagreement, noting that it wasn't certain that the Brothers would ever be taking the stand on the criminal matters they were facing.

"I mean all of this is up in the air. . . . Obviously these particular witnesses would have extremely helpful information for us. And if we can't . . . avail [ourselves] of it now, we might not ever hear of it in the future."

The final word was left to Sam Hughes.

"The concern with providing a proper environment for a fair trial is one that has always been in the minds of commission counsel and myself. And it is, I think, not our intention to call as commission witnesses anybody who is facing trial or the possibility of trial as a result of the inquiries of the commission and of the investigations made by the police."

The Commissioner then added a qualification that may have been in his mind when he ruled that evidence of sexual abuse by Darren Connors was irrelevant and forbidden.

"Not only has the protection of people facing trial been one of our primary concerns, but there is also the Section 13 of the Charter . . . the one that evidence given in one forum cannot be held against or produced in the courts. So I am concerned not only with a fair trial, but a trial which is fair not only to the defence but to the prosecution. And that is an additional reason for concurring with your views, Mr. Powell."

What part, if any, the earlier letter to the Hughes Inquiry from Newfoundland's Deputy Attorney-General, James Thistle, may have played in the eleventh-hour decision not to call accused Brothers is difficult to gauge. But not nearly as difficult as it is to understand the decision itself. After all, the commission had already decided to limit questioning of the accused Brothers to the circumstances surrounding the deal between the Catholic order and the Justice Department in 1975. If they now took the view that such testimony might jeopardize their right to a fair trial, why had they permitted a parade of male witnesses to describe in detail the sexual and physical assaults on their persons by various Christian Brothers? As one *Sunday Express* columnist put it, "The last time we checked, the Brothers were charged with sexual and physical assault, not obstruction of justice."

Regardless of the merits of the decision, which was reluctantly endorsed by David Day, its impact was crystal clear. The inquiry had voluntarily surrendered without a fight its right to put questions to various Christian Brothers on a number of crucially important matters. What, if anything, had Douglas Kenny done about investigating the complaints outlined in the Bradbury report? Had he been given the names of the alleged abusers by Frank Simms? What had the Brothers been told about the deal that sent them out of the province instead of into courtrooms? How adequate was the so-called "superb treatment" they received when they were sent to private Catholic clinics that put the most troubled Brothers back on the street in a matter of months? Were the schools that re-hired the Brothers fully apprised of their previous behaviour before the pair was placed back in the classroom? Did they know of other examples of child abuse at Mount Cashel that pre-dated the 1975 scandal?

Substantial public interest had been sacrificed for legal phantoms that grew paler and paler under close scrutiny. To some, the decision not to call the accused Brothers hinted at

psychic fatigue in the Hughes Inquiry, a dawn-grey softening of the will to get to the bottom of an ugly situation. But
the one thing most observers agreed on after hearing the
evidence of Gabriel McHugh was that Newfoundland's
Justice Department had unquestionably participated in a
cover-up of the debacle at the orphanage in 1975.

The only question left unanswered was how high up did
the travesty of justice go?

In one of the enduring ironies of the Mount Cashel story,
handyman Chesley Riche, teenager Brenda Lundrigan and
William and Carol Earle did more to seek basic justice for
the boys at Mount Cashel in 1975 than the entire Justice
Department. With the man who had executed the deal with
the Christian Brothers dead, almost everyone else in the
Justice Department took refuge in the argument that they
either hadn't been presented with sufficient information to
realize the seriousness of the situation at Mount Cashel, or
they assumed other officials more senior to themselves or
more directly involved had satisfactorily settled the affair. A
curious few testified that they saw nothing wrong with the
way the matter had been disposed of in 1975.

Before the Hughes Inquiry was convened, Robert
Hyslop was known only as the decisive Associate Deputy
Attorney-General who ordered the police to reopen the
Mount Cashel investigation in early 1989 as soon as he
became aware of Det. Robert Hillier's devastating and
long-buried police reports. But testimony before the
commission revealed that Hyslop, now a Provincial Court
judge, had in fact become aware of problems at Mount
Cashel at various times during his career in the Justice
Department.

In 1979, he viewed the oblique letters concerning Mount
Cashel that Vincent McCarthy left in the Justice files before
taking up his place on the bench; at the time of the Soper
Inquiry he heard news reports about the alleged 1975
sex scandal and cover-up at Mount Cashel; and in 1982,
he played a major role in the investigation of another
sex scandal at the orphanage, which led to the conviction
of Brother David Burton. Regrettably, Hyslop never

associated the two situations and never briefed the Crown prosecutor in the Burton case, Ronald Richards, about the events of 1975.

"My view of events [at Mount Cashel] was that they were concluded and that the Soper Inquiry had laid it to rest to the extent that the Justice Department . . . had not acted improperly in not laying charges, but that the only criticism was that the police may not have been told the reasons why," the former Crown attorney testified.

Mary Noonan, Hyslop's former colleague in the Justice Department and now a fellow judge, testified that Vincent McCarthy refused to give her the 1975 police report on child abuse at Mount Cashel that Newfoundland's Director of Child Welfare, Frank Simms, was so eager to see. The former legal adviser to the Director explained that she didn't pursue the matter beyond that single conversation with McCarthy because Social Services never repeated their request for the report and no one advised her that Simms and Devine had been unable to obtain the names of the boys involved in the police investigation.

While discussing McCarthy's refusal to hand over the Mount Cashel report to Noonan, Clay Powell asked if she might have been denied access to the document because the subject matter was too shocking. Noonan noted that in 1968, the Director of Public Prosecutions, James A. Power, would never permit her to see any police report dealing with a sex matter. But, according to Noonan, attitudes evolved and by 1975 she was allowed to read any police report she wished. It was a remark that allowed Sam Hughes to direct a barb at the host of previous witnesses who tried to portray sexual abuse of children as a concept that in 1975 had not yet dawned on the social work profession in Newfoundland.

"I am glad to hear your opinion about what prevailed in 1975 because honestly from the evidence I have been listening to, one would think it was 1066."

Allegations of child abuse at Mount Cashel surfaced again during the wardship hearings for Shane Earle and Frankie Baird in early 1976. A social worker reported that allegations of mistreatment of Shane had prompted his removal from Mount Cashel in December 1975. Ten-year-old Frankie

Baird, who was allegedly physically and sexually abused at Mount Cashel, attempted suicide twice in the two months following his departure from the orphanage. But the comments in the social worker's report never struck Noonan as a "red flag" leading back to the mysterious police report of 1975 that Vincent McCarthy had refused to give her.

Noonan noted that no charges had been laid against Christian Brothers and that the Director of Child Welfare hadn't stopped referring children to Mount Cashel, two facts that gave her enough comfort to stifle any lingering curiosity she may have had about what police had found during their secret investigation into the orphanage.

"I assumed that the matter had been satisfactorily dealt with at both the Justice level and the Social Services level. I had no reason to be concerned."

In 1982, Noonan had different reasons for adopting a passive role in the face of new and serious allegations of sexual abuse at Mount Cashel, allegations that this time she could not claim to be oblivious to. She had seen the official correspondence outlining the Justice Department's decision not to lay charges against anyone other than Brother Burton, even though there was abundant evidence that small children were being sexually abused by older residents of Mount Cashel. Testifying in 1990, Noonan said she felt charges should have been laid in 1982 against these older Mount Cashel boys. But when asked if she ever offered that opinion to Frank Simms in 1982, the former legal adviser to the Director of Child Welfare testified that she had not.

"No, because the matter was well in hand, I thought. The police were there investigating. The reports of the sexual problem were coming from the Director's own social workers. Once the matter was in hand by the Department of Social Services and the police, I would see no further involvement for me as a lawyer. . . . The genesis of this whole operation came from Social Services. They were aware that there were problems with the children. I trusted they were meeting the children's needs. . . ."

Once more, Noonan did not test her faith in the system by making independent inquiries of her own.

John Kelly, the former Director of Public Prosecutions in

the Justice Department, testified that the Mount Cashel affair was brought to his attention on three separate occasions – an informal conversation with Mary Noonan, Noonan's subsequent attempt to obtain details of the Mount Cashel report through Kelly and Staff Sgt. Arthur Pike, and the 1979 Soper Inquiry. Despite the repeated mentions of the mysterious case, Kelly never made a determined effort to get to the bottom of the 1975 sex scandal. Even by the time he took the stand in 1990, his command of the facts of the case was woefully incomplete.

"I didn't see it at that time, and I'm not certain I do now, as a matter of great consequence, of political and social significance. I think the significance of the report, the sensitivity and political potential of the report, perhaps comes from the way it was handled as opposed to what the report was at the time. There was an allegation, as I understand it, of sexual assault, breach of trust by two or three Brothers at the institution. . . . But it was against two or three Brothers at the institution. It wasn't an investigation into the total, the institution as a whole."

What Kelly apparently failed to grasp was that five Christian Brothers had been linked to sexual and physical assaults at the orphanage involving nearly one-third of the residents of Mount Cashel. And the number could conceivably have been much higher, since the other two-thirds of the boys hadn't been interviewed in 1975.

Noting that the sparse Mount Cashel file held in the Justice Department after McCarthy's elevation to the bench contained few hints that a major child abuse investigation had been handled improperly, Kelly, like Mary Noonan, took comfort from the fact that the system seemed to have performed normally in the disposition of the case.

"It was a matter that the Deputy Minister, fully informed, had made a decision . . . that was agreed on by the Chief of Police with certain undertakings from the Christian Brothers. And that was how I viewed the matter at the time."

The strangest testimony of the Hughes Inquiry was given by Herbert Joseph Buckingham, the lawyer who acted for the Crown in Shane Earle's 1976 wardship hearing. Although he had little to add to the facts concerning what had actually happened in the Mount Cashel case, the odd statement he read into the record after finishing his testimony yielded a fascinating insight into the mentality that condoned conferring a privileged status on the church even when the clergy broke the law.

Buckingham proudly explained that the male members of his family had been educated by the Irish Christian Brothers at St. Bonaventure's College in St. John's since 1904.

"I am a product of the Christian Brothers," he proclaimed, "and whatever good characteristics I have or demonstrate here today have in great measure flowed from the wise counsel that I have gotten from these men. . . . They taught me in a time when the rule was 'spare the rod and spoil the child.' "

With Buckingham grinning broadly, the light of the true believer flashing in his Mad Hatter eyes, Sam Hughes murmured, "Oh, that's obvious."

Since the Catholic church had historically fulfilled some of government's obligations by providing education and social services to its followers, it followed, Buckingham lectured, that government developed a protective stance about the church, which effectively placed that institution above the law.

"Added to this position of a need to guard the institutions was a realization that the public was settled into a position that accepted that any of the transgressions of persons of the cloth, as we refer to them, was not to be given public notice even though knowledge of such transgressions might even be widely known. But it was never to appear in our papers. It was never to be discussed in a public forum. It might be fair to say that there was a charitable understanding . . . which if considered in the light of present-day standards might be regarded as misguided."

Buckingham insisted that in 1975 Newfoundlanders still subscribed to the protective attitude towards the church, and ringingly endorsed the way that fellow Catholic Vincent McCarthy had disposed of the Mount Cashel affair.

"I have no hesitation in saying that if I had been in a position of authority in 1975 that I would have handled the situation exactly as it was handled."

Herbert Buckingham's bizarre and biased ruminations to one side, the only really interesting history lesson that the Hughes Inquiry received came on the last day of hearings on the Mount Cashel phase of the commission from the 177th witness to take the stand—T. Alex Hickman. The habit of authority was stamped on every feature of the Chief Justice of the Supreme Court Trial Division as he strode into the hearing room to give evidence for the first time in his life.

Dapper in a perfectly tailored navy suit, the youthful sixty-four-year-old whose expressive grey-blue eyes were magnified under his thick spectacles was a seasoned veteran of public life as a lawyer, a politician and a jurist. In 1966, Hickman entered the cabinet of then Premier Joey Smallwood along with two other rising political stars, John Crosbie and Clyde Wells. Two years later, Hickman, who was Attorney-General, contested the leadership of the provincial Liberal party with Smallwood and Crosbie. After losing to Smallwood, Hickman and Crosbie eventually made their way to the Conservative party, which ended the Smallwood dynasty in 1972 under the leadership of playboy-politician Frank Moores. For the second time in his political career, T. Alex Hickman became Attorney-General of Newfoundland. It was an unusual but not totally surprising feat, given that Hickman was often described as the most charming man in Newfoundland.

Heightening the interest in Hickman's testimony was the fact that he had just spent two years on the royal commission dissecting the gross miscarriage of justice against Donald Marshall, Jr. The fact that Hickman was now being linked to a grave miscarriage of justice in his own backyard struck some observers, including the Nova Scotia press, as hypocritical and newsworthy, even though there was no direct evidence of his involvement beyond the realm of emphatic speculation.

The predisposition to believe that Hickman had played a part in the unsavoury deal that allowed members of the

Christian Brothers to escape justice in 1975 was reinforced by a string of former senior Newfoundland Justice Department officials who testified that Vincent McCarthy would never have acted independently in the Mount Cashel affair. John Connors, the brilliant, irascible lawyer who served as Newfoundland's Director of Public Prosecutions until the fall of 1975, was categorical in his speculation that McCarthy hadn't acted alone.

"I'll stand here until hell freezes over before I think otherwise. . . . I think of necessity he would have to discuss it with Mr. Hickman, not so much as to pass the buck as to share the burden of the decision . . . I just can't see Vince McCarthy making this decision himself. He would at least have plugged the Minister in."

George Macaulay, the Assistant Deputy Minister in the civil branch of the Department of Justice in 1975, also adamantly rejected the notion that McCarthy had cooked the deal with the Christian Brothers on his own.

"It's just crazy," he testified, "It's just not Vince. I would be very, very surprised indeed if Mr. McCarthy ever did that on his own. No, I just can't see the man doing that. He was an experienced Deputy Minister. He knew the rules."

Beyond the rules, and the personal opinions of McCarthy's former Justice colleagues, departmental custom also suggested that Hickman as Minister would have known about the Mount Cashel affair. As a matter of course, he was regularly briefed on both criminal and civil cases affecting the community, even while police investigations were ongoing, provided the matter was deemed important enough. He was also briefed if there was any doubt about which policy the department should follow in a given situation—a qualifier that would certainly have applied in the Mount Cashel affair, particularly since Vincent McCarthy, as acting Director of Public Prosecutions, was not strong on the criminal side and ran a department of junior lawyers who could not be expected to give him much sage advice. Finally, according to former political colleagues, nobody enjoyed a juicy yarn more than Alex Hickman, and Mount Cashel, it was said, was exactly the sort of scandal that would never have escaped his attention.

But when the subject of all the pejorative speculation finally got the chance to speak for himself (unlike the royal commission Hickman had presided over in Nova Scotia, none of the Justice officials called before the Hughes Inquiry was represented by counsel) the drama surrounding his long-awaited appearance was quickly dissipated. In a measured and husky voice, Hickman flatly denied that he was ever informed of the orphanage investigation in 1975–76, claimed he was unaware of the meeting between Vincent McCarthy and Brothers Gabriel McHugh and Dermod Nash, and said he had neither seen nor ordered the March 1976 police report into Mount Cashel by Det. Robert Hillier.

"I learned of its existence, to my astonishment, when Supt. Power came to see me, it must be a year ago now, and asked me what, if anything, I knew of the Mount Cashel investigation," Hickman testified.

Hickman was particularly upset that a mysterious third party had apparently used his name to obtain the second report on Mount Cashel from the CID.

"I didn't see the report until you furnished a copy a month or so ago and I need hardly say I was not pleased. . . . I hadn't requested the report. I was unaware of any investigation going on. Nobody had suggested to me there was an investigation going on so I couldn't have asked for it, but I didn't. And one would not have to be very astute to immediately conclude that someone—who that someone is would not probably be appropriate for me to speculate—but that someone either erroneously or mistakenly or"—Hickman looked up from the report he was reading and sent a flinty glare over the rims of his glasses towards Clay Powell on his next word—"deliberately used my name and my office to get a report for whatever reason prepared by a detective in the Newfoundland Constabulary."

Hickman also made clear to the inquiry what would have happened had he learned about the unauthorized use of his name and office back in 1975.

"This may sound self-serving, but I can think, predict what my instructions would have been to the Deputy Minister: 'I want a meeting right now with you, the Chief, the Assistant Chief and whoever the investigating officers are. And I will have to have an explanation.' . . . And I would think that the person, whoever that person is who made that decision, that would be the end of his period of employment. . . . For someone to do that and to try to manipulate the authority and the office of the Minister for what . . . to me is not an appropriate way to deal with an investigation . . . no matter who the person is, what his or her record might have been, whether I respected them, that would be the end of their terms of employment. It flies in the face of everything I tried to accomplish while I was there."

Grand Bank's favourite son was also upset by the statement that three Brothers had not been interviewed because Chief Lawlor and Assistant Chief Norman had apparently ordered a "slowdown" in Detective Hillier's December 1975 investigation.

"I have never seen or heard before of a senior police officer directing an investigating officer to slow down an investigation. And that would strike me very quickly that a satisfactory explanation would have to be provided forthwith."

When questioned about the events of 1979, Hickman said he couldn't recall former D.P.P. John Kelly ever briefing him on Kelly's in camera testimony concerning the Mount Cashel affair during the Soper Inquiry. But he did remember hearing about the Mount Cashel investigation "in a very oblique sort of way" sometime in May 1979. Lawyer Michael Monaghan called Hickman to ask if the Justice Minister would review the Father Ronald Kelly case and consider granting the accused priest an unconditional discharge. Hickman firmly refused, but as the two men were signing off, Monaghan mentioned the Mount Cashel affair.

Hickman later called in his D.P.P., John Kelly, to advise him of the conversation he had just had with Father Kelly's lawyer. As the two men were walking out of the Minister's office Hickman told Kelly that Monaghan had mentioned something about Christian Brothers or the Mount Cashel Orphanage.

"John's reply to me was, 'Well, that was a case that was handled by Mr. McCarthy two or three years ago involving a Brother or Brothers at Mount Cashel.' He said, 'I don't know any of the facts surrounding the case, but as far as I know, it was properly handled.' And we parted company. That was the first time I ever heard of Mount Cashel, and, you know, he was very reassuring. . . . I would have felt very secure in knowing that if there was any problem with whatever it was that transpired at Mount Cashel, Judge Soper would deal with it."

Questioned about the policies of the Department of Justice in the mid-seventies, Hickman emphasized that the Crown certainly had no policy of allowing people to escape criminal charges in return for promises that they would leave the province.

During cross-examination by James Chalker, the lawyer representing the estate of Vincent McCarthy, a debate arose about the concept of prosecutorial discretion. It was Chalker's clear intention to defend the deal that McCarthy had executed, apparently on his own, on the basis that it is not always in the public interest to invoke the full process of the criminal law. But T. Alex Hickman made it very clear that McCarthy's handling of the 1975 case could not be legitimized by an appeal to prosecutorial discretion as he understood it.

"My view is, was, and has always been that if there is probable cause or a prima facie case . . . that the appropriate procedure is to lay the charge," Hickman testified, noting that the court could always adjust the sentence to accommodate any mitigating circumstances.

After Chief Justice Hickman's long-awaited but anti-climactic testimony, anyone who wanted to believe in a Mount Cashel conspiracy that reached all the way into the office of the Minister of Justice—and possibly beyond—had to rely on intuition nourished by common sense rather than direct evidence. After seven months of painstaking inquiries, responsibility for the deal that gave at least two Christian Brothers a free pass through the justice system in 1975 rested exactly where it had at the outset: with a retired police chief, two evasive Christian Brothers and a dead justice official.

As for the children of Mount Cashel, they had been swallowed up by a bureaucratic beast with no name, or so its saturnine keepers would have the world believe.

Epilogue

███████████

As if by magic, Newfoundland summer appears almost overnight. After the darkness of winter without end, the prevailing winds suddenly shift and the spring ice vanishes from hundreds of coves and inlets around the island. By late June, the gun-metal waters of the surrounding bays are dotted with brightly painted fishing boats whose owners tend to their nets and traps every morning at first light during the brief season of calm seas and mild weather. Forest trails, blocked for months by ice and snow, are suddenly open, tincted with the fragrance of wild roses and viburnum. Blueberries turn from powder-green to deep lavender under the gathering authority of the sun. Beside inland marshes and on windswept capes jutting out into the sea, partridge berries and bakeapples slowly ripen, to be picked and preserved for winter feasting or sold by the roadside for ready cash come fall. In the final weeks of June, pick-up trucks begin arriving at the makeshift market on the city limits of St. John's known as "The Overpass," their spring offerings of seal meat, rabbit and herring replaced now by fresh lobster, Atlantic salmon and turnip greens. The passage of the seasons on this desolately beautiful island is deliciously marked by the food on a Newfoundland table.

Before the first strawberries of the season had arrived from the lush gardens of the Codroy Valley, the Hughes Inquiry drew to a close. Like the world of T. S. Eliot's "The Hollow Men," it ended not with a bang but a whimper. For nine months, the dreadful revelations of Mount Cashel and other child care disasters had battered Newfoundlanders like a withering northeast gale. Numbed by the gaping weaknesses the royal commission had laid bare in almost every area of the establishment they trusted, Newfoundlanders were left with an ambivalent sense of approbation and of irritable exhaustion by the time the last of the 258 witnesses, including 31 former residents of Mount Cashel, had been heard.

Supporters of the inquiry praised commission counsel for exposing, despite the pain of revelation, the outrages of the past. David Day, whose hair went from black to grey over the 150 sitting days of the inquiry, was widely praised for his exhaustive research. He was also gently indulged by Commissioner Hughes when his monotone interrogations strayed into the pedantic barrens of the painstaking lawyer's methodical mind. Though Clay Powell scored points for his sometimes more incisive handling of witnesses, he never quite measured up to the awesome work ethic of his obsessed partner. Like Day, Powell too was marked by the evidence he helped present, claiming that the allegations of sexual abuse against children were more repugnant to him than the subject matter of a previous inquiry he had worked on dealing with Nazi war crimes. There was also public acclaim for the patient judge who, despite painful attacks of arthritis, sat day in and day out weighing the mountain of evidence that took shape before him, a Matterhorn of human misery consisting of 2,550 documents and 627 exhibits.

With the bouquets came some brickbats for the $2.3 million royal commission. Though much of the criticism was well founded, in some cases it failed to consider the amended and impossibly enlarged mandate the Wells government had handed to Samuel Hughes after the Liberals came to power. The commission was justifiably criticized for being unfocused, ill-organized and soft on witnesses during cross-examination. Rarely was testimony challenged by commission counsel, and witnesses were recalled only selectively, when new evidence contradicted previously sworn testimony. While the boys of Mount Cashel were called time and time again to give evidence, senior members of the Christian Brothers and the judiciary were not asked to reappear, even when circumstances appeared to justify it. Given that the people accused of physical and sexual abuse at the orphanage were never called as witnesses, there was a sense of incompletion hanging over the proceedings, of dire and unfinished business that would only be cleared up when the criminal trials of the eight Christian Brothers involved made their way through the courts.

Not everything about the Mount Cashel affair had to await the deliberate pen of Samuel Hughes or the slowly grinding wheels of justice long delayed. On June 1, 1990, the lone remaining resident of Mount Cashel was placed in alternate accommodation and the ninety-year-old orphanage closed its doors forever. The Christian Brothers made the decision to abandon Mount Cashel in late November 1989, because of what Brother Superior Timothy Turner described as the acute problems boys still living at the orphanage were experiencing as a result of publicity surrounding the reopening of the fourteen-year-old case.

"Some of the young people, they read the stories and they felt angry. . . . It left them feeling like they were thrown into the mix of the whole thing. If their friends read those stories, they would say that they were in the midst of it all. They felt that they were unfairly treated," he said.

In fact, there was a much more practical consideration that led the Brothers to abandon Mount Cashel. Basil Dobbin, a prominent St. John's businessman who was chairman of the Mount Cashel Future Options Committee, conceded that it might be difficult, given the explosive testimony at the Hughes Inquiry, to raise the $1.5 million in private donations needed to renovate the aging institution. Adding to the financial uncertainty, the provincial government had also made clear that it was moving toward the complete deinstitutionalization of the province's child care system, and couldn't be expected to contribute $3.6 million of the $7.5 million needed to modernize Mount Cashel. The order's handling of the Mount Cashel affair had simply sapped the Brotherhood of community goodwill, and with it the financial backing needed to operate the orphanage.

The Christian Brothers weren't the only ones who had to live with the fallout of the Mount Cashel affair. Although the

Roman Catholic church in Newfoundland had tried to distance itself from the scandal at the orphanage, stunning testimony in the dying days of the commission documented that, as early as 1954, the Archbishop of St. John's had been made aware of the sexual abuse of a boy at Mount Cashel. In that case, the victim's tormentor had been a civilian worker rather than a Christian Brother.

The 1954 case was brought at the time to the attention of the RCMP, the Christian Brothers and the Archbishop before it was finally disposed of by having the alleged offender dismissed from the orphanage. A year later, the same man was convicted of indecent assault on a twelve-year-old boy and given thirty days in jail or a fifty-dollar fine. The prosecutor in the case was a young Justice Department lawyer named Vincent Patrick McCarthy, who had also advised the police department on how to best handle the potentially scandalous situation.

During testimony about the incident, David Day clearly established that, according to Roman Catholic canon law, the Christian Brothers had a duty as a papal institute to report to the Archbishop if they could not handle such serious allegations themselves. Although he didn't explicitly say so, the import of Day's line of questioning was clear: if a lone incident had been brought to the attention of the Archbishop in 1954, how could an epidemic of sexual abuse that led to a major police investigation into several members of the Christian Brothers themselves not be passed on to the Archbishop in 1975?

Although Archbishop Alphonsus Penney initially resisted calls for his resignation, he did express regret for the way in which the church had abdicated its responsibility to victims of priestly abuse and to their families. As spokesman for the Archbishop, Father Kevin Molloy told reporters: "Looking back on it now, obviously it should have been approached differently . . . but the point is that advice at the time was to approach this [as] a legal issue and we apologize for that. We feel sorry this was the stand taken."

Archbishop Penney also established an eleven-member committee, including a high-powered advertising agency, to deal with the findings of the church's own investigation.

Vowing that convicted priests would never again return to parishes in his diocese, Penney said that he was not averse to sex offenders in the clergy being defrocked, though he quickly rejected the idea that celibacy should be reconsidered as a prerequisite of the priesthood. The Archbishop emphasized that he favoured adopting reforms that would allow the laity to play a bigger role in the church than they had traditionally assumed through the work of parish councils.

"There is a growing awareness on the part of the clergy," he said, "not to be threatened by accountability but rather to welcome it. . . . The church is not a democracy but there is a need within the church for co-responsibility and dialogue."

The reverberations of Mount Cashel and the epidemic of sex crimes involving priests reached all the way to the pinnacle of the Roman Catholic church in Canada. On July 12, 1989, the Canadian Conference of Catholic Bishops ended its silence on the scandal of pedophilia amongst its clergy. In an open letter to Roman Catholics across the country, James Hayes, the Archbishop of Halifax and the outgoing conference president, called for compassion and understanding in dealing with the "anguish" of sexual abuse. But the three-page letter concentrated on the pain and shock average Catholics were experiencing over the explosive issue rather than on the causes of sexual abuse or possible ways of dealing with it. The Archbishop specifically rejected "a variety of over-simplified theories" that had been written about in the media, a clear reference to the possibility of a married Roman Catholic clergy.

Judging by their response to the crisis, Canada's Roman Catholic laity was decidedly restless. An Ontario-based group called the Coalition of Concerned Canadian Catholics wrote an open letter to all Catholic bishops across the country, expressing distress and cynicism about the state of the church. "Our common theme is a wish to reclaim the church," said the group's spokesman, John McCrae. "The news about sexual abuse was the last straw."

The media coverage of Mount Cashel opened the floodgates for other men to tell their stories of physical and sexual abuse at the hands of Catholic Brothers. In the month after the *Toronto Star* uncovered the terrible secret of boys abused at St. Joseph's training school in Alfred, Ontario, police received 130 complaints from former residents, and another 10 complaints from men who attended a school also run by the Brothers of the Christian schools near Uxbridge, Ontario. One victim sobbed "they ripped the kid out of me. . . . It was nothing but absolute terror. That's the only way I can describe it." Documents in the Archives of Ontario showed that government investigators confirmed allegations of physical and sexual abuse at St. Joseph's in 1960, but the investigation ended with two offending Brothers being removed from the institution. No charges were laid.

Going into their national meeting in Ottawa on October 23, 1989, Canada's 129 bishops were completely over-whelmed by the controversy raging over sexual abuse by the clergy. The bishops had already decided to address the issue behind closed doors, but the press was there in force when they emerged. The bishops had elected a new president, Robert Lebel, the sixty-four-year-old Bishop of Valleyfield, Quebec. Bishop Lebel insisted that modern training methods would prevent sexual abuse scandals in the future. Questioned relentlessly about the church's muted response to recent revelations of sexual abuse by priests, Lebel said that no overall solution could come from the national conference and that the problem should not be approached in "an atmosphere of panic." Denying that celibacy was a factor in sexual abuse by priests, he pointed out that sexual abuse by married people in a family setting, particularly by fathers against daughters, was much more common. He did, however, promise to discuss the issue of married priests with the Vatican. "We raise the issue when we go to Rome," he declared.

A week later, the new president of the Canadian Con-ference of Catholic Bishops announced the formation of a committee to study the issue of sexual abuse by members of the clergy. The committee was charged with examining the lifestyle of priests to see if the root cause of sexual abuse could be found. Roger Ebacher, the Bishop of Gatineau–Hull who was chosen to chair the committee, told reporters that the vow of celibacy led to a life that was lived in virtual isolation from other people. A 1987 study in his own diocese found that two-thirds of the priests surveyed had no best friend. The man who conducted the study found an even grimmer statistic. Rev. André Guidon, a professor of moral theology at Saint Paul University in Ottawa, reported that one in four priests needed professional help with sexual problems. Faced with such a widespread and potentially disastrous problem amongst its clergy, the decision by the bishops to set up a study group didn't pour much oil on troubled holy waters. *The Globe and Mail*, for one, was not impressed:

"The bishops knew they had to do something about a scandal that has tainted the church's authority and made every priest either a suspect or a laughingstock. What they came up with yesterday, beyond an expression of their personal sorrow, was a committee.

"Astute politicians in need of a placebo to stave off criticism invent committees. Most Canadians who have taken an interest in the repugnant goings-on years ago at the Mount Cashel Orphanage in St. John's will not be impressed by a committee."

Detracting from the comfort such a committee might have afforded concerned Catholics and others were the facts that, first, no deadline was established for the completion of its work and, second, that committee members would not be investigating specific instances where dioceses allegedly participated in cover-ups by transferring suspected child molesters to other parishes, ostensibly because the Canadian Conference of Catholic Bishops had no power over individual bishops, who report directly to Rome. Nor was the public reassured when the Archbishop of Halifax, James Hayes, stubbornly insisted that after receiving therapy, priests who had been sex abusers would still be permitted to say mass. "We consider these people to be members of our family. You can't just put them out on the street."

The real reason the church stubbornly refused to face the fact that priestly pedophiles were morally unfit for their calling may have had more to do with a potentially devastating personnel crisis in its midst than with family feeling for the culprits. In a 1988 study entitled *The State of the Catholic Clergy*, researchers showed that the Roman Catholic church in Canada had 6,610 diocesan priests, approximately the same number as it had fifty years ago when the country's Catholic population was just half the size of today's flock of eleven million faithful. The study also showed that the number of parishes without priests is on the increase and is likely to get much worse. Three years ago, 34 per cent of priests were under the age of sixty-five and only 26 per cent were under the age of fifty. If the trends continue, fewer than 15 per cent of parish priests will be under the age of fifty by the turn of the century.

Clearly, church officials were reluctant to expel or defrock what is, by any corporate measure, an endangered species within the Catholic church – the parish priest.

But on July 18, 1990, when the report of the church's own commission into the sexual abuse of children by members of the Roman Catholic clergy in Newfoundland was made public, there was no way to save Archbishop Alphonsus Penney. Given the devastating contents of the Winter Report, the bewildered shepherd of Newfoundland's Roman Catholics had little choice but to tender his resignation to the Pope.

After conducting lengthy investigations, Chairman Gordon Winter and his four-member commission concluded that, contrary to Penney's earlier claims, the Archdiocese of St. John's had, in fact, learned about allegations of child sexual abuse on several occasions before the crisis of 1988, and that "the Archbishop did not take effective measures to address these issues, even after serious problems occurred with some priests who were acting out their sexuality."

The Winter Report found that the alleged sexual activities of at least five priests were personally known to the Archbishop, either formally or informally, but that nothing was done about the situation. The case of one of those priests, James Hickey, had been brought to Penney's attention a full four years before he was convicted on twenty counts of sexual assault involving young boys. In the 1984 incident, the Vicar General, Monsignor Raymond Lahey, informed the Archbishop that the Royal Newfoundland

Constabulary had concerns about an alleged sexual assault
Hickey had made on a juvenile in his Portugal Cove parish.
Instead of taking action, His Grace chose not even to raise
the matter with Father Hickey because he felt that would be
an invasion of the priest's privacy. The matter was dropped
without further investigation.

Given that Hickey's alleged sexual habits had been the
subject of informal complaints to the Archdiocese since
1975, and that Hickey was on a list of suspected homosexuals that was handed to Alphonsus Penney in 1979 when
he became Archbishop, his failure to act seemed indefensi-
ble. Perhaps that was why Penney's forced resignation
reverberated with a sense of the church's newly accepted
responsibility for the tragic turn of events in Newfoundland:
"We are a sinful church. . . . We are naked. Our anger, our
pain, our anguish, our shame, and our vulnerability are clear
to the whole world."

Since Mount Cashel was both a failure of the public child
care system and a travesty of the rule of law, the provincial
government was as obligated as the Christian Brothers and
the Roman Catholic church to respond to the tragedy
long before Commissioner Hughes tendered his report. At
best, the reaction of the Wells government was sadly
ambivalent.

As a direct result of Mount Cashel, the provincial
government acknowledged that Newfoundland needed new
child welfare legislation, more social workers and more
police officers. A little over a month after the Hughes
Inquiry began, Social Services minister John Efford
announced that a new child welfare act for Newfoundland
would be introduced. Such an act would require the
registration of all social workers in the province, who would
now be empowered to intervene in those cases where there
was even a suspicion of child abuse. He also recommended
that the Department of Social Services hire ninety-two
full-time child welfare workers over the next three years at a
cost of $3 million – an impressive 23 per cent increase in
field staff.

"I will make no bones about that at all: the social workers

and the child abuse workers are overworked, they cannot physically or mentally maintain the job put to them," Efford told the Canadian Press.

Efford's colleague in the Department of Justice took a similar approach. Justice Minister Paul Dicks, himself a former Christian Brother, recommended that sixty additional police officers and support staff be added to existing rosters across the province to deal with the explosion in the number of sexual abuse complaints from just nine in 1983 to over six hundred in 1989. But Dicks added a note of caution that proved to be prophetic: despite the obvious need, the government, he warned, might have difficulty coming up with the funding for so many new positions. His caution was demoralizing to the fourteen police officers and nineteen social workers who had to deal with the avalanche of child abuse reports that had surfaced since the Mount Cashel and Father James Hickey scandals became public.

On March 15, 1990, the wish lists of the departments of Justice and Social Services ran smack into fiscal reality. In presenting his second budget to the House of Assembly, Finance Minister Hubert Kitchen announced funding for only fifty new social workers (twenty-one would be allocated to the new child abuse unit) and a 5 per cent increase in the number of police officers across the province, measures the minister said were "a major step in the prevention of the abuse of children."

If these staff additions, such as they were, helped to convince Newfoundlanders that their government was serious about coming to grips with the ugly reality of child abuse, the effect was spoiled by the appointment of Beaton Tulk, a defeated Liberal MHA, to the powerful position of Assistant Deputy Minister of Social Services responsible for children and youth services. In the supercharged atmosphere of the Hughes Inquiry, it came across as a particularly tawdry example of political patronage, a charge the political opposition was quick to make. Tory leader Tom Rideout blasted the appointment on the basis that Tulk, a former president of the Liberal party in Newfoundland, was not qualified for the job.

"Mr. Tulk has a master's degree in education and

experience as a teacher and a politician, but he has neither the experience or qualifications essential to administering this crucial division of the Social Services department," Rideout accused.

Premier Clyde Wells had barely gone on the record to defend his former political colleague when the Newfoundland Association of Social Workers publicly denounced the Tulk appointment, warning that the defeated politician's complete lack of professional qualifications could have "grave implications" for the quality of service provided by the Department of Social Services. Remarkably, the government of the day had opted to staff a senior child welfare position with an unqualified political appointee who was expected to learn his profession on the job – a practice that had come under criticism at the Hughes Inquiry as a possible contributing factor to what had happened at Mount Cashel in 1975. It was a strange way to blaze a badly needed new trail in child welfare in Newfoundland.

Another weakness in government's response to the tragedy of Mount Cashel was the decision to remove the issue of compensating the victims of Mount Cashel from the mandate of the Hughes Inquiry. Questioned by reporters, Justice Minister Paul Dicks insisted that the compensation issue was better addressed by the courts than a royal commission. Opposition Justice critic and former Justice Minister Lynn Verge disagreed, arguing that it was grossly unfair to force victims to relive their traumatic experiences yet again and launch expensive civil actions to get just compensation. "If the commission finds the police, Crown attorneys and child welfare authorities did not do their duty and respond correctly to complaints of child abuse, then these victims should get special compensation," she said.

Despite taking the moral high ground at the outset of the controversy, and notwithstanding the deep and obvious involvement of the government in the events of 1975, the Wells administration refused to bend. If the former boys of Mount Cashel thought they were entitled to compensation, they would have to prove it in a court of law. Like the Roman Catholic church and the Christian Brothers before it, the provincial government adopted a position of strategic silence rather than moral leadership on the compensation issue, a prudent if uninspiring approach to a future liability in the Mount Cashel affair that could prove to be massive.

Shane Earle was the first Mount Cashel boy to inform the provincial government of his intention to sue, stating in his notice of claim that the Department of Justice, the Department of Social Services and the Royal Newfoundland Constabulary "failed to take proper and appropriate action" in response to complaints of physical and sexual abuse at Mount Cashel in the mid-1970s.

"The Director of Child Welfare and other officials . . . of the Department of Social Services . . . of the Department of Justice including the Royal Newfoundland Constabulary . . . knew or ought to have known that the Intended Plaintiff would suffer physical and/or sexual abuse and suffer irreparable harm and damages if they failed to take proper and appropriate action in accordance with their statutory and common law duties."

In the summer of 1989 the quiet ex-waiter whose explosive story had helped spark a royal commission into child abuse in Newfoundland expanded his civil action. During a trip to Toronto, Earle told reporters that he would be seeking $2 million in compensation for the "pain, emotional trauma, [and] physical and sexual abuse" he had suffered at the hands of certain Christian Brothers. In addition to the two provincial government departments he had already named in his intended action, his suit now included as defendants the Congregation of Irish Christian Brothers and the Catholic church. Within a matter of weeks, seven more victims of alleged physical and sexual abuse at Mount Cashel filed suits against the Christian Brothers, the provincial government and the Catholic church seeking $2 million apiece for the pain and suffering they had endured as children at the Catholic-run orphanage. In the end, more than twenty boys would launch lawsuits bringing the grand total of damages being sought in connection with the Mount Cashel affair to astronomical heights.

But outside the cold equations of judicial accounting, that

futile process of attaching a monetary value to a child's tears, lay the emotional wasteland inhabited by grown men in whom the broken boy would live forever, beyond the reach of cash settlements, retroactive justice and the heartfelt sympathy of strangers. Every one of them had known from the beginning that once the flash bulbs had faded and the old judge gavelled proceedings to an end, there would be a return to the here and now, that airless zone where life had to be re-invented out of the unholy memories of a childhood gone desperately wrong.

Paradoxically, for Shane Earle that meant both turning back the hands of time and looking ahead. Living now with John and Elizabeth Scurry, the couple that had wanted to adopt him as a small boy, the unemployed waiter could not decide whether to rejoin the work-force or go back to school. Although he acknowledged that the Hughes Inquiry did its best to recreate what happened so many years ago, the workings of justice delayed had not entirely impressed him.

"It [the Hughes Inquiry] leaves me somewhat discouraged because, I don't know, I just figure some of the key witnesses were given an easy ride and others weren't questioned enough, and others were there just for appearance and that was it. That was discouraging. The system is definitely not equal ...."

For Shane's brother Billy, out of work and waiting for his unemployment insurance benefits to run out, involvement in the commission had been emotionally disastrous. His attempt to help the other boys had inadvertently destroyed his always fragile world. Planning to leave Newfoundland to begin a new life somewhere else, Billy Earle was bitter about the personal consequences of the judicial forced march back to 1975.

"To be honest with you, I wish I had never got involved with this in the first place. I only did it to support the rest of the boys and Shane. But like I said, I never heard tell of none of them any more. It's the worst fucking thing that I ever got involved with. . . . I've left my wife."

Dereck O'Brien, the hefty former alumnus of Mount Cashel who for the past five years has been the chef at a school for the hearing impaired in St. John's, fights an uphill battle every day to deal with "flashbacks" from Mount Cashel. Married now, with two children of his own, O'Brien took part in child abuse demonstrations in St. John's and wrote a book about his experiences at Mount Cashel. But the boy who once accompanied Brenda Lundrigan and Johnny Williams to Social Services authorities to tell them what was going on at Mount Cashel admitted that the Hughes Inquiry had made it difficult to put the past behind him.

"I just try and turn it off and go on to something else, try to make myself busy so I don't dwell on it."

For James Ghaney, the little boy who developed a severe drinking problem after being subjected to years of physical, emotional and sexual abuse at Mount Cashel, life changed a lot after he left Newfoundland. Now the owner of a small contracting business near High Park in Toronto, the trained carpenter blocked out the past by keeping busy. Unlike Billy Earle, he believed some good had already come out of the inquiry.

"It does seem as though progress is being made. Already, it's out in the open now so it's something that the Catholic church has to face and deal with, as well as the Congregation of Irish Christian Brothers, and Newfoundlanders for that matter. . . . It's not over yet, you know."

Gerard Brinston, who claimed he was sexually abused by a Christian Brother in his very first week at Mount Cashel, now worked as a waiter in a gay bar in Vancouver called Papa's Place. The former male prostitute's involvement in the Mount Cashel case brought him national recognition after his appearance on "The Journal," as well as unwelcome changes in his personal life.

On one of several trips to Newfoundland during the Hughes Inquiry, Brinston was given a room in the Hotel Newfoundland, overlooking the Narrows. During the day before he had to testify, he sat by the window and enjoyed the view over coffee and cigarettes. But at night, old ghosts would ride up on the incoming tide and Brinston couldn't bear to be in the room alone. He would remember how he used to turn out the lights in the gymnasium and run headlong into the wall, hoping to get away from the orphanage by sending himself to the hospital. Or how he would fall asleep listening to boys crying in the middle of the night, unable to help them escape from the same nightmare in which he himself was imprisoned. Finally, there was the dark legacy of the abuse that so many of the boys suffered and that for Gerard left lifelong scars.

"I was really confused when I got out of the orphanage. I didn't know if I was gay, straight, bi or what I was. All I knew was I had no education. I had nothing to look forward to. And I was escaping into drugs and things like that."

After he had testified at the commission and returned to Vancouver, friends in St. John's sent him newspaper clippings about the trials of priests and the most recent developments at the Hughes Inquiry.

"Some days I just sit down and read all of them and cry. I just ask, 'Why?' "

Standing in the leafy coolness of the Mount Cashel grounds with the fog rolling in, the rest of the city is held magically at bay. The grass is knee-deep on the soccer pitch directly below and in front of the orphanage, and two sets of stands for spectators are slowly disappearing into the triumphant underbrush. The grass around the butter-coloured main building is still manicured, and the statue of the Virgin Mary to the left of the main door, with three children on their knees in front of her, flanked in turn by a pair of lambs, looks pristine from a distance. On closer examination, the gold, white and blue of her robe is cracked and faded, as is the whitewash on the barren flagpole on the front lawn. The high windows are curtained and silent and a lone light bulb burns above a side entrance, as if awaiting the return of a tardy resident. Behind the main building, a huge wild rose-bush blooms voluptuously beside Mount Cashel's deserted play-ground. Row upon row of empty swings sway by them-selves in the light breeze and grey-headed dandelions push up to fabulous heights through the cold geometry of the monkey bars. The laughter of unseen children, playing in the backyards of the bungalows that circle Mount Cashel, floats over the desolate grounds like a convention of ghosts. Then the caretaker opens the front door and makes his way down the steps to his pick-up truck, carrying something that looks like a statue. Obscured in swirls of fog rolling down over the east end of the city from Signal Hill, he puts the figure into the truck and climbs in. With the cough of the truck's engine, startled robins break from the bushes in front of St. Gabe's dormitory, complaining loudly before settling again in the double privacy of the fog-shrouded treetops. With the retreat of the glowing taillights down the driveway, the silence seeps back in. After a brief, shivery interval, Mount Cashel and its silent grounds disappear in the cold white light.

Back on the street, a teenage girl pauses for a moment at the gate, contemplating a short-cut through the deserted grounds. Deciding against it, she hurries up the sidewalk, the hollowness of her footsteps echoing through the fog like the ticking of a clock.